Buzz

Screen Classics

Screen Classics is a series of critical biographies, film histories, and analytical studies focusing on neglected filmmakers and important screen artists and subjects, from the era of silent cinema to the golden age of Hollywood to the international generation of today. Books in the Screen Classics series are intended for scholars and general readers alike. The contributing authors are established figures in their respective fields. This series also serves the purpose of advancing scholarship on film personalities and themes with ties to Kentucky.

SERIES EDITOR
Patrick McGilligan

BOOKS IN THE SERIES
Hedy Lamarr: The Most Beautiful Woman in Film
Ruth Barton

Von Sternberg
John Baxter

The Marxist and the Movies: A Biography of Paul Jarrico
Larry Ceplair

Warren Oates: A Wild Life
Susan Compo

Being Hal Ashby: Life of a Hollywood Rebel
Nick Dawson

Some Like It Wilder: The Life and Controversial Films of Billy Wilder
Gene D. Phillips

Claude Rains: An Actor's Voice
David J. Skal with Jessica Rains

BUZZ

The Life and Art of Busby Berkeley

Jeffrey Spivak

THE UNIVERSITY PRESS OF KENTUCKY

Published by The University Press of Kentucky
scholarly publisher for the Commonwealth,
serving Bellarmine University, Berea College, Centre
College of Kentucky, Eastern Kentucky University,
The Filson Historical Society, Georgetown College,
Kentucky Historical Society, Kentucky State University,
Morehead State University, Murray State University,
Northern Kentucky University, Transylvania University,
University of Kentucky, University of Louisville,
and Western Kentucky University.
All rights reserved.

Editorial and Sales Offices: The University Press of Kentucky
663 South Limestone Street, Lexington, Kentucky 40508-4008
www.kentuckypress.com

15 14 13 12 11   5 4 3 2 1

Library of Congress Cataloging-in-Publication Data

Spivak, Jeffrey, 1956–
  Buzz : the life and art of Busby Berkeley / Jeffrey Spivak.
     p.   cm. — (Screen classics)
  Includes bibliographical references and index.
  ISBN 978-0-8131-2643-2 (hardcover : alk. paper)
  1. Berkeley, Busby, 1895–1976. 2. Motion picture producers and
directors—United States—Biography. 3. Choreographers—United
States—Biography. I. Title.
  PN1998.A3B4885 2010
  791.4302'33092—dc22
  [B]
                          2010031653

This book is printed on acid-free recycled paper meeting
the requirements of the American National Standard
for Permanence in Paper for Printed Library Materials.

Manufactured in the United States of America.

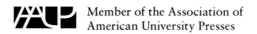 Member of the Association of
American University Presses

To Alysa

In an era of breadlines, Depression, and wars, I tried to help people get away from all the misery; to turn their minds to something else. I wanted to make people happy, if only for an hour.
—Busby Berkeley

Contents

Illustrations follow page 150

Acknowledgments

I am eternally grateful for the help, support, and advice of the following contributors, who made the writing of Busby Berkeley's life story a pleasurable experience:

Joe Franklin, for his witty Buzz Berkeley anecdotes and for putting me in touch with Hollywood personages he's known.

Sybil Jason, for her personal recollections of working with Buzz. His story is balanced and fair thanks in part to Miss Jason's first-person account.

Carol Jones, Program Director of the Peace Awareness Labyrinth and Gardens, for my personal tour of the magnificent Beaux-Arts mansion once owned by Buzz.

Miles Kreuger, President of the Institute of the American Musical, for his erudition, advice, and passionate adherence to truth.

Michael Kutza, founder and Artistic Director of the Chicago International Film Festival, for relaying humorous anecdotes of Berkeley and Ruby Keeler when they were feted at the festival.

Sandra Joy Lee, Curator, Warner Bros. Archives, School of Cinematic Arts, University of Southern California, and Jonathon Auxier, Curator, Warner Bros. Archives, School of Cinematic Arts, University of Southern California, for providing me access to the hundreds of files in the Berkeley archive.

Patrick McGilligan, the best mentor a biographer could ever ask for.

Susan Murray, my editor, whose suggestions and improvements were invaluable.

Teresa Neff, whose great-great-aunt was Nellie Gertrude Berkeley, for supplying me with the Berkeley family tree.

Dr. Shirley Radlove, for her cheerleading and heartfelt encouragement.

Debbie Reynolds, for clarifying some dim memories of Buzz and singing to me the little ditty quoted in chapter 13.

Jonathan Rosenbaum, for setting the record straight about a Busby Berkeley rumor I heard.

Donald Saddler, for his memories of a sad, somewhat dejected Buzz during *No, No Nanette*.

Leila Salisbury, for her support of and excitement about a Busby Berkeley biography during its earliest stages.

Rosalie Spivak, always there for me, always.

The staff at the Margaret Herrick Library of the Academy of Motion Picture Arts and Sciences, for graciously aiding me in my research.

The staff at the New York Public Library for the Performing Arts at Lincoln Center, for their help in obtaining rare Berkeley items.

The staff at the UCLA archives, for arranging screenings of rarely seen Berkeley interviews.

The staff at the Warren-Newport Public Library in Gurnee, Illinois, for their tremendous help with the hundreds of interlibrary loans I always needed at a moment's notice.

John Russell Taylor, for his amusing Berkeley anecdotes.

Joel and Carol Walner, for their long-standing friendship and kindness.

Marc Wanamaker, for providing Buzz's memoirs.

Anne Dean Watkins, acquisitions editor at the University Press of Kentucky, and her staff, for their belief that Busby Berkeley's life story needed to be told.

Frank and Dale Zirbel, for their never-flagging support and without whom this book would not have been written.

Prologue

Professionally, he used only half of his birth name. His real name, disjointed and clumsy, contained both parental surnames and tributes to a famous actor friend and a part-time soubrette. Contrastingly, his stage name was pleasing, rhyming, and alliteratively euphonious. Saying it out loud evokes scores of platinum, pulchritudinous chorines arranged in geometric, eye-appealing configurations. The name, a lowercase noun in *The American Thesaurus of Slang,* is defined as "any elaborate dance number."

Busby Berkeley was the premier dance director of motion pictures. His originality and sharply defined style brought him professional acclaim and financial reward. He saved a studio from bankruptcy and a doomed genre from senescence. Just don't call him a choreographer. According to "Buzz," his liberally used nickname bestowed by friends and colleagues, choreographers were defined with artists like Agnes de Mille. Buzz Berkeley wasn't interested in dance steps and didn't know a "buck and wing" from a "shuffle and riffle." He defined "dance-directing." Ascending a makeshift dumbwaiter twenty feet or higher above a cavernous soundstage, he peered into his large eyepiece and maneuvered his ensemble and his camera to the formations of his mind's eye as he dance-directed.

His early musical numbers were hermetic, existing outside the narrative of the films in which they appeared. They were often stacked together, one after the other, in a film's final reel. The brilliance of the numbers inadvertently created a side effect: they made a picture's story line wholly irrelevant and forgettable. The numbers were so ingrained that Buzz often received the lion's share of critics' kudos despite the fact that his musical digressions appeared in films directed by others.

Music has always been an essential ingredient in motion pictures. From the earliest days of the silent film, a Pianola assumed the role of the image's accompanist. When the movies found their voice in the late 1920s, Berkeley was toiling in a related profession and expressed no interest in working in motion pictures. He once said: "You can have your Hollywood musicals. They don't know how to do them out there." Stiff, wooden, with little directorial flourish, the musicals to which Buzz referred were photographed flatly, received passionately then indifferently, and yet, despite their blandness, formed a cottage industry. The problems encountered in the early days of sound recording dictated that audiences could barely distinguish a dancer's face. But in the talkies' early years, moviegoers were excited just to hear the formerly muted voices of their favorite stars. By 1932, however, the fickle public was voting with their pocketbooks, using their Depression dollars to view pictures of other genres in preference to the "all singing, all dancing" films. Some theater managers placed placards outside their box office assuring patrons their current presentation was *not* a musical. Yet, despite the overall diminishing interest, there remained a spark of ingenuity and creativity in those early days. Rouben Mamoulian's *Love Me Tonight* is a notable example.

Busby Berkeley was a specialist in the best and limiting senses of the word. For musical pictures he had no stylistic equal, yet the films he directed outside his purview were often middling and anonymous, lacking the imprimatur that defined his finest work. Studio bosses thought they knew best the projects in which Buzz could thrive, and after a fashion they imposed a creative ceiling that marginalized him and his career.

A witty and not wholly inaccurate description of a Busby Berkeley number comes from the poet and writer Sir John Betjeman, who wrote, "The decors display great ingenuity, but resemble, more often than not, a sort of drunkard's dream." In his most creative period, Berkeley's tableau featured expansive art deco formations and repetitive set decorations with the occasional use of gigantism for fantasy props. Conversely, when bowing to budget restrictions, Buzz created his most interesting work with minimalist trappings. Yet for all his notoriety, public success, and admiration, Buzz remained subservient to philistine studio executives. He took professional chastisement for perceived violations of Will Hays's production code of ethics and suffered personal grief from his battles with ladies and liquor that resulted in a fusillade of hurtful and shameful publicity.

The existing literature analyzing the life and works of Busby Berkeley is scarce and limited, consisting of only a few titles, most of them out of print. The details concerning his volatile existence are often contradictory and inaccurate. Quoted within the pages of this volume are colleague reminiscences, newspaper stories, legal documents, court records, studio memoranda, and never-before-published accounts from Berkeley's memoirs, unearthed here for the first time in more than three decades. The anecdotal and the quotable are sifted through the prism of veracity, providing a heretofore unseen portrait of the successes, failures, accolades, and tumult that comprised the disquieting life and art of the man who was . . . Buzz.

1

Actress and Son

In the northeast corner of New York State, on the western banks of Lake Champlain, lies the formidable town of Plattsburgh. On September 11, 1814, the Battle of Plattsburgh proved a crucial victory for the United States in the War of 1812. The fledgling U.S. Navy, under the command of Brig. Gen. Alexander Macomb, fought back an invasion from England, which, after defeating Napoleon, had turned its attention to retaking the northern states and possessing all navigation rights over Lake Champlain. The defeat of the British against overwhelming odds boosted national morale and was a chief catalyst in ending the war.

The town, named after the Continental Congress member Zephaniah Platt, was incorporated in 1815. The indigenous Iroquois had been driven from the area by Quebecers and other Canadians who journeyed south to settle there during the booming days of the fur trade. In the nineteenth century, the town welcomed a new breed of citizenry in the form of families from England, Ireland, and Scotland. Robert Barclay of Stirling, Scotland, settled in nearby New Hampshire with his wife, Rhoda Way, when they started a family in the late 1700s. By that time, Robert had adopted a new and similar-sounding surname, Berkeley, an Americanization perhaps of a family name dating back to the 1600s. He and Rhoda welcomed a son, Robert, on September 1, 1798. When Robert was in his twenties, he married a New Hampshire girl, Susan Woodbury, and together they had seven children. On December 5, 1848, their second-oldest child, Arthur Tysdale Berkeley (b. 1823) married Mary Jane Hooey of New York and moved to Black Brook, New York, in Clinton County, thirty miles southwest of Plattsburgh.

Over the course of twenty-four years, Arthur and Mary raised a brood of twelve, corresponding, almost exactly, to one newborn every two years. There was Susan Elizabeth (1850), George (1852), Edgar Eugene (1854), Susan Ella (1856), Alpheretta (1858), Billie May (1860),

Frank (1862), Nellie Gertrude (1864), Althea (1866), Mary (1870), Wales Oscar (1872), and Harry (1874). Records of the first six births indicate their locale as Black Brook. Beyond that, only the county (Clinton) is listed. Other documents claim that the eighth child, Nellie Gertrude, was born in the stronghold of Plattsburgh. For Nellie, life must have been confusing at first with seven brothers and sisters, two of them having the same name. Children from large families often find ways to overcome their early anonymity. For some, the pursuit of scholarly endeavors, or the engagement in the law or medical professions, distinguishes them from their siblings. For others, a talent and love for the dramatic arts can cause wallflowers to blossom. The life records of her eleven brothers and sisters are sketchy at best; it was Nellie Gertrude who distinguished herself with a passion for acting. The Berkeleys sent Nellie one hundred miles east to the Potsdam Normal School (formerly the St. Lawrence Academy), a facility known for sending its graduates out into the world as teachers for public schools. Training music teachers was the school's specialty. Nellie found interest not in music instruction, but in the thespian arts classes. There was an overall maturity in Nellie's appearance and speech, and she stood tall and walked assuredly through the hallways of Potsdam. Tellingly, at the age of seventeen, she was cast in the role of Mrs. Cregan, the mother, in a local production of Dion Boucicault's *The Colleen Bawn*. The highly melodramatic play of murders and marriages featured roles more in line with Nellie's age, but she was cast as the matriarch for her commanding presence. Nellie followed her passion, auditioning and winning roles in local repertory companies. She honed her skills in all types of roles including Shakespearian, where, quite convincingly, she played the bard's greatest harpy, Lady Macbeth. Nellie dropped the "Nellie" around this time and henceforth appeared on the stage from the east coast to the west as Gertrude Berkeley. In San Francisco, circa 1890, she found regular acting work with the prestigious Tim Frawley Repertory Company.

Francis Enos, an up-and-coming actor and director from the small town of Mansfield, Ohio, was working out comedy routines in nearby Van Wert for his "Enos and Wall's Model Comedy Company." Professionally, he adopted a number of names including M. Frank Enos, M. Francis Enos, Melzar F. Enos, and Wilson Enos. He settled on Wilson for the stage, while friends and family always called him Frank. In Van

Wert, it was Wilson Enos and his group presenting *Flirtation or a Wife's Peril.* Wilson kept the audience "in a roar" with comedy "that would shake down fences around the grave yard," according to the *Van Wert Republican* of February 1889.

About ten years earlier, Frank had started his career under the guidance of the "queer but talented" actor and manager Daniel Bandmann. While playing a role in *The Lady of Lyons,* he met and fell in love with the actress playing the lead, Ida Lewis. They married and had a son, George, but the marriage didn't last more than a couple of years. Ida later changed her name to Julia Arthur and found great success on the stage. Frank, with George in tow, played the circuit wherever actors, directors, or stage managers were needed. As George grew, he dabbled in small acting parts (sometimes under the name of George Arthur in a tribute to his mother), and gained some notoriety playing the title role in *Little Lord Fauntleroy* while Frank played the earl. Frank's Enos and Wall's Model Comedy Company found a bit of short-lived success, but not the kind to stake a future on. By 1890, he and George, a nomadic twosome, had traversed the country from Atlantic to Pacific, until Frank joined a well-known troupe originally based in Los Angeles. The company migrated four hundred miles up the coast to San Francisco, where a new home for the Tim Frawley Repertory was established.

It wasn't long before Frank Enos made the acquaintance of Gertrude Berkeley. They caught each other's eye and soon became a couple. Along with George, they took a road trip to Frank's home state, where all three performed what was defined as "an entertainment" at the Sandusky, Ohio, town hall on May 3, 1890. They were inseparable as they toured the country, and on Wednesday, June 17, 1891, Francis Enos and Gertrude Berkeley were married. She kept her maiden name for the stage, Frank still had Wilson, and George used Enos, Arthur, and Berkeley interchangeably.

Frank took on directing duties for Tim Frawley, while Gertrude toured the circuit, acting in one production after another, often starring with two dear friends in the company, Amy Busby and William Gillette. Amy was routinely cast in the role of a soubrette, the kind of maidservant who was pretty, coquettish, and flirtatious. William was a writer and actor whose parents were influential in Connecticut's early days. His mother was a direct descendent of Thomas Hooker, the Puritan minister who led seventeenth-century settlers to the state, and his father was a founder of Connecticut's Republican Party.

Frank and Gertrude enrolled George in Indiana's Culver Military Academy with the feeling that he should not have to endure the actor's life of transience and disappointment. In February 1895, while George was at school, Gertrude learned that she was pregnant with her first, and Frank's second, child. She hardly lessened her work schedule and appeared onstage often. By autumn, in her final trimester, Gertrude relinquished her spot on the stage to rest in Los Angeles with her husband. On Friday, November 29, 1895, Gertrude gave birth to a son. On the birth certificate, the name-of-child fields are empty, the father is listed as "M. Francis Enos," and the mother as "Gertrude Berkeley." They asked their best friends, Amy and William, to be godparents of the boy, and out of respect, admiration, and love, Frank and Gertrude gave their son the curiously disjointed name Busby Berkeley William Enos.

Gertrude returned to the stage soon after giving birth. She found her first marked success in the play *The Girl I Left Behind Me,* produced by the well-known Charles Frohman. Gertrude had assumed the lead role vacated by Blanche Walsh when the play had closed at New York's Empire Theatre. She toured in the role, eventually leaving Frohman's employ when the company came to San Francisco. There, she joined the Daniel Frawley Stock Company (no relation to Tim), and together with Frank they remained in the company for a couple of years. They toured the country yet again, but the difference this time was a "babe in arms" who accompanied his parents wherever they played. The couple found stage work in Woodward, South Carolina, with the Woodward Stock Company before heading west again. Fortuitously, they ended their trek in one of the country's most vibrant theatrical atmospheres of the late nineteenth century, Kansas City.

Frank left the family in November 1897 for an exotic acting assignment. In Honolulu, Hawaii, he costarred with the Tim Frawley Company in the war play *Shenandoah.* One daily said the audience liked the play immensely and was "more than pleased with the presentation of it." Wilson Enos was singled out as a "clever and quiet villain." The run was short for *Shenandoah,* and soon cast, crew, and Tim Frawley himself boarded a boat for the States.

The Woodward Stock Company mounted their productions at the

Auditorium Theatre in Kansas City until December 20, 1897, when fire
destroyed the building. The very next day, trucks moved props and wardrobe to the empty Gilliss Opera House, and that night, without missing
a beat, the curtain went up. It was a shivering audience that saw Frank,
Gertrude, and the Woodward Stock players, for the older Gilliss needed
more than twenty-four hours in order to reach a comfortable temperature.
It was a temporary solution at best, so the company ventured north and
west, settling in Omaha, Nebraska, for a spell. After the fire, Kansas Ci-
tians commissioned the building of a new structure to replace the burned
theater. The rechristened Auditorium was a modern marvel, complete
with what were euphemistically termed "retirement rooms" (rest rooms),
an attribute not shared with many theaters of the day.

On January 21, 1899, while baby Busby was being watched by Annie, his nurse, his parents were performing at the grand reopening of
the Auditorium in *Men and Women,* by David Belasco and Henry C.
DeMille. The credited Wilson Enos worked double duty as actor and
stage director, with Gertrude sharing his spotlight in front of more than
two thousand people. The second incarnation of the Auditorium was
such a success that the Woodward Stock Company was also referred
to as the Auditorium Stock Company. Regular attendees grew to know
the cast members as week to week they changed from role to role. Audiences enjoyed seeing the latest Wilson Enos disguise. His interpretation
of Cyrano de Bergerac was the highlight of the first season. The work
schedule for the cast was grueling. There was a different play each week,
performances every evening with four matinees, and rehearsals for the
next week's play scheduled on days off.

Annie was under strict orders from Busby's parents to keep the little
tyke away from the theater at all times, excluding Saturday matinees.
Although Frank and Gertrude had tried somewhat unsuccessfully to dissuade Busby's half brother from a life in the theater, they were more determined this time with their youngest. At the Culver Military Academy,
George thrived in athletics and horsemanship. He was the captain of the
prestigious Black Horse Troop (an Honor Guard and escort to kings,
presidents, emperors, and the like). When he graduated, he requested
from his parents a role in the Woodward Stock Company under the stage
name George Arthur, and after some pleading, they grudgingly agreed.

At one performance of A. Mitchell's Arabian-themed romantic play *Under Two Flags,* the littlest Enos was determined to get backstage. He sneaked away from Annie and passed the stage doorman unnoticed. The five-year-old stood in the wings and marveled at the pageantry. George, onstage dressed in an Arabian costume of flowing robes, caught Busby's eye. George made his exit and stood beside his little brother. Just as he was about to return to the stage, George, in a mischievous mood, persuaded Busby to stealthily accompany him. He lifted his enveloping burnoose, and a few seconds later a hidden child walked onto the live stage. With fright, Busby grabbed George's leg, shivered in place, and hung on. Had George's costume been a tad shorter, the audience might have been quite amused watching a robed Arabian with four legs limp offstage. Busby's debut was a shared secret, and George was spared his parents' wrath.

The strain of putting on a new production every week, of performing every evening and rehearsing when not performing, was taking its toll on Gertrude. She could handle things on the weeks when she played supporting roles, but when one leading role followed another, often with pages requiring intricate memorization, the pressure began to show.

The company was performing *What Happened to Jones* during the week, and Frank scheduled a Saturday rehearsal for their next play, *Darkest Russia.* That Saturday, Gertrude rehearsed all morning, grabbed a quick lunch, and took the stage for the matinee performance of *What Happened to Jones.* After a few hours' break, Gertrude was back for the evening show. Following that performance, another round of rehearsals was held for *Darkest Russia* that lasted until four in the morning. Gertrude was totally fatigued. She couldn't remember her lines from the first act of the new play. She mumbled, and the other actors complained they couldn't hear her. Somehow Gertrude managed to get through the rehearsals, and after a few hours sleep, she seemed to regain her faculties. On Sunday, March 17, 1901, *Darkest Russia* was staged for the first time as a matinee. Following the evening performance, Gertrude Berkeley Enos lost her mind.

Audience members had noticed the actress forgetting a line here and there and doing "strange things," but Gertrude had made it to the play's end seemingly unscathed. While walking his wife home after the performance, Frank was startled to find her in a highly agitated and paranoid state. She crouched behind him and begged hysterically that he not allow some imaginary persons to shoot her. Frank managed to get Gertrude home, humoring his wife's rantings along the way. Dr. D. H. Reigle was called to Gertrude's bedside and pronounced her utterly out of her mind. A newspaper account of the incident recalled that her ravings were the most horrific torture for her husband and "her little son, Busby." She screamed paranoid ravings that her life was in danger; she turned left and right, eyes wide with fear, looking for a gun. She recited passages from old plays and broke down in tears. Other doctors were consulted, and none could promise that she'd ever recover. Frank tried to work to keep his mind off Gertrude's condition, and he went back to the theater to rehearse his cast in their new play, *The Little Minister.* He sat in the darkness hiding his grief, occasionally uttering a halfhearted stage direction, but his thoughts were elsewhere. "My wife is mentally a wreck and there seems little hope that she will regain her composure," said Frank. To a reporter he promised, "If she ever comes out of this, I will take her away to some quiet country place where she can never think of the stage again." After a thorough review of Gertrude's condition, Dr. Reigle spoke on the record: "We have faint hope that she may, within a few weeks, begin to improve, but the outlook is very gloomy. She has been under such a strain that her mind gave way with a snap and such things are not cured immediately. One can make no promises as to the outcome of such cases."

While his stepmother began her arduous recovery, George Enos left the Woodward Company to venture out on his own. He rarely wrote to his parents, but when he did it was often for the purpose of obtaining funds. Ten months after her mental breakdown, Gertrude had recovered sufficiently to return to the stage, Frank's comments to the reporter notwithstanding. She joined the Columbia Theatre Stock Company in Brooklyn. The Columbia was an audience-friendly troupe. After Tuesday matinees, the audience was invited on the stage to drink hot chocolate, eat bonbons, and converse with the cast. They had group sing-alongs in between acts and gave away souvenir photos. In the January 28, 1902, edition of the *New York Times,* it was announced that *Shall We Forgive Her?* would be the next attraction at the Columbia and that Gertrude Berkeley, among others, would have "good parts." Gertrude didn't stay long with the company. Perhaps she regarded the Columbia as her way of making an out-of-town debut, much like a new play that would allow her to test her newfound resilience in front of unknowns. Her debut was a success, and with her mental stability holding steady, Gertrude returned to Kansas City that same year.

She couldn't have been greeted more warmly by Kansas City theatergoers. In the company's opening play of the season, *Hearts Are Trumps,* the audience applauded every time Gertrude walked onstage. In September, the Woodward Stock Company found itself in financial straits. Six members were fired with only a week's notice. The actors were extremely bitter, having been promised forty weeks of engagements. They could go to New York for work, but the firings occurred too late in the season to allow them to seek new employment. By November, all remaining members of the stock company had been dismissed. The beautifully refurbished Auditorium would now house only visiting road shows. Without a resident stock company, the new business plan lasted less than one season.

Gertrude was undaunted. In light of all the firings, she decided to form her own stock company to be called "Miss Berkeley's Players." They were to be the house stock company at the Century Theatre. The goal was to present a different play each week, mostly solid dramas. One of her leading actors, James Durkin, had worked his way from the stage to the back office, taking a management role in the company. He used his new influential position to try to fire some actors and lower the salaries of others. There was a festering rivalry between him and Gertrude, and arguments regularly ensued. Although recovered from the anguish she had suffered the previous year, Gertrude was in no condition to wage an ongoing battle within her ranks. She had made the decision to leave her own company. On the Century stage before the evening's performance, Gertrude was noticeably sobbing. To her faithful audience, she said: "Kind friends, I have done my best. I can say no more." Gertrude played her role one final time, and the audience was said to have been quite upset.

The family uprooted once again, this time to Washington, D.C., where Gertrude and Frank joined a local stock company. Illnesses of all sorts struck the beleaguered Enos clan; first, Frank was hospitalized with inflammatory rheumatism. Around this time, Gertrude learned that George had turned to morphine to lessen the effects of sustained unemployment. She placed him in a Stamford, Connecticut, sanitarium. Amid all of this, Busby was suffering through an acute case of influenza. In a touching puerile letter featuring watercolor drawings of flowers in vases, he wrote to Frank the following (spelling verbatim): "My Dear Father, Mother has bin wateing to hear from you. I have been sick with the gripp. George has been sick to, he in a sanitariun in Stamford . . . pleas write to us so mother won't cry so much . . . I did theas drawings."

During this difficult financial time, Gertrude accepted an offer to join the prestigious Castle Square Company based in Boston. She placed Busby as a day pupil in the Notre Dame Academy in Roxbury, Massachusetts. In the early part of 1904, she was working steadily when an accident occurred. While walking home one cold Boston night after rehearsals, Gertrude slipped hard and fast on the ice-covered pavement and tore her leg ligaments. For almost four weeks her leg was immobilized in a wooden splint. In February, Frank took an acting job in Canada, about a hundred miles north of Toronto. Soon after, his health became an issue again, and he was admitted to a hospital in Gravenhurst, Ontario.

On February 22, a hobbling Gertrude busied herself with preparations for the opening of *The Climbers,* by Clyde Fitch. Her character was a widow fresh from a funeral. Busby sat quietly in her dressing room as she donned her mourning garments. "You know Busby," said Mother, "I feel strange putting on this black veil and dress. It just doesn't seem right for some reason." He stood in the wings as his mother made her entrance. When she exited, she was given a telegram that she took unopened to her dressing room. Busby followed his mother, expecting her to change her costume for the next act. She sat at the lighted mirror and opened the telegram. Her face went ashen. In a whisper, she said: "My God. Oh my God." She turned to her son: "My darling Busby. Pray . . . pray as you have never prayed before." The telegram read: "Your husband died this morning. What shall we do with his remains?"

Gertrude was characteristically stoic. Living the adage that "the show must go on," she set an example for her son and composed herself. She returned to the stage to complete her performance; the cast and audience remained oblivious.

Frank Enos had passed away from complications of inflammatory rheumatism at the hospital in Gravenhurst. His funeral arrangements were handled by his brother, O. L. Enos, and it was decided to bury him in his hometown of Mansfield, Ohio. His body was transferred to the local undertaker, and on leap year day, seven days after his demise, a small service was held. Gertrude and her sons were not in attendance. In the *Mansfield News* coverage of Frank's funeral arrangements, it was reported that Gertrude did not attend because she was "injured by a fall several weeks ago."

Gertrude sent Busby to boarding schools during the next couple of years, along with camps in the summer, while she found work touring with various companies. She won the role of Mrs. Solness in Henrik Ibsen's *The Master Builder* in 1907. During casting she made the acquaintance of an unusual woman with a mysterious Slavic accent. Alla Nazimova used only her surname as her calling card and established quite a reputation in her native Russia before coming to America in 1905. She studied under Constantin Stanislavsky, the famed Russian director and teacher, and was the foremost interpreter of Ibsen. In late October and early November, Gertrude suffered bouts of insomnia and severe neuralgia pains. The curtain was held for more than a half hour before one performance of *The Master Builder* when the strain within her took hold and she fainted backstage. A doctor was sent for, and after a moment Gertrude regained her equilibrium. The impatient audience knew nothing of the drama taking place behind the curtain. The play eventually started, and Gertrude made it through without further incident.

Gertrude starred in the controversial *Myself Bettina* in October 1908. The story of two brothers (one, a clergyman), a woman who lives with them, and her sister (Bettina), who returns after a four-year absence, received scathing notices in the New York papers. The reviewer in the October 6, 1908, edition of the *Evening World* found the play's sexuality "excessive and gratuitous." "One of the season's worst offerings," grumbled another critic, who found the play vulgar and misogynistic. The furor was as short-lived as the play, which closed in less than a month.

Busby saw his mother as often as he could, and was impressed with her core strength and ceaseless drive. She fretted over which school she should send her son to during his teenage years. Her brother Wales suggested the school he had attended, the Mohegan Lake Military Academy in Peekskill, New York, a preparatory institution that taught military discipline along with academics. After successfully pleading with the school to reduce its fees based on a hardship, Gertrude enrolled Busby.

He was dreadfully homesick those first couple of days and cried in the privacy of his room. After a short while, though, he made friends and got into the spirit of the academy. At times he was a scamp, playing practical jokes with his buddies. He found a bunch of small alarm clocks and set the alarms for the middle of the night. He placed the clocks in the hot-air registers in the school's assembly hall, provoking instant panic from the startled cadets. On more than one occasion, Busby and a buddy tied bed sheets together, climbed out their windows, and went AWOL into Peekskill, looking for a little fun. He was expelled and reinstated three times with his friend Don Wray. Scholastic goals were met with only moderate success; he won a medal for Latin ("by hook and crook"), but the mathematics curriculum did not suit his temperament. Busby did find recognition in team sports, excelling as quarterback and right halfback in football, shortstop in baseball, center in hockey, and runner on the track team. He received medals for gymnastics and the manual of arms. In 1913 "B. B. Enos" was editor in chief of the *Moheganite*, the academy's student-published organ. In the Christmas edition (volume 12, no. 2), a short biography of each football player was included:

Busby B. Enos (Right Half)
"Buzz," who hails from New York, started in with the third team in 1909, and it looked as though there would not be many moons before he would be on the first and so it proved. In 1911 he was a "sub," but last year he made the team, playing quarterback, and this year as right half and sometimes quarter. "Buzz" is about 5 feet 10 inches and weighs 135 pounds. He is a good deal like a rubber ball, very lively, thus making him a hard man to tackle. His greatest strength lies in his intercepting or spoiling the forward pass while following interference and dodging are a couple of his good traits. Next year may see him at Princeton, or Penn., though as yet he is undecided. We wish him all success.

Gertrude kept herself busy with interesting stage projects and saw Busby on school holidays. Based in New York City, Gertrude would

occasionally travel out of state when the role demanded. She and Nazimova were paired again in Boston for Ibsen's *A Doll's House*. One day
while on leave from school, Busby, looking like a dapper little gent in
his cadet uniform, attended a Boston performance and stood silently in
the wings. Nazimova walked by with two young girls who were playing
her daughters. Without missing a beat, the famed tragedienne grabbed
the cadet's hand and led him and the girls onstage to a family scene
already in progress. Busby said nothing, stood stiffly, and exited when
he was prompted while the audience was none the wiser. After the play,
Nazimova told Gertrude what a natural actor her son was and what
great composure he possessed in his second brush with show business,
and the first with his face unhidden.

To his remaining family, the whereabouts of George Enos were a
mystery most of the time. When Gertrude learned that he was again
addicted to morphine, she had him placed in another sanitarium, this
one in New York. George was uncooperative with his treatment, and
he escaped the hospital repeatedly, only to return in a condition worse
than when he took off. He was a failure in the acting profession, and
he never sought solace or advice from his stepmother. During an acting
engagement in New York City with Buzz at her side, Gertrude received
another telegram backstage. The subject was George. Buzz stood behind
his mother, who was seated at her makeup mirror, and it was he who
read to her the words that sounded alarmingly like the horrid telegram
of a few years prior: "Your son, George has been found dead on a park
bench here in Plattsburgh, New York. What shall we do with his remains?" In a grisly coincidence, George Enos was pronounced dead of a
drug overdose in the town that was both the birthplace of his stepmother
and the stronghold of America's forces in the War of 1812.

She sobbed, she cried, she screamed in utter agony and grief. Buzz
never forgot the expression on her face as he saw it in the makeup mirror's reflection. It was now only these two. An extended family support
system just didn't exist. A resolve of life-changing significance took hold
of the teenage Busby as he witnessed his mother's deep sorrow. His sol-
emn oath: someday he will free his mother from her worries. A bond
that could not be torn asunder was established between mother and son.

Busby returned to the academy while a still-mourning Gertrude resumed her life on the stage. A "Miss Gertrude Berkeley" was listed in the

credit roll of William Vaughn Moody's *The Faith Healer,* which brought
the actress back to Missouri, but only as far west as St. Louis. In one of
her most praised roles, Gertrude starred as the mother, Mrs. March, in
Little Women at New York's Playhouse Theatre, which ran from October 1912 to March 1913. Costarring were Alice Brady as Meg, and
Gertrude's good friend John Cromwell in the role of John Brooke.

A man named Starr Lee approached Buzz one day at a school gathering with a post-graduation job offer. Mr. Lee's son Earl was Buzz's good
friend. Apparently Earl put in a kind word to his father, who owned a
shoe factory in Athol, Massachusetts. Buzz would apprentice and learn
the business that offered management potential. Buzz was convinced and
excited, and he relayed all the details of the position to Mother. When
Gertrude learned of her son's plans to work at the Lee Shoe Shop, she
was relieved that an actor's life would not be his. Following Buzz's gradu-
ation from the Mohegan Lake Military Academy in 1914, he moved
to Athol. He learned the shoe business as an apprentice at the Hobbs
Manufacturing Company (also owned by Starr). He was trained in the
manufacturing of paper shoe boxes. Buzz was so skilled that after a short
time he began making suggestions for streamlining the procedure. Simultaneously climbing the professional rungs of his industry as foreman and
then advertising manager for Lee Shoe, Buzz played semi-pro baseball at
Fish Park; opened a small, short-lived, dance studio; and did volunteer
work around town. The Athol Opera House on South Street was home to
Buzz's first attempts at "producing" and performing in stage plays. Three
nights a week Buzz led Athol's "Home Guards Unit," where 150 men
marched in the formations he had learned at Mohegan.

The Women's Club of Athol ran a benefit for a local charity. A
member of the club who had seen Buzz at the Opera House asked him
if he would recite something. With trepidation he accepted and selected
Margaret Manton Merrill's *The Soul of the Violin.* To stand and orate
was not enough for Buzz, and his creativity turned the recital into something memorable. He spoke to the violin as organ music accompanied:
"It has come at last, old comrade—the time when you and I must say
good-bye. God knows I wish I could sell myself instead of you." The
penniless violinist reflects his and his instrument's past while pondering
the future. With his hunger pangs diminished, he decides he won't sell
his beloved violin and begins playing the instrument with abandon. Buzz

mimicked a frenzied musician to the hilt. The recital ended as one violin string after another snapped off, and both the instrument and its player succumbed to a slow death: "One more rose, my beauty, my queen of all the world. The lights are growing dim. My sight is failing. I can see only you, only you." Buzz planned a dramatic finale to the recital. He had a friend man the light board, with the express instructions to cue the electrician on staff to cut the lights as the last violin string fell off and he dropped to the ground. Alas, an unprofessional unraveled Buzz's plans. He hadn't arrived at the emotional climax of the piece when the lights were cut prematurely. "No, goddammit, I'm not finished yet!" yelled the out-of-character narrator. The lights returned, the audience calmed down after some robust laughter, and Buzz resumed his death throes. "I learned a lot about show business that night," he reflected wryly.

The outbreak of World War I saw the birth of patriot and pacifist sympathies, most notably represented in the theater. President Woodrow Wilson promised the country's noninvolvement in the overseas conflict, but that didn't stop playwright Marion Craig Wentworth from writing a scathing indictment of the military, its soldiers, and the women they left behind. The thirty-five-minute one-act play *War Brides* was first produced on January 25, 1915, and starred Gertrude and Nazimova. Set in an unnamed country during the war, Nazimova (as Joan) played a bereaved woman who loses two brothers-in-law and her husband in the conflict. The king of the country soon declares that women must have more children in order to replenish the military ranks. Joan protests and finds needed support from her mother-in-law (Gertrude). When Joan learns of her pregnancy, she commits suicide rather than conform to the king's command.

A few months into the production, Gertrude suffered another personal loss. On May 7 her friend and mentor, the well-respected producer Charles Frohman, was killed. He was a passenger on the British ocean liner *Lusitania* when it was torpedoed without warning by a German submarine in the Celtic Sea.

Nazimova introduced Gertrude to a movie director friend of hers named Herbert Brenon. He admired Gertrude's performance in *War Brides* and asked her if she'd like a role in his upcoming picture, *The Two Orphans,* for Fox films based on the play *Les deux orphelines* by Adolphe d'Ennery and Eugène Cormon. Gertrude accepted, and the cast, led by actress Theda Bara, went to Quebec for the filming. This version of the story (it had already been filmed a few times) was released on September 5, 1915. The following month, Gertrude and Brenon's next collaboration, *The Soul of Broadway*, was in theaters. Neither her rookie nor sophomore efforts in the intimate medium of motion pictures drew great attention, but that changed in 1916, when the film version of the antiwar *War Brides* was released.

The film's producer, Lewis J. Selznick, had seen Nazimova in the lead role onstage. She had been offered other film roles prior to this, but had always turned them down. She changed her mind after Selznick's generous offer of thirty thousand dollars plus a guarantee of one thousand dollars for every day the production ran over schedule. She insisted that Gertrude Berkeley repeat her role and Herb Brenon direct. Richard Barthelmess, the son of an actress who tutored Nazimova in English, wanted a part in the picture. As a favor to her friend, she was influential in the casting of Richard for *War Brides,* his first film. The film ran in New York for several months and was placed in general release in April 1917. With the war fever that was spreading throughout the States that month, the pacifist *War Brides* suddenly went from admired to despised and was withdrawn from circulation almost immediately. As one critic put it: "The philosophy of this picture is so easily misunderstood by unthinking people that it has been found necessary to withdraw it from circulation for the duration of the war." And so it was, until Lewis Selznick came up with an idea: replace the titles and set the story in Germany. It evidently worked. The film was rereleased and continued to make money.

Onstage in January 1917, Gertrude acted in *As It Was in the Beginning,* another antiwar-themed production. The *New York Times* review praised Gertrude's "excellent work" and said the play was "told with unmistakable dramatic skill."

President Wilson asked Congress for a declaration of war against Germany on April 2, 1917. Buzz had his own thoughts about Europe's conflict and, despite his training in shoe manufacturing, the call to serve instilled by the Mohegan Lake Military Academy remained. He weighed the options of continuing work in the private sector versus military service and reasoned that he could return to the former once he had received an honorable discharge from the latter. A military registration card was signed "Busby Berkeley Enos" (with "Berkeley" squeezed in vertically, a last-minute addition) at the local board, Division #12, in Athol. He enlisted in the U.S. Army on April 5 at Fort Banks. His timing was incredible. Twenty-four hours into his enlistment, Busby Enos and the United States of America had officially entered the war.

2

In Formation

Gertrude was ready to quit the stage when Buzz entered the military, but there was an acting obligation in May. She starred in *Old Friends,* a premiere work produced, ironically, by Charles Frohman, Inc. His company had persisted long after his untimely passing. The play was by James Barrie, who had penned *Peter Pan* for Frohman in 1905. That same month, the dramatic film *The Iron Heart* was released to theaters. Gertrude played the devoted (and suffering) wife to a tyrannical nouveau riche factory owner. The owner is eventually given his comeuppance, after which his loyal wife welcomes the broken man with open arms.

Buzz wanted to go to France, and he had heard artillery service was the ticket. His goal was to be a commissioned officer. Buzz was one of two men selected for officer training in Fort Oglethorpe, Georgia. While down South he convinced the military brass that he was a bugler, a lie concocted to avoid the sweltering marching drills. Before Buzz played a rudimentary "Taps" one evening, a rowdy, lights-out pillow fight occurred in his barracks. He hadn't dressed yet, but he reached for his bugle. All of a sudden a bunch of his bunk mates pushed him out the door. There he stood, in nature's own, playing "Taps" for the company. He wasn't aware that he had an audience of one: the Officer of the Day. As the young enlistee turned on his points in a textbook military about-face, he came face to face with his superior. A bare Buzz was escorted humiliatingly to the gatehouse, stopping briefly to nervously don his standard-issue bronze collar and tunic.

Persistence paid off. He got his wish and was sent by ship to France to the Saumur Artillery School. A rumor that the purser on board willingly accepted bribes made Buzz and a friend seek out his company. They wanted some of the officers' chow as an alternative to the standard-issue gruel and were willing to pay for it. The purser lifted what he could from the ship's cargo, supplying the boys with French staples: champagne, bread, and cheese. They feasted privately while learning phrases in a new language.

Coincidentally, Gertrude was starring in the film *Over There,* a military drama whose title recalled the popular George M. Cohan song of the day. The story tells of a coward who refuses to enlist in the army only to change his mind when his fiancée volunteers for the Red Cross in France. He finds his courage over there, and regains the respect of his beloved.

The French howitzer was a nasty little cannon used in combat. The weapon's strength was that shells could be launched with a curved trajectory of up to sixty degrees. French officers at the Saumur Artillery School taught American infantrymen in the use of the "oweetzer." Before Buzz took his first lesson, he had a little sightseeing in mind . . . without permission. His unit landed in southern France near Bordeaux, where his camp was stationed. He and his friend (unnamed, but a safe guess is that he was the one who had shared Camembert on the voyage over) left camp for a rumored infamous underworld known as the "Apache" district. They had it planned: during roll call, a trusted friend would grunt "here" when either name came up. Had they known that the town was heavily infiltrated with the military police, they might have reconsidered. After a long hike, they found their first den of iniquity in the guise of a café frequented by the local *prostitué.* In broken French, they inquired about the notorious Apache, and in broken English they got their answer. Buzz saw the MPs and laid low. He and his partner in crime asked the girls to disguise them with lipstick and rouge. They covered themselves with some borrowed garments and walked with the ladies through the underground unnoticed. For forty-eight hours, Buzz learned the ways of the world, conferring and commingling with the French tarts. It wasn't until the MPs raided his hideout that he decided to hightail it back to camp. The two escapees returned unnoticed and unpunished.

Buzz's instructor at the Saumur School was Pierre Dreyfus, son of Alfred Dreyfus, the French captain who was wrongly court-martialed and later exonerated, but not before serving a hellish stretch at Devil's Island. It was a couple of months into his howitzer training that Buzz was awarded his commission. Second Lt. Busby Berkeley Enos of the 312th Field Artillery was now in command of Battery F. His primary job was to make his platoon into howitzer experts. It was an important position, to be sure, but the new lieutenant would have rather earned his gold bar as a witness to the madness at the front.

Overseas letters to Mother were delivered with regularity, and she responded in kind. The news of his commission was proudly acknowledged. In her correspondence, he learned of his mother's burgeoning film career. Gertrude's stage work after *Old Friends* had given way to motion pictures, and in the new year of 1918 she played an alcoholic mother in the melodrama *The Song of Songs*. The film, released in February, arrived shrouded in gloom; the director, Joseph Kaufman, had died on the first day of the month. In October, *Just Sylvia* opened with Gertrude again in the role of a nouveau riche woman. Here she intercedes in her son's life, playing the matchmaker with Sylvia, a dressmaker's model. When it's revealed that Sylvia has peerage, it proves of little consequence. She renounces her title, and love wins out.

For a man of imagination, repetition is an anathema. Second Lieutenant Enos loathed what he called "the routine" when referring to marching drills. The precise sound-off, count-off, was mastered quickly in Battery F. Parade drills, the closest thing to group manipulation on a large scale, were now in Buzz's hands. He moved from howitzers to marchers, directing all six batteries, 1,200 men in total, in "the routine." His colonel was pleased, but Buzz wasn't satisfied, and he came up with an interesting idea that would relieve the monotony. Each battery commander would be given a regimen in which the men marched silently to a prescribed count. The marching orders and counting schemes were unique to each battery; if handled correctly (and mathematically), the 312th Field Artillery would align majestically as disparate units seamlessly converged. Buzz worked it out on paper with lines and arrows representing the six groups of two hundred men each. He presented his idea to his superior and was granted permission. More than a thousand men marched in complete silence, moving to the count of the mind's metronome. Wordless batteries were arranged perpendicular to another group, some right-facing, others left until, like a deck of spread cards, they closed ranks in perfect formation. "It was quite something to see," said the second lieutenant understatedly. An acknowledgment of Buzz's cleverness came from commanders of the French army. They wanted their men to pull off the same stunt with Buzz waving the baton as the *chef d'orchestre.* The idea went no further than to Buzz's colonel, who refused outright.

His newfound celebrity brought Buzz little comfort as he still hadn't seen action on the western front. Buzz knew of the fledgling army air corps in France, and when he heard they were looking for volunteers, he requested and received a transfer. As an aerial observer, Buzz viewed the allies and enemies from a distinctive vantage point from which trenches snaked like black lines over long distances, and dead operators lay next to their demolished artillery. At 0500 hours on November 11, 1918, in a railroad car parked in a forest near the French front line, the armistice was signed, officially ending conflict in the "war to end all wars." It was great news to the world, and a disappointment to Buzz, who, knowing he'd never see combat, quickly sought an exit from the air corps and a transfer back to his old regiment.

If he had had his way, Buzz would've made another AWOL visit to the Apache district to relieve the boredom that a postwar occupation can produce. His marching stunt made him the perfect candidate to keep the men from restlessness, and soon after he returned he was told to produce shows in a decrepit barn that doubled as a theater. During the war, the touring groups of the YMCA entertained the troops, and Buzz arranged for the various factions to perform for his men. After a time, wanderlust or boredom, or both, made Buzz itchy for new surroundings. He was well aware of the army's strict enforcement of the AWOL statute, but he reasoned no harm could be done if deserting wasn't his intention. For the second time in his military career, the now commissioned officer, with duffle bag in hand, surreptitiously abandoned his fellow soldiers and made his way to the nearest train station, where he found refuge in an empty boxcar. The train's destination was a mystery to the absconder. Second Lieutenant Enos had crossed the line and committed himself to an enterprise that couldn't end well. While crouched in a corner of the car, he listened to the repetitive click-clack of the railroad wheels and imagined the court-martial awaiting him at the end of the line.

When the boxcar door slid open, Buzz was relieved to find no MPs poised for his arrest. He quickly identified his location as Chaumont, the headquarters of army Gen. John J. Pershing. He needed a cover story to explain his presence. As the so-called entertainment officer of his unit, he made up a perfectly plausible alibi. The name Dorothy Donnelly stuck in Buzz's mind. She was a stage actress, a writer, and a lyricist. Perhaps Gertrude had made mention of her (they were contemporaries, but had never appeared together), but it's more likely Buzz knew the name from the YMCA shows he mounted. Chaumont was home to the YMCA's entertainment unit in France, and it was run by Dorothy Donnelly. Armed with a cover story (flimsy though it was), he found the location of Miss Donnelly and arranged a meeting. Buzz told Dorothy that he'd like to direct some of these touring shows. He made his case, but she only feigned interest until Buzz name-dropped his famed mother. Instantly, her countenance became sunnier, and she gave Buzz a big hug. "You're just the one I'm looking for!" exclaimed Dorothy. "How would you like to be the Entertainment Officer here in Chaumont?" He readily accepted, believing his AWOL escapade had gone unnoticed.

It hadn't. Buzz was arrested and placed under guard. Dorothy Donnelly used her influence with General Pershing's administrative assistant. She pleaded Buzz's case, saying that the new entertainment officer was badly needed for the troops' morale in this postwar environment. Soon Buzz was transferred to Coblenz, Germany, his arrest countermanded thanks to Dorothy's assistance.

Buzz remained in Coblenz, acting as assistant entertainment director for the U.S. Third Army of Occupation. Not content just to arrange touring shows for the YMCA, Buzz rounded up men who were either actors in civilian life or who had stage-related careers. He followed in Gertrude's footsteps and built a new touring company of his own. Buzz staged shows, directed them, and occasionally took an acting role. They did musicals, comedies, and dramas all through Germany to receptive occupying forces. It was an exhilarating time in an otherwise dull postwar world, but after about a year, the excitement wore off for Buzz. He pleaded his case to the Third Army's adjutant general for an honorable discharge. He again used his mother as leverage, only this time he painted her as the aged widow and himself as her only descendant.

While Buzz was beseeching the adjutant general, Gertrude played the suffering mother in the film *Break the News to Mother,* released in June 1919. The story revolves around a series of inaccurate accusations. Gertrude's doting son in the film (Raymond Bloomer) thinks he shot a man when his gun and another happened to fire at the same time. His guilt forces him to flee, leaving his friends to tell the sordid tale to his mother. He joins the army, is eventually cleared, and reunites with his girlfriend and his mother.

Buzz planned his own reuniting when he obtained approval from his superior. He was sent to the Atlantic coast city of St. Nazaire, where he was to board ship for the States. Buzz was ready to embark when his orders were countermanded. The commanding officer needed Buzz to arrange entertainment for his men. He promised the anxious lieutenant a discharge from military duty provided he stay a bit longer in St. Nazaire and arrange entertainment for the troops. Buzz was disappointed but not insubordinate, and he accepted the temporary assignment with good cheer. It wasn't all hardship as Buzz staged shows in France for appreciative soldiers. One memorable occasion had Buzz and his group performing outdoors in front of an estimated crowd of ten thousand.

Buzz, after much pleading with his superiors, got word that his name was on the passenger list of a ship about to sail. First, he was to arrange a company of two hundred men and get them ready for the journey. In flagrant disregard for military protocol, he turned his command over to another lieutenant. As he did in the boxcar, Buzz sneaked onto the ship and quickly located a vacant hammock. It was a terrible hiding place, and the novice boatman was soon discovered. Buzz expected the worst: a loss of his stripe (certainly) topped with a nauseating ride home shackled in the frigid brig. He was totally taken off guard when he heard the ship's commanding officer speak to him in friendly terms. With Lieutenant Enos on the ship's manifest, the commander had an idea. Would the second lieutenant be kind enough to stage some shows during the long voyage? Affirmative! And so every evening the newly appointed "entertainment officer of the ship" put on an original revue. With the knowledge that he had narrowly escaped the brig, he took his role in stride until the ship finally docked in New York harbor. Second Lt. Busby Berkeley Enos was the very first soldier off the ship, and he "literally ran down the gangplank." If Buzz learned one thing in the service, it was that it's tough to hit a moving target. He dashed past the crowd and boarded a train to Ridgewood, New Jersey, where he'd see Mother (who was living in nearby Hohokus) for the first time in nearly three years. When he arrived at her residence, he was disheartened to find her gone. The phone rang, and he picked it up. It was Gertrude, still waiting at the dock! In his zeal to flee the ship, he had run past his own mother. An hour later, things were righted, and their reunion was deeply emotional. They hugged each other hard and shed happy tears years in the making.

Gertrude's demons were safely tucked away in one of the thousand dusty dressing rooms from which she made her nightly grand entrance in an anonymous theater in an anonymous role. By the time of her son's disembarkation, she had been retired from the stage for almost two years. At fifty-three, she gave a final performance in the same month as her birth. Perhaps it was the milestone of age. Perhaps, two months into her son's enlistment, she was under too much mental strain to concentrate on anything else. Her illness remained at bay as long as she stayed behind the footlights. New Jersey was her home now. Though close to New York, Gertrude entertained no thoughts of a Broadway comeback. Acting in pictures could well result in her accepting a short-lived part, but Gertrude's raison d'être was the guidance and nurturing bestowed with equal measure on her beloved Busby.

3

The Show Fixer

Buzz moved in with his mother and regaled her with military anecdotes. His successes with amateur theatrics fell on disapproving ears. Gertrude had hoped her soon-to-be-mustered-out son would find a job, any job, in any field except show business. The shoe factory apprenticeship in Athol was no longer an option: Starr Lee had died, and the company had gone out of business. Buzz also had no lady love in his life, a situation that caused no consternation in Gertrude; indeed, it suited her possessiveness.

Not yet in civvies, the uniformed second lieutenant and his beaming mother strolled through the Broadway theater district, past the William Brady Playhouse on Forty-eighth Street, with Gertrude doing the regaling this time, telling of past shows and past personalities. Approaching slowly from the opposite direction, a familiar face came into view. It was John Cromwell; seven years earlier, he had made his Broadway debut in the role of John Brooke with Gertrude as Mrs. March in *Little Women* at the Playhouse Theatre on West Forty-eighth. He was acting and directing now, staging Broadway productions and assembling casts for out-of-town shows. John looked quizzically at the dapper soldier, and an idea sprouted. Buzz was the perfect size and age for a part he was casting. Would he be interested in trying out for it? Gertrude was aghast! "No John, I don't want Busby going on the stage." Buzz, displaying the same excitement that fueled his gangplank run, was captivated by the idea. He begged Mother. "Just an audition . . . if I'm no good, then that's that." She let down her guard and acquiesced. Buzz auditioned and won the role. Within forty-eight hours, he had gone from veteran, to civilian, to actor.

On August 17, 1919, a week after Buzz had returned from France, a small headline in the *New York Times* read "A Soldier-Made Actor." The story was about Lt. Busby Enos, his wartime duties, and his commission at Saumur. His famous mother was mentioned, along with her having quit the stage in 1917. Dorothy Donnelly, the angel who had come to Buzz's aid in Chaumont, obviously planted the story as she's also named. Mentioning both Amy Busby and William Gillette, the piece stated that Buzz was "predestined for the stage," a proclamation that assuredly didn't register well with Gertrude.

The show was a drama titled, appropriately, *The Man Who Came Back,* by Jules Eckert Goodman. Buzz rehearsed, and his mother gave him pointers. She accompanied him on the road and coached him. She picked at his performance, tweaking his acting style. One night, Buzz, onstage and completely comfortable in his role, took the bows reserved for the great actors. Five curtain calls later, he came offstage self-satisfied and smug. "What do you think of that?" he asked Gertrude. She didn't return his smile. "Do you really want to know what I think? I think you're the worst dramatic actor I've ever seen." Now Buzz was aghast. He stormed away, angry and hurt. He pouted in his dressing room, deflecting his mother's criticism until it began to sink in. In a moment of personal reflection, he took her words to heart. In the service, his audiences had been boisterous; in drama, they were passive. His comrades had laughed up a storm watching his army shows. What great memories, thought Buzz. Henceforth, a dramatic actor no longer, he would only do comedies. For the stage, he dropped his surname, adopting as a tribute to his mother the pleasantly alliterative Busby Berkeley. It's not unlikely that Gertrude was deeply touched.

When *The Man Who Came Back* ended its surprisingly lengthy full-year run, Buzz found another show that caught his interest. The musical comedy *Irene* debuted at the Vanderbilt Theatre in 1919 and was a two-year success. With the hope of becoming part of the road company, he met the show's producer and pitched himself. Would he play the role of the effeminate dress designer? Without hesitation he replied, "Of course!" Buzz won the role as the London modiste, a character of dubious sexuality named Madame Lucy. From Biloxi, Mississippi, to Medicine Hat, Alberta, Buzz and his company never missed a performance. One local paper singled out Buzz as "a scream," describing his polished fingertips and "excruciatingly funny" manners. He danced with the two leads "the likes of which has not been seen before."

With Buzz on tour, Gertrude accepted a role as "the old woman" in the 1921 dramatic film *Suspicious Wives.* It's a story full of exaggerated histrionics. The married leading man is unfairly accused by his wife of carrying on with her sister. Later he loses his sight temporarily in a car accident. He's unknowingly nursed to health by his wife, with whom he reconciles in the final act. The film was released on September 1, and it was the final professional credit of Gertrude's life. She had come full circle in a lifetime of acting roles bookended with old woman parts, beginning at seventeen with *The Colleen Bawn* and ending here.

In October, *Irene* played at the Opera House in Mansfield, Ohio, the hometown of Frank Enos. The *Mansfield News* took notice and wrote of the prodigal son and his father's connection to the town. "Prominent member of *Irene* Company inherits dramatic talent from both parents," read the subhead. A short biographical sketch of Buzz and recollections of Wilson Enos on the stage were followed by a startling non sequitur. As reported, Buzz was more interested in management or of the "development of theatrical affairs." He was supposedly attracted to the newspaper business and was in negotiations to purchase a newspaper property. The show was a hit with the Mansfielders, and while Buzz was in town he visited with his uncle O. L. Enos and met some old-time friends of his father. No further mention was ever made of Buzz's professed connection to the fourth estate.

A cuddly picture was featured in the *Fayetteville Democrat* when the company played in Arkansas. Buzz and costars Mary Moore and Beatrice O'Connor were posed tightly together with their arms around each other's waists. *Irene* on the road ran for a couple of years with Buzz a constant, outlasting three leading ladies. One of the last, a young actress whose first name matched her character's, was Irene Dunne. Buzz had fun with Irene, and after playing Madame Lucy for so many performances, he decided to spice things up with a bit of mischief. One night as he pranced onstage, he reached for Irene's hand, gave it a kiss, and left a raw oyster in her palm. The leading lady desperately tried to stifle a laugh for almost two minutes.

Though show business had captured Buzz, he had had his fill of the demands of a long-running road show. He wanted to direct. At the Little Theatre in New York, Michio Itow's *Pinwheel Revel* was being staged for the second time, after premiering at the Earl Carroll Theatre only a couple of weeks before. Buzz landed a short-time job as general stage director and actor in different roles, each requiring extensive makeup.

He played a black man, a South Seas native, and a clown. Buzz was also the stage director for the annual musical review *The Greenwich Village Follies*. The Follies-producing team of Jones and Green was impressed enough with Buzz to offer him a job in their newest production. They wanted him to go to Chicago to stage the touring version of the long-running review *Hitchy Koo 1923,* starring the popular homespun comic Raymond Hitchcock, who had produced and acted in early versions of the review. Buzz did double duty on the show, appearing onstage with the star in seven sketches.

Buzz joined the Somerville Theater Stock Company in Somerville, Massachusetts, directing the musical farce *Going Up.* The play had been a big hit in New York and Chicago. In October 1923, the director began rehearsals for a three-day run in Fitchburg, forty miles west. On October 29, Buzz attended a luncheon where he met with twenty-five members of the Chamber of Commerce who had an interest in the success of the show. He discussed his plans and told the locals that *Going Up* would be the finest amateur production ever witnessed here and that the cast was by far the best he had ever worked with.

The stock life was the life of Busby Berkeley. He became a full-fledged director in Boston when the original director had to leave the show for a family emergency. He wasn't beneath advertising his own productions when the need arose. Once, in Paterson, New Jersey, Buzz took to riding shotgun on a biplane. Latching himself in place, he bent backward. With his head to the ground he let scatter little air balloons to which were tied tickets to an upcoming performance at Paterson's Lyceum Theatre.

Back in Boston, Buzz was associated with a dramatic, rather than musical, company. The producers had made a request that caused Buzz to scoff. Every Monday night he opened a new show. In two weeks, they wanted him to stage, act, and sing in a musical with his tone-deaf company. "Are you men crazy?" asked Buzz. "The leading man can't sing or dance, neither can the leading lady." The producers' rationale was that the audience would be in on the joke; knowing in advance that they were witnessing dramatic actors trying to sing would make for fun all around.

"Let me out. . . . [G]et somebody else to do the show," said a resigned Buzz.

The money men pleaded. Like his mother, Buzz softened. "What do you do about the dancing?" he asked. Their answer came in the form of a teacher from the Corbett School of the Dance. They assured Buzz he had nothing to worry about. With trepidation, he agreed. Right from the start, he had grief. In the middle of rehearsals, the Corbett teacher interrupted him with questions about staging and blocking. Who sings this verse, the man or the woman? Buzz didn't give a damn and told her as much. Do the girls come in from the right or from the left? "Have them come in from the ceiling. It doesn't make any difference to me; I don't know a thing about it."

Stressed and anxious, Buzz was not in good spirits on opening night. He had trouble memorizing lyrics. Because he was given responsibility for staging the book and not the musical numbers, he was worried that he'd bump into dancers entering from stage-left, stage-right, *or* the ceiling. "Next time you let me out if you do a musical," barked Buzz to the company manager, "either that, or I'll put it on myself."

The show was far from a fiasco. It ran its customary week, replaced by a drama on Monday. A few months later, management wanted another musical. Buzz's first impulse was to reject the idea, but they reminded him of his offer. Buzz staged and dance-designed his first musical with a resultant run of four weeks, unheard of in stock theater.

Other stock companies took notice. Buzz received offers in the form of letters, wires, and phone calls from up and down the eastern seaboard. He began contracting his services. Moneywise, it made sense.

At the Arlington Square Theatre in Boston, papers took notice of Busby Berkeley directing their next production of the Frank Mandel, Otto Harbach musical *Mary*. Following the opening-night show, some five hundred members of the Pilgrim Publicity Association staged a reception for Buzz and the cast, followed by a collation and dance on the stage. In early March, it was announced that a troupe named the Berkeley Comedians would star Busby Enos in a show with which he was familiar, *Going Up*.

In Baltimore, in order to save a play called *The White Sheik* from closing due to its poor theater location and weak ticket sales, Buzz had a prurient plan to forestall the inevitable. He went a few miles into the theater district and saw a show that was commanding respectable crowds.

Jules Eckert Goodman and Edward Knoblock's *Simon Called Peter* caused a rage when the play's villain tore off the leading lady's dress, exposing a breast. Buzz cleverly deduced the exploitable in the exposure and went on a talent hunt. From sleazy dance halls to New York's Ziegfeld Review, he recruited willing women who saw nothing objectionable in appearing clothesless onstage. One major change sealed the deal. *The White Sheik* was now titled, suggestively, *Seduction*. "See the Passionate Nautche Dancers of the Desert . . . See the Black Hat of Desire . . . See a Woman's Soul Laid Bare to Love . . . See the White Tent of Virtue!" wrote publicity man Buzz. Truckloads of sand were dumped on the stage. Sexy desert wenches danced in the dunes, their pretty faces hidden behind sheer veils. The climax featured the leading man tearing the leading actress's dress, doubling the exposure Buzz had seen downtown as both breasts were exposed momentarily before the lights were killed. Their display caused a *succès du scandale* with a run on ticket sales that kept the badly located house playing to capacity crowds for weeks.

Buzz regarded himself as a double threat. As director and performer he could command two salaries. He sometimes made upward of $250 per credit. With continuous work, his cash flow was flush, but very little was left over after sending a stipend to Mother back home. The balance was spent with no thought of a rainy-day provision. At this stage, Buzz needn't have worried. Word was getting around Broadway about this new dance director and "his intricate counter-rhythms and his unusual creative style." He moved into the St. Andrews Hotel at the end of September 1925 for the sole purpose of being close to the most exciting role of his career—dance director for a Broadway show.

"Dances and ensembles by Busby Berkeley," read the program notes to *Holka Polka,* a restaging of the Czech operetta *Spring in Autumn,* by W. Walzer. With *Rose Marie* a solid success the year before, operettas were again in favor. The show opened on October 14 at the Lyric Theatre and ran a scant twenty-one performances despite the good review in the *New York Times* and its praise for the "colorful chorus numbers" that included more than sixty dancers in the big *Holka Polka* finale.

Buzz's exuberance diminished when he became unemployed less than three weeks after his Broadway debut. Pride kept him from calling his scrupulously saving mother for a loan. In Brooklyn, a theater producer needed someone to stage dance routines for his show *Castles in the Air.* He contacted Buzz, who jumped at the opportunity after a pay-less month. He assembled what few coins he had and took the subway to meet one of the producing partners. Unfortunately, the partner told Buzz that his other partner had already hired a dance director. Buzz, out of cash for the return ride home and too prideful to ask the producer, made light of his situation and walked the eight miles back to Manhattan. Asleep for only a few hours, Buzz was awakened with a phone call from the producer with better news. He had convinced his partner to hire Buzz for the Chicago road production, and for several weeks he was kept on the payroll. The show ran for almost a year in Chicago. When it finally opened on Broadway in September 1926, it was a somewhat splintered show from the one Buzz worked on. In fact, Buzz's contribution to the show went uncredited; it was attributed instead to Julian Mitchell, who had died before the New York opening.

Almost a year after *Holka Polka,* Buzz handled the folk dances for another Broadway operetta, *The Wild Rose,* which ran sixty-one performances from October to December 1926. The show brought together the same creative talent that had been behind *Rose Marie,* with music by Rudolf Friml and lyrics by Oscar Hammerstein II, but without the same success.

At Broadway's Liberty Theatre, the show *Lady Do* opened in April 1927, with dances and ensembles staged by "'Buzz' Berkeley." The star of the show was Karyl Norman, a renowned female impersonator in vaudeville. One of the show's singers became ill the day after the opening, and Buzz took over the role for a week as the unofficial understudy. The *New York Times* reviewer was not enthralled, saying the show ran "two exceedingly long acts." Fifty performances later, it closed.

A lack of backing doomed Buzz's next project, *Sweet Lady.* It opened and closed before making it to Broadway when the funds ran out. A bright spot to the calamity came by way of Louis Shurr, a well-known theatrical and press agent. He saw the production and immediately signed the unrepresented dance director. He promised Buzz big things. The producer Lew Fields was casting a new Rodgers and Hart show that sounded perfect for his client. Louis went to Lew and pitched his new discovery.

Lew Fields wasn't immediately sold on Berkeley. He wanted the in-demand dance director Seymour Felix, but he wasn't available. Neither were Bobby Connolly, Jack Haskell, or Sammy Lee, three notable Broadway dance men. Fields signed Buzz to his production, and whether it was by default or through the incredible timing that blessed Buzz's life, he was now the dance director for the biggest-budgeted show of his career, *A Connecticut Yankee.*

Based on Mark Twain's *A Connecticut Yankee in King Arthur's Court,* the updated play was peppered with modern colloquialisms ("Methinks yon damsel is a lovely broad"). During the tryouts, Buzz, in the most pressure-packed of all his shows to date, received assistance from Seymour Felix, whose schedule had cleared once auditions began.

Buzz's inexperience with the machinations of the dance caused him once again to revert to his wits by bluffing his way through rehearsals. With relative ease he could masterfully maneuver his performers in circles, columns, and grids, devising complex pattern formations under the constraints of the proscenium, yet he was impotently ineffective when it came to defining specific dance steps. Buzz was thinking of a way to open the second act, which featured Queen Guinevere's dancing school at the king's court. Nothing specific was in the script, so Buzz came up with the idea of having the queen instruct her little subjects to arrange themselves in the first five classical positions of the dance. If Buzz had only known one of them he could have proceeded with some air of authority, but being completely unaware of all he let his bluster overshadow his ignorance. "What do you think we should do, Buzz?" asked one of the chorus girls. "Well, I think it would be nice to start with the first position," he said, bluffing. "Oh, you mean this . . ." replied the dancer as Buzz watched and took mental notes. Still not revealing his hand, he responded nonchalantly, "Well, I may do it or I may not . . . I don't know." The second through fifth positions were performed in the same manner, a seemingly bored Buzz wrapping his inexperience in false bravado.

Buzz was not linked romantically to anyone in the rehearsal phase of *A Connecticut Yankee* until he made the acquaintance of a pretty dancer in the chorus named Evelyn Ruh; shortly thereafter, the two became a couple. Less than a fortnight following the show's opening on November 3, Buzz announced that he and Evelyn would be married within the week. The November 15 edition of the *New York Times* wrote of the

coming nuptials, listing Miss Ruh's age as nineteen, and Berkeley's erroneously as twenty-eight (he was thirty-one).

When *A Connecticut Yankee* opened at the Vanderbilt Theatre on
Forty-eighth Street just off Broadway, it's a safe assumption that Gertrude
was a first-nighter overflowing with pride when she read the "Dances by
Busby Berkeley" credit in the third row below the title in the theater program. The show was a critical hit. Buzz's dancers received great praise
for mastering complex routines that sent them prancing over tables,
sofas, "over anything between them and the other side of the stage."
Robert Coleman's column in the *New York Mirror* succinctly put Buzz's
newfound fame in perspective when he wrote, "Berkeley's numbers were
a revelation except to the few who had witnessed previous products he
has directed." He went on to describe *Sweet Lady,* its premature closing,
and the loss to Broadway patrons of seeing an earlier Berkeley success.
The *New York Herald Tribune* of November 20 proclaimed "Rialto
Fame Comes Suddenly to Young Director of Dances" and included this
little description of one of the musical numbers: "The technique applied
by Mr. Berkeley is difficult to explain, it being a combination of the
classic, jazz, buck, acrobatic and pageant. For instance, one of the first
numbers in the show is with a chorus in modern dress, a conglomeration
of steps which combines jazz with individuality, a Charleston effect with
acrobatic leaps. It is a rushing, twirling affair with a tom-tom beat, leaving the chorus breathless and the audience applauding."

When the laudatory reviews came out, producer Russell Janney
asked to see the new wunderkind of Broadway. He immediately signed
Buzz to stage the numbers for *The White Eagle,* an operetta based on
Edwin Milton Royle's play *The Squaw Man,* scheduled to open in a
month. *A Connecticut Yankee* ran for 421 performances. A touring
company was created, and the play played in London.

The wedding never came off. For reasons unknown, Buzz and Evelyn proved premature in their announcement. Perhaps Gertrude had
expressed her disapproval. The net result of it all had Buzz living unencumbered on his ample salary while he routinely tithed his earnings to
Mother. The practical Gertrude saw value in real estate, and it's likely
that it was she who urged her son to purchase a twenty-four-room mansion in Dover, New Hampshire, and to record the title under her own

name. She moved from the Park Avenue apartment she shared with her son and began filling the new place with collectibles. Buzz raised no objection when Gertrude indulged her passion. Her happiness was his.

Buzz called himself "The One-Two-Three-Kick" kid, while another term, "The Big Four," grouped him with the top dance directors Sammy Lee, Seymour Felix, and Bobby Connolly. His name was routinely bandied about for future consideration. His next project was also big-budgeted. With a large chorus and ornate set decoration, he staged the dances for *The White Eagle*. Opening the day after Christmas 1927, it featured "spectacular stage numbers," including two mock Native American ceremonials.

Golden Dawn in 1927 and *The Greenwich Village Follies of 1928* were two projects where it was hinted that Buzz had lent his expertise. Because he also restaged shows that, in his words, "ran into trouble," he was known affectionately among his peers as "Doctor Buzz, The Show Fixer." He was now working at a brisk pace both on and off Broadway. At the midpoint of *The White Eagle's* run, it was announced that Buzz was opening a dramatic stock company of his own based in Plainfield, New Jersey. *The Little Spitfire* was the first production of "The Busby Berkeley Players," with Buzz himself directing and taking a dramatic role, his first since the epiphany backstage of *The Man Who Came Back*.

Lew Fields, Richard Rodgers, and Lorenz Hart (the creative force behind *A Connecticut Yankee*) wanted Buzz again for their next collaboration, *Present Arms*. Before the show reached Broadway in April 1928, it, like many others, was staged out of town in order to fix problems; one required a change of personnel. Lew fired the comedy lead and offered Buzz the role of a marine sergeant. It was the promotion that every actor dreams of. The decades of wandering that had characterized Gertrude's professional existence, the sacrifices made along the way, all seemed worth it when her son became a Broadway performer. Buzz was understandably under pressure, learning new songs and staging them at the same time. The story of a marine company stationed in Hawaii gave him the chance to mount some smartly styled military drills and what was called "high-brow jazz dancing."

If ever a problem plagued Buzz, it was his difficulty with memorization. Until he was comfortable with a role, he often lost track of his place in the script when facing a cold, staring audience. He relived his nightmare on opening night. Gertrude and everyone else in attendance witnessed a nervous Busby Berkeley going completely blank in the second chorus of his first song, "You Took Advantage of Me." He scatted and hummed when memory failed. Buzz noticed songwriter Lorenz Hart "running up and down in the wings almost apoplectic." Things naturally improved for the nascent Broadway thespian over the nine weeks of his performance. Reviewers were quick to cite "the 'whirling pace' of a chorus that met the tests of the eye and the stethoscope" and "the complicated and subtle rhythms that many a trained musician or trained artistic dancer would find next to impossible to perform." Buzz himself remarked on the unusual dance steps he sometimes employed: "Ordinarily you'd break a dance step on the eighth bar and go into a new step. I'd break it on the fifth bar and go into a new rhythm." A musical director who worked with Buzz said he never watched the dancing, for he'd lose the beat when contrasting rhythms were performed together. The *New York Times* commented on Buzz's technique: "He creates none of these dances in advance; in fact, his inspiration seems to come from having the girls in front of him on the stage ready for work."

In May, it was announced that the subject of jazz (that had supposedly "bewildered" the European continent) would be presented at the Salzburg Festival as American folk art. The Shakespeare Foundation of Stratford-on-Avon would be offering a series of the folk dances of various nations. Buzz was invited, and he prepared a jazz number that represented America (described as "mazes of syncopation"). An eight-girl troupe brought Buzz's ideas to life beginning with an Indian-themed number (with accompanying tom-tom beats) that metamorphosed, tracing the history of dance to the present day. Native Americans originating jazz was dubious ethnology, but such trifles mattered little to Buzz.

In the rush of recent successes and his ever-increasing commitment load, the Busby Berkeley Players were all but assigned to the back burner. After a few short months, his personal troupe was disbanded. Broadway was now his home base, and on off days he visited the famed vaudeville house the Palace Theatre. Much like a major-league scout, he'd watch New York's emerging talent with an eye toward future roles. Occasionally he witnessed a performance that was intriguing, appealing, and memorable. Alone on the Palace stage, a woman dressed in a flowing, airy gown played the violin while dancing and twirling in perfectly defined circles. In a controlled move, she raised her leg and flawlessly executed a high kick and a slow leg drop. Buzz was impressed by the inherent beauty of the move. At another show, four men were playing grand pianos simultaneously. "Someday I'll do that with fifty," said his inner voice. A tour Buzz took through the local Ford motor plant in the summer of 1928 also contained elements that he found recyclable.

An imitator of sorts of the lavish revues first staged by Florenz Ziegfeld in 1907 (which were themselves imitations of the French Folies-Bergère) were the Earl Carroll Vanities. The revues were of the vaudeville type, short skits or musical numbers unrelated to one another. The productions were lavish, containing dancing girls in skimpy outfits and, in the case of the Earl Carroll Vanities, quite risqué in their humor.

The *Earl Carroll Vanities of 1928* was named after the impresario who oversaw every aspect of his annual revue from casting to rehearsals. In this seventh edition of the vanities, W. C. Fields was the headline attraction. When it came to the dancing girls, Buzz was in charge. On the sweltering July nights that preceded the August opening, it wasn't unusual to see Earl Carroll in an operator's headset issuing orders to the backstage crew and electricians. Buzz worked his girls tough in rehearsals that sometimes lasted past 2:00 a.m. The final dress rehearsal had unforeseen problems: timing was off, and the whole production seemed lethargic. Carroll booked a one-week tryout at the Apollo Theatre in Atlantic City to open on July 30, 1928. On August 6, 1928, the seventh edition of the *Earl Carroll Vanities of 1928* opened at the Earl Carroll Theatre. The reviewer from the *New York American* certainly helped ticket sales when he wrote: "From the drop of the hat it is skin, skin, skin. Bare backs to the right of one, uncovered knees to the left, undraped thighs in unserried rank in front of one, and naked scapulae, patenae, and various odds and ends of anatomy in every nook and corner of the stage."

The number "Say It with Girls" opened the revue with an interesting use of light projection. Onto a large screen were seen close-ups of the pretty chorines, one by one, offering the audience an unheard-of intimacy. Pat Lee, a dancer in the show, was featured in an exotic number. Flanked by chorus girls holding batons, she walked down the center of the stage dressed in an Aztec sun god headpiece with her torso wrapped in a gem-encrusted nude body stocking. The audience loved it. In the second act (the "Machinery Ballet"), Buzz's Ford plant tour was envisioned as a high-tech assembly line with the females dressed in robot-like costumes. They moved in jerky motions from one end of the stage to the other while one factory worker slowly turned cartwheels, one after another. The number was widely praised, and one critic compared the mass anonymity of the assembly line to the faceless hoards in Fritz Lang's *Metropolis*. Lillian Roth, the famed singer (and haunted alcoholic), performed "I'm Flying High," a number that featured the chorus girls arranged in the shape of an airplane with one who formed the propeller. The positive reviews and naughty word-of-mouth made the *Earl Carroll Vanities* a success, playing to full houses for six months.

While he was rehearsing the *Earl Carroll Vanities*, Buzz was approached by writers from the *New York Times*. They had been impressed by *Present Arms* and told Buzz they'd seen the show four times. Buzz was flattered, figuring they had returned because they had liked the show. The writers disagreed: "The reason we have seen it four times is that we couldn't figure out how you create and break up your routines the way you do, and how you go into different tempos. So we wonder if we could interview you and ask you how you do it." Without a drop of false modesty, he replied: "If you can pick up anything, fine. But for me to try to explain it to you, I can't, because I know nothing about it. I create as I go along, and if this looks good, sounds goods, and feels good, I do it." On July 22, 1928, the *New York Times* printed a praise-filled, four-column interview titled "The Dance: New Musical Comedy Talent; Busby Berkeley's Direction Raises the Level of Our Stage Performances." Buzz appreciated the fact that the writers explained his own technique to him. "I thought that was wonderful."

He found his next job immediately. Just a month after the *Earl Carroll* opening, *Good Boy*, "a musical play," made its debut at Hammerstein's Theatre. On the surface, the show looked more like a revue (sixteen scenes in act 1, seventeen in act 2), but a linking narrative kept it closer to musical theater. To simulate the lead actress frantically making her way through Manhattan, Buzz ingeniously used treadmills and movable scenery to good effect where sidewalks came alive and arbitrary motion and direction were unnaturally rapid. Traffic noises and ambulance sirens added to the dizzying effect. Another winner, *Good Boy*, ran a half year, and one song, "I Wanna Be Loved by You," sung by Helen Kane became a hit on 78 rpm records.

The spell broke on Buzz's next project. He staged the numbers for Vincent Youmans and Oscar Hammerstein's American-style operetta *Rainbow,* a story of murder, wagon trains, and the California gold rush. Buzz staged a military-style march number and a "hoedown" dance for the song "Hay! Straw!" The critics were kind, but according to one report, the show never recovered from the miscues and mishaps evident on opening night. It ran six days shy of a month.

It's almost humorous that Busby Berkeley shared dancing credits with the similarly named Buddy Bradley for his next show, *Hello, Daddy!,* a Lew Fields production. Bradley, an African American, was a popular dance instructor at the Billy Pierce Dance Studio (he taught up-and-coming white stars) and was the perfect adjunct to Buzz, who was more interested in spectacular staging than intricate tapping. Written by Dorothy Fields and Herbert Fields (Lew Fields's daughter and son), the moderately successful show opened the day after Christmas and ran through June 1929.

In late 1928, Buzz was introduced to the brothers Shubert, the most powerful (and prolific) producers on Broadway. Older brother Lee produced dramas and Jacob (J. J.) handled musicals. They wanted Buzz to stage the dances for their newest show, *Pleasure Bound.* Actually, seeking Buzz's contribution was an afterthought. J. J. wasn't pleased with the way the production was developing and brought Buzz in to give it some "sparkle." The show was rehearsed in Newark, New Jersey, followed by a week of tweaking in Cleveland. The *New York Times* theater critic Brooks Atkinson called *Pleasure Bound* a "rough-and-ready" revue. Without naming Buzz directly, he went on to describe the dancing girls "who interpret their classical art as brisk high-stepping are never absent for long, and now and then display stunning visual effects." Two dancers in the show, Frank Veloz and Yolanda Casazza, were cited for the has-to-be-seen "centrifugal dance spinning feminine heels in the air." During the fine-tuning in Cleveland, Buzz received an urgent call from Arthur Hammerstein. His show *The Wild Rose* was playing in Springfield, Massachusetts, and having trouble. Would Buzz (who staged the numbers three years earlier) lend his expertise and fix what needed fixing? He left for Springfield and told Hammerstein to close the show for a week. He would work on restaging, and he urged Arthur to move the rehearsals to New York. As for *Hello, Daddy!* and

Pleasure Bound, both closed on June 15, 1929, but Buzz didn't care. By that time, his next show for the Shuberts had already opened.

A Night in Venice was the third in a series of similarly titled projects (*A Night in Paris, A Night in Spain*). In this version, two Lotharios pose as "Lindbergh-style" pilots to gain the affections of a couple of show-girls. The ruse is eventually revealed in the tuneful final act. The story was thin, and the production was again tipped toward a revue, with twenty-five scenes over two acts. Ted Healy and his Stooges, a wrestling bear, and semi-nude posers were just a few examples of the show's diversity. On May 21, *A Night in Venice* played Broadway, but not before a tryout across the Hudson in Newark.

Buzz was known as a jokester to the chorus girls. He'd tell a smutty joke just for their reaction. The ongoing treasure trough of beautiful women gave Buzz ample opportunity to savor a flower or two (if not an outright bouquet), but he wasn't truly passionate about any of them. Gertrude wasn't pushing marriage, and Buzz's increasingly hectic schedule didn't allow it. He went to Philadelphia to oversee the road show of *A Night in Venice,* and just as he did with his time off in New York, he perused the local theaters. At one show, a tall blonde caught Buzz's discerning eye. He was, in his own words, "smitten from the moment she walked on stage." Backstage, Buzz politely introduced himself to Esther Muir.

She was a model in high school, a nascent actress when she won a role in *Greenwich Village Follies* (not the same revue with which Buzz had been associated), and a young divorcée. Their paths didn't cross when Esther played a bit part in the *Earl Carroll Vanities* either. But in Philadelphia, a smitten Buzz and a statuesque Esther became an item.

Gertrude and her beloved antiques were far away from Buzz, Esther, and the Broadway lights, but eventually the two women met, most likely at the time Buzz was rehearsing the ensemble in the Shubert brothers' next production, *Broadway Nights.* The show, in the same vein as *A Night in Venice,* was more revue than plot. Buzz directed his dancing girls in a routine that had them bouncing big rubber balls and tossing them into the audience. Another number featured the chorines assembled in the form of a train, prompting the *New York Times* to include the show in its description of "The Big Railroad Year" when referring to musicals. Buzz claimed to introduce the concept of the perennial underdog in musical comedy. He had the shortest chorus girl placed at the end of the chorus line. She would struggle about, trying to kick as high as the other girls, following their lead and doing whatever it took to fit in. Buzz knew it was guaranteed to get the audience's laughter, sympathy, and applause. Financially, *Broadway Nights* was a short-lived disappointment, closing after only forty performances.

His next show was monumental. The Shubert brothers agreed it was time for Busby Berkeley to wear the producer's hat. Buzz took it three steps further. He would design the dance numbers, direct the show, and command the credit "Presented by Busby Berkeley," an accomplishment never before achieved by anyone. *The Street Singer* drew upon *Pygmalion* with its young millionaire eager to transform a Parisian flower girl into his personification of the "perfect lady." Buzz led an ensemble of seventeen dancing girls, twelve show girls, and eight boys in more than ten numbers. Broadway dancing star Queenie Smith, who played the flower girl, performed one of the more interesting dances. Set in the Green Room of the Folies Bergère, the dance Buzz designed was a lyrical, atypical ballet. During rehearsals, the Shuberts liked the rapidity of Buzz's ensembles and had the show advertised as the "fastest dancing chorus ever." He opened *The Street Singer* on September 17, 1929, with Gertrude and Esther in attendance. The reviews were some of the best of his career. One critic admired what he called "the fastest-stepping throng of pretty girls ever to enliven a stage" and spoke of Buzz's "tireless, peppy, pulchritudinous chorus [that] won salvos of applause." Author and critic Gilbert Seldes was effusive in his admiration: "The dances Busby Berkeley arranged for *The Street Singer* were so numerous, intricate, exciting and well done that nothing else in the show mattered. . . . [T]he novelty and the assurance of the entire chorus body were all exciting and gave specific character to the show." *The Street Singer* was a financial success and ran through the rest of the year. Its frazzled creator needed time off. The stress and strain of putting on his own show—the headaches, mistakes, missteps, and last-minute improvements—led Buzz to the Shubert Theatre's liquor cart on several occasions.

The Shuberts called Buzz and asked him to show up at the theater at midnight. When he arrived, he was surprised to see the noted composer Sigmund Romberg poised and ready to conduct a twenty-four-piece orchestra. J. J. had wanted Buzz to listen and comment on Romberg's

new numbers for his operetta *Nina Rosa*. The grand treatment of a full
orchestration for audition purposes was extravagant since normally it's
only the songwriter and piano accompanist (often one and the same).
Buzz listened, nodded appreciatively, and told J. J. that he liked what
he heard. "Glad you like it because you're going to stage and direct it,"
said J. J. The show needed tinkering and didn't require Buzz's services
immediately, which for Buzz was a godsend. J. J. had left for London,
The Street Singer was breathing on its own, and Esther and her beloved
spent quality time with each other as things were getting quite serious.

Buzz had a discerning eye for beauty and a tin ear for romance. He
proposed to Esther, she accepted, and neither could set a wedding date.
Too busy was the excuse. He's dance-directing; she's acting at another
theater. J. J. cabled Buzz with an invitation to join him in London, where
he was auditioning local talent. Buzz called Esther and sold her on the
idea of a romantic ocean cruise. She melted and wrangled her way out
of her contract for a few days' leave. Dutiful Buzz called Mother and
invited her along, too. How Esther reacted is better imagined. Buzz and
J. J. did their business during the day, and it's a safe assumption that
when he, Esther, and Gertrude were together in the evening—every
evening—three was a crowd. The cause of the eventual row and general falling out between the engaged isn't known, but it was one ship
that brought them eastward and two that brought them home. Esther
sailed solo, while the more demonstrative actress and her rising-star son
cruised home together in continental style.

They patched things up, but a wedding date hadn't been selected. Esther drew the line; a date had to be made before she would see Buzz again.
Meanwhile he was assigned his next project by the Shuberts, *The Duchess of Chicago*, a musical comedy with operettist overtones. It tested in a
number of cities. Buzz figured by the time the show played in Baltimore,
he'd have a free day or two to get married; reality proved otherwise.
The Duchess of Chicago was having problems, first in Springfield, then
in Newark and Philadelphia. Now in Baltimore, the high-strung dance
director was distracted with wedding plans. On Friday, November 22,
1929, weeks after the devastating stock market crash that left Eddie
Cantor, the highest paid star on Broadway, a virtual pauper, Buzz was
all aflutter. In the afternoon, J. J. Shubert saw him making a mad dash
for the exit. He asked Buzz where he was going. "I'm on my way to City

Hall to get a marriage license," he yelled. "What a damn fool you are!" yelled J. J. back. Buzz was panicking. He got the marriage license and was now in a rush to find the right ring. He bought a stone and setting, and raced to meet Esther at the train station. Time was ticking, and Buzz had to be back before the curtain rose. He shuffled Esther in his car and they rode at a clip, arriving at the Maryland Theatre in time to hear the opening notes of Pierre de Reeder's orchestration. A couple of hours after the curtain dropped, in the private office of Leonard B. McLaughlin (the manager of the Maryland), Buzz and Esther were married. Present were J. J. and a few other theatrical friends. A party was thrown for the newlyweds on the same stage where *The Duchess of Chicago* was floundering. Conspicuous by her absence was Gertrude.

Buzz and bride settled into the Lexington Hotel, while Gertrude lived comfortably at Ninety-first and Park Avenue. No time for a real honeymoon, so the new Mr. and Mrs. returned to work, with Buzz fighting a lost cause. The trades bemoaned the stock market crash and its effect on theatergoers. Just one day into their marriage, it was reported that Broadway impresario Florenz Ziegfeld had to close his show *Whoopee* starring the *nouveau pauvre* Eddie Cantor. *The Duchess of Chicago* might have well remained there for she never saw the lights of Broadway. The failed show closed after its Boston run.

Buzz staged the musical numbers for *Ruth Selwyn's Nine Fifteen Revue,* a production that was overstuffed and overblown with an elephantine budget. The producer, Ruth Selwyn, was the young wife of actor, writer, and Broadway producer Edgar Selwyn. He pampered his wife with a six-figure production budget and a name preceding the title. No less than Earl Carroll himself was brought on board to direct (though he wasn't listed in the opening-night program). Buzz led his all-female ensemble through some suggestive staging. Lingerie-clad cuties tiptoed across the stage in one number, and a takeoff on "Goldilocks and the Three Bears" was quite risqué when "who's been sleeping in my bed" comically questioned the heroine's virtue. Songs such as "How Would a City Girl Know?" "Boudoir Dolls," and "Gotta Find a Way to Do It" were all aimed at the lower instincts. The *New York Times* called the show "noisy and speedy" in its review of February 12, 1930. The tune "Get Happy," written by a young, new songwriter named Harold Arlen, made quite a splash on its own. It was sung by Ruth Etting to close the show, and George Gershwin commented that it was "the most exciting finale he had ever heard in a theatre." But for all its effervescence and peekaboo production numbers, *Ruth Selwyn's Nine Fifteen Revue* was a colossal flop, opening on February 11 and closing on February 15 after only seven performances.

Lew Leslie, the Broadway producer and director, had made his name staging revues with all-black casts. His *Plantation Revue* and *Blackbirds of 1928* were resounding successes. Buzz declined a new contract from the Shuberts when Leslie made him a more intriguing offer. With a cast that included Gertrude Lawrence, Jack Pearl, and Buzz's wife, Esther, *Lew Leslie's International Revue* opened ten days after the *Nine Fifteen Revue* closed. The opening night for *International Revue* was described as "disastrously disorganized," and Lew Leslie immediately retooled the show. Buzz's numbers included "Keys to My Heart," where his chorus, in half-black, half-white piano-key costumes, dances across a giant keyboard, and a mock Indian number, "Big Papoose on the Loose," with girls war-chanting in elaborate headdresses. One interesting number, "The Rout," featured the denizens of Montmartre's Apache district. Drunks mingle with dope addicts, swells walk the avenue, and organ grinders crank their music past flower girls. A gun goes off, and a woman jumps from the second-story set into the arms of a young lothario. A fight ensues between two men, resulting in the accidental stabbing of the woman. The "street" empties, save for an old gentleman, who silently walks across the stage as the curtain closes.

International Revue gave birth to two hit songs, "On the Sunny Side of the Street" and "Exactly Like You" and garnered its fair share of positive reviews. In March, Buzz, Esther, Guy Lombardo, and other swells were first-nighters at Duke Ellington's new revue (his sixth) titled *Blackberries of 1930*. Playing at Harlem's Cotton Club, the show featured singers, dancers, and two dozen chorus girls that Buzz didn't fail to notice.

Since he was no longer associated with the Shuberts, it wasn't surprising that Sigmund Romberg's *Nina Rosa* opened without Buzz receiving a credit. Sources disagree as to the level of Buzz's involvement in the show, but it did feature an Indian-style number called "Peruvian Sun Worship" that bore a resemblance to "Big Papoose on the Loose" and the mock ceremonials he staged for *The White Eagle*.

Buzz's agent in New York was William Grady Sr. He worked for the William Morris Agency and fielded requests for the talented dance director's services. During rehearsals of *The International Revue,* Bill Grady rushed into the theater and interrupted Buzz, who was directing from the theater box. Eddie Cantor had contacted William Morris, who had in turn contacted Grady with an incredible opportunity.

"Buzz, how would you like to go to the West Coast—I mean Hollywood," said Bill.

Buzz, who wasn't at all impressed with musical pictures in the new era of sound, replied hastily: "No you can have your Hollywood musicals. They don't know how to do them out there. They show a lot of girls dancing and then cut to the milkman kissing the maid 'good morning' and then cut back to the dance again. That's no way to do musical sequences."

Undismayed, Bill shot back, "Would you be interested if I had a good star?"

"Yes."

"Okay, how about Eddie Cantor?"

"Yes, that's all right. Who are the producers?"

"Ziegfeld and Samuel Goldwyn."

Buzz bit Bill's lure: "That's good . . . what's the show?"

"*Whoopee.*"

Whoopee was the big hit of Broadway's 1928–1929 season. It was typically Ziegfeldian, with sparkling costumes and spectacular stagings. The luster dulled after the market crash, and the legendary impresario lost more than $1 million. "Ziggy" told his wife, stage star Billie Burke, "I'm through. Nothing can save me." That's when Samuel Goldwyn swooped in like an angel. He was looking for a good story to film, and his timing couldn't have been better. Ziegfeld disdained Hollywood vulgarity and already carried a grudge when some of his biggest stars, such as Will Rogers and Fanny Brice, bolted for Los Angeles. But Ziegfeld's bargaining power had diminished, and he sold *Whoopee* to Goldwyn with the guarantee that Eddie Cantor would remain with the show. It was also agreed that Cantor would remain with the road show through March 1930. In one of the many notes that Eddie wired to Goldwyn, he urged the hiring of Busby Berkeley, and shortly thereafter Bill Grady gave Buzz the news.

Bill escorted his client to the William Morris office. A phone call was made to producer and studio founder Samuel Goldwyn in Hollywood. Goldwyn confirmed that he had purchased the rights to film *Whoopee* and that Eddie Cantor and Florenz Ziegfeld were attached to the project. Buzz thought more money would be in the offing, but Goldwyn promised him nothing beyond his current Broadway salary of a thousand dollars per week, and he let Buzz know that working in Hollywood was a priceless opportunity. Actor, singer, and motion picture star in talking pictures Al Jolson, who had wandered into the area where Buzz, Bill, and Sam Goldwyn were conversing, helped seal the deal. "Go on, Buzz, take the thousand. What do you care? They've got golf courses out there five minutes from the studio, the ocean at your back door, beautiful beaches, sunshine every day." On Jolson's prodding, Buzz accepted a one-picture deal from Goldwyn. He told Gertrude of his plans to work on just this one film and return to New York when he was finished. Esther was thrilled with the news, for she imagined her career trajectory included motion pictures.

She and Buzz were in Cleveland with Eddie Cantor when *Whoopee* closed, and they went to Childs Restaurant, where, on the back of a menu, Buzz sketched designs for the major dance numbers. The next day they, along with Thornton Freeland, the film's director, boarded a train for Hollywood. Berkeley would revolutionize the making of musical films, said Eddie. Buzz, Eddie, and Thornton spoke together frequently during the three-day trip about the many changes that would be required to take *Whoopee* from stage to screen.

The *New York Herald Tribune*'s theater critic Ray Colman had a notion when he wrote presciently the previous year: "What that boy Buzz Berkeley would do in pictures if they ever give him the reins and holler 'Gid-dap!' He sure would make a few of those boys and girls out there raise plenty of Hollywood dust, or I don't know that Christmas comes in December."

4

A Cyclopean Vision

Before Buzz arrived in Hollywood, Sam Goldwyn had him privately investigated. He was hesitant to hire him because of an alleged drinking problem. Whoever relayed that information to Goldwyn is a mystery, but Ziegfeld knew Berkeley prior to his involvement with *Whoopee!* He had wanted Buzz to dance-direct a show a couple of years earlier, but Buzz had been busy with the *Earl Carroll Vanities*. It's quite likely that anecdotal accounts of Buzz's indiscretions were passed between Sam and "Ziggy" in private dinner conversations. Goldwyn overlooked his trepidation and sent a greeting party from his studio and the West Coast office of the William Morris Agency to meet Buzz and Esther at the Los Angeles depot. The couple checked into the Hollywood Roosevelt Hotel, and later both were driven to the Goldwyn Studios to meet its founder. Goldwyn told Buzz he was glad to have him on board for his (Sam's) first musical picture. He instructed Buzz to learn the studio ropes, wander about the sets, ask questions, and observe.

Buzz walked on the set and studied the lights and cameras. The picture's art director, Richard Day, came up to him when he saw the cinema neophyte looking perplexed. "Buzz, they try to make a big secret out of that little box, but it's no mystery at all. All you have to remember is that the camera has only one eye, not two. You can see a lot with two eyes, but hold a hand over one and it cuts your area of vision." Buzz thought that, instead of being restricted by the single eye, there were unlimited things you could do with a camera. But Goldwyn hired Buzz to stage the musical sequences, not shoot them. He soon approached the studio chief and made his case for directing his own numbers. Goldwyn balked somewhat before asking Buzz if he thought he could handle it all. "Mr. Goldwyn, I don't think I can, I *know* I can," said Buzz. Sam gave him the benefit of the doubt and made Thornton Freeland aware of the personnel change.

On the first day of shooting, Buzz walked onto the set with the same braggadocio he had displayed in *A Connecticut Yankee*. He saw four cameras in different areas of the set, each manned by its own crew. When he had spoken with Richard Day, he hadn't thought of *four cameras* with a single eye. He asked his assistant why so many were needed. He was told that the cutters (editors) would assemble the footage from each camera and splice together the finished product. "That's not my technique," announced the braggart. "I only use one camera so let the others go." Buzz never revealed to the crew that he couldn't get his mind around four cameras rolling at once. Unrecognized, even to him, was that his "technique" was pure and unencumbered. He envisioned his numbers being captured by the single eye to the point that a cutter needn't bother with footage from other cameras. Buzz planned to direct *in the camera,* complete and in sequence. It was a remarkably austere method. Shoot a segment, move the camera, and film another linearly until the number was finished. Surely, Buzz was urged, the four-camera setup could have accomplished the same thing once the editors assembled individual takes, but Buzz didn't think along those lines. The single camera was his appendage, an extension of his mind's eye, and the tool that carved the cornerstone of his art.

A brief exterior shot of cowboys on horseback opens *Whoopee!* and the action moves to an obvious stage set, nicely dressed in warm colors with an artistically rendered sky of deep blue. It isn't long before a young cowgirl (an unbilled thirteen-year-old named Betty Grable) shows her lasso prowess while belting out "The Cowboy Song," Buzz's first filmed dance number. It's a full-ensemble piece as Grable and the other identically dressed cowgirls maneuver in regimented line formations across a wood floor with alternating brown hues. Joining the girls are the uniformly outfitted cowboys, and as Buzz films them from various angles it's a thrill to hear and see the dancers' feet stomping in unison. Buzz's first top shot shows two concentric circles moving in opposite directions as the girl in the center stares upward toward the lone camera. A new formation has each man holding up a cowgirl, and in a move known on the stage as a "wave," each girl in quick succession bends downward to the waist and up again, giving the dance line an appearance of a sine wave on an oscilloscope. A second top shot is even more impressive as the circling dancers wave their giant Stetson hats back and forth. A final shot of the men lifting a half-dozen cowgirls is peered through the spread legs of hoisted girls in the foreground. Only four minutes into the film, and camera angles, points of view, blocking, dancing, and other accentuations announced a distinctive cinematic arrival.

And then *Whoopee!* begins in earnest, and Thornton Freeland's pedestrian directing brings the opening frenzy to a deflated stop. Eddie Cantor is Henry Williams, a hypochondriac who would always try to best someone complaining of their surgical scars. He accidentally gets between the soon-to-be-wed Sheriff Bob Wells (Jack Rutherford) and Sally Morgan (Eleanor Hunt). Sally really loves the half-Indian Wanenis (Paul Gregory), and runs away with Henry, leading to a series of misplaced assumptions and identity changes, as Henry assumes disguises in Indian garb and blackface.

The writing is witty, and Cantor delivers many sharp jokes, but Freeland's conception of the action never escapes the tacit boundaries of the stage. Characters enter from stage left, say their lines, and exit stage right. Jokes are told and paused for expected laughter. Only when the ensembles take center stage under Berkeley's command do the cinema and the cinematic converge.

In Buzz's second filmed ensemble, the short and lovely "Mission Number," church bells herald a wedding processional as the Goldwyn Girls in bridesmaids dresses pass before Buzz's singular eye in pleasing formations. They move in slow, tightly defined, circular groupings tossing flower petals and providing a path for Betty Grable as she leads other dancers past the girls out of camera range. There's restraint in the staging as Buzz keeps the camera grounded while making the performers' movements symmetrically interesting.

The "Stetson" number opens as singer/dancer Ethel Shutta performs a few steps with six whoopin' cowboys. The scene shifts to center stage as Stetsons are placed, one at a time, on a ledge, and then the empty hats pop up, each with a smiling girl underneath it. In single file, they jump, jump, jump down the staircase and assume a new interesting position. With his camera low to the ground and the girls standing, they spread their legs into an archway formation. Buzz's camera rests passively as the arch of legs moves in front of and passes the camera in little jump steps. A grid pattern is then formed, and each girl cleverly passes and retrieves her Stetson while tapping to the score. Then a simple but profound setup that Buzz claimed to be his singular contribution to the movie musical up to that point unfolds: "I introduced the big close-ups of beautiful girls," he boasted. "It had never been done before in musicals." As he was setting up his shot one day, Sam Goldwyn came to the set and asked Buzz what he was doing. "Making close-ups of the girls as they come into the camera," he replied. And the result of that planning is one of Buzz's immortal cinematic epitaphs. One at a time, in medium close-up, a girl inches toward the camera, a Stetson hiding her face, and in turn each moves the hat to her head, revealing a big smile before the next hidden face is unveiled. This seemingly simple act, a close-up of a succession of faces, somehow was never considered filmable in the stiff and stagy musicals that Buzz had seen and disdained. On a 1930 theater screen, it was a revelation of sorts to view glamorous film dancers desirably up close and almost obtainable.

"The Song of the Setting Sun," Buzz's fourth and final number for *Whoopee!* is a staging of an ersatz Indian ceremonial dance. Another visually dynamo top shot features the girls raising and lowering their feathered headdresses while moving in clockwise formation. Following next is a passing parade of girls, each adorned with elaborate feathers, posing as if they were models in a Native American fashion show. Then girls on horseback enter, led down a fake mountainside, the copious feathers on each head ample enough to threaten a winged species with extinction. (One has her feathers carried by two men like a long bridal train.) For his final shot, Buzz placed the camera in an ideal position to view the spectacle as if seen from the vantage point of a Broadway audience. As the entire ensemble is positioned in every area of the frame, Busby Berkeley established the clearest link between his theater staging and the newfound freedom that only the camera can define and celluloid can capture.

As filming progressed, it was Buzz who often gave Sam Goldwyn advice. He instructed his boss on ways to save money on wardrobe and accessories (avoiding real materials like leather whenever possible). Buzz and other studio employees found Sam an irresistible target for practical jokes. In a reply to Mr. Goldwyn on why shooting hadn't begun for a particular scene, Buzz said that wardrobe hadn't sent down the leotards for the horses. Sam didn't question the inanity of Buzz's reason. He immediately phoned the wardrobe department and demanded the horse leotards. Befuddlement surely struck the recipient of Sam's frantic call.

Even as Buzz was finishing *Whoopee!*, on June 12 it was announced that he was to sign a year's contract with options for Paramount Pictures. Reportedly, Buzz would move to the Paramount lot after staging dances for Irving Berlin's *Reaching for the Moon* at United Artists, starring Bebe Daniels and Douglas Fairbanks.

The Technicolor *Whoopee!* completed filming in late June, seven days behind schedule, and was previewed in San Diego in July. Apart from the invigorating contributions of a nascent motion-picture dance director with a funny name, the title's appended exclamation point is about the only thing that changed from stage to screen. Flo Ziegfeld went with Eddie Cantor to the preview and urged him to give up Hollywood for another stab at Broadway. "Wait till we see the picture, Flo," said Cantor; "If I squeeze your hand, we'll talk about another show." There was no squeeze. The Berkeley numbers sold the film. Cantor's original contract with Goldwyn stipulated one additional picture if *Whoopee!* was successful. On July 19, he received a new contract for three films. "There is much for the eyes to feast on in the various scenes," wrote Mordaunt Hall in the *New York Times*. Audiences enjoyed the unusual perspectives in Buzz's numbers. His top shots were exciting and unique, with interesting, eye-appealing formations in the best use of the effect to date.

Buzz left Sam Goldwyn's employ on good terms. He let Goldwyn know of his new job at Paramount, and at the time of his departure there was no talk of a future association with the studio or Eddie Cantor. Though *Whoopee!* was regarded as a success upon its release, musical films in general were suffering a steep decline in interest. Buzz went to Paramount, got introduced all around, and spent his first two weeks on salary in a quiet office twiddling his thumbs waiting for something to do.

Billy Rose, the famed lyricist, called Buzz long distance. He was producing his first show, *Sweet and Low,* and needed Buzz's expertise. Buzz sought and received permission from Paramount to return to New York. Esther remained in Hollywood waiting to be cast in her first film role. Buzz contacted Mother soon after his train pulled into Grand Central Station. He rehearsed at Chanin's Forty-sixth Street Theatre, working on dance numbers that the original dance director, Danny Dare, didn't. Rose, like any self respecting impresario whose wife is a stage star, gave Fanny Brice (Mrs. Rose) the lead role in the show that was supported by actor George Jessel. On November 17, 1930, *Sweet and Low* opened to middling reviews. The *New York Times* called it audacious, not on the dainty side, and "an extravaganza of the rough-and-ready sort." Buzz was no longer required after the opening. He returned to Paramount with the hope that an assignment was forthcoming. Gertrude was unconvinced that her son's Hollywood career could sustain him like Broadway.

Reaching for the Moon's producer, Joseph M. Schenck, didn't require Buzz's services. Buzz learned that none of the five Irving Berlin songs written for the film would be used. He waited for work that wasn't coming. One day, perhaps at the urging of Schenck, the seldom-used telephone rang in Buzz's quiet Paramount office. Quite surprisingly, at the other end of the receiver, Buzz heard a high-pitched friendly greeting of introduction from "America's Sweetheart" Mary Pickford. United Artists, the studio Mary cofounded with Charlie Chaplin and Douglas Fairbanks, was doing a remake of David Belasco's comedy *Kiki*. Mary would play the role originated by Norma Talmadge. Few knew that *Kiki* was the part Mary had always longed to play. She offered Buzz the dance director position, and with his never-failing gift of luck and timing, he severed his fruitless contract with Paramount and graciously accepted Mary's offer.

For Buzz, *Kiki* was a straight dance-directing job requiring little of the magic a Doctor Buzz would've brought to Broadway a few years earlier. But within him the seeds of inspiration were germinating, and he wanted once again to press his eye on the viewfinder of the cyclopean box and create anew. He received a "Dances staged by" credit, and brought back the uncredited Betty Grable and some other Goldwyn Girls for the dance number. The film's opening sequence, not credited to Buzz, has the look and feel of Berkeley inspiration. The fact that it stands apart from the balance of the picture makes Buzz the likely director. As music is playing, an elderly man is shaking his foot and whittling in time; the single camera pulls back to a poster being glued to a wall; the camera continues backward, revealing a man hammering to the beat; another is sawing, and a man wearing a giant elephant costume enters the frame.

The camera pulls back further to show a stage in disarray. It's a marvelous little self-contained sequence that has Buzz's telltale fingerprints. About fifteen minutes in, the comedic dance number is featured with every girl outfitted in tuxedo, top hat, and cane. Buzz, acknowledging the comedic angle, shoots the number without any special adornments that would distract from the laughs. For the first time, he employs the "domino effect" of staging, where one dancer drops to the ground while the camera moves to follow another and another in quick succession. All in all, it's an entertaining seven minutes due to Buzz's blocking and staging. The film opened on March 14, 1931. In spite of receiving good notices, *Kiki* lost almost $400,000, a first for a Mary Pickford movie.

Buzz's marriage was in trouble. Esther was often alone, and she still hadn't found Hollywood work, not even an unbilled walk-on. Buzz was simply a contractor for hire in an industry that seemingly had lost interest in his brand of entertainment. Together, they made a miserable couple. Buzz chewed Gertrude's ear off with his marriage woes in their scratchy transcontinental conversations. He didn't want her to relocate just yet, at least not until his career prospects solidified. With a bit of fortuitous timing, good news came by way of Sam Goldwyn. Based on the success of *Whoopee!* Goldwyn signed Eddie Cantor for another picture called *Palmy Days,* and both wanted Buzz on board.

Eddie Cantor punched up the *Palmy Days* script with more gags, and Buzz expanded his repertoire with a couple of cleverly executed numbers. The setting was Clark's Bakery ("Glorifying the American Doughnut"), an interesting business whose staff is made up of pretty dancing girls. Leading them through calisthenics in the company gymnasium is the high-steppin' comedy actress Charlotte Greenwood. Her opening number, "Bend Down Sister," allows Buzz some creativity in the staging. He keeps true to his creed of showing faces with a quick "passing parade" shot of the girls. A visually interesting effect occurs as the girls, armed with long wooden sticks, line up single file, with only the first one visible. Betty Grable, in her third go-around with Buzz, heads the front of the line. She raises her stick in an arc formation around her head, immediately followed by the next girl, and then the third, etc., making the sticks look like sky-reaching tendrils. Little Betty proffers a suggestive wink, and a cleverly arranged top shot closes Buzz's first major number since *Whoopee!*

Buzz had nothing to do with the film's second song, "There's Nothing Too Good for My Baby," featuring Eddie in blackface. The number was tacked on following less-than-stellar audience previews. Director Mervyn LeRoy was called in to do retakes and film the number, which added seventy-five thousand dollars to the production cost. The film's final song, "Yes, Yes (My Baby Said Yes, Yes)," had Cantor singing, rolling his banjo eyes, and mirthfully bouncing while clapping his hands. Buzz simply recorded the number without regard for the time/space incongruities.

In New York, Sam Goldwyn threw *Palmy Days* one of the great advertising campaigns in movie history. On Broadway from Forty-second Street to Fifty-ninth, 250 lamp posts had attached flags that read "Eddie Cantor Palmy Days 'Buy Now' campaign." There was a parade of trucks almost two miles long with life-size pictures of the Goldwyn Girls and Cantor lining the route.

Buzz mentioned that he made his first appearance on film as an actor in *Palmy Days*. In an early scene that introduces Eddie Cantor's character, a fake séance is being led by a shifty fortune teller (Charles Middleton). According to Buzz, "one of the actors playing the part of a fortune teller was supposed to be a comedian and he was pretty bad. This fact irritated director Eddie Sutherland so much that he fired the man and asked me if I wouldn't mind stepping into the comedy role, since I had played these kinds of parts in stock. So, I took over the brief part and made my first screen appearance." That scene might have been shot as Buzz described it, but the released print shows no such thing. However, one of the non-speaking participants in the séance is wearing glasses and appears to be him. A quick profile and a brief full-face shot almost certainly identify the dance director as the accidental screen actor.

A syndicated newspaper item, more fluff than actual news, mentions that fifty girls were selected for *Palmy Days* from more than five thousand applicants. It said Buzz drew up a chart showing that thirty-seven of the fifty were blondes. Buzz reportedly said that of the thirty-seven, fewer than 10 percent were natural blondes (and some with fair hair used bleaching preparations for an even lighter effect). "With the new lighting for talkies, peroxide hair stands out on the screen and enables girls to steal scenes."

After July, Buzz was at loose ends again, and he thought about a move back to New York and Broadway, where at least he wouldn't have these feelings of not knowing where the next job would be. Buzz made the acquaintance of Mervyn LeRoy during *Palmy Days*. LeRoy had subbed for Eddie Sutherland when he was briefly called out of town. Mervyn liked Buzz, and liked his approach to filmmaking. He urged Buzz to stay in California. LeRoy felt musicals would come back big again. According to Buzz, Mervyn was "very persuasive." Buzz remained, but without an immediate director's job he signed with a production house called Fanchon and Marco. *Variety* called the company "the world's most famous brother and sister producing team" and "the standard by which stage shows are judged." The production house staged prologues (short, live-action playlets) that preceded the main feature in movie theaters.

The Howard Hughes production *Sky Devils* afforded Buzz a quick dance number that lasts barely longer than a minute. In the story of World War I army fliers, the idea of a stage show for the entertainment-starved men was a natural for Buzz. The only dance number in the picture is brief, with little in the way of spectacle. Mary (Ann Dvorak) and six "Parisian girls" entertain the men at the army canteen. A nice shot behind the footlights keeps Mary's legs framed in the foreground as she moves across the cramped stage. Her dancing is less than graceful (and the audience wasn't too picky), and soon she exits stage left. The supporting Parisian girls were actually male soldiers sporting ladies' masks. They enter the stage single file, form a dance line, and high-kick a few times. The action cuts away and never returns. In *Sky Devils,* Buzz's talent was underused and underappreciated, and he never made mention of the picture that was in production from May to June 1931 and released a lengthy eight months later.

Amid the hoopla surrounding the postproduction work on *Palmy Days,* the Associated Press on July 8, 1931, ran a story with a small headline that read, "Actress Divorces Dress-Ripping Mate." Esther had had it with Buzz. Mrs. Enos requested and was granted a divorce. She told the judge a story that, on the surface, sounded ridiculous: "My husband almost embarrassed me to death. We were at a hall and he became very angry and came up to me and ripped my dress right off me. I had hardly anything on and there were a lot of people there I didn't know." She also blathered, "[Buzz] was a lovely person but a real mama's boy." She also felt that most of the time she was "more his keeper than his wife." Assuming Esther's ripped dress story is more fact than fiction, it points to a disturbing character flaw of Busby Berkeley. It's conceivable that prodigious liquor consumption fanned the flames of rage. His history with the bottle had made Goldwyn suspicious. But Esther, on the record, never mentioned Buzz and alcohol in the same sentence. Gertrude was in Los Angeles to soften the blow after the divorce decree was signed. But Buzz was too busy to grieve for an abbreviated marriage; he was now freelancing in one of America's most exciting and restrictive professions.

In August, Esther litigated for alimony. Buzz filed a legal paper in which he claimed the woman could and should support herself. He also admitted to a $250-per-week salary. The court granted Esther $300 a month. There was a matter of $3,700 in arrears claimed by Esther, but the court refused an opinion, saying only that it will be decided at "later hearings."

That same month, Buzz, now contracting at MGM, allowed his flight of fancy to take wing in the aerial comedy *George White's Flying High*. White had produced the show on Broadway, and per his contract with the studio he retained his name in the possessive above the title. Bert Lahr played the lead onstage and reprised the role in this, his first film. The elastic Charlotte Greenwood took the female lead, her first role since high-kicking for Buzz in *Palmy Days*.

At this point in his career, Buzz's musical numbers were experiments in camera placement and movement, ensemble blocking, and set manipulation. In *Whoopee!* the high camera angles and unique chorus-girl positioning yielded interesting results. For *Flying High,* Buzz, with commanding control, expands upon his initial preoccupations and creates a couple of numbers, all identifiably the work of a singular artist.

With the airplane as the focal point, "I'll Make a Happy Landing" allowed Buzz to indulge his variations on a theme, first as miniature planes flying through slatted floors, to ensembles positioning themselves as cogs in a human airplane as cleverly envisioned from above. The dancers rapidly tap in unison as they climb stars, rotate in groups of five, and form other appealing patterns that bear Buzz's stamp. A nod to the famous flyers of the day finds the arranged dancers spelling out the names of Byrd, (Frank) Hawks, and Lindy. A final close-up of the dancing girls as they grin into the camera ends the imaginative number.

On a chalkboard is written, "Girl's Examination 2 p.m." This is all the suggestiveness Buzz needed for a number that pushed the boundaries of the MPAA's (Motion Picture Association of America) censorship board. The girls gather in the large waiting room of a physician (Charles Winninger). He tells them to strip. "Hooray, we gotta strip!" says an agreeable chorus girl. They lose their skirts, and on display are leg pairs of every length. With the girls clad now in identical black undergarments, the doctor wants to find out their aptitude on curves. The girls nod—they're good on curves! The double entendres continue until a head nurse yells, "Forward, march!" causing the dancers to take their marching positions. There's no song actually credited to the examination scene, but Buzz's handiwork is apparent.

"We'll Dance until the Dawn" is an inventive number. Armed with his arsenal of forty women and sixteen men dressed in identical garb, Buzz fashioned fascinating patterns that eclipse one another. In a scandalously sexually charged image, a double row of men is moving forward and backward, while girls positioned in circles revolve in counterpoint to the men's movement. A final top shot held for almost forty-five seconds (longest to date for Buzz) features tight inner groupings of dancers moving in opposite directions, raising and dropping propeller props, enhancing the image with a strange, undeniably hypnotic effect.

To judge by some of the reviews of the day, *Flying High* was strictly earthbound. *Variety* said that if the public heard that the film was a musical, they would stay away unless they'd seen everything else in town. In his first starring feature, Bert Lahr wasn't a draw, and by November 1931 (the film's release date), if a musical didn't have a big name, it was doomed. The work of Buzz Berkeley was noticed and complimented, but a full-time dance-directing career in Hollywood remained outside his grasp.

Vivian and Rosetta Duncan (popularly known as the Duncan Sisters) toured together in the roles of Topsy and Eva, two characters from Harriet Beecher Stowe's *Uncle Tom's Cabin*. The 1931 version of their musical/comedy show was held at Los Angeles's El Capitan Theatre. Buzz supervised and staged the dances, and it was announced that a new specialty number for the last act would "outshine any of their previous productions." On Sunday, November 22, the largest matinee audience in the theater's history came to the opening of *Topsy and Eva*. Running almost three-and-a-half hours, the show received ecstatic notices. Calling it farce, melodrama, music, opera pageantry, burlesque, and dance rolled inextricably together, the *Los Angeles Times* lauded Buzz and his forty-member cast, but balked at what they called "some ragged formations . . . that will undoubtedly be straightened out at successive performances."

Mother remained in Los Angeles by her son for the year-end holidays. The East Coast had no hold over Gertrude, and she abandoned the home in Dover, New Hampshire, for the warm weather she fondly remembered and for the son who now needed her. Four days into 1932, Esther Muir announced her engagement to Rex Lease (a movie "cowboy"). She loved him but couldn't marry the cowboy until papers dissolving her marriage from Buzz were received and notarized. The alimony promised to Esther the previous summer was not being paid at regular intervals. She dragged Buzz back to court and had him cited to show cause why he should not pay the required amount. Buzz told the court that he had lost his automobile, was about to lose his home, and could not meet the demands of the payment. The court suggested the couple reach a compromise, and it appeared to all that the order for alimony would be modified.

Prologues were also known and advertised as *ideas,* and Buzz staged an idea for Fanchon and Marco in January 1932 while in between assignments. The title *Chains* came from Buzz. He was asked by the producers for a name, and only when he entered a men's room and saw the commode's pull-chain did an idea for the *idea* strike him. Slave-girls bounded by chains, chains of pearls, and swinging chains were all Buzz-devised. At Loew's State Theater (thirty-five cents until 1 p.m.), *Chains* was advertised as having a cast of forty while Buzz's name (its main selling point) was featured prominently.

In February, *Variety* announced that Buzz would be working on the film *Girl Crazy,* a takeoff of sorts of the 1930 George and Ira Gershwin musical. It was updated to play on the strengths of the hot comedy team of the day, (Bert) Wheeler and (Robert) Woolsey. Buzz's involvement with the film was to take place *after* filming had finished. Earlier in the year it was screened for a Glendale audience that gave it a "chilly reception." Executive producer David O. Selznick immediately ordered new scenes and retakes. Norman Taurog, a director since 1920, was surreptitiously signed to handle the new footage. Although production reports have Taurog being reimbursed, there's no paper trail that indicates Buzz had any involvement with *Girl Crazy* despite *Variety*'s blurb. Yet the visually exciting "I Got Rhythm" number stands incongruously apart from anything in the film. Attributing the number to Buzz's budding creativity in both editing and composition isn't much of a stretch. In a western-style nightclub setting, singer Kitty Kelly (a former Ziegfeld girl) belts out the first verse, with only her face lit. Then the lights are turned on, then off, and a traveling spotlight focuses on one table, then another while in the background "rhythm, rhythm, rhythm" is chanted. The spotlight pans and tilts, illuminating and darkening the patrons as forceful editing rhythms drive the number onward. The camera is focused everywhere, on legs beneath tables, on musicians' instruments, on pretty faces, from table to table in an agitation of spotlights, quick cuts, and music. Soon everyone and everything is singing and bouncing to the main lyrics including the stuffed owls, buffalo heads, and the cacti on the plain. Performed at a breathless pace, "I Got Rhythm" is two-and-a-half minutes of visceral excitement. If the number was a retake as Selznick ordered, its new director remained anonymous. As for Buzz, he never spoke of it.

He bounced to a different studio for his next assignment. Carl Laemmle's Universal Pictures (which had had successes with *Dracula* and *Frankenstein*) was filming a dark melodrama titled *Night World*. In January 1932, Buzz came on board thanks to Laemmle's insistence. The one-picture deal gave him screen credit ("Dances staged by"). A nightclub is the film's only setting as its denizens deal with violence, duplicities, romantic entanglements, and the occasional musical number. Buzz makes the best of a small, cramped stage at the nine-minute mark when the "Who's Your Little Who-Zis" number begins. The dancing girls align in two rows as they tap toward the camera. They separate and then arrange themselves in single file. While they're dancing, Buzz gets close enough to hear them commenting on all the club's customers. Then, reminiscent of *Whoopee!*, Buzz visually reiterates the "arch of legs" as the girls bounce toward the camera and separate (one lascivious customer sports a big grin while kneeling and looking up). The camera follows the girls in a 360-degree shot that is followed by a bit of Buzz magic. The girls sit in a circle, legs together, knees bent. Cut to a Buzz high shot. The legs move left, then right, and back again while the girls lift and drop their heads. Buzz then takes the opposite view as the girls stand in a circle. With the camera on the floor shooting upward, the girls bend over in unison, stand upright, kick their legs in unison, and repeat. It's a great effect, another in Buzz's maturing arsenal. Released in May 1932, *Night World* clocked in at just under fifty-eight minutes and had a brief theatrical run.

RKO studio's *Bird of Paradise* was a story of forbidden love amid the splendor of the South Seas. The David O. Selznick production was without a desired director until the producer asked his father-in-law (Louis B. Mayer, head of MGM) for the services of King Vidor (well regarded for his previous films *The Big Parade, The Crowd,* and *Hallelujah!*). Vidor wasn't particularly enamored with the original play on which the film was based. Through Selznick's encouragement to "just give me three wonderful love scenes . . . I don't care what story you use so long as you call it *Bird of Paradise* and [Dolores] Del Río jumps into the volcano at the end," Vidor came on board as director. According to reports, Selznick admired Buzz's work on *Whoopee!* and *Palmy Days* and signed him to a one-picture deal in February 1932. (Buzz said it was King Vidor who asked him to help out.) His role was not as director of the native dance numbers but, more accurately, to "put a chorus through its paces" during the production.

An independent yachtsman (Joel McCrea) and his sailing friends drop anchor at a Polynesian island. Soon McCrea falls in love with the daughter of the local king (Del Río), but cultural differences (along with the fact that the daughter is promised as a sacrifice to the gods in a volcano ceremony) drive a wedge in the romance. Dolores Del Río, with her exotic appeal and fluttery eyelashes, was well cast as Luana, the free-spirited native girl who doesn't think twice about frolicking nude in the balmy waters. Buzz took the short-lived role and arranged the girls (some of them native Polynesians) in various march-like positions with numbers of small groups maneuvering in concentric circles. Since he was more consultant than director, the finished film reveals little of his influence (although an archway made of native spears was referential). In the final cut, the numbers did not exist in unbroken sequences. They stopped in the middle for dialogue passages, the kind of interruption that Buzz greatly abhorred.

After about a year of parlaying his experience at various studios into projects key to his development, Buzz was again in the employ of

Sam Goldwyn. With Eddie Cantor on board, their third collaboration was titled *The Kid from Spain*. Leo McCarey (a prodigious filmmaker with almost ninety pictures to his credit by the time he signed on) sat in the director's chair while Buzz was the dance-routine designer. The songs (all of them with clever risqué lyrics) were by Harry Ruby and Bert Kalmar, the team that had composed witty tunes for the Marx Brothers. Sam Goldwyn borrowed $1 million to produce the film, the first seven-figure loan given by Bank of America for a motion picture. He wanted it shot in Technicolor, but he had a spasm when he learned the cost: $225,000 more than black-and-white (an elevated price to reflect the improved technology not available in *Whoopee!*). Sam nixed the process. As it was, his payroll was high, and often his talent would seek remuneration up front. Buzz was one who did so. Two petty-cash vouchers were made out to him for $16.67 and $25.00 respectively, the latter amount reflecting a daily salary of $41.67, less an earlier advance.

On July 18, rehearsals began. Soon after, Eddie Cantor learned that Flo Ziegfeld was ill. On July 21, he went to visit the old impresario at the Cedars of Lebanon Hospital in Los Angeles. Ziegfeld was asleep, and Eddie hung around for a while, but left before the patient awoke. The next day, Florenz Ziegfeld, the premier showman of his day, with a name forever synonymous with stage shows of glamour and uncompromised ostentatiousness, passed away.

The first ten minutes of *The Kid from Spain* are all Busby Berkeley. The setting: a college girl's dormitory. Not just any dormitory—a libertine's seraglio composed of dozens of silk-sheeted beds butted together to form a circle with a Goldwyn Girl in an enticing stage of undress on each mattress. The action begins as one student awakes, rubs her made-up eyes, and lets us in on a little secret:

> We're opening this story
> By giving you a peek
> Into a dormitory
> Where all the pretty co-eds sleep.

And peek and ogle we do as Buzz's mobile camera moves from bed to bed, each Goldwyn Girl reciting delightfully suggestive lyrics:

I'll be here till I'm twenty
I'm only seventeen
By that time I'll know plenty
Of course, y'all know what I mean!

In unison the girls rise, put on their pumps, and shoulder to shoulder they dance around, climb some stairs, and encircle an ornate Olympic-sized pool. Off come their outer wrappings as the identically clad bathing beauties take position on the side of the pool. In his first use of what can be described as Buzz's domino effect with regard to stage action, he shoots two angles of girls as they dive in the water. One immediately follows the other like tipped dominoes. The first group has the girls diving toward the camera, the second away, and both are eye-appealing.

Water in a confined space doubling as a celluloid canvas had never been attempted before. The possibilities of weightless pool-bound girls in manipulated shapes sparked the eager dance director, pushing himself harder with every new large-scale production number. Buzz was up to the challenge. His single camera rises high to reveal the inherent patterns only a visualist can unearth and enliven. On display are concentric circles, swimmers in pairs, leg pairs opening and closing, multiple diamond shapes spinning clockwise and counterclockwise. Buzz reverses the action as a trio swim in circles that open and close like a flower petal. Sufficiently bathed, the girls leap from the pool and slide down back to their room as Buzz's leering camera catches them in nude silhouette as they dry themselves. The voyeuristic camera wanders just past the blocking scrim, the girls utter a mock shriek, and it's back to bed to continue dressing. Buzz, tireless once inspiration struck, kept all seventy-six Goldwyn Girls working through the night on the pool sequence.

Cantor's blackface number, "What a Perfect Combination," gets an invigorating jolt from Buzz and the Goldwyn Girls. They pop up from below tables arranged in a nightclub setting. They dance on the tabletops and collect around a circular, stationary dance floor with a raised tier. The girls spin and move, lift and lower their hats, sit and spread their legs, bob their heads to and fro, and from Buzz's perch fifteen feet above, the view is attractive. One interesting effect has the Goldwyn Girls passing in front of a circle made of sleeved arms, opening and closing like a camera's iris. By the number's end, the focus is on Cantor singing the final verse. Surrounding him are the girls. Their heads are down, the tops revealed to show a face made up in burnt cork! In a reverse shot, the camera rises swiftly above Eddie Cantor as the girls carry different sections of a large puzzle-prop that when joined reveal a gigantic bull's head. Buzz wasn't totally satisfied with the way the number turned out. He wanted the stationary center stage to revolve and he asked Goldwyn if studio technicians could make it happen. "No, I don't want them to revolve," said Goldwyn. "Do it the way it is now, and if you must revolve them, do that at some other studio." Buzz was indignant. "One of these days I'll have them revolve."

The Kid from Spain met with good reviews and box-office success. In some theaters, Goldwyn sent sixteen of his girls to perform in prologues before the picture. Goldwyn wanted to present the film in Los Angeles as a "road show" engagement (which meant exclusivity in distribution during its first few weeks). But the road show in LA was canceled as audiences balked at the $1.50 ticket price (in New York, where it did play, road show tickets were $2.20).

Mervyn LeRoy, who urged Buzz to remain in Hollywood, was directing pictures at Warner Brothers. He had had a big success with *Little Caesar* in 1931 and had been busy ever since. By 1932, the Depression resulted in Warner Brothers and its competitors bleeding red ink. In three years, weekly movie attendance had dropped by 40 percent, from 10 million to 6. The studios laid off employees. In January, Warner Brothers posted losses of $7,918,604. It was evident that the studio couldn't survive on the successful gangster pictures and rapid-paced comedies it produced. The head of production was Darryl F. Zanuck, who had been hired as a staff writer in 1923. He honed his craft writing clever plots for the successful *Rin Tin Tin* German shepherd films, and worked his way up through the company. In 1928, he was promoted to studio manager. A year later, in his late twenties, he was made chief of production, answering only to the brothers. Zanuck, in no small way, was responsible for the advent of talking pictures. It was at his urging that studio cofounder Sam Warner moved ahead forcefully with the Vitaphone process that resulted in the release of the seminal *The Jazz Singer*. He embraced the advent of sound and helped wean the studio from silent pictures.

But musicals, by and large, were a losing proposition. The novelty of sound had quickly exhausted the musical (a genre, ironically, birthed by sound), and it got to the point that some theater owners placed a "Not a Musical" sign outside their box office if their latest picture might be mistaken for one. Mervyn LeRoy commanded the ear of Darryl F. Zanuck, and he energetically made the case for a new type of musical. Zanuck did have a project in the wings, a gritty backstage Broadway story told from an insider's point of view. The story was loaded with prurient subject matter including drug addiction, aberrant sexual desire, and adultery. Originally adapted as a drama (with Loretta Young penciled for the lead), Zanuck saw the possibilities of a re-adaptation where the Broadway show envisioned in act 1 is realized glowingly in act 3. He was also aware that the studio had purchased a music publishing house once talking pictures became the standard. A little tweaking and his backstage story could be turned into the kind of musical Mervyn LeRoy envisioned. Without hesitation, LeRoy recommended his friend Busby Berkeley to the studio chief. Zanuck had seen *Whoopee!* and he contacted Buzz directly. They immediately struck a rapport. Buzz was asked if he'd be interested in directing the musical sequences for a film called *42nd Street*. The evocative title appealed to Buzz. There was no question of acceptance, but before he drove to Mr. Zanuck's office on the Warner lot, Buzz made sure Gertrude learned the good news.

5

The Cinematerpsichorean

On August 11, 1932, a Warnergram (interoffice memorandum) was delivered to M. Ebenstein from Jacob Wilk asking him to prepare a contract for the world motion picture rights of the unpublished novel "42nd Street." Warner closed a movie-rights deal with former chorus boy–turned-novelist Bradford Ropes for six thousand dollars. The film was scheduled to start shooting in mid-September to coincide with the publication date of September 15. As of September 1, Buzz was still under contract to Sam Goldwyn until September 18, but that didn't inhibit Warner Brothers' plans. Mervyn LeRoy would direct the book; Buzz, the fifty-seven chorines. It was reported that Buzz studied his girls' knees before making his final casting selections. A couple hundred dancers auditioned. If Buzz liked the girls' faces and ankles, they made the cut. The 120 semi-finalists were whittled down to 57 (selected by the attractiveness of their knees) and were awarded contracts of sixty-six dollars a week. Buzz quite confidently said that any person in the audience will be able to find at least one girl who conforms to his or her idea of beauty.

One of the music publishing houses that Warner Brothers purchased was Remick in New York. Songwriter Harry Warren worked for Remick, and he was Zanuck's choice to compose *42nd Street*. He partnered Warren with lyricist Al Dubin, who had started his career on New York's West Twenty-eighth Street (the Tin Pan Alley district), writing special material for vaudevillians. It was a simpatico collaboration, and they worked at a brisk pace. Four songs were written, and Harry also composed the film's incidental music.

A studio executive viewed a 1928 two-minute Fox Movietone short featuring a tap dancer that showed how the sounds emanating from the dancer's feet could be captured on film. The executive liked the test and offered its "star" a contract for *42nd Street*. The actress, Ruby Keeler, had had small parts in a few Broadway musicals and was cast in the out-of-town tryouts of *Whoopee* (but did not appear in the show when it played Broadway). She married singer/actor Al Jolson, Warner Brothers' biggest star, on September 21, 1928, and moved to Hollywood. The following year, "Ruby Keeler Jolson" (as her name was listed in the program) returned to New York for Flo Ziegfeld in *Show Girl*. After her short-lived Broadway comeback, Ruby returned to California, and with encouragement from her husband, she dropped her married name professionally.

On September 28, production officially began on *42nd Street*. LeRoy was indisposed with tonsillitis, and Lloyd Bacon, a Warner's contract director known for his rapid shooting style, took over. Buzz and Bacon worked different days with different units at separate soundstages; the only constant was prolific studio cinematographer Sol Polito. Bacon shot on six soundstages at First National Studio, while Buzz filmed his numbers at Warner's Sunset Studios from October 19 to November 16. The total cost of production came to $340,000.

Shot in the Warner Brothers house style, *42nd Street* is as gritty, streetwise, and contemporary ("stories ripped from the headlines") as the studio's gangster dramas *Little Caesar* and *Public Enemy*. "Jones & Barry are doing a show" is the exciting rumor being spread in Depression-struck Broadway as *42nd Street* begins. A new show, "Pretty Lady," is the production, funded by Abner Dillon, an "angel" (Broadway slang for a backer) and letch, played by Guy Kibbee. He's being used by actress Dorothy Brock (Bebe Daniels), an unscrupulous actress willing to be "kept" in order to win a fat contract and the starring role in the show. Directing the production is the broke and ill Julian Marsh (Warner Baxter), who realizes this show is his last chance at the big time. At the rehearsals we meet a stage neophyte, Peggy Sawyer (Ruby Keeler), a young performer, Billy Lawler (Dick Powell), along with wisecracking showgirls Ann (nicknamed "anytime Annie"—"she only said 'no' once and then she didn't hear the question") and Lorraine (Ginger Rogers and Una Merkel). The night before the opening, a drunken Dorothy falls and injures her ankle, leaving Marsh at wit's end. Ann selflessly recommends newcomer Peggy Sawyer. Marsh mercilessly drills the stage virgin on the songs, steps, and phrasings. It's now opening night for "Pretty Lady," and as the chorus line takes the stage, Marsh picks this moment, one minute before Peggy is to step out in front of an audience for the first time in her life, and gives her this passion-laden "pep talk" while she waits in the wings:

> Sawyer you listen to me and you listen hard. Two hundred people, two hundred jobs, two hundred thousand dollars, five weeks of grind and blood and sweat depend upon you. It's the lives of all these people who've worked with you. You've got to go on and you've got to give and give and give. They've got to like you. Got to! Do you understand? You can't fall down. You can't because your future's in it, my future, and everything all of us have, is staked on you. All right now, I'm through, but you keep your feet on the ground and your head on those shoulders of yours and go out . . . and Sawyer . . . you're going out a youngster, but you've got to come back a star!

And thanks to Buzz Berkeley's tutelage, she does. Onstage, the Niagara Limited's caboose has newlyweds Ruby Keeler and Clarence Nordstrom singing of their upcoming honeymoon to the Falls (a "Shuffle Off to Buffalo"). Then the couple appears to separate, but it's really a Busby Berkeley device that could have been presented in his Broadway days. The train opens up wide on a real stage as the wheels and curtained cabins are revealed. He follows the newlyweds as they sing and dance their way to their cabin, and except for his liberal use of close-ups of the other passengers (all of them chorus girls, strangely enough), the number remains within the physical boundaries of the proscenium.

Sequentially, "You're Getting to Be a Habit with Me" was Buzz's first number at Warner Brothers, and was placed some forty minutes into the film. In her only song in the film, Bebe Daniels sings of the similarity between an embrace and a fix:

> Every kiss,
> Every hug,
> Seems to act just like a drug,
> You're getting to be a habit with me.

The number is strictly stage-bound, but Buzz keeps the camera moving as it follows the star and her paramours skipping and stepping to both ends of the stage. A Berkeley joke (it couldn't have been scripted) ends the number as a Mahatma Gandhi look-alike whisks Bebe off the stage to the disappointment of the boys. One commentator noted that the young men dancing with Bebe Daniels (who represented the old, established stage star) could be viewed metaphorically as Warner Brothers infusing new blood into a tired genre.

Be they Goldwyn Girls or Berkeley girls, all dozen or so regulars went unidentified in the credit rolls and remained anonymous when Buzz filmed them in admiring close-ups. In the number following "Shuffle Off to Buffalo," a chorus girl equally commands the stage with Dick Powell, a first. Her name was Toby Wing, and she was the embodiment of the Busby Berkeley chorine. She was sixteen when Buzz hired her as one of the Goldwyn Girls in *Palmy Days* (where she was known as "the girl with a face like the morning sun"), and, along with her sister Pat, she appeared in a number of musicals for various studios. In "Young and Healthy," Toby, dressed in a bareback outfit trimmed in white fox, gets serenaded by Powell, and soon the cinematic pyrotechnics of Busby Berkeley take over. The bench where the couple is sitting slides down flush to the floor, and the prop of tiered revolving stages (the kind Buzz begged for with Sam Goldwyn) becomes the focal point and locale of the number. First it's Powell and Wing in the top center, with chorus boys on their stomachs in the outer ring turning in the opposite direction. Buzz's parade of faces follows as Powell sings to each one passing his way. As Toby glides by, she disembarks, they kiss, and Buzz closes in tight. After separating, the Berkeley girls arrive and position themselves as Buzz's passive camera catches their outspread legs that move past our view on the revolving stage. The effect of viewing positioned people from a high angle and the resultant patterns achieved through the originality of a visual imagination are realized in the two stunning high shots that follow. The 1933 audience was thrilled to the point of applause when they saw the unusual patterns that could be generated from a vantage point fifty feet in the air. The number ends as the camera passes through Buzz's "archway of legs" toward Toby and Dick, who are captured in a cute close-up. Although she inadvertently glanced to her left for an instant, Buzz liked the take, and it was a wrap.

Attempted assault, a woman stabbed to death, a drunkard, and a nursemaid spanking a doll do not sound like the standard ingredients of a musical number—unless, of course, they're products of the stylized imagination of Busby Berkeley. The presentation of the titular song borrows the best from Buzz's stage years while infusing the number with the kind of cinematic staging that Zanuck encouraged. It's Ruby Keeler, purportedly on center stage, singing the first chorus. She removes her lower-body covering and does a nice buck-and-wing dance. Buzz cuts to a different angle, and it's revealed that Ruby was singing on the roof of a New York taxicab. From there, a street scene reminiscent of the pantomime dance Buzz directed for *International Revue* ("The Rout") is revealed as a microcosm of the "naughty, bawdy, gaudy, sporty" world that is this thoroughfare. The number's narrative, written totally by Berkeley, contains an eyeful of interesting vignettes before the magic begins in earnest. As Ruby descends from the cab, we see the neighborhood denizens all moving to a snazzy beat; a barber shaving; a nursemaid spanking a doll lifted from a carriage; fruit vendors leaving their stand carrying golf clubs; and traffic conductors keeping cars at bay. A crowd forms around two black children as they street dance; a drunk stumbles out from a basement tavern; a cigar-store Indian comes to life; and then violence. A dapper gent is nodding to the line of women entering a hotel. A scream is heard, and he looks up. Buzz moves his camera to the second floor, where we see a masher assaulting a terrified woman. She pushes him into a lamp and the room goes dark. She exits the window, just missed by two gunshots fired from the darkness. Another scream and she jumps from the landing into the arms of a waiting lothario. They dance a few steps before the second-floor brute returns and stabs her dead with his knife. Dispassionately, Dick Powell is viewing the scene from his second-floor vantage, a drink in his hand and background bartender in view, and he sings his few lines before the Berkeley girls arrive in formation. A moment hence, and the mixed ensemble enters from stage left and right, their backs to the audience and each carrying a hidden placard. When the many rows are filled in, the ensemble turns to reveal the New York skyline, buildings of all sizes and shapes with what appear to be lighted windows in a few. The chorus exits, and the perspective shifts to an unusual angle of a skyscraper. As we move "up" the building (in reality, Buzz is shooting horizontally, but the effect is all that matters), we see Ruby and Dick together (they never were for the entire number, but no matter), singing the final lines and pulling an asbestos curtain down past the camera's eye. Buzz's work was finished, and the story's bittersweet coda had theater patrons praising Peggy Sawyer while castigating the weary Julian Marsh, who's smoking and listening within earshot.

The filming went well for Buzz. Interference was minimal from Zanuck, who gave his director free rein to pursue his vision. One evening Zanuck and other studio executives paid Buzz a visit while he was creating "Young and Healthy." Buzz took great pains to describe the continuity of the scene and how he filmed in snippets. He instructed Dick Powell and the male dancers to arrange themselves according to different sections of the number. According to Buzz, Zanuck was quite pleased with his staging. "Give Berkeley whatever he wants in the way of sets, props, costumes. Anything he wants, he can have" were Zanuck's marching orders. On November 16, one day after his work on *42nd Street* was completed, Buzz received a tangible expression of Darryl Zanuck's faith. He was presented with a thirteen-page, seven-year escalating contract at a starting salary of $1,750 per week. Buzz signed without regard for any previous arrangements he had made with Sam Goldwyn. In a Warner Brothers memo, studio employee R. J. Obringer grants Goldwyn the use of Buzz's services. Goldwyn is to give forty-five days written notice when he needs Buzz, and the studio is to receive the same compensation from Goldwyn as they paid out to Berkeley. To Buzz, Sam was relegated to the past. Sam was cheap, and Sam thought small. Buzz's dream of a revolving stage came true at Warner Brothers without question after he gave his specifications to the studio's crack engineering team. The rotating platforms worked so well that in December 1932 he applied for a patent for his invention. Detailed descriptions of the tiered, concentric "revolving stage" wherein "two lines of performers are made to pass each other without apparent movement on their part" were included in the application.

Buzz also took credit for another invention that simulated the effect of a large boom without the need for six to ten men to operate it. This "monorail," as Buzz described it, was designed to simplify the camera's vertical and horizontal movements while allowing a dolly speed that could never be accomplished with a lumbering boom. "It was actually two rails, way up high in the rafters. Then they [studio technicians] put a rigging that went straight down, just like a frame rigging, and the camera car went up and down the side of that rigging," described its inventor. The benefit of the design allowed him to use only two operators positioned above his platform. One had the lever that raised and lowered the camera, and the other had the lever that moved the camera back and forth. Buzz was most proud of the monorail's swiftness of movement. "I pioneered it," he said immodestly.

It was no secret that the liberal Warner brothers were enthusiastic supporters of President-elect Franklin Roosevelt. The film's poster identified *42nd Street* as "Inaugurating a NEW DEAL in ENTERTAINMENT!" capitalizing Roosevelt's radio speech of July 1932, in which he championed a "new deal for the American people."

The studio, in collaboration with General Electric, customized a seven-car train in gold and silver, christening it "The 42nd Street Special." A huge press event complete with a marching band was held for the train's send-off: one hundred cities on the way east with an arrival in Washington, D.C., to coincide with inauguration day, March 4, 1933. At the event, Los Angeles mayor John C. Porter broke a champagne bottle on the caboose railing, while Darryl Zanuck accepted KFWB radio's live microphone from Jack Warner and stated, "The train is almost as good as the picture."

Zanuck knew he had a winner in postproduction. What few knew was that he hedged his bet. *42nd Street* could have easily been released as a drama if the musical sequences didn't work. Back-loading the major numbers to the end of the picture made them easy to excise. But the work of Busby Berkeley was not to be denied, and Zanuck was more than pleased. While *42nd Street* was in post, Buzz, Mervyn LeRoy, and Zanuck discussed their next project, tentatively titled *High Life*. It was to be the third version of Avery Hopwood's play *The Gold Diggers*. Filmed twice as *The Gold Diggers of 1923* and *Gold Diggers of Broadway*, this version was to be announced only after *42nd Street* was released per Zanuck, who demanded the project be kept hush-hush. Conference notes between the three called for a semi-documentary opening, various shots of closed theaters, deserted buildings, and empty ticket agencies.

In February, Buzz's name was mentioned as part of the creative team for the film *Blondie Johnson*, but by the time of the film's release, he went uncredited. From March 6 (just days before *42nd Street* was to be officially released) through April 13, the Berkeley unit (he now had one) shot the musical sequences for Warner Brothers' newest picture, retitled *Gold Diggers of 1933*.

The semi-documentary opening originally envisioned for *Gold Diggers of 1933* was scrapped in deference to Buzz's staging of the opening number, "We're in the Money." The irony of the song (also known as "The Gold Diggers Song") is soon made evident when the dress rehearsal under way is abruptly terminated due to the producer's insolvency. Although Buzz has stated that he's loath to end a musical number prematurely, he does have fun with the abbreviated song that opens the film. "The long lost dollar has come back to the fold," sings Ginger Rogers, decked out in an outfit of silver coins. She sings adieu to "ol' man Depression" (a most potent send-off to the strapped audiences of the day). Buzz moves the action to his parade of faces, each girl momentarily hidden by a large imitation coin. Then a *Palmy Days* trick as Ginger heads the front of a single-file line, raising her hands that hold enlarged 1933 silver dollars, each girl following close behind. A fashion show of sorts follows with outrageous costuming when Ginger returns to sing the opening verses, every line—in Pig Latin.

Erway inhay the oneymay
Erway inhay the oneymay
Eveway otgay a otlay ofway atwhay itway akestay otay etgay
    alongway

Soon after, the law intervenes, and Buzz's gauche ode to prosperity ends ungracefully, the long-lost dollar having left the fold.

The deliciously suggestive "Pettin' in the Park" reteamed Berkeley, Keeler, and Powell, last seen on a Forty-second Street skyscraper. The "park" is a lively place thanks to Buzz, and he pulls off some nifty meteorological effects amid the tracking of a comic foil: a dwarf dressed as a baby.

Light judgmental banter between the charismatic couple opens the number:

POWELL: Pettin' in the park
KEELER: Bad Boy!

POWELL: Pettin' in the dark . . . Bad Girl! First ya pet a little, let up
a little, then you get a little kiss.

Buzz, needing a transitional image, focuses on a box of animal crackers
with a drawing of monkeys behind bars. He segues to the real thing,
then to couples old and young sitting on benches in Buzz's multitiered
"park." A pea-shooting "infant" misfit (eight-year-old actor Billy Barty,
best known at the time as Mickey Rooney's little brother in the *Mickey
McGuire* short-film series of the late 1920s and early 1930s) is introduced in the number. Next, a visibly angry Ruby exits a cab with Powell
in the back seat (pettin' in the cab was evidently a poor idea). Officer
Aline MacMahon points her to a roller-skating service "for little girls
who have to walk home." She's almost trampled by the multitude of
angry women on skates. Billy the baby lands a pea on a police officer's
neck, jumps out of his baby carriage, and skates away with the law in
pursuit. The whole environment is suddenly transformed into a snow
scene complete with sleigh bells, snowball fights, and a wintery top shot
using large prop snowballs. The weather changes on a dime, and now
it's a summer scene, but only briefly, as the rains begin to pour. The girls
run to their own private dressing rooms (a two-tiered set subdivided into
individual quarters) and change out of their wet things. Buzz allows a
voyeuristic view of his girls hidden by a curtain, lit in silhouette, while
little letch Billy Barty raises the curtain (and his eyebrows). Recalling
a similar peeking that Buzz almost got away with in the opening number of *The Kid from Spain*, the girls are dressed in swimsuits before
anything is revealed. Their outfits, made of tin, register a group disappointment among the men who are "locked at the front gate." Leave it to
crafty Billy to provide Powell a can opener, which he employs forthwith
ratcheting upward on Ruby's tin chastity cage.

"Pettin' in the Park" was witty and inventive, with the most extravagant production design that Buzz had worked with at his new studio.
"Pettin'"—as term or act—is never defined explicitly. Adults possessed
more worldliness in the Depression years than is routinely attributed to
them. They often sought relief from their Depression doldrums not with
pure entertainment, but with diversions that were impure and brazen.
Buzz, Jack Warner, and the audiences of 1933 were partners in this little
act of complicity that allowed the overtly blue nature of the number to

remain in the picture unexpurgated. As for the children who watched Buzz's pretty pictures unfold, the only thing they took away from "Pettin' in the Park" was the imitative toddler named Billy Barty, the pea-shootin' marksman.

All that Buzz needed was a good melody for inspiration to strike, but if Al Dubin wrote lyrics that instantly lent themselves to cinematic transfer, so much the better. The melodic "Shadow Waltz" had to have been a transliteration challenge. There was difficulty in visualizing "In the shadows let me come and sing to you. Let me dream a song that I can bring to you." But Buzz had an idea that had percolated for years; the Palace Theatre . . . the lady with the violin . . . that controlled high kick of hers. What if, on a mass scale . . . ?

A white-tuxedoed Dick Powell takes the stage, which is minimally dressed with a bench and theatrical picture window, and sings to a platinum-coiffed Ruby. A dissolve, and four Berkeley chorines are seen behind the faux glass repeating the opening refrain as Powell accompanies on violin to a gliding Ruby. She receives his boutonniere, and its close-up is the transitional point to a unique and fanciful production. A chorus girl wearing sequins in a white, three-layered hoop dress is playing a white violin as the camera pulls back to an image of a dream in graceful fluidity. There on a winding platform is Buzz's germinating idea in full fruition. Dozens of identical girls, violins on chins, are playing, twirling, and performing to Buzz's exacting standards the controlled kick he found so effective "if done right." They move gracefully along a winding bridge that resembles a gigantic curved ribbon; an imitation palm tree and moon in the background are the stage's sole dressing. Audaciously, Buzz cuts all the studio lights, the illumination provided by neon tubing attached to the contours of each violin. The effect is magical. As the theme saws away, Buzz's top shots are even more impressive as a neon-lit violin spins in the center of a circle of other violins. The technical wonderment of the number is the remarkably composed top shot in which the individual violins position themselves into one enormous instrument, its super-elongated neon bow moving rhythmically over the bridge. Buzz exploits the tri-hoop outfits of his girls in floral-effect top shots. When the girls spin in place and contract the circle, the effect from up high is beautiful and graceful. An impressive change in perspective occurs as the girls appear to be dancing sideways from the top of the screen to the bottom on the right half of the frame while their image is reflected on the left. It's just the kind of invention Buzz was proud of. The trick was simple. The camera is placed on its side. The girls were filmed dancing off the winding staircase while their movements were reflected in the pristine black floor. When projected they defied gravity. A low-mounted parade-of-faces shot (similar to the ending of "Young and Healthy") brings us back to Dick and Ruby. In another Buzz sleight of hand, we watch as the two embrace. Ruby tosses the boutonniere, it lands in water, and only when the boutonniere's splash causes water ripples to fill the screen do we realize we've been looking at their reflection.

In a speech from April 7, 1932, Franklin Roosevelt (then governor of New York) mentioned the lowly forgotten man as an entity worth remembering during the country's economic distress at the time: "These unhappy times call for the building of plans that rest upon the forgotten, the unorganized but the indispensable units of economic power, for plans like those of 1917 that build from the bottom up and not from the top down, that put their faith once more in the forgotten man at the bottom of the economic pyramid." "Remember My Forgotten Man" is a musical number of social conscience, a serious depiction of war's effects and society's apathy for the plight of returning World War I veterans. Its inclusion was disconcerting in an otherwise lightweight musical comedy. While adhering to the Warner house style that catered to the proletariat, "Remember My Forgotten Man" empathized with them as well. Buzz, with his firsthand knowledge of the returning vet's plight, transformed the number into an emotional plea of staggering force.

Under a street lamp, Joan Blondell (who, it's hinted, might have succumbed to life as a streetwalker) trades her cigarette with a down-on-his-luck man and speaks of tragedy that is her life: "I was satisfied to drift along from day to day, till they came and took my man away. Remember my forgotten man. You put a rifle in his hand. You sent him far away. You shouted 'Hip hooray' but look at him today." And in conclusion: "Forgetting him you see, means you're forgetting me, like my forgotten man."

Buzz raises the camera to second-floor window (recalling the *42nd Street* number) as a grieved singer (Etta Moten) soulfully sings Blondell's monologue. The camera moves from image to image: a bereft woman holding a fatherless infant, and an elderly woman looking forlorn. A homeless man sleeping on the sidewalk is tapped awake with an officer's billy club when Joan intervenes by showing the policeman the pinned service cross on the veteran's lapel. A blackout, and the curtains part to a scene of revelry as the young doughboys march to war, flanked by cheering crowds shouting "hip hooray," throwing paper streams, and waving flags, their uniforms matching exactly the one worn by 2d Lt. Busby Enos sixteen years earlier. He captures the marching from different angles until a black curtain parts and another transition takes place. The grim reality of the marching men is now seen as they trudge through a downpour (the cinematic effect of the men walking on runners is revealed, a shot that tethers the number to the stage). The casualties of battle are reflected in all forms; soldiers on stretchers, the walking wounded, bandaged and bloodied men barely able to move, some of them propped up by their buddies as the march continues. Next, a transition to a sight Depression-era audiences knew all too well: the war heroes, wounded not by enemy fire but by an economy in collapse, are queued in a long breadline, one by one receiving the minimal sustenance of a sandwich and cup of coffee, their faces reflecting their plight. A final change of scene and a powerfully envisaged tableau (within the physical constraints of the proscenium) is presented in the kind of spectacle that Buzz could have designed for Broadway. A large tri-level arch shows marching men in silhouette, while women with outstretched arms plead, "Oh bring them back," as a group of societal downcasts march toward the camera and sing in unison these emotionally wrenching lyrics:

We are the real forgotten men,
who have to lead this life again.
We sauntered forth to fight,
for glory was our pride,
but somehow glory died.
Remember your forgotten men.
You've got to let us live again.
We came, we marched away,
to fight for USA,
but where are we today?

Joan, in speaking for every suffering woman, concludes the number as the camera pulls back, displaying the crowds, the marching men, and the outline of the doughboys in a spectacular finale, the kind Buzz always believed gave a number its lasting impression. His direction of the vignettes reveals a sympathetic force behind the camera. The story, all his own, is told with the recognition of a tragedy that only an active participant in those fateful years could have conceived. That the number is told in somber images is an acknowledgment of the growing acumen of its creator, who could, with equal fervor, film ladies with coins and neon violins, while envisioning the citizenry of the day in an empathetic portrayal of combined despair.

"Remember My Forgotten Man" is as powerful an ending as any in musical pictures, but "Pettin' in the Park" was originally supposed to close the film. Backstage, following "Young and Healthy," the chorus girls waited in the outfits they were to wear for the roller-skating sequence, but after viewing the "Forgotten Man" number, it was evident to the directors that it belonged as the finale.

At the cast screening, a big laugh came from the chorus girls who recognized Buzz onscreen. Before the final number, he's seen in the cameo role of "call boy," urging the cast to make haste: "Hurry up, boys. Snap it up, will you? Onstage, Forgotten Man number." A couple of cuts, and Buzz appeared again in a tight profile that called attention to his swarthiness; his bushy thick eyebrows, pronounced nose bump, and jutting lower lip filled the screen: "All right, Miss Carol, Forgotten Man number."

Buzz filmed his bit part a day before Warner Brothers was supposed to close for inventory purposes. The studio didn't want the expense of actors for a quick line, so Buzz was ordered to shoot the few bits with personnel on the lot. He inserted himself, and by the time of the final cut, he was the only one who made it onscreen.

Buzz's working methods, those that featured him at an altitude greater than anyone on the lot, found interest in the press. "He blows his shrill whistle," wrote one reporter, "and 80 girls run to their positions." The syndicated Hollywood columnist Robbin Coons caught Buzz preparing the rain portion of "Pettin' in the Park." In his column of May 4, 1933, Buzz was described as hopping on his boom, shooting down from up high, and repeating the procedure. His style on set was to grab an amplified megaphone and bark his orders: "Fast, there, girls! Watch that step! How's the lighting, Mike? Quiet, Quiet! I've got to have quiet! Music, now, get ready . . . GO!" Five rehearsals and Buzz was ready for the take. The camera was hooded to keep it dry, and as Buzz called for rain, the mimicking water pipes obeyed. Impressionistic lightning flashes appeared, followed by the music playback, and it was a take. "Good," said Buzz. "Now we'll start the next number. Fast, now, fast!"

To get those great top shots, Buzz used a wide-angle lens when he was sixty feet up. But there were many times he wanted the camera higher than the ceiling allowed. Buzz took aside some studio craftsmen and told them to bore a hole through the roof. Newly drilled holes appeared in five different soundstages. The camera, no longer subjected to the ceiling's limitation, was covered with a tarpaulin once it escaped the physical boundaries of the soundstage. "The front office was a little upset," said Buzz, possibly understating their position. A new soundstage with a ceiling of ninety feet was being built around this time. Jack Warner, in Europe when the work was completed, left word with an underling: "Now that the new stage is finished, don't let Berkeley on it!" Warner envisioned bore holes ninety feet up, and he would have none of it.

On March 6, in the midst of shooting, President Roosevelt declared an unprecedented nationwide bank holiday for four days, halting all bank transactions in an effort to prevent a widespread run. At the same time, all of the studios (in agreement with the Motion Picture Academy) initiated an eight-week pay cut of an astounding 50 percent for salaried employees earning more than twenty-five dollars a week. Buzz was certainly affected, but not Darryl Zanuck, who somehow skirted the edict.

Everything dealing with the violins of "Shadow Waltz" was of Buzz's making, including the neon. Lighting the violins was an afterthought, but all were retrofit when a prototype model with neon tubing on its perimeter proved successful when filmed in the dark. Unfortunately, wires connecting the neon to its battery often came in contact with the outer metallic coating of the chorus girls' dresses, resulting in minor electric shocks. Yet nothing could have prepared Buzz and his violinists for what happened on March 10, when, at 5:55 p.m. at a late rehearsal, a magnitude 6.4 earthquake occurred with its epicenter in Long Beach. There were seven quakes in total, the second at 6:06; a third, four minutes later; another at 6:12, diminishing in intensity until 7:25. All around Los Angeles, buildings swayed and glass windows shattered in a swath two hundred miles long and thirty miles wide. As the ground and ramp shook on the "Shadow Waltz" set, some girls fell, and one was seriously injured when cracked neon tubing punctured her skin. There was a total blackout on the set, and Buzz, dangling from his camera boom some thirty feet in the air, required immediate assistance. Cinematographer Sol Polito pulled him up to the platform. Once upright, Buzz ordered the girls to stay put and wait until the stage doors were opened and light was let in.

Joan Blondell was a terrific actress who couldn't sing. She talks her way through the opening of "Remember My Forgotten Man," usurped by the emotionally delivered strains of contralto vocalist Etta Moten, who adds a passionate level of despair to Al Dubin's haunting lyrics. In the number's finale, Joan's voice was dubbed by a nightclub singer named Jean Cowan, who, for a few years, was under contract to KFWB, the Los Angeles radio station owned by Warner Brothers (and present at the "The 42nd Street Special" christening).

In May, just two months after *42nd Street*, *Gold Diggers of 1933* was released and met with positive reviews and substantial box office. Relma Morin in the *Los Angeles Record* described the perfectly amazing job of Busby Berkeley, though she erred on Buzz's nonappearance: "It's a dazzling, eye paralyzing, ear tickling creation that makes all the other musical films look like Delancey Street peep shows. The star of the picture is the gentleman who does not appear in it. Busby Berkeley, the geometrically-minded lad who created the dance sequences, has done a perfectly amazing job."

For "We're in the Money," fifty-four girls were dressed in costumes of fifty-four thousand "silver" coins. The number also used five silver dollars, twenty-eight feet in diameter, and dozens of gold pieces ten feet wide. As a promotional giveaway, the coins were duplicated in chocolate. The hoop-skirt costuming for "Shadow Waltz" (designed in part by Buzz himself) was made of two thousand yards of white China silk. The Warner Brothers press book for the film notes that "75 women worked eight days to make these costumes and at the last minute, two milliners sat up all night to create 54 silver wigs of metallic cloth with little sequin tendrils in front giving the appearance of curls."

A prologue designed by Buzz, the kind that he dabbled with at Fanchon and Marco, was set for the Los Angeles opening. It was scrapped abruptly when Buzz let the word out what was being done. He had been told by the studio to keep quiet about the prologue, and failing to do so lost him the opportunity to show the film colony what he could devise for the stage. The dancer and dance director Albertina Rasch was awarded the assignment after Buzz's indiscretion.

With two strong showings of directorial finesse, Buzz made his case to Darryl Zanuck. He wanted to direct an entire feature, both the book and dance numbers. Zanuck wasn't entirely convinced on a solo shot; after all, Buzz's numbers had always existed autonomously from the rest of the pictures he was involved with. Nothing that Buzz had done thus far (impressive as it was) made Zanuck think that he could handle the day-to-day banality of filming dialogue passages. If Buzz was teamed with a mentor, however, Zanuck would sign off on a tandem director assignment.

Gold Diggers of 1933 had its first screening at Grauman's Chinese Theatre in Hollywood. As Buzz and Jack Warner were exiting the theater, owner Sid Grauman came up to them and asked, "Buzz, how the hell are you going to top 'Shadow Waltz' and 'Forgotten Man'?" Buzz gave an answer that, according to him, came out of nowhere. "Sid, I can see a big waterfall coming down through the rocks, with girls sliding down the rapids in a huge Ziegfeldian pool with twenty-four gold springboards and a gold fountain telescoping into the air!" Jack interrupted, "Sid, don't pay any attention to him, he's just blown his top." On the way home, Buzz thought his aquatic idea sound and filed it away, just as he did during his Palace Theatre excursions.

Like every Hollywood director, Buzz met many people during the course of his early years at the studio. In Buzz's case they tended generally to be female, many looking to be the next Berkeley girl. At dinner, cocktail, and pool parties, Buzz was delighted to meet industry professionals, along with actors and actresses he'd never otherwise work with. One was a petite redhead with a sunny smile named Merna Kennedy. Her calling card was her starring role five years earlier in Charlie Chaplin's *The Circus,* though she had appeared in twenty films to date. Buzz was quite taken by the former Maude Kahler of Kankakee, Illinois, and soon after making her acquaintance they became a couple in love.

The news was good for *42nd Street.* It was one of the top money-making films of the year and won Academy Award nominations for best picture and best sound recording. The success paved the way for Buzz to land a full-fledged directing credit. The first directorial assignment promised by Zanuck had come to pass, and, as stipulated, it was to be a shared effort. With *Gold Diggers* editor George Amy, Buzz received codirecting credit for a brisk sixty-two-minute drama that revolved around managers, buyers, and secretaries titled *She Had to Say Yes*. When lonely buyers arrive in town on a business trip, the company's managers scramble to find them "accompaniment" during their stay. A naïf in the secretarial pool, Florence (Loretta Young) gets caught up in the side business, first through a cheating fiancé, then a buyer of some repute (Hugh Herbert), and finally smooth-talker Daniel (Lyle Talbot), who whisks her away in his arms by the closing credits.

In the standard dialogue sequences, it's difficult to discern where Buzz's directing ended and George Amy's began. There are, however, moments when Berkeley's contributions are quite noticeable. The opening montage that sets the tone and place features the workings of the garment industry from designer drawings, to seamstresses sewing, to models traipsing in front of a tri-paned mirror. Another scene opens with a Berkeley specialty—ladies' legs. He shoots the crossed legs of one secretary, then turns his camera to catch the gams of the other girls. A nightclub sequence begins with a close-up of shaking maracas. They're replaced with the hands of a violinist playing his instrument, and focus shifts to a solo dancer on a circular stage.

She Had to Say Yes had a modest budget of $111,000 and a short shooting schedule of two-and-a-half weeks. Buzz said he learned a lot from George Amy. Amy's tips helped as Berkeley's technique was still evolving. "It was a routine picture," confessed Buzz, "but a pleasant one to do. I learned not only that I could direct, but that I liked it."

A personnel shift at the highest level of the Warner Brothers management hierarchy occurred in the summer of 1933. Darryl Zanuck quit his job when a Warner brother told him that he had reached the limit of his earning potential. He started the Twentieth Century Company soon after and never looked back. His job was filled by former publicity man Hal Wallis, who had been with Warner Brothers since the silent days. Wallis had taken charge of the Burbank studios when Warner Brothers purchased the First National Company, and until Zanuck's departure he was an associate producer. The news could not have been received well by Buzz, who lost his mentor and chief champion.

Soon after the Wallis announcement, Merna and Buzz solidified their relationship, evidenced by an engagement ring that was reportedly "the size of a chunk of coal." They were to be married in the fall, according to reports.

In August, Buzz was preparing his next film, *Footlight Parade*. At the same time, Sam Goldwyn was arranging the next Eddie Cantor vehicle, *Roman Scandals,* with Berkeley in mind for the musical numbers. In a preemptive move, Buzz sent a legalese letter on August 17, 1933, to Samuel Goldwyn, Inc., Ltd. in which he enclosed a check for $708.37. Buzz claimed the money was an overpayment for his services (now that he was in Warner Brothers' employ). Sam Goldwyn was not pleased and was not about to relieve Buzz of his obligations. *Roman Scandals* was in production, but by this time Goldwyn's hold on Buzz was tenuous. He'd seen what Buzz had accomplished at Warner Brothers, but for some reason he never extended his contract to the man he rightly felt was his discovery.

Roman Scandals and *Footlight Parade* had similar shooting schedules. Warner Brothers wanted Berkeley just at the time when Goldwyn needed him. Goldwyn had a loan-out arrangement with Warner Brothers for Buzz's services. He could shoot two pictures at Warner's if Goldwyn didn't require him in the meantime. From Sam's point of view, Berkeley was his property. He didn't imagine (and had no knowledge) that Buzz would work both studios simultaneously; mornings for him and nights for Warner Brothers. In a concentrated period of three months, Buzz made an almost daily trek to both studios. Goldwyn never let go of his suspicions about Berkeley's proclivity to strong drink, but made no bones about it, as he always found Buzz fine in the morning. Then things started to change. Buzz was becoming listless. He looked tired and overworked. Goldwyn again hired detectives and had him followed. It wasn't drinking, as Goldwyn had feared. Buzz was simply burning the candle at both ends. The detectives tracked him to the Warner Brothers studios, where, for several evenings, he was seen entering the studio at dusk and exiting in the wee hours. Goldwyn now knew, but said nothing. Buzz, for his part, couldn't carry on the charade any longer. He made an appointment with Goldwyn. After entering the studio chief's office, Buzz just stood there, head down. "I am ashamed to come in," began Buzz, "I know you will be angry with me." There was silence. Then Buzz dropped his bombshell. "I have signed a long-term contract with Warner Brothers and I am to direct pictures. But I told them I was obligated to do the next Cantor picture."

Goldwyn didn't take his anger out on Buzz. It was the Warner brothers he disliked. He thought they were "guilty of the most reckless star-raiding that the industry has ever known." The AMPP (Association of Motion Picture Producers) worked on behalf of studios and producers as an ombudsman of sorts, resolving contract conflicts and other studio/ employee issues. Sam brought Jack Warner before the AMPP. He charged that Busby Berkeley's services had been pirated. He looked around the room, seeking support from his fellow members, and received none. In exasperation, he got out of his chair and headed for the door, but not before uttering the following: "How can we sit together and deal with this industry if you're going to do things like this to me? If this is the way you do it, gentlemen, *include me out!*" The AMPP resolved nothing, but Sam Goldwyn didn't let the matter die. He wanted the Warner brothers in court.

In *Footlight Parade,* James Cagney played "Dr. Buzz, the Show Doctor," and nobody knew it but Buzz. It was a story of the emergence of sound pictures, the decline of vaudeville, and the staging of prologues. Chester Kent (Cagney) is practically jobless when the stage shows he produced gave way to talkies. Enter the Fanchon and Marco angle. Kent stumbles on the idea of creating and directing live prologues before the feature. They would play in cities all over the country simultaneously, where franchising allowed for greater profits at lower cost. Success is seemingly his until he learns that a competitor has been stealing all his ideas. A mole in the cast is revealed, and in an effort to win a large contract for his prologues, Kent keeps his girls under house arrest. They are to rehearse his new numbers without leaving the premises. In 1933, audiences accustomed to Buzz's film magic might have had an inkling that something spectacular would be unveiled. A patient wait was amply rewarded with perhaps the finest musical production number ever conceived and executed.

Wedged in the narrative of *Footlight Parade* is "Sitting on a Back-yard Fence," the dance devised by Chester earlier in the film. It's a piece without resolution (as was "We're in the Money"), but Buzz has some fun with his tomcat- and pussycat-clad dancers while a life-size mouse enlivens the action. The Sammy Fain/Irving Kahal ditty, in consort with Warren and Dubin's suggestiveness, opens with a mating call:

Come out, come out, come out and get your lovin'
Now don't you keep me in suspense.
Come on, come on, we'll do our "turtle dovin'"
Sitting on a backyard fence.

Billy Barty, back from his turn as the provocateur in "Pettin' in the Park," plays the oversized mouse with thievery in his eyes. His role in the number is quite odd (there's no logic in his appearance, not that that ever gave Buzz concern). The mouse's lair was filmed on a stage with oversized props (milk bottle, mousetrap), and Buzz must have been pleased when Billy, salivating over the milk, rolls his eyes and smacks his lips in close-up (one can faintly hear the director urging the dwarflet to "open your eyes . . . let me see them"). Billy's screen time is brief, and an anticipated cat-and-mouse interaction with the purring chorines never materializes. Nonetheless, Buzz keeps things cinematic with a pa-rade of smiling feline faces as Ruby Keeler reenters the number through a painted mouth (made to hide the trap door) on the stage floor. She dances a bit, Frank McHugh calls cut, and the number ends abruptly. It's hard to believe that, with the costumes, sets, and staging, "Sitting on a Backyard Fence" was not intended to be more robust. The resultant edits leave the piece truncated and half-finished. An educated surmise is the number was clipped for time.

The commerce transpiring in the "Honeymoon Hotel," Buzz's first of the film's purported three prologues, wasn't much of a secret to the day's audiences. Defined as a lover's idyll, a place where the "bridal suites are never very idle," Jersey City's Honeymoon Hotel boasts a guest list where "Smith" is predominant (making one wonder why "Honeymoon" is part the establishment's title). Dick persuades Ruby that a tying of the knot goes hand in hand with a honeymoon, and they're off to New Jersey.

Next, they're checking in, but not before participating in a quickie wedding in the back office (a special effect has the hotel's postcards arranged to form an image of the justice of the peace and the couple). As they enter their connubial room, they're surprised to find Ruby's entire family in attendance, warning them of marriage's tribulations (with Billy Barty, the youngest member of the clan). The uniformity that was a Busby Berkeley stalwart extends itself to the hotel's guests—a nightgown-wearing chorine in each room down the long hallway, while their "husbands" march in tandem toward a changing room in preparation for the night's festivities. Amusing Billy darts from one room to the next, settling in the one without a do-not-disturb sign. Obliviously, Dick enters the same room and gets into Billy's bed. Al Dubin's witty lyrics spice up the situation with a clever closer:

> DICK: Kiss your little honey boy good-night, girl,
>   Now we're married, dear, and here we are.
>   I've a right to be beside the right girl.
> BILLY: But you're in the wrong boudoir!

A minor misunderstanding and quick make-up between Ruby and Dick has them in bed, under the covers (scandalous, but not intolerable for its day) as the room light is extinguished. The ever-clever Buzz pans to a magazine whose pages are flipping in the breeze. Just then, the winds calm, and the magazine stops fluttering, landing on a page containing a photograph of a cute infant. Buzz's cautionary foreshadowing is clearly unambiguous and unapologetic—a blue visual joke for the adults that was indecipherable for the kiddies.

Buzz's water ballet in *The Kid from Spain* was a prototype for a more expansive treatment. His Warner Brothers successes gave him carte blanche to pursue the cinematic aquacade on a scale grander than Sam Goldwyn would have allowed. According to *Footlight Parade*'s story, the three sample prologues were meant to seduce theater owner Apolinaris (Paul Porcasi) into signing a contract to produce these shows in all his houses. As the second prologue begins, Cagney leans over to Joan Blondell. In referencing Apolinaris (but speaking to us), he delivers what could be the understatement to end them all: "Well, if this doesn't get him, nothing will." Unfolding in the next eleven minutes was the most expensive and extravagantly conceived number of Busby Berkeley's career to this point. In a memo dated June 20, 1933, Hal Wallis refers to the water number as "By a Mountain Stream." The song's catchy melody and romantic lyrics (by Sammy Fain and Irving Kahal) lent themselves to a kind of visual interpretation and experimentation unexplored at this level by Buzz until now. He took full advantage of the studio's attributes (and largesse) in creating a spectacular tableau of cataracts, waterslides, and pools, all attended by mythical water nymphs. In a setting of trees and streams, Dick Powell opens "By a Waterfall" (as the song was officially titled) singing of "love in a natural setting." He is joined by Ruby, singing of the waterfall and the whippoorwill:

> There's a magic melody,
> Mother nature sings to me,
> Beside a waterfall,
> With you.

Powell falls into slumber, and the balance of the number is, ostensibly, his dream as realized in Buzz's prismatic vision. The water nymphs beckon Ruby, and she dives into one of Anton Grot's designer pools. Berkeley girls sporting bathing caps of imitation hair and identically sheer swimsuits (exposing their flesh while hiding their navels) surround the busy water slides. From this point forward, Buzz's captures the swimmers and their milieu from a myriad of angles and the most impressive top shots heretofore witnessed in motion pictures. His custom pools featured windows on the sides and bottom, allowing for both unusual camera setups and impressionistic lighting. One of the girls dives into a zipper-type setup where two facing rows interlock in a human zipper display (and unzip themselves as she swims through). Underwater shots of Ruby give way to over-the-waterline images of formational swimmers, followed by Buzz's parade of grinning chlorinated chorines. Next, the camera poised below the swimming tank offers Buzz one of his greatest little inserts. As the girls stand on the bottom, they open their legs in the arch formation, but from this angle a unique image develops. Entering from the bottom of the frame, a Berkeley girl gracefully floats to the top, seemingly in front of the legs in a resultant effect both imaginative and erotic. The song saws away as Buzz's next bit of inventiveness takes his top shot to the next level. Viewed from on high, the swimmers in concentric circles form lovely images (each swimmer is partnered with a "holder" whose job it is to position her in Buzz's defined patterns). Suddenly, a negative lighting cue, and the studio's overhead lights are switched off, leaving the pool's side lights as its sole illuminating source. The effect in the top shot is enthralling, making the swimmers look like a colorless mass. The lights illuminate, and a lengthy top shot, trumping any that Buzz had ever made, unfurls. His regimentation, his chalkboard drawings, and his detailed rehearsals make this particular top shot (in this case, a "snake shot") an unqualified success. Two lines of swimming girls, their arms outstretched to grab the shoulders of the one in front, maneuver themselves in the pattern of a slithering snake on its way to consuming its own tail. It's quite startling to behold and a bit bewildering in its conception. To give life, movement, and visual splendor to an arrangement of such complexity, and to make it all look effortless, is the very definition of Busby Berkeley's regimented art. As the snakes "recoil," they're redistributed into other pleasing formations. Next, a circular ziggurat is seen, populated with water nymphs on each tier. A top shot that almost tops the snake shot has the girls, one tier at a time, kicking and spreading their legs, and the resultant effect is nothing short of dazzling. Buzz goes to the well once again for a quick top shot, followed by a glimpse of Ruby standing beneath a waterfall. A matching dissolve has Ruby flicking water on Powell's ankles as his dream gives way to the final chorus. In Buzz's closing shot, four (mechanical) baby whippoorwills open their hungry mouths in turn to the last four notes of the song. A humorous coda has the audience members (even the imperturbable Apolinaris) applauding as if they were privy to the ne plus ultra expressionism of Busby Berkeley.

A squalid den of iniquity is the setting for *Footlight Parade*'s bombastic finale, "Shanghai Lil." Cagney plays Bill in his only number in the film. He's a sailor who jumped ship in a heartfelt quest to find his life's love, the girl in the port he couldn't forget, the mystifying Shanghai Lil:

I've covered every little highway.
And I've been climbing every hill.
I've been looking high, and I've been looking low,
Looking for my Shanghai Lil.

In a Chinese saloon catering to prostitutes and their navy clientele, Bill, drunk, meanders from table to table, pausing to examine each girl. Various ethnicities (Frenchman, Jew, Asian) are lined up at the bar, allowing Buzz an unglamorous "parade of faces" while his camera slowly glides past each customer commenting about the unseen Lil. Bill leaves the bar and enters an adjacent opium den lined with languorous addicts (a smoker's pipe clearly in the foreground). His Lil isn't here. "She's every sailor's pal, she's anybody's gal," yells a table-standing ruffian, and Bill slugs the guy in the chin. A melee ensues (Buzz intensifies the action with quick cuts and interesting camera placements). Bill stands clear of the fighting, and as the bar empties, a large basket opens, revealing Shanghai Lil (Ruby Keeler in eye-slitting makeup and tapered fingernails). In an accent far from native, Lil sings to her sailor:

I miss you velly much a long time
I think that you no love me still

But Bill sings of his sincerity, and soon the two are dancing together on the bar. Cagney, in the light-footed approach that he displayed on the Broadway stage, moves with a delicate grace complementing Ruby's more forceful taps. The tapping abruptly ends as a military trumpet sounds the call to embark. In full lieutenant mode, Buzz masterfully arranges the groups of marchers, and the ensemble looks like the navy in a passing parade. Bill, along with the rest of his shipmates, proceeds with a display of the manual of arms (another regimented series of moves that inspired Buzz). Lil implores Bill to take her "on great big steamboat" with him, but since the ship isn't his, he can't. Bill marches on as Buzz, camera up on high, films a group of sailors holding placards (the first since the *42nd Street* finale). Together they form the picture of the American flag and Franklin Roosevelt. Next they're arranged in the formation of the National Recovery Administration's New Deal eagle (complete with a 21-gun salute). A final march to the ship has Bill and Lil (disguised in a sailor suit) together. Before they sail, he pulls out a deck of cards and flips the backs to reveal an animated ship sailing toward the horizon, and Buzz's jingoistic number comes to a rousing end.

Buzz boasted to the press: "We've got a waterfall number in the picture that is one of the high spots of the show. We sort of let ourselves go crazy over that number; it's not just a waterfall you know, there's lots of other aquatic stuff in it as a setting for one of the songs. Well, all the girls had to be able to swim. I expected that probably fifteen or twenty of them would have to fade out and be replaced. Not a bit of it. Every single one of these girls could swim well, not like Eleanor Holm of course, but they could take care of themselves in the water. They teach it in the schools nowadays and it's a good thing, especially when you're staging a number like the one I was worrying about. We spent a whole week shooting that one number. The girls were in the water for most of each day. When it was all over none of us thought we would ever want to go swimming again. But I believe it's a great sequence." Buzz agreed that his swimming sirens worked harder than any of the principals did.

Buzz the coddler listened sympathetically when Ruby Keeler told him she could swim *a little,* didn't dive, and didn't like being underwater. "You'll be able to do it. Get in the water with the kids, get used to it," he said. "Yeah, but after that, what do I do?" asked Ruby. "For the first show you'll go down to the other end of the pool and do a porpoise dive." Ruby held a blank expression as Buzz explained: "You dip your hands and you dive then you swim underwater to this end of the pool with your eyes open because there's a window here with a camera. You have to time it so when you pop out of the water you're smiling." Buzz might have been piling on the dread for his own amusement, for he was quite aware of Ruby's trepidation.

Buzz wrung $38,000 from Jack Warner for the "By a Waterfall" pool, originally budgeted for $16,000 ($10,000 construction, $2,000 labor, $1,550 electrical, $2,450 miscellany). "It was built like the hold of the [SS] *Bremen,* pumping 20,000 gallons of water every five minutes," said Buzz. He designed the set, the backdrop, and the foliage. With the studio's best electricians, engineers, and art directors, he brought his vision to life. The pool was eighty feet by forty, and featured plate-glass openings at the sides and underneath. Buzz said that visitors were constantly on the set to see if what they'd heard was true. Buzz's bathing beauties wore a special bathing "costume" designed by Milo Anderson that offered a semi-nude effect when the rubber headpieces ran down the length of the girls' bodies. George Groves, chief sound engineer for the studio (and the man responsible for recording *The Jazz Singer*), noted that the lengthy wait for Buzz to get his camera setup just right had caused some water-girls to faint; they were revived with smelling salts. "I have the greatest admiration for Buzz," said George. "He was an extremely well organized man. Wonderful ideas of course; he's a great guy to work with. Buzz was extremely talented . . . just marvelous."

It seemed the toughest part of the entire number was not the elaborate dressing of the full soundstage set, but finding the right song. The pool was hydrated, and Buzz had no number to film. According to him, Warren and Dubin were on vacation (more likely in an unpaid time-off between projects as was studio policy), so he sent out word to other composers to come see him. Song after song was performed, and nothing sounded pleasing, nothing in the water ballet vein that Buzz envisioned. Anxious to find something, he auditioned a songwriting team with whom he was unfamiliar. Sammy Fain played the piano, and lyricist Irving Kahal sung the opening verses of "By a Waterfall," and before they finished, Buzz knew he had his water ballet song.

In the first two days of rehearsal, before the Berkeley girls entered the pool, they studiously watched Buzz at the blackboard, where, like a football coach, he white-chalked the patterns and movements the girls would undertake in the pool. Before they could don their swimsuits, Buzz had the wardrobe department drag out every smock they could find. The girls wore the smocks while Buzz, wooden pointer in hand, referenced the circular chalk marks. By his order, Buzz kept the stage doors closed. The girls knew he did it on their behalf. They worked long hours in the pool with no labor laws to protect them. Sometimes they broke for dinner. It was often six hours between calls to the set. "A thirty-two hour day was nothing," said studio still photographer Madison Lacy. Daily production reports show that it took from 9:00 a.m. to 2:48 a.m. (the next day) to complete one underwater shot. Other reports show a shooting schedule of almost twenty-two hours, from 10:00 a.m. to 7:40 a.m. The arduous parts of their day were the long waits between takes. Buzz would meander back and forth (and up and down) pointing to a girl, instructing her to reposition herself, and then continue devising in silence. With so many women in "By a Waterfall" and the many days required for rehearsal and shooting, it was bound to occur that some girls couldn't enter the water. A rehearsal in the pool meant standing in waist-high water for hours. It was a quiet set save for the water pumps, and the stage lights were cut unless Buzz demanded otherwise, and the girls stood in place, their fingers and toes resembling raisins. No one had the good taste to inquire if lavatory breaks were circumvented. Buzz was high up on his monorail when he instructed the waders below: "Okay girls, now spread your pretty little legs" and the naughty-minded responded with giggles and twitters.

Lorena Layson, a Busby Berkeley girl since *42nd Street,* got punched in the face and was knocked out cold during the filming of "Shanghai Lil." When filming action sequences, Buzz wore a whistle around his neck and blew it rather than yelling a sometimes unregistered "cut." In the fight portion of the number, Buzz warned the stunt men to be careful with his girls. As the fight became intense and complex with action at every corner of the set, Buzz reached for his whistle. He asked the assistant director about the girls' well-being. Everyone seemed to be fine except for a passed-out Lorena Layson. She had evidently stepped into a fist, but fortunately she recovered quickly. Stuntman Harvey Perry was asked by Buzz if he wanted to rehearse the fight scene prior to shooting. "Skip it," said Perry. By noon Buzz was ready for a take, but decided to call lunch. Back on the set, Buzz instructed Harvey and fellow stuntman Duke Green how he wanted the men to fall down a staircase. Buzz said it had to be spectacular from the camera's viewpoint or they'd do it over. "All right," said Buzz. "Camera!" Perry and Green fought at the top of the stairs and tripped on purpose. They plunged down the stairs and wound up in a heap, bumping into the camera. The men untangled, dusted themselves off, and asked Buzz if they should do it again. "Nope, that was good. You're through," and Buzz moved on to the next setup.

The Chinese Council in Los Angeles was promised a screening of *Footlight Parade,* but Hal Wallis was hesitant. He was a tad disingenuous in a memo to production manager Bill Koenig when he advised Bill to tell the council that the "Shanghai Lil" number wasn't ready to be shown and that the number wasn't at all disrespectful to their people.

Daily Variety reported that dance director Larry Ceballos had brought a lawsuit against the studio and Buzz. He was suing for $100,000, claiming he had not been given the opportunity to direct *Footlight Parade*'s special dance numbers per his contract with Warner Brothers. The suit was quickly dismissed.

Footlight Parade was another ringing success for Buzz despite the *New York Times* labeling it a "dull and turgid musical film." Cagney received praise for his light-footedness, and Buzz's complex geometries were "enough to sink the unmathematical mind." The best review of all, unwritten, occurred at the New York premiere, where patrons gave "By a Waterfall" a standing ovation. Some in that opening night audience were so giddy they tossed their programs in the air.

From July to October 1933, *Roman Scandals* was in production, and Buzz was busy with it and his Warner Brothers assignment. How he managed to find time for Merna is anyone's guess, but around then he made the acquaintance of two of Merna's friends, Etta Dunn and Leonard Judd. They made a friendly foursome, and it was no secret that Etta and Leonard had their sights set on the altar. From their point of view, the coosome Buzz and Merna might just beat them to it.

Buzz's numbers in *Roman Scandals* border on the scandalous, with barely hidden nudity and suggestive lyrics. Early in the film, Eddie (Eddie Cantor) finds himself among a group of residents in New Rome, Oklahoma, who have been dispossessed and now find themselves living on the street. Timely of the hardships still being suffered in 1933, Warren and Dubin's "Build a Little Home" is also eerie in its thematic association with the *Communist Manifesto*'s abolition of property ownership. Eddie, making light of the residents' plight, urges the homeless group to think of the positives that come with communal living:

> It's not a palace or a poor house,
> But the rent is absolutely free.
> This is my house, but it's your house,
> If you'll come and live with me.

Buzz follows Eddie around the indoor/outdoor set as he helps the little group with various chores. The lyrics make mention to an "optimistic feeling," and that's precisely what Buzz's contribution gave the number. Soon after, Eddie falls asleep outdoors and dreams the balance of the picture, finding himself in ancient Rome playing the role of taste-tester to Emperor Valerius (Edward Arnold).

Buzz's surreal slave auction sequence begins with the torch song "No More Love," sung by Ruth Etting. The scene shifts to the royally staged auction where, on a multi-tiered pedestal, slaves are on display. At the top of the pedestal stood chained and sad-looking Goldwyn Girls. Said Buzz, "I thought it would be a very lovely thing for the top row to be all nudes, with long blonde wigs almost down to their knees. I was going to try to photograph them nude." Buzz really didn't think he could pull off the nudity, long hair or not. He thought a flesh-colored body suit (a "fleshling") would be needed. But how would he handle close-ups? The body suit would surely be visible, so he asked the girls outright if they wouldn't mind being undressed. He stressed the fact that everything would be shot tastefully, and the hair would cover breasts and other regions. The girls agreed with one stipulation: they demanded a closed set and that filming be done at night to avoid the nuisance of dealing with visitors. Buzz shifted his schedule with Warner Brothers to film the slave auction. At night, only he, cinematographer Gregg Toland, and the girls were on the set. Buzz completed his work with the knowledge that he had pulled a fast one. Nobody would ever guess the girls were completely nude except for the long blond wigs. The number proceeds with a minor story of its own as a brunette is brought to the tier and forced into a tawdry dance on the very top. A lascivious-looking Roman gives her the eye, and she spurns him from a distance. Eventually she tires of the dance and drops facedown, whereupon she's kicked off the pedestal by a Roman guard and falls to her death. Ruth Etting returns for the final verse, and Buzz ends the number with a lingering close-up of the expired slave-girl's face.

Fifty women were chosen for the slave-girl scene after viewing several thousand screen tests. Alfred Newman, the music director at United Artists, recorded the music and singing first, and Buzz whittled the number down to its bare components (one to four bars at a time). He then progressed from shot to shot, filming the Goldwyn Girls lip-synching to the record. At the time, Buzz remarked that he depended on the camera rather than the girls for the suggestion of dancing. The beauty parlor set (where the girls are prepared for the slave market) had its units partitioned with plate glass. It was necessary to turn on the set lights slowly and, at the end of the scene, turn them off one at a time to prevent the glass from breaking under the radical temperature change.

Eddie turns a lady's mudpack into an Ethiopian disguise (more blackface than African) for the delightful "Keep Young and Beautiful."

He urges the girls to look their best if they want to be loved. The Goldwyn Girls chime in, singing and glamorizing their look through hand-held mirrors and powder puffs, while Buzz shoots them in vertically aligned poses, in groups of two and three, with ample skin on display. Eventually the girls take their positions, arms stretched and interlocked, and do a high-kick/step, high-kick/step. Out from behind revolving doors come ten "Ethiopian" women (a stark visual contrast to the overly blond Goldwyn Girls) doing a dance routine of their own. Buzz makes great use of the revolving doors as the Goldwyn Girls enter and the black dancers exit in a number of repetitions.

In Hollywood, was there anyone better suited than Busby Berkeley for discovering the glamour girl of tomorrow? Sam Goldwyn sought Buzz's opinion on some test footage he shot in New York. Goldwyn filmed a number of girls with the intention of bringing them to Hollywood and placing some of them under contract. They sat side by side in the projection room watching the footage. There was one girl whom Goldwyn didn't care for, but Buzz liked. A newcomer to pictures, Lucille Ball was cast in spite of Goldwyn's objection. "That's how Lucille got her first break in films, because Sam respected my judgment," said Buzz. One day Lucy had a bad cough on the set and couldn't control herself. Buzz, patient to a point, glared scarily at Lucille and seethed a shuddering, "Please!" She apologized. Someone gave her cough syrup containing codeine, and she wound up drinking half the bottle. The active ingredient made her very drowsy, and she slipped away to an empty corner of the set. Under makeshift blankets, she drifted off to sleep. Hours went by before she was discovered, and an angry Sam Goldwyn never let her forget it.

The scene in the slave market and the "Keep Young and Beautiful" number made *Roman Scandals* the most expensive musical ever produced to that date. The song "Put a Tax on Love" (nonspectacularly filmed by Buzz) was strictly an afterthought. It was placed in the picture after a test screening in San Francisco, and it required the film to go back into production. The picture finally premiered at the end of 1933 as Goldwyn envisioned a Christmas release. The trades said he made more than $1 million profit on the film. For Buzz, the egregious schedule of round-the-clock shooting for two studios was finally over. He turned his attention and talents to his new employers, while Sam Goldwyn, still stewing over Warner Brothers' perceived thievery of *his* discovery, planned his revenge.

In September it was announced that, at the behest of Warner Brothers, Buzz was leaving for New York "to raid all the choruses to find girls for Broadway and back." Buzz, reportedly, was to sign up every pretty girl and buy a one-way ticket for each to Hollywood. The girls would form a new chorus for the studio that, in 1933, had Buzz Berkeley musicals in its plans. In a lightweight supportive story syndicated on September 23, Buzz said, "All beautiful women can be divided into two groups—like houses, furnished and unfurnished." "Unfurnished beauty," he clarified, "is mere prettiness without the high order of intelligence which makes for personality behind it." According to the article, Buzz said that no woman living could claim perfection in all these qualifications for real beauty and that, while he never would give up looking for such a woman, he never expected to find her. In his own words, he was "only interested in furnished beauty."

Busby Berkeley was a frequent guest in the skinny columns of the syndicated press. In November, hometown newspaper readers learned of Buzz's regimen for "keeping young and beautiful." With tips that smelled more fictitious than practical, his sixty chorus girls were told what they could and couldn't do if they were to keep their jobs. They were handed a copy of Berkeley's Beauty Commandments: (1) three square meals a day, with a steak or chop once a day when working; (2) one quart of milk and one glass of orange juice daily; (3) cold showers every morning; (4) daily sunbath when not working; (5) open-air exercise—golf, tennis, or swimming, daily; (6) a minimum of makeup, except for screen work, and no mascara; (7) no high-heeled shoes while working or exercising; (8) eight hours of sleep a night starting before midnight; and (9) one late date a week, when working. Buzz, the didactic and naughty gleamer, observed: "Dancing is strenuous work, as strenuous as playing football. Strict observance of these rules will result in better health for the girls, better dancing, and it will help them to preserve their beauty and freshness." Commandment 8 might've raised the eyebrows of the girls who worked until the wee hours while Buzz was creating and perfecting.

Buzz and Merna remained in New York through Christmas. A postholiday dinner at Sardi's restaurant (in the heart of the theater district) found the couple sitting alone in a far corner paying attention to no one but each other. Soon after 1934 rolled in, Buzz and Merna took a train west, back to work and warm weather. On January 7, it was erroneously reported that a project initially titled "Radio Romance," now identified as "Hot Air," would have Berkeley numbers in them. With music by Warren and Dubin, the picture was to star Dick Powell, Ann Dvorak, and Ginger Rogers. Buzz was assigned two pictures whose production had started at the end of 1933, *Fashions of 1934* and *Wonder Bar,* the latter starring Ruby Keeler's husband, Al Jolson, and featuring a supporting role for Merna.

By now it was apparent that Merna and Buzz were altar-bound. On the *Wonder Bar* set, Ruby and Al were witness to Merna being referred to as the fiancée. But it wasn't official until the last day of the month, when Buzz and Merna appeared at the marriage license bureau and filed a notice of intention to wed. The ceremony was scheduled for February 10.

What nobody knew, except for those intimate participants, was that Buzz had arranged an unusual financial arrangement between him, Gertrude, and Merna that required Merna's unconditional acceptance before a wedding could commence. Buzz, now earning a respectable salary of $1,500 per week, supported Gertrude monetarily, a perfectly understandable gesture and tribute. What was unusual was the condition under which his mother received his largesse. Buzz didn't hand Gertrude cash or checks; he tithed half his funds to her. In a letter dated April 4, 1933, Buzz wrote to William Dover of Warner Brothers requesting that half his paycheck be sent regularly to his aging mother: "This is requested with no desire or effort to dodge any financial debts or responsibilities in any way whatsoever. It is simply requested so that my mother, who is well on in years, may have peace of mind, that she will receive the same amount each week without any unnecessary worry due to my negligence to give her the amount of money promised her for her support as she is dependent entirely on me." On April 18, it was agreed in a phone conversation that Warner Brothers would send 50 percent of Buzz's salary to Gertrude at 608 Sierra Drive, Beverly Hills (the residence they shared). Merna signed her name to a paper that, though not exactly a prenuptial agreement, authorized Buzz to continue making direct payments to his mother. As far as Buzz was concerned, this condition was non-negotiable.

The "News from Hollywood" columns were already predicting that the Berkeley-Kennedy nuptials would be the biggest church wedding in years. More than three hundred invitations were sent. As planned, Buzz and Merna were married at noon on February 10. Rev. Glenn Randall Phillips officiated at the Hollywood Methodist Episcopal Church. Many of the studio's stars were present, and Jack Warner was Buzz's best man. The bride wore a gown of ice green satin designed by Hollywood's prolific costumer Orry-Kelly. The official photograph has the smiling couple with hands interlocked, the bride holding a bountiful bouquet, her boutonniered husband in a tailed tux and collarless shirt as a Rembrandt self-portrait watches dispassionately from above the bride's right shoulder. A champagne breakfast arranged by Etta Dunn was held the next morning at the Uplifters Club in Santa Monica. For a wedding gift a guest presented Buzz and Merna with a deed to two lots on Lookout Mountain in the Laurel Canyon neighborhood. After the breakfast, the newlyweds left town. Heading north, they honeymooned in San Francisco.

The two didn't move to Lookout, but leased a residence in Beverly Hills. The home that Buzz and Gertrude shared was sold. The proceeds went to a new residence for his mother in Redlands, California, some seventy miles east of Beverly Hills. It was a large house with a swimming pool, horse stables, and acres of orange groves.

With the whirlwind of a wedding behind him, Buzz could concentrate on his demanding work schedule. Shortly before the ceremony, *Wonder Bar* was sneaked in Santa Barbara, and a New York showing was fast approaching. In the papers, Buzz was quoted as wanting "something new, something different." It was reported that Buzz had supervised the construction of a circular revolving soundstage with sixteen immense glistening sheets of glass enveloping a revolving black floor. Engineers, carpenters, electricians, ironworkers, and prop men worked for weeks. An iron track was built near the roof of the soundstage to carry the derricks, machinery, camera, and sound equipment to make those top shots. The restaurant where Dick Powell sings and Dolores Del Río and Ricardo Cortez dance occupied an entire First National soundstage. Seven hundred great lamps as well as numerous spotlights were used to light the set.

Fashions of 1934 was released on Valentine's Day 1934, and its credits indicate that the dance numbers (plural) were directed by Buzz, but his only contribution was the feather-heavy "Spin a Little Web of

Dreams." The number is pure folly, an oasis of ostrich plumes, beholden to the slimmest referential point in the plot. Disreputable huckster Sherwood Nash (William Powell) slithers his way into the world of Parisian fashion, co-opting couture dress designs and selling them as his own. Along the way he meets Joe Ward (Hugh Herbert), a down-on-his-luck salesman of ostrich feathers. A deal is struck, and the feathers become the primary props in a fashion review produced by Nash. The sure hand of Berkeley takes over at this point with one of his most fascinating stagings.

Verree Teasdale sings the tune on a bare stage with closed curtains. We then see a seamstress working with ostrich feathers. The losing-consciousness transitional device Buzz was fond of takes place as the young girl falls asleep at her sewing machine. The sky is the limit in Buzz's impressionistic dreamworld, where, among other things, a dozen human harps (with beads for strings) are plucked in a surreal setting. The swiveling camera leaves this idyllic interregnum to concentrate on the Berkeley girls, all carrying large white ostrich plumes. When bunched together, the plumes simultaneously hide and reveal their holders (à la Sally Rand, the famed naked fan dancer), who are brought into close-up as strategically placed feathers are pulled away. The effect reaches its zenith in the beautifully designed top shot as the ostrich plumes slowly close and slowly open, rendering the look of a flower petal captured in time-lapse photography. The feathers give way to the girls rowing a large galley on a simulated sea of movable material. For the effect, Buzz had the floor bored with holes. Air was pumped through the holes on an alternating basis, giving the illusion of waves and wind as the ostrich feathers billowed. The screen fills with feathers, and the transition moves full circle back to the sleeping seamstress as the number comes to a close.

Buzz's seven-minute contribution to *Fashions of 1934* was well received by Warner's management. They might have been blinded by the magnificence of Berkeley's work in contrast with the film's pedestrian story line. Before the film's general release, Warner Brothers planned a road show engagement in Cleveland, Philadelphia, Pittsburgh, Washington, and Boston. The studio's desire to showcase *Fashions of 1934* reflected its esteem for the work of its high-profile dance director.

The Production Code of 1930, in effect when *Wonder Bar* was filmed in late 1933, specifically states: "The sanctity of the institution of marriage and the home shall be upheld. Pictures shall not infer that low forms of sex relationships are the accepted or common thing." With regard to crime the code states: "[They] are not to be presented in such a way as to throw sympathy with the crime as against law and justice." If ever there was a film that thumbed its nose at the Studio Relations Committee, it was *Wonder Bar,* an adult-themed update of the 1931 Broadway play.

Al Jolson is Al Wonder, the proprietor, emcee, and performer of the notorious Parisian nightclub where drinking, dancing, and assignations of all types take place. Assisting him in the club is Dick Powell in a decidedly minuscule role as his backup singer. The dancing couple Ynez and Harry (Dolores Del Río and Ricardo Cortez) perform at the Wonder Bar, while getting into romantic entanglements with Al, Dick, and Liane (a dour Kay Francis). Hugh Herbert and Guy Kibbee, along as comic relief, play henpecked husbands who rely on strong drink to help them tolerate their harridan wives. In the club they meet a pair of Parisian tarts (Fifi D'Orsay and Merna Kennedy) who have gold-digging ideas for the drunken twosome.

Buzz's work on *Wonder Bar* consisted of two major productions. The first, "Don't Say Goodnight," is a magician's trick of epic proportions. With an imagination fueled by his recent major successes, Buzz takes the number into a dimension as vast as the reflection of two facing mirrors. The staging is pure escapist, purportedly at the nightclub as Harry and Ynez perform a *dance amoureuse.* The sequence segues to a set filled with dozens of movable white columns from which some sixty masked chorines appear. But are there really sixty dancers? Buzz asked Warner Brothers' property department head Albert Whitey for twelve mirrors, each of which was to be twenty feet high and sixteen feet wide. The mirrors were placed on revolving floors in an octagonal arrangement. The columns slide in and out as masked male dancers join the girls. So brilliant is the conception that one scarcely realizes which dancers are mirror images. At the apex of the number, one black curtain is raised to reveal more reflections, followed by a second curtain and a third revealing the manufactured image of thousands of dancers, all caught with an incognito camera that, by all the laws of reflective physics, should be seen in the octagonal mirrors. This kind of visual spectacle is one of Buzz's very best, heartbreakingly beautiful in its technique.

When the magician reveals his secret, the effect is no less impressive. "The cameraman and the front office thought I was crazy because they thought the camera would show in the mirrors, but I tricked it so it would never show," explained Buzz. With a miniature set of mirrors in his office, Buzz experimented with a pencil that had a small strip of white tape on it. He moved the pencil around to the point where he could look at the tiny mirrors and not see the white tape. The camera would act like the white tape. Buzz had it placed on a piece of pipe (the pipe acting as the pencil). Where the mirrors butted together stood a narrow white column. If the camera was placed in just the right position facing the column, its reflection wouldn't be seen. But what about the camera operator? Per Buzz: "We finally had to dig a hole through the stage floor and we put the camera on the piece of pipe. The operator laid flat on his stomach underneath the stage and crawled and moved around slowly with the turning of the camera." It's a splendid, awe-inspiring effect whose power and trickery isn't diminished even after multiple viewings.

"Ever since I was a little pickaninny, I rode an old Missouri mule," begins the second of Buzz's contributions to *Wonder Bar,* the interesting, controversial, offensive, and blatantly racist "Goin' to Heaven on a Mule." Jolson, in blackface, straw hat, and overalls, sings to a young child of Judgment Day when he passes away and how he wants to arrive at the pearly gates with Zeke, his mule, by his side. A moment later the lights turn low (Judgment Day has evidently arrived), a choir hums in the background, and the image blends to a beautifully rendered effect when, in the distance, Jolson and Zeke cross a long rainbow-style archway into heaven. Jolson is admitted, meeting and greeting Saint Peter, who announces his arrival: "Here you is in da hebbinly land where da good folks go." Jolson gets introduced all around to Gabriel and three little seraphs (harps, wings, and blackface). He's fitted with his own wings and witnesses an angel being sent by chute to hell because he passed some bad liquor to Peter. "Oh, Saint Peter is I goin' to where da pork chops am a growin' on da trees? Tell me is I goin' where da watermelon vines are blowin' in da breeze?" asks Jolson. "Yes you is and da chickens am free," says Peter. He's then directed to the "Pork Chop Orchard and the Possum Pie Grove," where indeed, the thin trees (resting on porcelain pigs) have pork chops hanging from the branches. He recognizes acquaintances like Ol' Black Joe and Uncle Tom on his way to the chicken area, where they're plucked and rotisseried in the blink of an eye. Rubbing his hands in anticipation, he takes a quick bite. Jolson then boards the Milky Way/Lenox Avenue Express, and the action shifts to a bustling street scene. Stopping for a shoe shine, he whistles for a newspaper (a Yiddish newspaper!) before journeying to the "Big Top Cabaret." There he shakes hands with Emperor Jones and grabs some dice, hoping to roll some sevens. The camera does a swift pan to a winged Hal Le Roy (a Warner Brothers' actor-dancer) as he taps in front of a dozen blackfaced ladies holding up human-sized watermelon slices. The cabaret customers go into a final chorus of the song while Zeke reappears sporting wings of his own. The ensemble sings with a choir's passion, arms outstretched (à la "Remember My Forgotten Man"), as the number ends with a close-up on a decorated Al Jolson, who obviously made good at the heavenly crap table.

"Goin' to Heaven on a Mule" was not prerecorded as many musical numbers were by that point. It was usually a director's decision to do a "standard record," where the orchestra is playing out of camera range, and this is what Buzz preferred. He didn't want Jolson tied to a playback. So cast, crew, and orchestra all worked on Warners' stage 2.

It would be disingenuous to laud "Goin' to Heaven on a Mule" for its directorial wizardry without noting the inflammatory nature of its racist imagery and derogatory lyrics. Buzz Berkeley's numbers up to this point (and indeed most features from any studio) featured Negro performers in denigrating roles such as butlers, maids, field hands, and Pullman porters. Complaints from moviegoers of color regarding their depiction in feature films were seldom voiced, the exceptions coming from the NAACP and publications such as *Norfolk Journal and Guide*. (Conversely, when asked about her numerous servant roles, actress Hattie McDaniel, with a touch of realistic cynicism, once said she'd rather play a maid than be one.) The tolerance of the nation (or, more accurately, the lack of intolerance) for blatant stereotyping is most revealing in *Wonder Bar*'s March 1934 *New York Times* review by Mordaunt Hall, when he cites the "several amusing features" of the number while blithely ignoring its racism. A rumor that Warner Brothers completely excised the number from the prints that ran in theaters primarily patronized by minority audiences is without substantiated proof. Buzz himself referred to "Goin' to Heaven on a Mule" only in regard to the octagonal mirrors that he employed on this and "Don't Say Goodnight." But as Buzz was a literalist (in the most spectacular fashion) with lyrics that supplied the base to his concoctions, it's somewhat understandable that his visuals complemented the words without obscuring their meaning. The number's link to nineteenth-century minstrelsy and Jolson's black-face embodiment of the lowly sharecropper were the skeletal elements with which the number was built. Its dreamlike set pieces (the tree of hanging pork chops, the life-size watermelons) were never designed to be hateful. The reality of Buzz's relatively staggering budgets meant eschewed sensitivity to any one group; his true goal was "to get the shot and make it pretty." (If one adds Jolson's knowing glance as he's seen reading the Yiddish newspaper, you now have two affronted minority groups.) But the responsibility for the number is Buzz's, and the final word on its inclusion was the studio's, and even an image as lovely and haunting as Jolson and his mule walking on the rainbow bridge to the "hebbenly gates" cannot justify its overall prejudicial imagery.

Wonder Bar could have been the impetus for the Studio Relations Committee changing its name (and authority) to the Production Code Administration in 1934, when moviegoing was at pre-Depression levels. Soon after *Wonder Bar* was released in March 1934, the Catholic Church's Legion of Decency was established, and within a month it had 3 million members. There were certainly enough objectionable elements in *Wonder Bar* to fuel their wrath:

1. A man and woman are dancing when a mustachioed dandy taps on the man's shoulder. "May I cut in?" he asks. "Why certainly," says the woman. But the questioner takes hold of the man, and they dance off together. With a hand on his hip and a limp-wristed outstretched arm, a fey Al Jolson quips, "Boys will be boys, wooo!"
2. Jolson's opening number, "Viva La France," boasts that in gay Paris, "The wine is stronger, the kisses last much longer," among other suggestive lyrics.
3. For two of his American customers, Jolson defines the word *boudoir*—"In America it's a place to sleep. Over here, it's a playground."
4. The dance of Dolores Del Río and Ricardo Cortez is undisguised sadomasochism, as Cortez repeatedly cracks a long bullwhip at

the head and shoulder of his partner. At the number's end, she stabs him with his knife and never pays for her crime, in direct violation of the 1930 Code.

Joseph Breen, the head of the Studio Relations Committee, strongly objected to *Wonder Bar*'s many salacious elements (and, as *Variety* expressed it, the film's "panze humor"), but Jack Warner never responded to them. Executive producer Hal Wallis didn't bother to show the SRC "Goin' to Heaven on a Mule," instead telling them "there was nothing to worry about."

The Catholic Legion of Decency staged a boycott of all films that were playing in Philadelphia at the time. This brought the Hollywood studios to their knees. Joseph Breen was contacted in an effort to end the boycott. He did, and an industry-wide change was ushered in. First, all films must abide by the 1930 Production Code. Second, in the future, no films could be made unless their scripts were approved, and henceforth a new body titled the Production Code Administration would be the final arbiter in the making and releasing of feature films. With rules such as "nudity is not allowed in part or in silhouette," the images of the risqué "Pettin' in the Park" became a part of history, and films from this point forward were defanged. A new term, "pre-Code," was defined nostalgically as a time when Depression-era adults seeking their escapist fare could find an outlet at their local movie house. From this point on, "Dance numbers created and designed by Busby Berkeley" had to have the naughtiness implied.

In April 1934, Sam Goldwyn would not let the matter of Busby Berkeley linger any longer. He filed suit against Warner Brothers, demanding that Berkeley be released to him for two pictures in accordance with a contract he claimed to possess. On May 5, in court, Eddie Cantor came to Goldwyn's defense. Cantor said he was partly instrumental in bringing Berkeley to Hollywood. Goldwyn told the court he had arranged with Warner Brothers to "sub lease" Berkeley for two films, but Warner Brothers had reneged on the deal. Also taking the stand on Goldwyn's behest were Irving Thalberg, Lou Brock, and Winfield Sheehan, all executives at rival studios. Goldwyn said Warner Brothers promised him Berkeley's services when the director was not engaged in actual rehearsals. They all supported Goldwyn's contention that a rehearsal is the filming of the actual story. Dick Powell claimed that Buzz had been steadily employed at the studio and at no time was he idle. Buzz testified he didn't like to work for Sam Goldwyn because he (Buzz) didn't get enough publicity. On May 18, Superior Court Judge Frank M. Smith ruled that Warner Brothers held Berkeley's regular contract and that he was invalidating Goldwyn's, which called for the studio to lend Berkeley to Goldwyn for part-time services. The titan tug-of-war had finally ended, but Buzz faced one more defamation. Lou Brock (who took the stand against Buzz in Goldwyn's suit) claimed that he had planned a South Seas bolero six weeks earlier for "Down to the Sea in Yachts" and that Buzz had stolen all his ideas and his dance steps. Buzz wired Lou back: "How could I possibly put on a Hawaiian bolero when I don't even know what a Hawaiian bolero is and besides, I don't dance."

Warner Brothers' biggest hit of the previous year had been *Gold Diggers of 1933*. Six weeks after its release, Hal Wallis wanted more of the same. Buzz had his own unit at the studio, a group of familiar artisans that accompanied the director on each film. He was in complete control, answering to no one except Wallis and the brothers. Producer Robert Lord and Buzz worked together on the story angle, and soon Wallis told Jack Warner to register the title *Dames*. Hal Wallis tugged the financial reins tighter than Darryl Zanuck. He frequently sent memos to Buzz castigating him for his spending. He overruled Buzz's casting decisions, and insisted that Buzz never cast without consulting him.

Dames was advertised as Warner Brothers' "5th Musical Triumph," though it could have easily been named "Gold Diggers of 1934" for all the affinities it shared with the studio's previous films. The most flippant of all the backstage musicals, *Dames* is built on the most artificial of premises. Sausage-casing king Horace P. Hemingway (Guy Kibbee) is meeting his wife's cousin, the eccentric multimillionaire Ezra Ounce (played to perfection by Hugh Herbert, his character's name based on that of poet and critic Ezra Pound). Cousin Ezra announces he'll liquidate some of his assets, bestowing $10 million on Horace and his wife (and Ezra's cousin) Mathilda (Zasu Pitts). First, Horace must pass a test written by Ezra that attempts to categorize Horace's morality. Ezra's goal is to enlist Horace in the O.F.E.A.M (the Ounce Foundation for the Elevation of American Morals), to stamp out lewd behavior, liquor, cigarettes, and immoral plays. One of those plays, written by black-sheep-of-the-family Jimmy Higgens (Dick Powell), has Ounce enraged. The fact that Jimmy is dating his thirteenth cousin Barbara (Ruby Keeler), and that Barbara happens to be Horace's daughter, spells trouble for Horace when trying to conceal the facts from Ezra.

Ezra decides to spend a month at Horace's house to judge for himself the morality of his family. On the train ride to his home, Horace encounters a strange woman in his chamber. Mabel Anderson (Joan Blondell, lately known as "the me me me girl" in the studio's advertising) knows a good fleece when she sees one, and she blackmails Horace with a scream and a phony confession, leaving the poor guy at her mercy. At the Hemingway house, Ezra, on account of an unpleasant encounter with Jimmy, winds up with a severe case of hiccups that only "Dr. Silver's Golden Elixir" (106 proof) can cure. The balance of the film has Horace reestablishing contact with Mabel as she blackmails him into financing Jimmy's new show (in which she has a part). Once the show begins, a new golden elixir (158 proof) is imbibed by all. The ramifications of the plot have all led to one destination: three stacked numbers by Busby Berkeley, two of which are bona fide spectaculars.

Ten minutes into *Dames,* a non-stacked "When You Were a Smile on Your Mother's Lips and a Twinkle in Your Daddy's Eye" (Sammy Fain/Irving Kahal) is sung by Dick Powell as he professes his love to Ruby Keeler. A pleasant enough number (and exceedingly brief by Buzz's standards), it's filmed without fanfare in standard over-the-shoulder reaction shots. Shot outdoors next to a calm stream, it lacked the potential for the extended treatment a previous water setting had provided for Ruby and Dick.

"The Girl at the Ironing Board," the first of the three stackings, is quite amusing thanks to the spirited non-singing of Joan Blondell and Buzz's special effects. It's set in the Gay Nineties, with horse-drawn carriages and tandem bicycles competing for space on the boulevard while a mustachioed policeman pounds the beat and twirls his billy club. Watching an embracing couple wistfully is Joan, a loveless laundress who daydreams of having a man of her own. As she washes and darns men's unmentionables, she knows not who wears what, but her fantasies are enough to sustain her. Wrapping the sleeves of an undergarment around her shoulders, she sings:

And because it's part of you
I'm learning to love you

Joining her in song are her fellow laundresses (no glamour here as Buzz dresses them down in appropriate washerwoman attire), who lament their "scrub and rub" drudgery. In the laundry's courtyard, where long underwear hangs from clotheslines, Joan muses on the cute men who inhabit the skivvies, and they return the favor with some serenading of their own. They sing admiringly of her fastidiousness with buttons, ironing, and starch. Each hanging undergarment was attached with thin strings at the shoulders and sleeves, allowing for marionette-type manipulations. The song diverges into a single line sung to the melody of "Shuffle Off to Buffalo," followed by Mendelssohn's "Spring Song" and Saint-Saens' "The Swan" (the latter, imaginatively staged by Buzz, has the white-sleeved girls mimicking swimming swans as they glide above a tall fence). The song winds down, and the hanging clothes, en masse, fall to the ground, burying Joan. She pops her head up, readjusts her hair, and in her speaking voice recites the final witticism:

And when I'm off on Sundays,
I miss all these undies.

Buzz closes the clothes number with chirping birds (similar to "By a Waterfall") who sing their approval.

Buzz, for all his creativity, required the impetus of a good song to set his imagination ablaze. His numbers, for the most part, shared a common attribute: they began in a recognizable milieu, and once established, transformed the banal into glorious ostentatiousness. So it is with "I Only Have Eyes for You," the most surreal of all Berkeley productions to date. In this second number of the stacked trio, a common street scene provides the launching point as Ruby Keeler patiently waits for boyfriend Dick Powell, a ticket seller, to end his shift. He sings to her of the singularity of his obsession:

Are the stars out tonight?
I don't know if it's cloudy or bright.
'Cause I only have eyes for you.

Buzz, in a special-effects fadeout, removes all pedestrians from view (save Ruby), then reinstates them as they recite the song lyrics. The couple soon ducks into the subway and boards a train where product advertisements confirm Dick's feelings as each image changes to a headshot of Ruby. Another Buzzism occurs as the couple drifts off into slumber, creating a launching point for the magic that follows. The surrealism takes hold, first in the images of seven cutouts of Ruby's head, then, repetitively, dozens more. Then Buzz, at his most theatrical, reveals a startling set where a white, human-sized Ferris wheel turns and spins. On each stair of the wheel are Buzz's beauties, all made up as a clone of the star. As Ruby walks toward and over the camera, a transition occurs. Now the multiple Rubys are seated on the stage in outstretched dresses.

Similar to his "Shanghai Lil" top shots, Buzz arranges his placard-carrying girls into a gigantic Ruby Keeler headshot. Between close-ups of Ruby herself, and group shots of dozens of Rubys, Buzz shifts our frame of reference with no single image on which to tether. Following the top "puzzle shot" of Ruby's face, the image dissolves into a close-up of the puzzle's eye. Perspective is suspect as Ruby herself rises through a hole in the pupil of her own eye! Another Berkeley sleight of hand has Ruby posed on the backside of a handheld mirror. As the mirror turns toward the camera, the frame of reference shifts back to the "reality" of the subway car, where Ruby and Dick awaken from their nap realizing they've come to the final stop in the line. They leave the train and exit the train yard in a perfectly composed shot in which the couple walks diagonally from the top right to the bottom left of the frame.

A refreshing pause from Ruby Keeler idolatry finds Dick Powell in a boardroom flanked by members, each with his own opinion of what makes a show great. Powell rejects the notion of writers, stars, and songs and offers his suggestion:

> What do you go for?
> Go see a show for?
> Tell the truth, you go to see those beautiful dames.

Over his intercom, his secretary announces some male visitors (George Gershwin among them), but Powell refuses to see them. A woman's name is uttered, and Dick livens up by responding "Send her in!" The boardroom desk splits in two and moves out of frame as more names are announced: "Miss Dubin, Miss Warren, Miss Kelly" in a nod to the songwriters and costume designer Orry-Kelly. Soon the office is filled with girls, and Buzz obligingly ogles each one. Powell tells the girls of the upcoming rehearsal and to set their alarms "no later than ten."

The scene shifts to a stage filled with half-moon clocks that slide away into slats on the stage floor (an old Broadway trick). Next are rows and rows of beds, two girls per, stretching and exercising. The beds are moved together (in Buzz's "zipper" effect). A transitional shot finds the girls in a myriad of neon-lit bubble baths, each with bather and attendant. A powder puff into the lens signals another transition as we now see the Berkeley girls sitting in front of makeup mirrors. The mirrors are false (the girls are facing each other), and one picks up a bottle of perfume and "sprays" the camera as we transition from this scene to the girls, dressed and marching to work. Multiple stage doors (half-moons like the clocks) open, and the girls enter. At this point, Buzz's fertile imagination takes hold, and he arranges the girls in different formations until he begins his next sequence. The chorines crunch together in a circle as they appear to toss a girl toward the camera. It's a reverse shot in which a girl smiles into the camera and is slowly brought down to the floor. Buzz amplifies the effect using a large black ball that drops down to a circle of girls. When the ball descends, the girls are moved to the kaleidoscopic shapes that the high-positioned camera captures. Pure cinema magic closes the number as a spinning camera catches the image, mirror image, and upside-down perspective of the chorus line. For a final effect, the girls are placed in a multi-tiered set, some sitting, standing, reclining, or positioned with their backs together. The image is frozen and then, with the illusionist's surprise, Dick Powell pops his head through what is now a photograph of the posed girls. It's a great effect, and totally disarming.

Buzz now had to fight for the ingredients that made his numbers so special. "I Only Have Eyes for You" was budgeted for thirty-six performers and a set costing $15,000. Buzz wanted 250 chorines and a $50,000 set. Wallis wrote, "We have been warned not to have this kind of number in the picture, and I personally will not approve anything of this kind." Inevitably, Wallis conceded with a $40,000 budget for "Eyes" and gifted Buzz a hubless Ferris wheel loaded with girls that rotated in a geared cradle. The stage was lit in the manner to suggest that the girls on the device were moving through the air without support. For the title number, synchronized treadmills with moving scenery follow the girls. The music and voices are recorded first. Then these records are played back over the sounds of noisy machinery (recordings of gears, driving shafts, and motors) as the girls mouth the words and dance. The sets were suggested by Buzz and designed by art department chief Frank Murphy. Nearly all the machinery was built at local ironworks.

Hal Wallis, who had the studio install a projection system in his home, screened footage daily. He took pains in describing even the most mundane issues such as billing: "The title *Dames* is to be followed by the name of the director and Busby Berkeley in equal-size type," wrote the production head in a postproduction memo.

For *Dames,* Buzz had a threat to his autonomy more powerful than either Wallis or Warner Brothers. In the summer of 1934, the Motion Picture Production Code was toughened and strictly enforced after protests from Catholic groups. Among the targets of their attacks were the musicals of Busby Berkeley. One of the raciest numbers Buzz planned never made it to the soundstage, much less past the Code's censors. He wanted Joan Blondell to perform a number about a battle between a cat and a mouse that would end with Blondell inviting all to "come up and see my pussy sometime." Wallis nixed this number completely in a memo he sent to Buzz, on March 19, 1934: "we are accused of obscenity in our pictures enough as it is without reason, and besides there is no use besmirching the name of Berkeley with filth." As a replacement, Berkeley devised "The Girl at the Ironing Board." Having Blondell washing and ironing was not just an illustration of the song. At the time of shooting, she was seven months pregnant, and careful camerawork, handled by her husband, cinematographer George Barnes, was required to disguise her condition. "Berkeley had a great sense of humor, but he worked us to the bone," said Joan. "It was even worse for his girls. I don't think they ever had any time off."

All the attention on Blondell may have caused Buzz to overlook a rare onscreen goof. He recalled that after the picture opened: "Over her right shoulder in the distance I see outside on the lawn where the clotheslines were hanging, one of my property men nailing up a clothesline. I had never noticed it, and no one else did until a week after the picture had opened."

On July 2, Eddie Cantor, Ted Healy's "Three Stooges," Dick Powell, and others packed the Biltmore Bowl for the Marion Davies Foundation charity drive. Powell unintentionally reawakened the Sam Goldwyn/ Warner Brothers competition for Buzz's services when he recalled the "By a Waterfall" number and its glorious swimming pool. "Yeah," said Cantor offstage, "a pool of Goldwyn's blood."

Dames was in final cut mid-July, and it opened on August 16 at New York City's Strand Theatre. It was the first Warner Brothers film to require the Production Code Administration's approval. A month before opening, Jack Warner received a letter from Joseph Breen that said "the version we saw this morning in your projection room of your production *Dames* is acceptable under the provisions of the Production Code." Soon thereafter the studio rushed to theaters *And She Learned about Dames*, a nine-minute promotional for the feature. Its hackneyed story has a "Miss Complexion of 1934" winner (Martha Merrill) given a studio tour by the always available Lyle Talbot. In a soundstage, they see Buzz ascending on what Lyle calls his "flying trapeze" (the monorail). Later, the director (in ascot, coat, and white pants) has an uncomfortably un- natural dialogue scene with the contest winner that fades into a sneak peek of "I Only Have Eyes for You":

> MISS COMPLEXION: I've often wondered where you get those beau- tiful girls.
> LYLE: Buzz, what have you got up your sleeve for *Dames*? Think you'll top the numbers in *Wonder Bar* and *Footlight Parade*?
> BUZZ: Well I don't like to make any promises, Lyle. But I really think this picture is going to top anything we've ever done. We have a very huge set over there, and practically everything moves, this being moving pictures. And the stage begins to move, the girls begin to go up and . . .

Buzz, superstitiously, always started a new picture in the same old sneakers, old linen trousers, and sweatshirt. He directed his first stage success in the garb and wore it on at least the first day's shooting of every new picture. His latest promised to be his most ambitious, for not only would Buzz handle the musical numbers, but he would also command the title of *director*. A little tease from a United Press story had Buzz waxing poetic over Washington, D.C.'s Elinor Troy. He described her as "the most perfectly formed girl" he ever saw and signed her for his new picture titled *Gold Diggers of 1935*. According to Buzz, Elinor was a brunette beauty, five feet nine inches, 132 pounds. She left Washington with the avowed purpose of getting a job with Buzz, who signed her after one look.

Gold Diggers of 1935 was the apex of Busby Berkeley's professional arc. He received two credits—direction and dance direction, and though wildly divergent, Buzz handled both with acuity and aplomb. The year in the title capitalized on the studio's previous success, while the term "gold digger" was a misnomer of sorts, a marketing of the *idea* of the gold digger. There are no chorus girls in the film, leaving the gold digging to the employees of the Wentworth Plaza Hotel who work for tips, and tithe their remuneration to their greedy bosses.

The clientele of the Wentworth are the crème de la crème (or the cheap of the cheap) who spend their summers pampered in the hotelier's lap of luxury. Early on, we're introduced to some of the guests: a widowed mother, Matilda Prentiss (Alice Brady); her son Humbolt (Frank McHugh); and daughter Ann (Gloria Stuart). Mother's a profound tightwad (tipping a bellman a quarter, she tells him to split it with his coworkers), while her son is four times divorced. Ann has been promised (against her will) to an absent-minded millionaire and friend of the family, T. Mosley Thorpe (Hugh Herbert), who is writing a monograph on the history of snuff and snuff boxes. Ann, desperate for attention from someone closer to her age, finds a simpatico friend in Dick Curtis (Dick Powell). Matilda bribes Dick to look after Ann, and so they skip arm in arm to the hotel's arcade shops, where Ann gets a complete hat-to-shoes makeover. Their number together, the bouncy "I'm Going Shopping with You," arises innately through the narrative, and though enjoyable, it is comparatively unspectacular in relation to others in Buzz's oeuvre. Their other number, "The Words Are in My Heart," is suitably downplayed in its first incarnation as Buzz bypasses the overt for romantic atmospherics.

A stenographer (Glenda Farrell, the only female gold digger in the film) assists Mosley in his monograph, and it isn't long before she hatches a blackmail scheme against the eccentric snuffer. Meanwhile, Mrs. Prentiss, in staging the annual summer talent show, meets stage director (and swindler) Nicolai Nicoleff (Adolphe Menjou). He tries fleecing

Mrs. Prentiss with boastful claims and promises, and soon she agrees to let him direct. A friend of Nicoleff's joins the action as a costume/set designer, and together they try their best to milk the widow at every opportunity.

The alacritous summer show opens with the reprise of "The Words Are in My Heart," a number Buzz pushes to the extreme. His memory served him well once again as the piano quartet he saw years earlier increased fourteen-fold. Buzz called Whitey Wilson and asked for fifty-six ivory-colored grand pianos that do not have to play, but must be able to dance. Whitey had the pianos created by a large piano company. Buzz's idea was to have a small person, dressed in black, positioned under each piano. The instruments were only facades, so manipulation was easier than one would expect. In a great effect, a woman is seen dancing on a piano as all the pianos in the number move to the center, creating a perfectly enclosed rectangle. It's projected in reverse, making it look as if the instruments had come together unencumbered, when, in reality, the pretend pianos were already positioned properly and moved out of place as the scene was shot. The little men beneath each soundboard are briefly visible in some angles, and their silent contribution results in the number being one of Buzz's most memorable.

The first evening star is visible amid a black velveteen sky; a pinpoint of light is adrift in the darkness; a voice in song emanates from the white dot. Slowly, meticulously, either we are moving closer to the image or it is approaching us. . . . Such are the opening moments of Buzz's disturbing and fascinating film-within-a-film, the incomparable "Lullaby of Broadway." The singer, Wini Shaw, becomes identifiable as the monorail-mounted camera inches its way closer to the source. There's passion in her singing as she slows her delivery for the maximum effect of the song's final syllable: "Listen to . . . the lullaby . . . of . . . old . . . Broad . . . way."

She pivots her head 180 degrees, her chin now at the top of the screen, and places a cigarette in her mouth. Buzz freezes the image into a close approximation of a well-known photograph, Man Ray's unofficially titled "Women Smoking a Cigarette" from 1920. The face now morphs into a representative New York City, and the number's narrative begins in earnest.

Working from farthest to closest for the second time in the number,

Buzz obliterates time and spatial concerns. Service workers are hustling in the early morning; women are upped and dressed, and placed on busses and streetcars as they begin their day. A taxi pulls up, and two night owls (Wini Shaw and Dick Powell) decked in fancy evening garb alight; their day is ending. A brief kiss sends Powell on his way, while Wini, back at her flat, removes her nylons and prepares for slumber. She pulls down her window shade and sleeps during the day. At around 6:45 p.m., Wini arises (the "Credit Jewelers" clock acts as the impassive overseer of her life). As the artificial sun descends, Wini prepares for new nocturnal festivities. The carpet is unrolled at the "Club Casino," and Dick and Wini, the only customers in the place, are seated in what appears to be a loge. The set is cavernous and nightmarish in its grand design, scaled with thousands of steps spread among dance stages and various vertical mounts. With merriment, Dick and Wini view the opening floor show, a pas de deux by Ramon and Rosita (a well-regarded dance duo of the 1930s), oblivious to their stature as the club's only paying customers.

The dancers exit at opposite ends of the stage floor and reemerge, each leading hundreds of dancers of their own sex in a sort of stampede. The regimented look and the echoing sound of tapping heels reinforce the strangely expansive set. Working with ensembles this large was no small feat, but the dancers were under the direction of a second lieutenant who knew the group manipulations required to make the number a success. The dancing is captured at various angles, including one clever shot of a high-speed hoofer filmed from the underside of his shuffling shoes. Soon the entire group, captured perfectly in long shot, is imitating him. Powell picks up his glass and offers a toast.

"Come and dance!" the ensemble orders Wini.

"But baby won't let me," she responds.

She joins in the dance. The crowd is loud and boisterous as they gather around her. She dances a bit and runs behind a glass-paned door. Stepping backward, she kisses the glass that separates her from Dick. The door opens, and Wini is pushed back, back, back, to a development conceived in a dreadful nightmare. One final step and she tumbles over the balcony's retaining wall toward the pavement below (and another musical murder is attributable to Busby Berkeley).

Wini's fall is captured through her eyes. The approaching ground spins around and around, blending into the image of the jewelry clock.

The "Lullaby of Broadway" is heard as the little kitty waits for a sample of milk that isn't forthcoming. The night owl's day ends as the sun rises, and Buzz, as is his wont, neatly wraps the number by reversing the opening sequence. The image of New York changes back to "Woman with a Cigarette," and Wini spins herself again to face us. She repeats the closing refrain as Buzz's monorailed camera rapidly retreats to its opening position. The white blip in the far distance disappears as the extraordinary, unsettling, and unforgettable fourteen-minute playlet ends with grand approbation.

Heretofore, none of the numbers that Buzz conceived could be defined as having a structured narrative. "Remember My Forgotten Man" came close, with its short history of the ebullience that led to war and the postwar neglect of the disenfranchised casualties. Buzz's dreamy "By a Waterfall" supports the same somnambulistic logic of "Lullaby of Broadway." In a number bereft of top shots, Buzz refocuses his directorial extravagances to new ensemble blocking on a mass scale. He was blessed with a massive set, the skillful uniformity of his dancers, and live music accompaniment, each ingredient necessary for the trick to work. With the "Lullaby of Broadway," the maturation of the magician was complete. The press and public justly lauded Buzz's first authorship of all creative aspects of *Gold Diggers of 1935*. The Academy of Motion Picture Arts and Sciences found both "Lullaby of Broadway" and "The Words Are in My Heart" worthy of nominations in the dance direction category. But Buzz's masterpiece, though heralded, went unrewarded. Surprisingly, Dave Gould took the Oscar home for the less accomplished "I've Got a Feeling You're Fooling" from *Broadway Melody of 1936* (an ersatz Berkeley-styled number featuring stage props that instantly popped up from the floor) and "Straw Hat" from *Folies Bergère de Paris*. Buzz was a bridesmaid and never a bride when it came to awards, and one can guess that he was bitterly disappointed at not winning the Oscar. On the record, without hesitation, Buzz declared that of all his musical numbers the "Lullaby of Broadway" was his favorite.

Gertrude visited the set of her son's first complete authorship almost every day, according to sources. Seldom saying much, she was driven from Redlands to the set, where she sat quietly for about an hour or so before returning home.

When filming "Lullaby of Broadway," Buzz wanted the taps for his large ensemble to be heard, but there was a problem. When the rows of dancers faced each other and tapped, the whole floor shook, and the dancers could hardly hear the music playback. Buzz had the Warner orchestra positioned on one side of the set, while microphones placed at the stage level captured the sounds of the dancers. Soundman George Groves recorded it all perfectly on a single track, and he called the fix "an example of standard recording by necessity."

A dancer in the chorus, Jack Grieves, died on the set while Buzz was directing "Lullaby of Broadway." The cause was labeled "acute indigestion," rare and strange for a man of only twenty-six. Alice Brady, who, coincidentally, starred with Gertrude in *Little Women,* gave the studio a bit of a scare when she disappeared on an unscheduled leave of absence. One report said incorrectly that Brady was kidnapped.

In November, Buzz was in between projects when a bit of good news came his way from the United States Patent Office. He was awarded Patent Number 1979363 for his invention of the revolving stage. Buzz couldn't take his idea to any studio, however. Though the patent was drawn in his name, he was beholden to Warner Brothers, who legally held claim to it.

By the year's end, Busby Berkeley was one of the studio's most popular "stars," reflected by the amount of received fan mail. His schedule was oppressive, and the double-duty work he did for *Gold Diggers of 1935* didn't lend itself to harmony at home. Increasingly, Buzz was seen alone at functions where couples were in attendance. Bad domestic news was withheld from the public until a demonstrative action took place. In the new year, rumors replaced whispers that Buzz and Merna's marriage was in trouble.

Alone, Buzz attended "The Warner Club—First Annual Dinner Dance" on February 21. Held at the Biltmore Bowl, Biltmore Hotel, the Warner Club had been established the previous year for the social and athletic entertainment of its members. Stars, including Buzz, Errol Flynn, Paul Muni, Al Jolson, Dolores Del Río, Bette Davis, Joan Blondell, Hugh Herbert, and others, worked on various committees. Strangely, on page three in the ornate program that was handed out to all attendees were the photographs and regrets of the surviving Warner brothers: "We can't tell you how deeply we regret being unable to be with you tonight at the Studio's first Warner Club Dinner and Dance, because it is one affair we had set our hearts on attending." A couple of sentences later they ended with, "Eat, drink, dance and be merry!" with the names Harry M. Warner, Jack L. Warner, and Major Albert Warner printed below.

Buzz was pontificating for the press while at the same time promoting *Gold Diggers of 1935* when, in spring, he gave his thoughts on wedding betrothals. His diatribe, with little subtlety, never fails to mention his two stars:

> Proposals this year will mostly be made in the Dick Powell–Gloria Stuart manner. A year or so ago it was Clark Gable or Jimmy Cagney who set the styles in the delicate business of asking a girl to marry. But the Dick Powell–Gloria Stuart way is the most popular right now. The old "Down-on-your-knees—Will-you-marry-me" formula has been outmoded for years—just because early motion pictures showed how ungainly and funny such a proposal really was. Then John Barrymore, Douglas Fairbanks and others brought in an era of adventurous romance—climbing to balconies to plead with the lady, galloping a hundred miles to return a handkerchief and plight a troth. Young people have to have a pattern to follow when the time comes to pop the question. Years ago the cue came from the romantic novelists. That was the "knee-bending" period. Now they unconsciously study the lovemaking methods they see on the screen—and choose the one they like the best. And this year, at least, it is Dick Powell and Gloria Stuart who are setting the pace which lovers will follow. Dick's love scenes are gentle, sincere and unaffected. Next year George Brent or Cary Grant or Jackie Cooper may set the styles in the world's lovemaking. But right now it is Dick Powell and Gloria Stuart.

While *Gold Diggers of 1935* was in the final editing stage, Buzz learned of his next project, *In Caliente*. He was given a breather from the emotional toll a first feature can take and assigned only the musical numbers, while his friend Lloyd Bacon directed the balance. With a total of four writers, it's disappointing that the story isn't wittier and more in line with the Warner Brothers house style. The luminous presence of Dolores Del Río, and the studio's version of Caliente, Mexico, couldn't compete against the eminently more interesting contributions of Busby Berkeley.

The first of three Buzz numbers, "In Caliente" is a one-minute gem, six minutes in, coming after a quick montage of Caliente's assets (horse racing, casino gambling, etc.). Buzz's number takes over as we see a close-up of a spinning white Mexican sombrero, then thirty girls identically dressed twirling in the center of the hotel Agua Caliente. The scene is lively, with marimbas, dancers, an upright bass, and smiling singers lining the stairs. A quick reverse shot ends the number as all the white sombreros fall down in perfect position surrounding a Berkeley senorita.

"The Lady in Red" takes place in the nightclub and begins in darkness. Each Berkeley girl (dressed in blue to approximate the look of red in a black-and-white film) lights a center candle at each table. Wini Shaw, fresh from her "Lullaby of Broadway" fall, takes the lead vocal, until comedienne and pretend-bumpkin Judy Canova (in her first feature) warbles and yodels to a discomforted Edward Everett Horton. The specialty dance team of Tony and Sally De Marco perform their pas de deux until Wini reappears, pulling the reluctant Horton up from his chair for a final go-round.

"Muchacha" is pure Berkeley sleight of hand, an autonomous number existing outside of reality's confines. The setting is a bandit cave with a roaring fire and a mountain range in the background populated by local Latin cowboys. One of the men sings the opening bars ("Muchacha, tonight I gotcha where I wantcha") as the action shifts to the nightclub (made up to look like a giant western saloon). Soon the horse-riding men with snapping whips and firing pistols invade the club. The rowdy action follows the horsemen up and down stairs and abruptly shifts to the dancers on the tables and bar. The number ends with a busy shot of all the Berkeley girls, the banditos, and Dolores Del Río spinning and singing in unison as the curtain closes on this improbable scene.

The inner circle of the Berkeley girls, his "close-up" girls, were kept on set the longest. They were Buzz's skeleton team, the ones he used when working out a number. He would say, "stand here, stand there, I'm trying to get an idea about this or that." For "The Lady in Red" number, Buzz wanted the studio to provide him with a couple of horses. He told the close-up girls that he probably wouldn't get his wish, but he did have an idea. "Come here I want you to hear this," said Buzz to the girls. He dialed Hal Wallis's number. "Now Hal, for this thing with Dolores Del Río I really want to make a barnyard scene out of it. I'd like some pigs, two or three, and I think I'd like a dozen or more white chickens, and I think we ought to have an ox in there too. And some little animals, some dogs or something like that!" The girls bit their lips to keep from laughing. They could hear Wallis yelling through the earpiece: "No! No! You can't have any of this. No!" Buzz calculatingly compromised: "Well, I'll tell you, if I can't have any of those, how about just a couple of horses?" His ploy went unnoticed, and the horses were his.

One day Buzz was visibly upset over the way a segment of "The Lady in Red" was being shot. Three girls were singing the number when offscreen a yell of "Cut!" was heard. Buzz took his ire out on Sol Polito, the director of photography. Buzz's tone was sharp and his voice raised and demoralizing. It was an easterner's high-pitched castigation that sliced like a knife and deeply embarrassed the recipient:

BUZZ: All right, cut it, cut it. Wait a minute, listen Sol, where are you cutting her, here (*points to the middle of one girl's back*) or here (*points to just below her buttocks*)?
SOL: No, no, no.
BUZZ: (*louder, impatient voice*) Well, WHERE? I don't want it cut up here. I want it cut down here.
SOL: (*he comes up to the girl and points*) Right here.
BUZZ: (*much louder*) Sol, for God's sake, I said cut it down here!
SOL: You told me to cut it right here . . .
BUZZ: I did not, you were standing right here. (*Yelling*) I SAID CUT IT DOWN HERE! RIGHT HERE!

The "Muchacha" number was bound to have problems with galloping white horses in a closed environment. Add in the dancing girls and guys, two hundred in total, and it was a very crowded set. The shooting continued near lunchtime when Buzz saw something in the distance not to his liking and blew his shrill whistle to stop the action. The horses, spooked by the whistle, became uncontrollable. They stampeded out of the set, down a side street, past the commissary, and to the studio back lot. Buzz remembered one man commenting to another: "There goes Berkeley's horses. He must have dismissed 'em for lunch. Look at 'em go.

He must be working their tails off!" According to Buzz, it took hours to collect and calm the horses and return them to the set.

In the rare moments when Buzz wasn't filming, he was engaged in what he called "hanging the dollies." He had a big easel on which white chalk lines were drawn. At each intersection of the lines was a small wall hook. On these hooks Buzz hung small, fluffy dolls that represented his Berkeley girls. By changing the position of the dolls, he was able to visualize how the real girls would look during filming.

Bright Lights was a sometimes warm, sometimes amusing story of vaudevillians on their career ascent to Broadway. Joe E. Brown, the actor/comedian with the wide grin and cavernous mouth, played stage comic Joe Wilson, with Ann Dvorak as Fay, Joe's wife and "straight man." The story was another natural for Buzz, who was often assigned projects that (purposely or not) matched his own life experience. While *Bright Lights* does not have musical numbers, Berkeley deserves credit for the lively pace and for providing the show biz insights and subtleties that make for an entertaining experience. But in so many ways, this effort carries the comparative burden of a previous success without the resources that could have forged new ground.

Buzz shot the stage scenes in an abandoned theater on Main Street. Gertrude attended the filming, and a flood of memories rushed back. After cast and crew were dismissed, Gertrude asked Busby to walk back with her to one of the long-unused dressing rooms. She had acted in this old theater with Frank in the late 1890s, when Buzz was just a baby. She smothered a sob in her handkerchief when she described for her son the little crib that had rested on her clothes trunk.

There was a good reason why Buzz and Merna hadn't been seen together in ages. By June 1934, only four months into their marriage, they had become estranged. Merna officially left her husband a year later, on June 26, 1935, and sued him for three thousand dollars a month separate maintenance through her attorneys Roger Marchetti and A. V. Falcone on the grounds of extreme cruelty. Merna claimed that Buzz drank to excess, left her alone for two and three days at a time, and spent that time in the company of other women. The final straw was Buzz's request that she accompany him to his lawyer's office, where property rights were to be settled with divorce as the next logical step. Merna said that

Buzz used "violent and opprobrious language" when he spoke to her and that for several days at a time he remained in an intoxicated condition. The complaint stated: "Throughout the marriage of the parties hereto, and as a continuous course of conduct, the defendant has maintained an indifferent and aloof attitude toward plaintiff, especially concerning defendant's business affairs and his earnings, concealing knowledge of the same from plaintiff."

Merna also contended that on numerous occasions Buzz escorted her to public places of entertainment and upon their arrival became intoxicated and "carried on open flirtations with other women," leaving her alone and unescorted. Sometimes Buzz came home drunk while Merna was entertaining friends (perhaps Etta and Leonard), and his rudeness caused her guests to leave. One stretch of four days found Buzz away from home. Merna and her friends saw him at Santa Catalina Island drunk and in another woman's company. The assertions continued when a bill was sent to Buzz for nail polish he had purchased in the name of another woman. When Merna confronted him with the bill, he quickly snatched it from her hands and ripped it up. She contended that her husband had "deeply wounded her feelings, humiliated her, and caused her to become ill and nervous."

With her litany of accusations, Merna practically validated Esther Muir's outrageous claims. On July 3, Buzz made his case in front of Superior Court Judge Valentine. He brought up the subject of the agreement Merna had signed stipulating that a portion of his earnings went to his mother. The judge asked why Buzz shouldn't pay the $3,000 monthly maintenance requested by Miss Kennedy. In a surprising move, Buzz said he owed his mother $65,000; that she was past seventy years of age; and that, for other personal reasons, he had assigned her $540 each week of his net salary. "If Miss Kennedy had not signed the agreement, I would not have married her." More dirty laundry was aired in court when it was learned that Merna had spent $500 on clothes and $72 on shoes subsequent to their separation. Buzz "appeared shocked" to learn that Merna was having a mink coat made up at a cost of $2,750. "He told me I could order it," said Merna. "I did not!" responded Buzz vociferously. Another matter of $5,000 in overdue bills was brought to light. Buzz's attorney, Milton Cohen, argued: "It seems to me that $400 a month would be more fair than $3000. Somebody has to pay these bills and my client is civilly liable for them." During lunch Judge Valentine deliberated the case, finally awarding Merna $100 per week.

Scarcely a month went by before Buzz grabbed the director's megaphone for the declaratively titled *I Live for Love* (changed from the passive *Romance in a Glass House* as *Boxoffice* magazine called it on July 6, 1935). The film was a musical without any *real* Berkeley numbers, a comedy with few amusements and a telegraphed love story. A stage diva (Dolores Del Río) and baritone street singer (Everett Marshall) clash onstage and during the radio broadcasts in which they are forced to appear. They hate each other immediately upon meeting and, expectedly, fall in love in the third act. Del Río is solid and sensual as the tempestuous Donna Alvarez. As for Everett Marshall (whose film career stalled after this), Buzz should have explained to the singer the definition of modulation. Every time he opens his mouth in song, it's at the volume of an operatic solo at La Scala. (When he sings to Del Río in close-up, it's a miracle her hair isn't blown backward.) The title is something of a misnomer (neither of the principals actually "live" for anything but their egos), and the film barely made a blip at the box office when it was released in early autumn.

In 1935, the name Busby Berkeley was so well known to movie fans that his last name was linked to projects in which his participation was limited to the musical numbers. A Lloyd Bacon or Mervyn LeRoy picture was a Busby Berkeley movie to them. His recent marital woes and excessive imbibing made not a ripple in publications east of California. The fan letters continued to pour into the studio, and Buzz's popularity had never been higher. Studio records reveal that the Warner Brothers publicity department came up with a neologism to describe the uniqueness, distinctness, and inimitable nature of its star director. A man who combined groundbreaking technique in the artistry of film while seamlessly merging his craft with the classicism of dance was designated by Warner Brothers a cinematerpsichorean.

6

The Cancerous Tire

The movie-going public, those who paid eighteen cents for a thinly padded balcony seat and purchased a tawdry movie magazine afterward,
didn't know the real Busby Berkeley. On his own he was increasingly
drawn to liquor's potent comfort, though on-the-set colleagues swore to
his sobriety when he was on the clock. The blistering details of scandalous anecdota from two bitter ex-wives were known only to the closest
of colleagues and, of course, his mother. Mother, with her son's interest
at heart (balanced with bitterness toward her latest ex-daughter-in-law),
might have been the author of Buzz's $65,000 defensive plea. Who could
disprove such a tall tale?

In August, Buzz contributed a witty number to *Stars over Broadway,* the only-in-Hollywood story of the meteoric rise, fall, and rise
again of a bellhop with a remarkable tenor voice. James Melton, fairly
new to pictures, was known for his concerts, radio performances, and
operas. Along with the renowned radio singer Jane Froman, they star
in Buzz's comedy vignette "At Your Service, Madame." It was another
ditty in the Warren/Dubin canon (who are, as an inside joke, mentioned
twice in the picture), describing the lady of leisure with a butler whose
job description matches the song's title.

The curtain opens to Berkeleyville, a street scene as a dozen black-
suited applicants outside of a job agency watch a lady customer through
the glass. She leaves, and a sign is posted: butler wanted. Buzz moves
his camera in tight to a screen-filling shot of a man's coat, then back
out again to reveal the same men dressed impeccably in black tie and
tails. They sing their service motto in Madame's circular, two-tiered,
glass-lined apartment (a very impressive-looking set). Melton and Jane
Froman take over the number, singing and dancing around each other
on the oval stage. A close-up of two hands yields a sequence change in
which a humorous reversal of roles occurs. Now it's James Melton being

123

waited on by Miss Froman. It's all done well, filmed with Buzz's light touch that complemented Al Dubin's witty lyrics.

Buzz had an interesting idea for another song in the picture, "September in the Rain." The imaginative literalist wanted an elaborate setting filled with silver trees that moved independently (recalling the moving columns in "Don't Say Goodnight"). The number was nixed, with budgetary limitations to blame.

Buzz, stag, attended a big Hollywood-type home party on September 8 in the Pacific Palisades area of Los Angeles. Hosted by Warner Brothers production manager William Koenig, the soiree was held in honor of Koenig's new bride, Barbara, a former Berkeley girl. An estimated two hundred guests clinked glasses and spoke freely without intrusive cameras. The studio-centric guest list included Pat O'Brien, Glenda Farrell, Guy Kibbee, Frank McHugh, cameraman George Barnes, musical director Leo Forbstein, and fellow dance director Bobby Connolly. Holding punch in his right hand, Buzz circulated among his Warner brethren and walked outdoors to the patio, where he grabbed a seat for a bit of chatting with Guy and Pat. His plan was to stay only a few hours, then head down to Santa Monica along the coast road to see bandleader Gus Arnheim, with whom he had an appointment. Piano music wafting from indoors drew Buzz's attention, and he excused himself from the patio and joined in singing with some other colleagues near the keyboard's open hood. Some moments later, half of a second glass of punch wound up on Buzz's white linen suit when a man bumped into him. The guest had sprung from a trick electric chair when a jokester in attendance flipped the switch that gave the unsuspecting dupe a shocking jolt. Apologies all around, and Buzz, in good humor, did his best to tamp out the stain.

It was a bit after ten, a warm, dry night, when Buzz said his "thank yous" and "good-byes." He drove his green convertible roadster toward Gus's, taking the winding roads of the Roosevelt Highway. Without warning, his right front tire blew. Buzz braked and pulled his car delicately into a gas station that was fortunately close to the road. When he exited his car, he accidentally stubbed his toe on the cement base near a gasoline pump on his left and caught himself by placing his hands on the pump's face. He was lucky that C. J. Box was on duty that night. C. J. swapped the useless tire for a new one, and as soon as it was balanced and mounted, Buzz proceeded on the snakelike Roosevelt.

With the wind in his hair, Buzz maneuvered the unlit twisting road-way near the Santa Monica Canyon as best he could. A hard left and a hard right, and another as Buzz took the curves faster than the law allowed. With a loud, instantaneous pop, wholly unexpected in light of what had already occurred, Buzz lost control of his car. Panicked, he turned the steering wheel this way and that like a helmsman in a torrential storm, and never gained control. At more than forty miles per hour, the roadster's *left* front tire had inexplicably blown, causing Buzz to cross the center line and charge blindingly into an oncoming vehicle.

William A. Hudson, a junior college student, and his friend Clarence Burtless Jr. were driving in the opposite direction toward William's home in Santa Paula when they saw the convertible heading straight toward them. William turned hard to avoid it, but the cars collided. Buzz's car careened directionless headfirst into another car with five occupants before it came to rest. The other vehicle was struck so forcefully that it flipped over, entrapping its passengers. The cars, as all on the road in 1935, had no safety devices, padding, or restraints. Glass was not safety glass, and when it shattered the shards were lethal projectiles. Buzz, dazed, but otherwise lucky to exit the smashed roadster, staggered toward William Hudson, who, lucky himself, had pulled the unconscious Clarence from his car and laid him on the pavement. Buzz looked down at them to gauge their condition and surely noticed William touching his chin with a grimace. Moments later the green convertible roadster burst into flames before their eyes.

Still shaky on his legs, Buzz walked five hundred feet from the wreckage to the Lighthouse Café, where, in a crazed state of mind, he attempted to get a customer, any customer, to drive him away. "I have to get away. They will be looking for me soon," said the distraught Berkeley to Lighthouse employee L. M. Bunn. Buzz walked over to an occupied car, talked to its driver a bit, and climbed into the rumble seat. A minute passed, and when the driver exited his vehicle so did Buzz with a thump. L. M. saw him stumble and walk on all fours.

Police, ambulances, and the Pacific Palisades Fire Department responded to the call. Claud Hart had just driven past the accident scene and saw cars hurtling through the air in his rearview mirror. He stopped his car and helped upright the overturned vehicle. The passenger doors were stuck shut.

Police officer A. M. Sheets from the West Los Angeles station was one of the first to arrive on the scene. Inside the café he found Buzz, unbalanced and sporting a cut over his eye. He questioned him. At first Buzz deliriously claimed he wasn't driving the car. Later he changed his story. "Why did you leave the scene of the accident?" asked Officer Sheets. "I was going to phone my mother," said Buzz.

The immovable car door was opened with mechanical help. Fire Department Captain Ora W. McKillip was the first to see the end result of a five-person rollover. Moments after the impact, backseat passenger Ada von Briesen died horribly . . . agonizingly . . . inverted. Her son, William, the assistant auditor for the City of Santa Monica, was driving. He, along with his wife, Manon, and his two sisters-in-law, Laura von Briesen and Peggy Daley, were breathing and unconscious. Before the roadster interrupted their lives, William had been driving from Santa Monica to Topanga Canyon cautiously "because the women were nervous."

Buzz was taken to St. Vincent's Hospital in West Los Angeles with head and leg injuries; the other survivors were ambulanced to the Santa Monica Hospital. The accident closed the Roosevelt Highway for hours. The green convertible roadster was indistinguishable from a box of charred metal. Before he was admitted to his room, Buzz lay motionless on a white gurney. Still clad in his black shirt, white tie, and white suit (stained with punch and blood), he wore a thick white bandage that encircled his forehead. Visibly exhausted with eyes partially closed and right arm outstretched, Buzz held a lit cigarette between his first and second fingers and reran the evening's awful incidents in his mind. There remained the dreaded business of informing Mother.

"GET GIESLER!" Such was the command of the Warner Brothers front office. Jerry Giesler (pronounced *geese-ler*) was a short, balding, nondescript little man who just happened to be one of the shrewdest defense attorneys in the state. In protecting their self-interest, it was Warner Brothers who sought and financed Giesler's council for Buzz, whose accident made for nasty copy in periodicals and sleazy tabloids throughout the country. By 1935, Giesler's reputation preceded him. He had made his name some six years earlier, when he successfully defended the self-made millionaire, theater-chain owner, and lifelong illiterate Alexander Pantages from a charge of statutory rape. A seventeen-year-old with theatrical ambitions named Eunice Pringle had accused the sexa-

genarian of luring her to his flagship theater at Seventh and Hill streets
in Los Angeles under the pretext that he could help her career. There,
he supposedly forced himself on her in a small office on the mezzanine
level. Pringle, disheveled, ran out onto Seventh some moments later, and
concocted a story that made headlines. When she took the stand, she
looked years younger than seventeen (hair in pigtails, no makeup, clad in
a schoolgirl getup). Giesler needed to convince the jury that Pringle was
not quite as prim as she appeared. He told the court that it was necessary
for Miss Pringle to wear the dress she wore on the day in question. The
judge didn't overrule. Pringle reappeared looking quite ripe in a bright
red, low-cut, snug dress that caused eyebrows among court spectators
to arch. Under questioning from Giesler, Pringle admitted to wearing
lipstick to Mr. Pantages's office, that she studied dramatics, and was
reasonably athletic. The law in 1929 governing statutory rape prevented
Giesler from introducing testimony that might have impinged on Eunice
Pringle's chastity (or lack thereof). Working with limited testimony, the
jury bought the teenager's story and found Pantages guilty of rape. Soon
after, Giesler wrote an appeal brief attacking the state's rape law. So brilliant was his legal reasoning that the state supreme court annulled the
verdict and ordered a new trial. There Giesler, fangs bared, went after
Eunice Pringle's moral character in order to destroy her believability.
On the witness stand he unearthed a conspiracy between the undulat-
ing Pringle and her near forty-year-old boyfriend, Nicholas Dunave, to
frame Alexander Pantages into a phony compromising position. The
second verdict was not guilty, and Giesler set a legal precedent for rape
trials in California that still stands.

Two days after the accident, Peggy Daley, William von Briesen's
sister-in-law and a graduate of Beverly Hills High School, died of injuries sustained in the backseat of the overturned vehicle. The second
victim was only eighteen.

So Giesler was got, and on September 17, a preliminary hearing
was held in the West Los Angeles branch of the municipal court to try
Busby Berkeley on two counts of vehicular manslaughter. In a stunning
entrance, the defendant in a polka dot robe was wheeled in on a stretcher
and remained supine for the duration of the hearing. Some twenty-five
witnesses took the stand; a few testified that Buzz had been driving er-
ratically. Most damning was William Hudson. Looking somber with

his bandaged chin, he testified that he smelled liquor on the defendant's breath. Buzz winced and tossed on his stretcher when he heard this. Municipal Judge Joseph L. Call then made a startling decision from the bench. He said, "The evidence in the case has clearly shown that a greater crime than manslaughter has been committed." For the deaths of Ada von Briesen and Peggy Daley, Busby Berkeley was now charged with two counts of murder in the second degree. Arraignment was ordered for October 7, with a bond of $10,000. Said Giesler, "We feel we have a complete defense which we will present at the proper time in Superior Court." The next day, William von Briesen filed a $150,000 damage action suit against Buzz based on the injuries he had suffered that horrible night.

Second-degree murder is first-degree murder without the premeditation. If Buzz was aware that his conduct (i.e., his driving) was injurious to others and death could occur as a result, he was guilty not of involuntary manslaughter, but of murder; his weapon, his car. Jerry Giesler was collected and composed. High-profile clients were often viewed with adulation then contempt when an incident involved injury and death. And Hollywood had been a hotbed of scandal with headlines full of innuendoes going back to when films were mute. But Giesler knew two things: If the original charge of vehicular manslaughter were allowed to stand, Busby Berkeley would definitely be facing hard time, and it was much harder to convict someone for second-degree murder in the scenario of a car accident. Giesler's tactic was simple and profound: blame the front left tire for the accident.

Buzz telephoned Jack Warner on September 20. He made it clear he was ready to return to work. The next day, Warner wrote an unambiguous memo to Hal Wallis:

> I talked to Berkeley on the phone last night. It is needless to say how I felt about it. He wanted to return to work here Monday the 23rd but I definitely told Mike Levee [Buzz's manager] on the phone later that Berkeley should go away somewhere for a week—preferably with his mother at Redlands—and come to work a week later. By all means do not permit Berkeley to come to work this coming Monday as I know it will do him more harm than good as he feels very badly. If he came here Monday he wouldn't be any good himself and will feel that everyone is

staring at him. The man is so hysterical that it would be foolish having him around next week. Then, too, the week following the papers will all be quieting down and Berkeley will be himself. Have Obringer advise Levee's office that we don't want him to come to work this Monday definitely. Let me know some time today that this has been done. J. L. Warner.

Copies were sent to Bill Koenig and Roy Obringer. Jack Warner's feeling for Buzz was quite telling. Leo Forbstein once described Buzz as a "highly nervous and excitable" person, and Warner, in the memo, trumped that assessment, calling Buzz "so hysterical."

A studio memo from Hal Wallis was sent "To All Departments" and dated earlier that month (September 6, 1935): "The title of the next Al Jolson picture hitherto known as *Little Pal* is now *The Singing Kid*." A follow-up memo from Hal Wallis to Bill Koenig dated October 2, 1935, read: "William Keighley will direct *The Singing Kid* and Busby Berkeley will do the numbers." Buzz tried contacting Wallis, but was put off ostensibly by the producer's busy schedule. In referring to the premiere of *Stars over Broadway,* he wrote Wallis the following, dated October 15: "I probably won't see you unless I trip over you tomorrow night accidentally or maybe purposely, so here's wishing you the very best of luck—you deserve it, and I mean that from the bottom of my heart."

On October 21, one month to the day after Jack Warner's memo, the state's case against Busby Berkeley grew even more ominous. William von Briesen died of his injuries. He was twenty-three. A third count of second-degree murder could now be appended to the district attorney's complaint.

Warner Brothers was beginning to sweat. The nationwide news was increasingly dour. On October 24, Producer Robert Lord, in a memo to Hal Wallis, let his anxiety show: "What had we better do about Berkeley? Just when he really starts working won't he have to stand trial? I suspect that his trial will be a very serious and long drawn out affair. It is not really reasonable to expect a man to stage musical numbers when he has 3 murder trials hovering over him. You and I had better discuss this matter."

Court was held in Mrs. Manon von Briesen's hospital room in early November. The widow's testimony was taken. News came midmonth that Buzz's trial had been postponed until December 2 in order to permit the filing of the second-degree murder charge.

As a relief to the encompassing strain Buzz was under, the studio allowed him to continue work on *The Singing Kid*. On location at the Franklin Canyon Fishing Pier between November 9 and 16, Buzz directed Al Jolson and child actress Sybil Jason in the number "You're the Cure for What Ails Me." Jason had come to the United States via Cape Town, South Africa (her birthplace), and London nightclubs, where she sang and danced at the tender age of five. It was the studio's desire to counter the 20th Century Fox gold mine named Shirley Temple with a child star of its own. Sybil Jason, petite with a charming smile and dark hair in a Dutch bob, had the talent to fill the bill. Jack Warner brought Sybil from England and made her the first child actress under contract at the studio.

While shooting "You're the Cure," Buzz sent a memo dated November 11, 1935, to studio employee Max Arnow. In it, Buzz stated that he had interviewed 250 girls in the past four weeks and selected 47 for tests "as in all probability I will produce and shoot the first production number before I do the last big number."

That same day, more trouble befell Buzz when a small headline announced, "Busby Berkeley Named in Federal Tax Lien." The amount of $1,448.91 was mentioned, as was the estranged Merna Kennedy, who was named in a separate lien of $1,490.88.

Professionally, Buzz found no consolation when *Stars over Broadway* was released later in the month. Buzz and Bobby Connolly shared the "Numbers staged and directed by" credit due to Buzz's inability to complete the picture. With the trial just days away, he, Gertrude, and Giesler honed a strategy that aimed to divert the jury's attention from the driver to the exploding tire. Giesler got in touch with the special-effects department at Warner Brothers. The same crew who created miniatures of the "Shadow Waltz" and "Don't Say Goodnight" sets made a lifelike scale model of the accident scene complete with road markings, foliage, and small cars. A special axle was put into Buzz's miniature roadster that allowed its front left wheel to swing out in a demonstration. Jerry looked at it, liked it, and after some consideration, decided not to use it. His reasoning was simple. Parading a detailed professional model to the working-class jury was akin to flaunting your wealth. In its stead,

Giesler had an aerial photograph taken of the road to be used as visual evidence.

Scandal was rife in 1935. On December 16, the day Buzz went on trial, the actress Thelma Todd was found dead, slumped over in the front seat of her Lincoln Phaeton convertible. This was not the diversion Jerry Giesler had envisioned. The law of chain of events could work miracles in a courtroom, and that was the crux of Giesler's defense. If Giesler could persuade a jury to believe that the blown tire was responsible for the accident, then Buzz's condition at the time would be of no consequence. Giesler reasoned that if a person was indeed driving drunk and a car smashed the drunk driver from behind, causing the drunk to hit someone, his drunkenness could not be held accountable as there was no legal connection.

Presiding in the trial was Judge Charles Burnell. Representing the state was David Coleman, a member of the district attorney's staff and Deputy District Attorney Dionizio DiVecchio. In his opening statement, Jerry Giesler declared that Busby Berkeley does not want sympathy, but he does not want prejudice either. Many attendees at Bill Koenig's party were called to the stand. Producer Bryan Foy was asked by Giesler to describe Busby Berkeley as he knew him. "He's very high strung and walks around at times as though he was a little bit nuts." A roar of laughter overcame the courtroom.

Actor Frank McHugh, a Buzz regular in a few pictures, said under oath that he didn't see anyone in particular drinking the night of the party. Judge Burnell was angered when he heard this, and his tone betrayed his emotion when he usurped David Coleman's questioning and asked incredulously: "This cocktail bar must have been like an altar, because no one got near it. Here were 200 people at a cocktail party and all they had to drink was milk. Was that it?" Bobby Connolly swore to Buzz's sobriety. When Coleman asked Connolly if everybody was drinking, Connolly replied drolly that he couldn't see everybody. Judge Burnell inserted another prejudicial question when he asked the witness, "It wasn't a cocktail party given by the W.C.T.U. [Woman's Christian Temperance Union]?" "No," was all Bobby Connolly said. Actor Addison Randall elaborated, "Cocktails, all kinds of cocktails were served." He also said he didn't see Buzz take a drink, and that Buzz was sober when he (Addison) left the party at ten.

Giesler brought the party's stars up for questioning. One by one, Guy Kibbee, Mervyn LeRoy, Glenda Farrell, and others towed the party line and were in agreement: Buzz was absolutely sober when he left the party and had no more than two drinks in the course of the evening. Buzz and Gertrude listened attentively to the testimony at Jerry Giesler's side behind the defendant's table. Wire images sent nationwide from the *Los Angeles Times* to the *New York Times* showed a subdued man under extreme duress.

Buzz recognized some faces as they took their oaths. L. M. Bunn of the Lighthouse Café told of Buzz, his attempted getaway, the rumble seat, and his crawling on hands and knees. L. M. heard Buzz telling an officer that he was planning to call his mother. Claud Hart recounted his own involvement with the accident, and that, though he had stood close to Berkeley, he had noticed no alcohol odor. Service station employee C. J. Box played into the prosecution's hands when he characterized Buzz as "somewhat intoxicated" when he drove into his station. "His speech was irregular," according to Mr. Box.

On December 19, Judge Burnell moved the trial to the home of Manon von Briesen. Attending at bedside were the jury, Buzz, Giesler, Coleman, a court stenographer, and the judge. Mrs. von Briesen described the crash in as much detail as she could. Later that day, the group was taken to Santa Monica Hospital to hear the testimony of Laura von Briesen, who was still in serious condition.

Giesler worked the angles. If he encountered witness resistance, he remedied the situation behind the scenes. He was aware that the Pacific Palisades Fire Department was called to the accident scene, and he sent a couple of his men to interview the firemen. After they were introduced at the stationhouse, Giesler's guys couldn't help but feel strong hostility from the firemen. The firemen had been there on that dark night and had seen the carnage and the wavering instigator stumbling as if in a stupor. Giesler had his investigators return to the station, two, three, four times. Repetition and recognition allowed the firemen to gradually open up to the investigators, yielding Giesler a tidbit or two and a bit of goodwill.

Back in court, no fewer than five tire experts offered their testimony, three of them for the defense. M. B. Briggs of the Goodyear Tire and Rubber Company said the tire's failure "was not a spontaneous blowout, but looked as though it was caused by an impact." His coworker, chemist G. A. Bolazs, remarked that he could detect no weakness that could have caused the tire to fail without an impact with some heavy object. Giesler wanted his witnesses to testify that the tire had an inherent weak spot, whether chemically or structurally. He used the frightening word "cancer" to describe a tire that was gradually, but obliviously, compromised by a spreading fault that mirrored the disease's pathology. A. H. Eagan said the blowout was spontaneous and occurred before the crash. B. W. Cunningham, the store manager for Hollywood's Frank W. Dillin Tire Company, testified that the tire's failure was caused by a previous injury. Finally, defense expert R. L. Blankenship said with certainty: "I am sure the tire blew out before the accident because, among other things, I found a mark on the tire where it had struck the bumper of the Ford coupe [William Hudson's vehicle] in the accident. The mark indicated to me that the tire had been flat when it struck the bumper."

The testimony of a dead man was read in open court. William von Briesen's statement, taken from his hospital bed, mentioned his passengers' nervousness while recounting the lead-up to the accident. "About a thousand feet ahead of me I saw a car on the wrong side of the road coming toward me. I thought it was somebody trying to find a place to park. I lost track of the car then, until it came right up in front of me. The lights were so strong I couldn't see. I was knocked unconscious for a few moments. When I came to, I was perfectly helpless. I could not use the right side of my body. The car was overturned."

Buzz took the stand in his own defense, and Judge Burnell, who didn't suffer wealthy Hollywood hotshots gladly, was ready to pounce. Under direct examination, Buzz testified that the driver's side front tire had gone flat just prior to the accident and that he had tried desperately to gain control of his car when it veered into the oncoming lane. Again beating the prosecution to the punch, the judge, in a derisive voice, questioned the accused:

"The tires on your car, they were of the most expensive make, weren't they?"

"I couldn't say as to that. They were four or five months old."

"They were in good shape then?"

"I didn't notice particularly."

Giesler asked Ben Koenig (Bill's brother) to take the stand. Ben revealed that Buzz had circulated around the party. He mentioned Buzz by the patio and piano, with the director singing along with some other guests.

"What were they singing?" asked the judge immaterially, "Sweet Adeline?"

When the state and defense rested their cases on December 20, DiVecchio summed up the prosecution's charge with a denunciation of the defendant, calling Berkeley "a drunken motorist who committed a triple murder on Roosevelt Highway." "I think we have proved beyond a reasonable doubt," he continued, "that the defendant was intoxicated when his automobile collided with two others," and he repeated out loud the victims' names.

On Christmas Eve 1935, a hung jury voted ten to two for acquittal. Buzz and Giesler regarded the verdict as a moral victory, feeling the judge's harsh treatment of defense witnesses had backfired with many jurors. "They could have convicted me, but it seems too bad those two had to hold out for conviction," said the weary defendant. The court set February 24 for a retrial. Milton Cohen, assistant to Jerry Giesler, told Buzz that "we will surely win the second trial." "I'm sorry my son can't be free for Christmas," said Gertrude. On the record she praised the jurors: "You were wonderful. Thank you so much."

That evening, Hal Wallis sent Jack Warner (who was traveling during the trial) a radiogram with the verdict. Warner wired Buzz: "Merry Christmas. Awfully sorry that you weren't completely exonerated. Have felt certain . . . that you should have no fear . . . if there is anything I can do . . . waiting to hear from you." One of the things Jack Warner couldn't do was erase Busby Berkeley's opprobrium with moviegoers who, in the court of public opinion, found him guilty.

Meanwhile, *The Singing Kid* was precipitously moving along and the question of Buzz's involvement was subject to a host of back-and-forth memoranda. Eleven days before the jury made its decision, Wallis made his. In a memo, he stated the numbers credit would read "Numbers Staged By Bobby Connolly." The day after Christmas Robert Lord wrote to Hal Wallis: "Do you want Berkeley to do the 'Save Me Sister' number or do you want Connolly to do it? I talked to Buzz Tuesday night and he told me that you had told him to go ahead with the number. Is this the case or not?" Wallis responded the same day: "I met Buzz after the jury disagreed the other day and he told me he was extremely anxious to get busy again as he feels he should be doing something. . . . If you figure that Berkeley is still in too nervous a condition—we don't have to be bound by this." Such were the inner workings of the people who doled out screen credits. It didn't take Hal Wallis more than twenty-four hours to make his decision whether or not Busby Berkeley would receive acknowledgment for his work on scenes that were clearly intended to be in the final released print. To a "Mr. Selzer" at the studio he commanded: "On *The Singing Kid* we will give credit for the stage numbers to Bobby Connolly. No credit is to be given to Berkeley."

On the second day of the New Year, out of court, Buzz settled seven damage suits now totaling $250,000. When the court reconvened, details of the settlement were disclosed. With an agreed-upon reduction to $95,000, the distribution was divided thusly:

Mrs. Manon von Briesen, $29,400 for her injuries.
Laura von Briesen, $30,000 for her injuries.
Heirs of the deceased Mrs. Ada von Briesen, $2,500.
Heirs of the deceased Peggy Daley, $2,500.
Heirs of the deceased William von Briesen, $10,000.
Clarence Burtless Jr., $19,400 for his injuries.
William Alvin Hudson, $1,200 for his injuries.

On January 11, the "anxious to get busy again" Buzz returned to the studio to film the number "My How This Town Has Changed," starring the comedy/singing quartet the Yacht Club Boys (George Kelley, Billy Mann, Charlie Alder, and James V. Kern). It was shot and completed in two quick days. Was Buzz aware of Wallis's no-credit edict? Did anyone tell him? Would anyone dare?

Something unsavory was amiss in the superior court. On January 14, Judge Charles S. Burnell was ousted from the criminal court bench and demoted to the civil branch of the superior court within an hour after he received an anonymous telephone call criticizing his handling of Busby Berkeley's murder trial. Burnell wrote a letter to his forty-nine colleagues on the bench and said the mysterious caller identified himself as "a friend of Busby Berkeley." The caller criticized the judge, warning him to "fix up your instructions and talk to the jury (at the forthcoming trial) so there'll be no danger of Busby getting into a jam."

The caller asked "if it was true that Berkeley was to be tried again before [Burnell]," and the judge said it was. "Busby's friends want you to give him a break," the caller said, and Burnell was quick to counter that "Berkeley would have a fair trial such as I endeavored to see that every defendant before me received. That was all the break I would give." The man snapped back: "That is what we mean. You know damn well you can fix up your instructions and talk to the jury so there'll be no danger of Berkeley getting in a jam." Judge Burnell told the party where he might go, and the caller forcefully ended the intimidating discussion: "All right if you feel that way about it, we'll see that you are yanked out of that court and someone put in who is more amenable to reason." An hour later, Burnell received a visit from Superior Court Judge Douglas L. Edmonds (the presiding judge-elect), and then the presiding judge, Edward L. Bishop. Burnell said Judge Edmonds urged him to relinquish his criminal court because he was "greatly needed in civil work." Burnell vehemently rejected the proposal but to no avail. When Buzz's February retrial date was moved to April, it was Judge Vickers who presided.

As stated, Buzz justly received Academy Award nominations for his ingenious "Lullaby of Broadway" and "The Words Are in My Heart" numbers from *Gold Diggers of 1935*. On March 5, the Frank Capra–hosted awards banquet took place at the Biltmore Bowl in the Biltmore Hotel. What seemed like a shoo-in turned into a rebuff, as Dave Gould won the award for his work in *Broadway Melody of 1936* and *Folies Bergère de Paris*. Was it inconceivable that Busby Berkeley was overlooked by the haughty Academy voters from the moment William von Briesen's car overturned? Or was Dave Gould's work really more inspiring, accomplished, and of an intrinsically higher artistic value? If Buzz commented at all on the oversight, he did it in private and off the record.

Any trial attorney will tell you a retrial is drudgery. The same witnesses recite the same testimony to the same questions. Giesler likened it to watching a movie you've seen before with the hope that somebody tacked on a new ending. On April 4, Clarence Burtless was unable to describe the accident. The speed at which Buzz's car was traveling was now reported at more than sixty miles per hour.

Hal Wallis's decree held firm. *The Singing Kid* was released around this time sans Buzz's credit. Regarding his delightful contribution "You're the Cure for What Ails Me," Buzz confessed to Sybil Jason:

"Nobody but you will ever know that I worked on this picture. Nobody would believe me." Buzz, apparently to keep himself busy and escape his troubles, worked with Sybil on a Technicolor short called *Changing of the Guard* made right after *The Singing Kid*. The delightful two-reeler, directed by Bobby Connolly, features a fabulous dream sequence where Sybil (in a plaid kilt) leads the palace guards in formation at Buckingham Palace. As the guards march past the camera, we see that they're actually Buzz's girls! Sybil was coached in her steps by Buzz, and the Berkeley Beefeaters were trained by Connolly. It all blended seamlessly. Buzz took no credit, nor did he want any, for his little contribution. As Sybil learned firsthand, there was often no real division of labor between collaboratively creative people.

On April 14, the same celebrities who had taken the stand in the first trial redoubled their efforts. Still in agreement, they all said Buzz was sober when he left the party. The next day Buzz took the stand and, among other things, told of the party's electrified chair and his spilled punch.

Three days later the case went to the jury. After eight hours, they were deadlocked at six each. The next day they resumed, but reached an impasse when seven jurors voted for acquittal. The jury was dismissed, and the prosecution did not indicate whether Buzz would be brought to trial again. Less than a week later, the DA's office recommended that the charges of second-degree murder against Busby Berkeley be dismissed. Superior Court Judge Thomas Ambrose (now assigned) said he would proffer a decision the following week. On April 26, Buzz left the courtroom but remained the state's captive. Judge Ambrose surprised everyone by ordering a third trial.

In May, Buzz was directing again thanks to the assistant treasurer and studio comptroller, Paul Chase. After the trial, Chase submitted an affidavit to California Superior Court to allow a continuance so Buzz could work. Innocent is not the same as being found not guilty, so the stigma of another looming trial was made somewhat bearable while Buzz kept busy. Two weeks after the second verdict was pronounced, production on a new film, *Stage Struck,* began with Buzz as the megaphonist. Casting problems plagued *Stage Struck* as the always reliable Dick Powell (marked for the lead) was given strict orders by his physician to rest his throat. Warner Brothers thought they had an ace in the hole

with Rudy Vallee as a backup. Powell eventually convinced the studio
that his singing voice was as good as ever, and accepted the Berkeley-like
role of a Broadway dance director who creates spectacular productions.
The ubiquitous Joan Blondell was cast as the supreme actress/diva and
much-married Peggy Revere (a character many in Hollywood recognized
as spoofing real-life gold digger Peggy Hopkins Joyce).

The film is watered-down comedy with little of Buzz's directorial
magic (showing, perhaps a real auteur whose despondency affected his
work). The script allowed for broad comedy (forearm on the forehead in
mock grief) and digressed into slapstick whenever the Yacht Club Boys
were on screen. There's also a surprising lack of musical interludes (especially with the story's Broadway background), and in only one number
does Buzz evoke his innate brand of artifice. "Fancy Meeting You" and
"In Your Own Quiet Way" were written by E. Y. (Yip) Harburg and
Harold Arlen. The first is staged rather blandly as Powell and painfully
obvious newcomer Jeanne Madden sing to each other while strolling
through a museum. The second, "In Your Own Quiet Way," gets the
Berkeley touch when it's sung by Madden as part of a supposed dress
rehearsal. As the number begins, Buzz cleverly shifts perspective as we
think we're watching the camera panning down the stage curtains, when
in reality we're viewing the long train of a nineteenth-century hoop dress
resting on the floor. The camera tilts up to reveal a long shot of Madden
in a room with sparse furnishings (divan, large windows, upright lighting fixture). A series of close-ups carries the balance of the song, ending
with a reverse shot of the opening.

Stage Struck ends with a disappointment. As the mechanical, *42nd
Street*–inspired plot comes to its obvious conclusion, Powell and Madden decide they'll put on the show together. Anticipation of a finale in
the Berkeley bombastic tradition soon gives way to an anticlimactic final
shot of comic actor Frank McHugh looking flustered and embarrassed
after receiving a kiss from Miss Madden. The film's final sin was the
absence of a production number (of any scale) to send the picture off
with a bang. In spite of those shortcomings, Dick Powell did his best to
promote *Stage Struck* by making recordings of the two Harburg/Arlen
songs that received radio airplay during the film's release.

In July 1936, Buzz turned his attention to *Gold Diggers of 1937*,
the dreariest of the series. Lloyd Bacon directed the book while, like old

times, Buzz swooped in and out with his own unit and created one of the most amazing minimalist numbers of his career. Berkeley wasn't at all thrilled with the two original songs already assigned to the film, "Speaking of the Weather" and "Let's Put Our Heads Together," composed by Harold Arlen and Yip Harburg. Buzz sought the assistance of Warren and Dubin, and their contributions "With Plenty of Money and You" and "All's Fair in Love and War" greatly enhanced the film.

Gold Diggers of 1937 opens with "With Plenty of Money and You" as a mustachioed Dick Powell in a white tuxedo sings the bouncy verses (while a previous Berkeley foray with the filthy lucre brought to mind "We're in the Money"). The second time the song is performed the filming is restrained by Berkeley's standards as Powell croons to Joan Blondell on the front steps of her building, featuring light dance work up and down the stairs. "Speaking of the Weather" is also sung twice, first in the small setting of an office with minimal extravagance, and opened up in its reprise as Buzz's recognizable technique takes over. The lyrical ballad "Let's Put Our Heads Together" follows the Berkeley pattern of tracking singing couples at a grand outdoor party while the camera floats between them and close-ups of his chorines. Without a beat, the temperature is raised as the reprise of "Speaking of the Weather" is performed, giving ample screen time to the actor and fine tap dancer Lee Dixon (whose character wears the improbable moniker of Boop Oglethorpe). The sequence features a short stop at a pool as Buzz films his girls in medium close-up while they back-float past the camera, one smiling face after another. Dixon then gets to shine as he fast taps his way around a makeshift tennis court. At the number's peak, the Berkeley girls face each other and interlock their arms while Dixon, in a display of strength and control, walks on the girl's arms using nothing but his hands.

"All's Fair in Love and War" is a marvel of creativity in the face of a tight budget. "We don't want any more of these big expensive sets," barked Hal Wallis (a subtle reminder to Berkeley that the days of Darryl F. Zanuck's blank checks were long over). Buzz, ever the jokester and prankster, was enraged at Wallis's edict. He walked into the production chief's office, reached over his desk, and flipped all the levers on his intercom. It must have been quite humorous to hear every yes-man on the Warner Brothers lot replying in unison, "Yes Hal. What is it Hal? Right away Hal!"

The "no expensive sets" command was enforced, but this kind of limitation fueled Buzz's imagination. He told Wallis: "All right, don't give me any set. Just give me a black floor and a black cyclorama. If you give me fifty boys and fifty girls, I'll do the number."

The curtain rises to reveal Dick Powell in the far distance, wearing a white tuxedo amid a void of total blackness (think Wini Shaw's face in the opening and closing of "The Lullaby of Broadway"). Buzz then takes full advantage of his monorail-dolly system rapidly moving forward as Joan Blondell, Lee Dixon, and Rosalind Marquis (who had an unbilled role of a chorus girl in *Stage Struck*) pop out from behind him. The song is a pastiche of the eternal male/female struggle as love is lyrically linked to war. As he had in previous numbers ("By a Waterfall," for one), Buzz takes the literal approach to his conception of the number (based on lyrics) while his surrealistic vision paints the number in dazzling images of outrageous scale:

> The battlefield's a rocking chair
> Look out look out for all is fair
> In love and war

Soon there are about fifty rocking chairs on the black stage, one white-clad couple per each, as the tune begins one of many repetitions. A pause as Blondell speak-sings her desire ("a nice old man with lots of wealth, who isn't in the best of health"), and Buzz is on the move again. The monorailed camera swiftly pulls back far then reverses itself as Lee Dixon is seen tapping on the seat of a twenty-foot-high rocking chair. The camera in motion tilts down as Rosalind Marquis lights the fuse of a human-size bomb. The resultant explosion leaves a cannon in its wake, firing cannonballs to the camera (à la *Dames*). Three firings reveal two Berkeley chorus girls and Joan Blondell wearing World War I army helmets (and smiles, of course). They're used as a transition to a mock battlefield featuring a row of chorus girls/soldiers equipped with white rifles; on the right, a sign proclaims, "No Man's Land." The women face a row of men (in "No Woman's Land") equally equipped. The combatants fire on one another to no avail until the women pull out their secret weapon (perfume) and spray the enemy. As the demilitarized zone gradually recedes, the women claim their victory with a kiss as the men wave white handkerchiefs in surrender. The scene shifts to a marching band with drummers and flag holders (with Blondell as the majorette) in the regimented formations for which Berkeley had no equal. The girls line up single file and twirl their flags around, one immediately following the other, as Buzz repeats the theme with two rows of girls, then the entire company in a stunning long shot. We then see the reverse of the bomb explosion as the cannon now rematerializes. The camera pulls in to reveal the stars singing the final chorus and, finally, a symmetrical shot (the reverse of the opening) as the camera rapidly leaves Dick Powell, pulling back until he's a white speck in the darkness; then he, too, disappears. The dance director is given the final word, so to speak, as another film ends with a bombastic Busby Berkeley number, leaving most of what preceded it a blur.

Joan Blondell on Buzz: "He was a wild man. He had to be"; "He was fabulous and strict. He had to be"; and "I always liked Buzz very much." The "wild man" presented itself on set during the "All's Fair" number. The long and seemingly endless rehearsals were finally finished, and it was time to shoot. Buzz was airborne and going over last-minute details with his cameraman. Onstage, an anonymous chorus girl became dizzy and sick and needed to be replaced. Blondell's stand-in was quickly grabbed by assistant director Richard Maybery to replace the ill girl, and Buzz wasn't informed. Had he been, he would have nixed the idea of substituting a girl who didn't know the routine and couldn't dance. Buzz called for action, and his camera swooped and swayed. As the boom got close to ground level, Buzz "screamed bloody murder." Apoplectically he yelled, "That stupid fool down there, she's out of step!" When he was told of the ruse, he turned his anger against Maybery. The poor stand-in's story was the opposite of Peggy Sawyer's in *42nd Street*. She went out a youngster and didn't come back a star.

On September 16, Policeman A. M. Sheets, for the third time, told a jury that Buzz was intoxicated the night of the crashes. He said that Berkeley's speech was thick and he was wavering on his feet: "In my opinion he was intoxicated." He said he detected an "alcoholic odor." When a wearied Jerry Giesler put the screws to the officer and suggested that the smell came from his client's clothes, Sheets reluctantly agreed that this was possible.

Joan Blondell and Dick Powell, lovebirds for a quite a while now, wanted to finish *Gold Diggers of 1937* in a hurry so they could marry. On September 19, Buzz, along with Jimmy Cagney, Glenda Farrell, Mervyn LeRoy, and Hal Wallis, attended the Blondell/Powell nuptials on a yacht called the *Santa Paula* at San Pedro. No one could say if Buzz had been cognizant that the yacht's name eerily matched the town of William Hudson's destination on that infamous night.

Back in court the following week, tire experts took the stand again with some for and some against the theory of the cancerous tire. But no matter, this time Jerry Giesler believed Buzz would be acquitted fully and soon. He reckoned the jury this time knew of the last jury's verdict and was predisposed psychologically not to contradict their decision.

The nightmare of more than a year ended on September 25, when, after an hour and a half, a Superior Court jury acquitted Busby Berkeley. He wept openly. In a quivering voice, he said to the press, "Thank God, justice at last." A photo of Buzz holding Gertrude by the arm was taken shortly after the reading of the verdict and was captioned, "A Happy Reunion."

Jerry Giesler never lacked for work. The Berkeley case instilled in every Hollywood powerbroker the two-word commandment that had the authority to squash a legal discomfiture—"get Giesler." From time to time, he once admitted, he would reach across his desk and touch the miniature roadster with the swing-out axle that he saved for his own private pleasure.

7

Post-Traumatic Inspiration

Buzz and Gertrude posed for acquittal photos for the Associated Press. The accused wore suit, tie, and artfully folded handkerchief; Mother was decked out in hat, brooch, and spectacles, looking very much like a doting grandmother. The grueling hours between court and set weighed heavily on Buzz. *Stage Struck* was shooting on an inflexible schedule when the superfluous third trial was under way. A Dick Powell sequence wrapping at 2:00 a.m. was followed by a look-your-best appearance in front of judge and jury at 9:00 a.m. sharp. But Buzz looked at his oppressive schedule in a positive light: "I was lucky that I had so much work because it helped keep my mind off the accident. Even though I was found innocent, it was a shocking and terribly depressing thing to have been involved in the death of three people. I think it was the heavy work commitment that saved my sanity."

The legal expense, the pages of billing minutiae to the quarter hour, came due on the heels of Buzz's $95,000 settlement. Giesler's fees amounted to almost six figures—worth every penny to keep Buzz from losing his sanity and facing hard time for murder.

No one snapped pictures or took statements of the victims and their relatives. The cash settlements may have come with restrictions against on-the-record comments. To learn their feelings about Berkeley's final verdict would have been enlightening, if not profoundly saddening. Judge Burnell's unusual ouster never attracted much attention, and he and the threatening voice that led to his reassignment disappeared from public consciousness. The identities of the caller and the one who hired him were never revealed.

When it takes three highly charged murder trials to affirm innocence, human nature is loath to accept the final verdict. Those pronounced innocent can't return to the state they inhabited one second before the alleged transgression. Just ask Fatty Arbuckle. Found innocent of scan-

dalous charges that left his career in tatters, he was guilty, not of the
crime, but of being charged in the first place. So it was with Buzz. The
trial had tainted his name; in the minds of some, his reputation as a
boozer made a car accident inevitable regardless of the law's last word.
Fortunately, he wasn't looked upon with suspicion by his coworkers.
It was the public perception of the name Busby Berkeley that changed
following three deaths to which he was permanently linked. A coincidence perhaps, but by the time of the third trial, the kind of musical
Buzz had been making was facing extinction. To call it a transformation
would be equally correct. A new naturalness where songs would spring
from between lines of dialogue rather than being compartmentalized at
a picture's climax was the direction musical films were taking. At RKO,
Fred Astaire and Ginger Rogers were its chief proponents, with dance
numbers filmed in a style antithetical to Buzz's.

He rested in Redlands and was given no work from the studio while
the dust from the final trial settled. The case of Merna Kennedy was also
legally sealed. When all was said and done, the trial-weary Buzz agreed
to pay annual alimony of $7,500.

It seems Buzz wasn't the only one in Hollywood who believed he
deserved the recognition the Academy refused to bestow at the March
awards. Less than two months after his acquittal, Buzz was made the
guest of honor at the first annual dinner dance of dance directors at the
Trocadero. More than 250 people attended, including top studio personnel and just about every Hollywood dance man. A framed certificate was
awarded to Buzz by the Academy of Motion Picture Arts and Sciences
"in recognition of his outstanding contribution to the pioneering and
development of musical productions in motion pictures." In the award's
border were black-and-white images from Buzz's numbers along with
the signatures of all the leading dance directors in attendance. "I ap-
preciate it as a very nice tribute," said Buzz, "because they all thought I
was the best of the bestest."

Feted one day, undercut the next. On January 6, 1937, Jack Warner
sent a memo to studio counsel and contract negotiator Roy Obringer:
"In the next four or five days get hold of Buzz Berkeley. Instead of him
going up $500 I want him to stay another year for the same money. Let
me know."

Buzz's *The Go Getter,* his next film as director, was a tepid hybrid, a drama lacking dramatics and a light comedy that wasn't very funny. George Brent plays the indefatigable Bill Austen, whose motto, "It Must Be Done," inspires him to overcome an amputated leg suffered in a navy dirigible accident. Persistence leads him to a lumber broker owned by the irascible Cappy Ricks (Charles Winninger, typecast). A lengthy diversion occurs midway as Cappy sends Austen on a wild goose chase to test the go-getter's mettle. What he goes through pales to what happens later, when the poor guy is told to leave his cruise ship honeymoon to handle a problem at the office. He dives overboard, flags a rowboat, makes it to work in record time, and still his boss yells at him! Brent and female lead Anita Louise had worked for Warner Brothers, but they had never worked together and had never met socially. Their very first scene together was bound to be awkward—an intimate love scene where the stars had to embrace and kiss and repeat. Buzz may have claimed to film his musical numbers only once, but he took his time here and shot the scene five times before he was satisfied.

The Go Getter amounts to a film of little pleasures, with Buzz's personality all but missing. It may be damning the film with faint praise to call it a nice time-waster, but any film that required Buzz to rein in his overt impulses while honing his dramatic technique was personally worthwhile.

Frank Borzage, who had directed films going back to 1913, and most recently for William Randolph Hearst's Cosmopolitan Pictures (a distribution entity of Warner Brothers), was set to make *The Singing Marine*. He didn't stay long on the project and soon signed on with MGM. Ray Enright, *Dames'* book director, was given the assignment. Buzz lent his expertise to the staging of a couple of numbers, including the show-stopping "Night over Shanghai" (evoking "Shanghai Lil," albeit with less of Lil's blatant patriotism).

The title pretty much delivers what you'd expect: Dick Powell, in his third stretch in the military (he'd already been a sailor and West Point cadet in other pictures), plays the title role—a marine whose popular singing voice leads him to New York on a furlough, where radio exposure brings him success. His popularity goes to his head, causing him to go AWOL. His platoon, seething with resentment, does everything in their power to keep the singing marine from ever performing again (including a sentence in the brig).

Buzz brings his usual pizzazz to the proceedings, first with the clever "The Lady Who Couldn't Be Kissed." In Buzz's favorite milieu, tuxedoed Dick Powell performs in a stylized nightclub (pristine central dance floor, tables encircling it, a small stage). The patrons (mostly Berkeley girls) turn their chairs around as Powell croons. In a simple, yet effective waist-high shot, Dick sits next to a pretty lady, takes her number, gets a kiss, then moves his chair backward to the next table, where the same transaction occurs, and on to the next table and the next. As the number continues and transforms, Lee Dixon (Buzz liked him in *Gold Diggers of 1937*) takes the reins and gets to tapping, accompanied by four Berkeley beauties dressed in white outfits, all pushing push brooms. There's a bit of magic as the brooms dance out of sight, leaving the girls and Lee to tap a great routine that Buzz captures from advantageous angles. The number ends with a laugh when Dixon (in fast motion) gets wrapped up in a carpet and the girls roll him offstage.

A sprawling nightclub in Shanghai is the setting for Harry Warren and Johnny Mercer's "Night over Shanghai," another of Buzz's great directorial efforts. Here, as in *42nd Street*, Buzz evoked the "Rout" number from his Broadway staging of *International Revue* with the denizens of life's underbelly subsisting in a gritty environment. As the fanlike curtains open, we see a world in black with a starkly lit image in the far distance (an opening Buzz obviously embraced, having used it twice already). The image doesn't register at first. Riding the Buzz monorail, we now decipher two hands moving together like a fluttering bird. Closing in tighter, the hands are shown to be wrapped around a harmonica played by virtuoso Larry Adler. The camera lifts off the ground to an open window, and a Shanghai street scene with Dick Powell comes into view. Next we're in a dive saloon (not nearly as depraved as Shanghai Lil's), where onstage the film's female star, Doris Weston, is singing. Behind her are black curtains from which eight sets of white arms protrude, moving rhythmically as if performing a disembodied hula dance. The self-contained number continues as Powell fights to protect Doris. As he walks her out of the saloon a gun fires a fatal shot into her back—another death in a Busby Berkeley musical number. Larry Adler appears and reappears throughout like a roving commentator as his harmonica plays a decidedly downbeat melody. A final close-up and Buzz ends as he begins. The monorailed camera gracefully returns to its original position: Adler's expressive hands are again in the far distance, and the curtains close to applause.

Warren and Dubin's "The Song of the Marines" was actually embraced by the Corps, and they kept it. Buzz filmed the formations to the patriotic finale as the men in their dress blues march here and there while Powell belts out the tune. It's reverential in the best tradition, and it gets the sincere treatment that a nostalgic World War I second lieutenant could apply.

A bridesmaid again, Buzz received another Academy Award nomination for dance direction for "All's Fair in Love and War." On March 4, 1937, he attended the ceremony, held at the same venue as the previous year, with George Jessel acting as MC. In a roundabout way, Buzz's path recrossed with Florenz Ziegfeld; this time it was MGM's loosely biographical *The Great Ziegfeld*. Dance director Seymour Felix took home the award, beating Buzz with his staging of "A Pretty Girl Is Like a Melody." When one learns the budget each had at his disposal, a naked set was, evidently, no match to the extravagance afforded Felix at Metro.

By midsummer, the conflict festering in Europe brought to the fore a Busby Berkeley fan of unusual repute. The created post of Reich Minister of Public Enlightenment and Propaganda for Nazi Germany was held by Josef Goebbels. He'd obviously seen Buzz's stylish abstractions, the anonymous masses reacting as a tight-knit unit under a forceful command, and created a diary entry on June 1937 that made oblique reference to his enjoyable perceptions. He wrote that Germany's largest studio, U.F.A., was making a dance film: "I prohibit it from showcasing the philosophic dance of [Gret] Palucca, [Mary] Wigmann, and others. Dance must be animated and display beautiful women's bodies. That has nothing to do with philosophy." Buzz would no doubt have agreed. German director Leni Riefenstahl, who made the highly artistic (and propagandistic) *Triumph of the Will,* was told of the comparison of Berkeley's regimented ensembles to the thousands of soldiers she had filmed in uncanny similarity. She didn't disagree, saying she had learned much from the early Warner Brothers musicals and that she was an admirer of Busby Berkeley.

Buzz welcomed a change to the musical. The stress of designing upward of twenty numbers in a year's time was no longer his. He fought the pigeonholing of his talent with the firm belief that he was more than top shots, patterns, and pulchritude. He could, and did, direct comedy. He wanted to stage dramas. But now, with his trial tribulations behind him and years of contract work ahead, the free-and-single director sought some Hollywood real estate to add to his portfolio. A Beaux-Arts–style villa, built in 1913 and scene of many parties (Benito Mussolini was once an honored guest), went on the market in 1937. Located at 3500 West Adams Boulevard, the villa was owned by Secundo Guasti, the founder of the Rancho Cucamonga winery. The property was magnificent. Its entrance hall had an inlaid marble floor while overhead hung a giltwood chandelier. Paneled walls were of Peruvian mahogany, and red and yellow Italian marble was accented in the salon and dining room fireplaces. A curved and dramatic oak stairway led to an elegant second-floor solarium. A frieze in mock Renaissance style featured cherubs carrying grapes; in the dining room, they held glasses of wine. When the property owner's widow passed away, the house was auctioned. Buzz won with a $200,000 bid. One of his first bits of interior design was converting the wine cellar into a screening room for Gertrude. She loved the house. Her objets d'art and antique furniture had space to breathe in the villa's expanse. "It looked more like a museum than a home, but it made her happy *and that's all I cared about*," said Buzz with face-value honesty and dutifulness.

Buzz was conducting summer auditions for a new picture called *Varsity Show*. He'd walk in front of the line of hopefuls and check their legs and smiles. Sometimes he unfairly used his position and invited a pretty naïf to his office, where she was asked to lift her skirt higher than the call of decency. "Oh, I have to see more than that," teased Buzz, and he'd wink at the others in the office. "Come to work, come for a fitting" was Buzz's way of saying, "You're hired." For *Varsity Show*, Buzz's eye fixated on one particular beauty in the chorus line who was wearing a tight, form-enhancing sweater. When the unknown began her athletic dance routine, Buzz remarked to a colleague, "Oh yes, we want her." A private skirt-lifting audition wasn't required for the girl who identified herself as Carole Landis. Buzz, smitten again, hired Carole on the spot, and according to studio contemporaries, a sexual relationship ensued that very day. At the audition Buzz gave Carole a line of dialogue, a ruse often used as a director's bedding scheme. Give dialogue directions, promise an onscreen close-up, edit it out later (dancers rarely spoke on screen), and no one's the wiser to the perennial ploy.

Buzz and Carole kept company from that day forward. Within a few weeks, Buzz used his influence to grant Carole a seven-year contract with Warner Brothers, starting at the standard rate of fifty dollars a week with options that could escalate to five hundred. Carole was Buzz's protégée and paramour, but there was something in her past that she feared would reemerge; a teen marriage, not exactly annulled or divorced, had the power to kill a budding romance. A suspicious stint in San Francisco was also something Carole would have rather kept under wraps.

In 1934, when Carole was only fifteen, she had married Irving Wheeler, a neighbor of hers. They lived together for three weeks. After an argument she ran home to her mother. The couple never again lived under the same roof. For years she tried in vain to contact Wheeler. She figured, incorrectly, that a divorce had occurred automatically through a provision in the marital code dealing with desertion. The contract that Buzz arranged for her couldn't be signed as she was technically a minor. Carole's lawyer, Sidney Wetzler, could not find Wheeler either, so on July 8 she was forced to petition the court to approve her contract. On August 2, a court order was issued validating it. The court felt a married woman of eighteen was equivalent legally to one who was twenty-one, so she soon signed the contract and became a fixture at the forty-one-year-old director's side. Her first role was as a student (no credit) in *Varsity Show*.

"Buzz's Boola Boola" is what the finale to *Varsity Show* could have been called, filled as it was with an overabundant dose of school spirit. He directed the final number only, infusing it with great visuals including subtle reverse shots and appealing patterns in group blockings. The highlight (which garnered cheers in the theaters) featured a medley of fight songs of famous institutions with the Berkeley dancers in regimented formations spelling out school names, one after another.

The finale begins with Buck and Bubbles, a talented singing/dancing act used too sparingly in Hollywood. There's great tap work in their short routine. Bubbles (John W. Sublett) peers from behind a gigantic prop of sheet music. He then stands on a wooden board as it descends on a track encircling the band. He stops and slides his way onto the top of the piano played by Buck (Ford Washington Lee), and together they perform an invigorating routine to "On with the Dance." Next is the giant sheet music for "Love Is on the Air Tonight" spreading apart in a "V" shape as dancers are led by a baton-twirling majorette. Singer/actor Johnnie Davis intercepts the action in his quick "Old King Cole," and the action shifts as the film's stars reprise "On with the Dance." Buzz again employs the reverse-shot effect (used so effectively in *Dames*) for the "rah rah sis boom bah" finish. Fred Waring and his Pennsylvanians provide the spirited school-themed sound track. From a high shot, we see one of the stars catch a football from Waring and throw the ball into a compact, circular dance group. When the football is caught, the dancers instantly take their places, forming the letters of a particular school (Notre Dame, Wisconsin, USC, Army, Navy, etc.) The reverse effect allowed Buzz to place his dancers in precise formation (for example, in the shape of ND). He films the formation and then instructs the group to close ranks and form a tight circle. The group, now compacted, is the last setup Buzz shoots. When played back, it appears as if the tight group moves backward into the exact complex formation that Buzz had filmed in the first place, making the effect totally seamless. His fertile imagination is on display in every college-themed grouping. The inspiring music and eye-enticing arrangements end *Varsity Show* on a rousing note. The Academy of Motion Picture Arts and Sciences agreed, and Buzz received his third Oscar nomination in as many years.

On July 8, Hal Wallis received a memo from Warner Brothers production assistant Walter MacEwen. The subject was the title of the studio's latest project. In the memo, MacEwen mentions Buzz's suggestion to title the film "Hollywood Band Wagon" instead of the already agreed upon *Hollywood Hotel.*

Buzz and Carole Landis made the publicity photos in the late summer of 1937. One caption refers to him as her fiancé. But Buzz kept his marriage impulsivity at bay while he concentrated on the new film he was slated to direct that was based on a popular radio program. His suggestion for a different title was not considered. The studio would go with the one that Jerry Wald and Maurice Leo wrote in their initial script of February 8.

In the fabled Orchid Room of the magnificent Hollywood Hotel, a queen routinely held court. The biggest show-business stars of the day

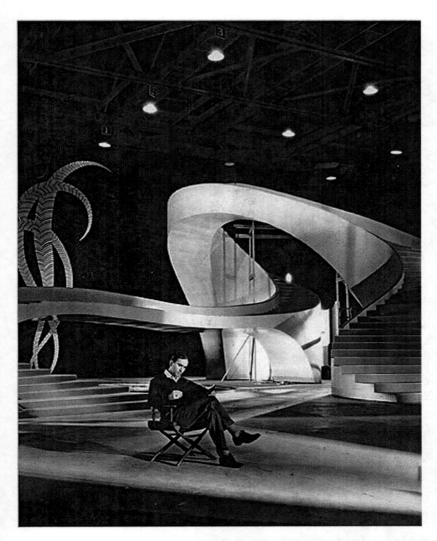

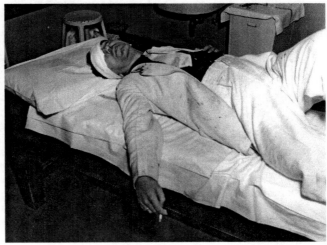

(Above) Buzz in front of the white ribbon staircase for "Shadow Waltz" before the earthquake. Publicity photo from *Gold Diggers of 1933*. Copyright Warner Bros. Pictures, Inc., 1933.

(Right) September 8, 1935. Hours after the car accident, his wracking ordeal had just begun. Photofest, New York.

(Above) Nellie Gertrude Berkeley, actress, mother of Buzz, circa the Gay Nineties. The New York Public Library for the Performing Arts/Billy Rose Theatre Division. (Right) Francis Enos, director, actor, father of Buzz. He went by the name Frank and, at times, Wilson Enos. The Etta and Busby Berkeley private collection.

(Left) Amy Busby, soubrette. Her surname launched a legend. The New York Public Library for the Performing Arts/Billy Rose Theatre Division. (Right) William Gillette, distinguished actor and family friend. His forename rests comfortably in Buzz's between the last names of his mother and father. Publicity photo of William Gillette, photographer unknown.

Busby Berkeley William Enos. The Etta and Busby Berkeley private collection, from *The Busby Berkeley Book* by Tony Thomas and Jim Terry.

Second Lieutenant Enos, World War I. The Etta and Busby Berkeley private collection, from *The Busby Berkeley Book* by Tony Thomas and Jim Terry.

War Brides, 1916, a "photodrama" starring Gertrude Berkeley and Nazimova.

(Left) Busby Berkeley: "Buzz" to everyone except Mother. Studio publicity photo, circa mid-1930s. (Right) Esther Muir, the first of a half-dozen spouses. Publicity photo from *A Day at the Races*, copyright Loew's Incorporated, 1937.

Realizing perspective while setting a shot for *Whoopee!* 1930.

Top shot from *Whoopee!* 1930. Buzz didn't invent it; he mastered it.

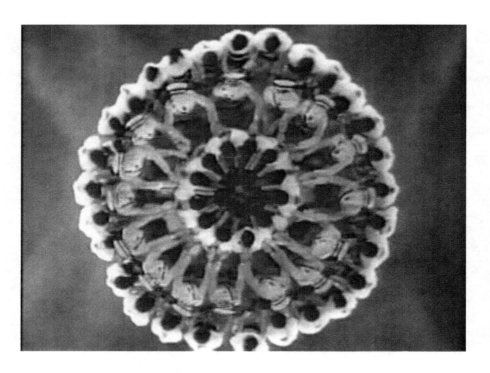

Flying High top shot, 1931. Dismal receipts kept the film earthbound.

Buzz posed and pointing to the calf owned by a *Flying High* chorine who has his eye, 1931.

Buzz (*in back*) at the rehearsal of "Who's Your Little Who-Zis" for *Night World*, 1932.

The Kid from Spain, 1932. His first water ballet, a foreshadowing of grandiose cinematic aquacades.

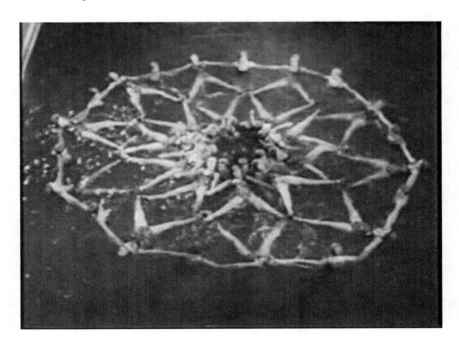

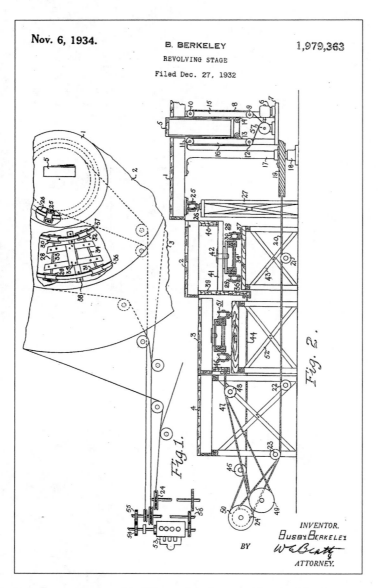

Nov. 6, 1934.

B. BERKELEY

REVOLVING STAGE

Filed Dec. 27, 1932

1,979,363

INVENTOR.
BUSBY BERKELEY

BY

ATTORNEY.

Fig.1.

Fig. 2.

Buzz's patent, owned by Warner Brothers and inspired by Sam Goldwyn's frugality. Patent filed December 27, 1932.

The world takes notice of Busby Berkeley. The first top shot of "Young and Healthy," from *42nd Street,* 1933.

More inventiveness with movable platters. The second top shot of "Young and Healthy," from *42nd Street,* 1933.

Women, violins, and the elegant raised kick. "Shadow Waltz" from *Gold Diggers of 1933*.

A violin of violins. "Shadow Waltz," from *Gold Diggers of 1933*.

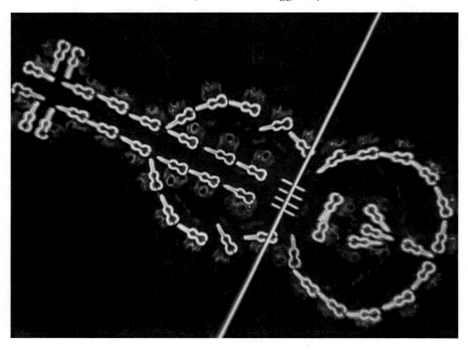

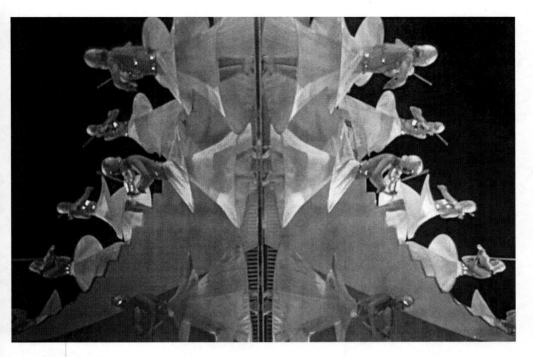

Tilting the camera on a reflective floor from "Shadow Waltz," in *Gold Diggers of 1933*.

A neon violin saved
from the earthquake.

Social consciousness in the cinema. The powerful final image of "Remember My Forgotten Man," from *Gold Diggers of 1933*.

Merna Kennedy and Busby Berkeley, the official wedding photograph, February 10, 1934. The Etta and Busby Berkeley private collection.

Roman Scandals, 1933. The Goldwyn Girls agreed on nudity, but only if they were filmed at night.

Buzz diagrams his water ballet for his apprehensive "swimmers" in *Footlight Parade*, 1933.

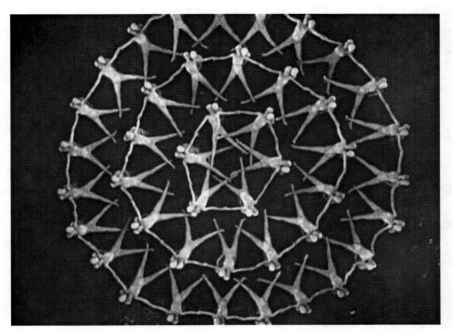

The finest of all water ballets, "By a Waterfall," from *Footlight Parade*, 1933.

Tier and set for "By a Waterfall," from *Footlight Parade*, 1933.

Above the tier, looking downward, in "By a Waterfall," from *Footlight Parade,* 1933.

Studio and director's patriotism worn on their sleeves. The thirty-second president, Franklin D. Roosevelt, reproduced in "Shanghai Lil," from *Footlight Parade,* 1933.

(Above) Magnificent
detail—top shot from
Dames, 1934.

(Left) Buzz on the make-
shift Ferris wheel directs
Ruby Keeler in "I Only
Have Eyes for You," from
Dames, 1934.

Image infinity. "Don't Say Goodnight," from *Wonder Bar*, 1934.

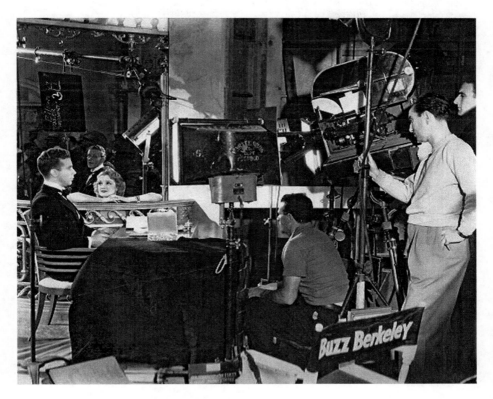

An empty monogrammed chair, Buzz, Dick Powell, and Dorothy Dare, *Gold Diggers of 1935*.

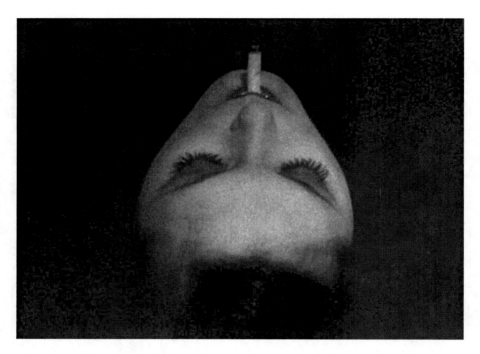

Buzz does Man Ray: "Lullaby of Broadway," from *Gold Diggers of 1935*.

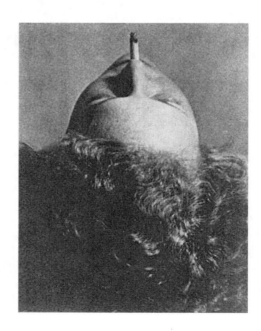

The original *Woman Smoking a Cigarette* (Man Ray, 1920). Copyright Man Ray Trust/ARS-ADAGP, The J. Paul Getty Museum, Los Angeles, California.

"Lullaby of Broadway," a nightmare musical number, and Buzz's favorite, from *Gold Diggers of 1935.*

An exploitative entrance? Buzz listens on a stretcher as William Hudson testifies that he smelled liquor on the defendant's breath the night of September 8, 1935. Acme Newspictures, Inc., 1935. New York World-Telegram and the Sun Newspaper Photographic Collection, Library of Congress.

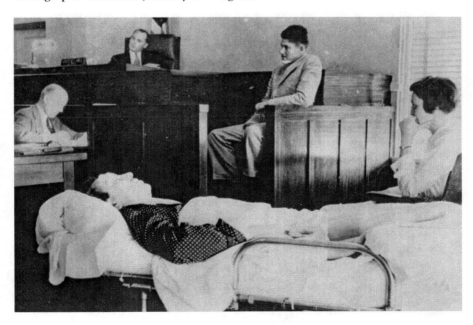

Pianos en masse as Buzz (*standing*) sets up a shot in "The Words are in My Heart," from *Gold Diggers of 1935*.

Despondency. Buzz and lawyer-to-the-stars Jerry Giesler at trial. Photofest, New York.

A Plexiglas ceiling in his makeshift frame has Buzz setting a peeping shot for *In Caliente*, 1935.

Hand holding: Buzz and Gertrude, with Jerry Giesler in court. AP WirePhoto, 1935.

Buzz's Beaux-Art mansion, 3500 West Adams Street, Los Angeles, as it looked when Secundo Guasti had it built in 1910.

Buzz and Carole Landis. Gertrude intervened and a wedding was thwarted.

Buzz directing soon-to-be Mr. and Mrs. Dick Powell in *Gold Diggers of 1937*.

The battlefield's a rocking chair. From "All's Fair in Love and War," in *Gold Diggers of 1937*. Copyright 1936, Warner Bros. Pictures, Inc., and The Vitaphone Corp.

(Above) Happy birthday. Gertrude, Buzz, Mickey Rooney, and Judy Garland. Photofest, New York.

(Left) MGM studio chief Louis B. Mayer with his employees.

Wife number three. Claire James and Buzz, circa 1942. Photofest, New York.

His favorite feature. Buzz rehearses Judy in *For Me and My Gal*, 1942.

Bananas ad infinitum. "The Lady in the Tutti Frutti Hat," from *The Gang's All Here*, 1943.

Heads on parade: the finale from *The Gang's All Here*, 1943.

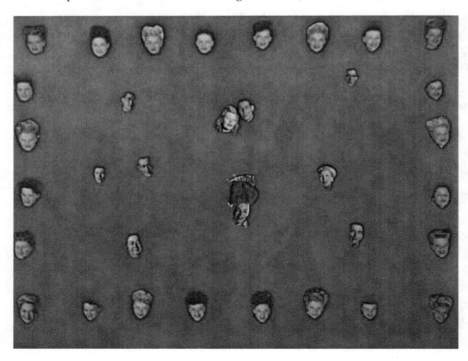

Buzz and Myra Steffens (his fourth wife). He once remarked that he had a hard time remembering all their names. This annulled union was particularly short-lived. AP WirePhoto, 1944.

Producer Sam Spiegel and "Mrs. Busby Berkeley" (Marge Pemberton), photographed in December 1948, a couple of years after Buzz's supposed divorce from her. Peter Stackpole/Time & Life Pictures/Getty Images.

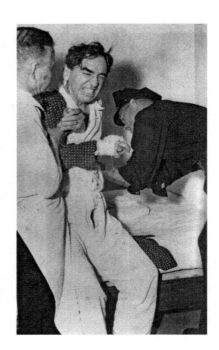

Complete emotional breakdown. Buzz
restrained after his suicide attempt,
July 17, 1946. UPI Bettmann Archive.

Ann Miller on top, while
an unheralded crew
reveals the trick behind
"I Gotta Hear That Beat"
from *Small Town Girl*,
1953.

(Above) He saved the best for last. Etta, Buzz's sixth and final wife, with her husband at the Berlin Film Festival, 1971. Erika Rabau, Berlin.

(Left) Buzz oversees a standing ovation at a 1969 film festival appearance. Warner Brothers Seven-Arts Film Festival, 1969.

Credit Etta for making Buzz's last house in Palm Desert his first real home. Author's photo, 2009.

The headstone reveals far more than its inscription.

made a pilgrimage to see the queen. Those who were in the queen's good favor (as Buzz was) received good press. They returned the favor by whispering juicy gossip in the queen's ear. The diminutive "Lolly" was uttered only by the closest of friends. To her enemies (or anyone she held in disfavor), the words written under the byline of Louella O. Parsons could have a devastating effect. Her columns could shape or decimate careers. In a country glued to the radio for news, information, and entertainment, the *Hollywood Hotel* radio show hosted by Ms. Parsons presented all three with a popularity other gossip shows couldn't match.

Buzz helmed *Hollywood Hotel,* a charming, fast-paced story based on the radio show where the establishment was used as the central gathering point of the film. The famed "Orchid Room" was created by Warner Brothers solely for the film. Working with the great actors in the Warner stable, Buzz crafted a fine musical comedy in spite of ongoing budget tightening. The thin-as-a-razor-blade story concerns itself with Ronnie Bowers (Dick Powell), a saxophone player for Benny Goodman's band, off to the West Coast for a ten-week movie contract. In the opening scene, Buzz cleverly shows the handiwork of Powell's friends in handmade posters taunting Hollywood stars ("Clark Gable beware!" "Olivia de Havilland, Your Midsummer Night's Dream is on his way!"). This sequence segues to Johnnie Davis performing exuberantly the song that would define the industry and become a huge hit, "Hooray for Hollywood." By the time Buzz got attached to the project, he had more than twenty-five motion picture assignments to his credit. His artistic technique and perfectionist temperament had completely forged; it was clear to insiders (if not the public at large) that Busby Berkeley was a chameleon among directors. Generally, when a picture fails financially, it usually is an indicator of a bad film or poor publicity; it is not necessarily reflective of the director's skill. This rang true with *Hollywood Hotel.* Buzz had repeatedly shown his employers his willingness to compromise when budgets were tight. Though there were no archly designed musical numbers in the film (save for the infectious "Hooray for Hollywood" opening), Buzz's direction was as sharp and crisp as that of any of his peers on the lot. As for Queen Louella, Buzz gave her the chance to act on camera. She wasn't photogenic, nor was she a competent actress. Her one great bon mot came at the expense of Ted Healy (playing Powell's agent). He asked Louella why he wasn't featured in her column. "I guess a guy has to bathe in champagne to get noticed," said Healy. "Just soap and water will do," snapped the queen.

Hollywood Hotel had its share of grief and scandal. Campbell Soup, which sponsored Louella Parsons's radio show, sued Warner Brothers for using the title without authorization, as did the owners of the Hollywood Hotel. Ted Healy died under mysterious circumstances a few hours after attending the film's preview. When the film returned lukewarm box-office receipts, Parsons privately remarked that Buzz Berkeley's drinking problems were to blame for *Hollywood Hotel*'s flop. Who in Hollywood wasn't aware of Buzz's drinking proclivity? Though off the record, the remark was uncharacteristic of Lolly. The name Busby Berkeley was always mentioned positively in her column. Louella kept a secret of her own, and fortunately it wasn't revealed to the public at large. Buzz and his girls were witness to a device that was firmly on the set and out of camera range. Parsons had weak kidneys, and while seated at a table, she wore rubber pants. Below the table a chamber pot waited, just in case.

On November 7, 1937, Buzz heard some news that undoubtedly affected him. Mrs. Manon von Briesen, the twenty-six-year-old widow of William von Briesen, died in a Monterey Park hospital, the fourth person injured in the car accident to perish. Five doctors were called into consultation, but they declined to go on record to reveal the cause of death. The coroner ordered an autopsy. Mrs. von Briesen had suffered concussion of the brain. She died within twenty-four hours of being stricken. Her mother, Mrs. Jeannette Daley, said her daughter had been suffering aftereffects of the accident, having alternate periods of hilarity and depression. The previous month she had asked the court to give Manon a sanity hearing. The widow von Briesen was paroled to the county psychopathic probation officer. It was a sad decline for Manon, living with the psychological and physical shrapnel of September 8, 1935. Poor Jeannette Daley, by proxy, was twice a victim of the accident. Her other daughter, Peggy, had been one of the nervous girls in the backseat.

That same month Buzz and Carole posed together for fluff pictures, and in one caption, she calls him her fiancé. A syndicated gossip column described the couple as looking like they were "running a temperature." When dining out at Ciro's or the Trocadero they were often photographed.

Near Christmas, Buzz went to LA's Calvary Cemetery for the funeral of actor Ted Healy. He, Dick Powell, studio executives Eddie Mannix and Harry Rapf, and director Charles Reisner were pallbearers. Healy was only forty-one, and he never learned that he was a father (his wife had given birth the previous week). His death was another Hollywood mystery shrouded in rumor.

A week later, the mercury that measured Buzz and Carole's temperature dropped precipitously. Now rumors announced a breakup. Suggesting teenagers in an ongoing love/hate dynamic, talk of a makeup occurred soon after the holidays. New films, *Men Are Such Fools* (with her boyfriend directing) and something about *another* Gold Diggers project kept Carole at Buzz's side. Buzz promised her on-screen time, but he invariably made promises to almost every actress at every audition.

Men Are Such Fools is both the title and final line of a blithe romantic comedy. The milieu is the advertising world rather than the nightclub, and Linda Lawrence (Priscilla Lane) is a secretary with ideas and ambition. Her boss is the squirrelly Hugh Herbert, and through easy manipulation Linda ascends the company ladder. Her boyfriend, Jimmy (Wayne Morris), is an up-and-comer himself. They marry, and he soon forces his wife to abandon the office for a domestic life. That lasts only so long: Linda leaves Jimmy (due to his sudden lack of ambition) to return to the business world. Back at the office, Linda fends off the affections of a powerful colleague, Harry Galleon (Humphrey Bogart). She eventually succumbs to his advances, and Linda plans for a divorce from Jimmy so she can marry Harry. True love is victorious at the end, however, as Jimmy and Linda reconcile, and Harry becomes the odd man out.

Men Are Such Fools was amiable and light on its feet and a picture Buzz could be proud of. His direction is assured and precise, but as the film remained firmly on terra firma, no digressions into Buzz's imaginative fancy were allowed. The interesting casting of Humphrey Bogart allowed Buzz to again work with another of Warner's higher-echelon stars. Both Bogie and Buzz felt they should be involved with higher-quality material, but they espoused the same work ethic. "Bogie was never any trouble to me at all," said Buzz. "He felt, and I agreed with him, that he should be working in better films, but whatever discontent he felt, he took out on the bosses, not on the people he was working with. As far as I know, he never refused to play a part. His credo was to keep working, and I agreed with him on that point too."

Buzz was always aware of his standing within the studio's directorial hierarchy. Despite successful attempts to the contrary, he remained pigeonholed with the chorus girl and the top shot. With barely a fortnight off from *Men Are Such Fools,* Buzz turned his attention again to creating imaginative musical numbers. His next assignment was in familiar territory. Another Gold Diggers picture was ready for the cameras, and it needed Busby Berkeley's singular talent.

Evidently Warner Brothers thought there was enough life left in the ol' gold-digging gals to make a promising revival, but good intentions don't always yield good results. The production of *Gold Diggers in Paris* began in January 1938, with Ray Enright again responsible for the book and Buzz for the dances. Warren and Dubin, a gold digger's best friends, were employed as well. Buzz called on George Barnes for his sequences while Sol Polito shot for Enright. The film's fluffy plot of mistaken identity where nightclub dancers (at the club Ballé) are thought to be members of the American Ballet is but an excuse for Buzz's inventions. His first big number, "I Wanna Go Back to Bali," is Buzz on a budget. We follow a sailor's cap as it's handed to all the musicians; then to customers, waiters, and more musicians; then to the Berkeley girls wearing flower leis and native Indonesian garb, to finally rest on Rudy Vallee's head. Buzz's camera follows him around the small set (cost cutting is quite obvious here), then onto his girls, who do their best to imitate native dancing. The company and Vallee move behind a bamboo-pole curtain to reemerge as the novelty act the Schnickelfritz Band, and there Buzz's inventiveness stops cold. As it happened so often when Buzz was confronted with the direction of specialty acts (*Stage Struck*'s the Yacht Club Boys among many others), he lost his identity in service to the act. But the belief in Hollywood was that specialty acts add value to a production, especially when it came to promotion. Vallee gets to showcase his Maurice Chevalier impression in the witty "A Stranger in Paree," and the bouncy number moves on to the bus as the full cast joins in and merrily sings its way to the hotel.

"The Latin Quarter" number follows a painter (Rudy) as he sings through his gallery and points to his paintings while Buzz quickly pans right to reveal the human subjects behind the art. The scene shifts to the Berkeley girls again in line (on an empty soundstage) and tapping to the song as Buzz shoots them in canted angles for an interesting visual effect. The number winds up again on the shoulders of the Schnickelfritz Band, and they bring up the reprise of "I Wanna Go Back to Bali." The entire company joins in, and Buzz revives the earlier image of the captain's cap when a gigantic prop of the same appears high up on the set, lowering itself to the point of enveloping everyone onstage. Rudy and actress Rosemary Lane rise from the back of the prop, smiling and singing in close-up as the number ends. The Gold Diggers series had run its course. For five years, the prurient ensembles that Busby Berkeley had elevated to filmic fantasy had tapped their last chorus line at Warner Brothers. For Buzz's part, he saw the writing on the wall. He believed his deliverance would lie in directing drama.

The Tenth Academy Awards ceremony, on March 10, 1938, was held again at the Biltmore Bowl of the Biltmore Hotel, and history repeated itself when Buzz, attending on behalf of *Varsity Show,* left empty-handed. His finale lost to Hermes Pan's "Fun House" number from *A Damsel in Distress.*

Carole Landis was in a bit of distress herself. Her bit roles for Buzz amounted to nothing, and she claimed no screen credit. A renewal of her contract was due soon, and she feared the studio would drop her. What made matters worse, Gertrude was now involved in her life. When she heard rumors that Carole was a call girl in San Francisco, she urged Buzz to drop any notion of marriage. Gertrude's opinions were tantamount to orders, and her son was pliable and receptive. The last public mention of Buzz and Carole was in the March 16, 1938, edition of the *Los Angeles Times,* when they attended a costume party at the Hawaiian Paradise Café. Soon after, things cooled off permanently. But Buzz didn't pine for Carole; she had been supplanted. During the casting of *Gold Diggers in Paris,* Buzz took notice of a beautiful young auditioner named Claire James. At only fifteen, she had been crowned Miss California and had come in second in the Miss America pageant. The director was smitten once again, and per his pattern, he hired Claire as one of the unidentified gold diggers. Flying in the face of convention, the forty-something Buzz and the teenage Claire began dating exclusively.

LA's Cocoanut Grove in the Ambassador Hotel, with its constant stream of celebrities, politicians, and potentates, was rife for spoofing. A month after *Gold Diggers in Paris* wrapped, Buzz was on to his next full directorial project. *Garden of the Moon* was the name given to the

Grove's fictional equivalent. In a setting largely confined to the night-club, it shares only a passing resemblance to *Wonder Bar,* with none of the film's extravagant musical numbers. Instead, it's a brisk, perky comedy-with-music owing to Buzz's expansive experience and talent. Johnnie Davis and Mabel Todd were both back for their fourth film with Buzz. Jerry Colonna, whose bug eyes rivaled Eddie Cantor's, and who had a singing voice that sounded like an ambulance siren simultaneously approaching and passing, had a fan in Buzz and was given more-than-ample screen time.

Pat O'Brien is John Quinn, the nail-spitting manager of the Garden. He's gruff and tough, keeping his underlings in terror with a shattering voice and a crudely rude manner. His dilemma—Rudy Vallee's bus was in an accident and he has two open weeks he needs filled. Enter up-and-coming bandleader Don Vincente (John Payne in a role Dick Powell refused that resulted in Powell's layoff by the studio) and his cast of eccentric band members.

It isn't long before Quinn and Vincente dislike each other while Toni Blake (Margaret Lindsay after Bette Davis refused the part) gets caught in the middle. Her boss is Quinn, leaving her questioning her loyalties to her boss and her new love interest.

Buzz lets loose with "The Lady on the Two Cent Stamp" and "The Girl Friend of the Whirling Dervish" numbers. In typical Berkeley fashion, he introduces the musicians in complementing cuts, left and right, closing in on Payne singing the lead. He maneuvers and spins his camera around the bandstand like a dive-bombing bird. Interesting also is Buzz's method of lighting the band members. Often they're purposely underlit, thanks to a bulb placed in each music stand. It gives a flashlight-under-the-chin look that is remarkably effective in the stark black-and-white photography.

During the filming, Buzz learned that his now-estranged Carole Landis was to be separated from the studio as well. Warner Brothers informed her on May 13 that her contract, due for renewal on June 1, would not be picked up. Understandably, she was upset. A week later Buzz again found himself the defendant in a major lawsuit.

It was one of the last days of filming *Garden of the Moon,* and John Payne was singing "Love Is Where You Find It." Buzz wanted John's performance to be lightly burlesqued. After a couple of takes, Buzz wasn't satisfied, so he demonstrated what he wanted by acting and singing the scene himself, reviving the old stage mannerisms he hadn't used in years. He gestured and smiled at the attentive Margaret Lindsay, and went down on his knees for a big finish. No one would have guessed that the animated director had withstood a bombshell that morning.

The mocking headline screamed "Busby Berkeley Named in $250,000 Love Theft Suit." Irving Wheeler, Carole Landis's husband for all of two minutes, had appeared from out of nowhere, claiming Carole had left him on account of Busby Berkeley. In his suit, Wheeler alleged that Buzz enticed and otherwise persuaded Carole Landis to transfer her affection. He was asking for $150,000 direct damages and $100,000 punitive damages. The timing of the lawsuit painted Carole Landis as the obvious provocateur. After losing her studio contract, she and Wheeler might have concocted a means of legally fleecing Berkeley. But it was not so. Carole told reporters the short story of her brief marriage: "I married Irving in 1934 when I was 15. We only lived together three weeks. Then we had an argument and I ran home to mother. I did not see him again until last fall when he called me to ask about a divorce. He said he had a friend in Nevada who could get him one quickly." She said the suit was "silly" and that for three years she had tried to find Wheeler. If and when the case went to court, she told Louella Parsons, she would testify for the dance director despite their breakup. Buzz added to the fray, barking, "I'll never pay Wheeler a penny!" He countered Wheeler's suit with a demurrer requesting the case be thrown out.

Buzz's old friend Mervyn LeRoy was producing at MGM. On the same day Irving Wheeler's lawsuit made the headlines, LeRoy wrote a letter to songwriter and (uncredited) associate producer Arthur Freed, in which, among other things, he mentioned Buzz for a new MGM movie based on L. Frank Baum's turn-of-the-century children's book, *The Wonderful Wizard of Oz*. Freed expressed interest in bringing Buzz to the studio. In later correspondence with Freed, LeRoy added this reminder: "Also I presume that you are following through on your idea of getting Buzz Berkeley to direct the musical sequences."

Buzz finished *Garden of the Moon* at the close of May 1938. There were no new musicals in his foreseeable future. The studio was getting reluctant about producing them (again). They believed the second renaissance for the musical picture given life by Busby Berkeley was coming to an end. But the pigeonholing was giving way, and they now saw more than a one-trick-pony in Buzz. In June, Louella Parsons ruffled some feathers of the Warner Brothers brass when in her column she wrote that Buzz's next picture, *Comet over Broadway,* was in for a rewrite job. If Buzz finishes in time, wrote Louella, he will go to MGM to direct *The Wizard of Oz* for Mervyn LeRoy, who wants Buzz for the intricate special numbers.

The title belies the melodramatic underpinnings of a syrupy story in *Comet over Broadway.* A small-town wife, mother, and part-time actress with the Genesis-inspired name of Eve Appleton (played stoically by Kay Francis) soon finds trouble when a visiting New York thespian woos the naïf into his motel room with implied promises of an audition. Her husband finds the couple, misunderstands the situation, and accidentally kills the actor. He's sent away for life as Eve vows to live her days raising both her daughter and the necessary funds to someday extricate her spouse. Her career eventually takes off, but not before extensive traveling forces her to leave her child in the care of a vaudeville friend, "Tim" (Minna Gombell, a live-wire actress in a role of equal parts tart and tenderness). Years later when Eve returns to the States after a successful engagement in London, she's unrecognized by her daughter (Sybil Jason). These and other messes eventually work their way through the molasses of plot to a happy, unrealistic conclusion where Eve (eschewing her career) and her daughter (who now calls Eve "Mommy") are walking together, head high, toward the prison from which husband and father finally gets released.

The maudlinism is thick in *Comet over Broadway,* undercutting its best intentions with a cloying score that permeates almost every scene. Buzz's direction, though, is assured and competent, with a reined-in flashiness (in deference to the story) that still allows for the occasional inside joke (in a scene set in a vaudeville house one can clearly hear the orchestral version of "Dames"). Minna Gombel is the film's comic relief, and her running gag of describing herself as "almost turning 40" finds a nice payoff at the end. The film was a serendipitous melding of director and subject, filled with the kind of backstage drama that the nostalgic Buzz knew well.

Kay Francis had a reputation for being difficult, but Buzz saw none of it: "I had been told by other directors that she had sometimes been tactless with co-workers and studio executives, but I saw no evidence of it on this picture. I do know she was unwilling to participate in the publicity game. That didn't interest her at all. And it seemed to me she lacked that driving ambition an actress needs in order to get the best parts in the best films." When some visitors from Kansas came on the set, Buzz and Kay staged a "show" for them. Unbeknownst to the Kansans, Buzz pretended to bawl Kay out, and she stormed off to her dressing room where she proceeded to tear up all her dresses. One visitor turned to another and said, "You see, that's what I told you about these movie people!"

In mid-August, John Farrow took over directing duties on *Comet over Broadway* for a couple of days because Buzz had to appear in court to answer Irving Wheeler's charges. From August 15 through 19, Buzz, Wheeler, and Carole Landis appeared before Judge Robert Kenny. Carole reiterated that there hadn't been any affection or consortium between her and Wheeler since September 1934. "I didn't think anyone knew I'd ever been married. I thought Irving had forgotten our marriage too. I've only seen him once since then and that was when he told me he wanted a divorce. I can't see how he figures anyone stole me from him." Carole said that Mr. Berkeley and she were good friends, but certainly not in love. Buzz concurred, describing her as a protégée and star pupil and that there was no romance between them. Judge Kenny sustained Buzz's demurrer, and once again, a court verdict favored him.

Buzz was finished with Carole Landis once and for all and took no time off in August as he began preproduction on a drama that strongly piqued him. *They Made Me a Criminal* was a remake of 1933's *The Life of Jimmy Dolan,* which starred Douglas Fairbanks Jr. in the role of an up-an-coming prizefighter who, in a case of murder and mistaken identity, is forced to go on the lam, change his name, and start a new life. John Garfield as the lead in his first starring role was on-spot casting. Comedic support was supplied by the Dead End Kids, whose recent success in *Angels with Dirty Faces* made them a hit with audiences. Gloria Dickson as the sister of one of the Kids played Garfield's love interest. Buzz loved the fact that the film wasn't a musical and that pugilism was at the story's core.

Risk-taking cinematographer James Wong Howe manned the camera, in his and Buzz's second collaboration. Howe was a simpatico fit for

the experimentalist director. Most of the outdoor shooting was scheduled for Palm Desert, 120 miles east of Los Angeles. It was assumed
that all involved knew that weather conditions in the desert would be
oppressive, but the production manager would not change his mind. At
times, the intense heat caused the film stock in the camera's sound-tight
magazine to melt. Gabriel Dell of the Dead End Kids fainted in one of
Palm Desert's many 110-degree days in the shade. It wasn't unusual for
a heat-stroke victim to succumb, and Buzz, sympathetic, often called
off production at 1:00 p.m. to the distress of his bosses. He was flooded
with memos from the front office belaboring his shooting "at a snail's
pace." To Buzz's credit, he ignored them all.

The atmosphere on the set was generally light and professional without the stresses found in the tightly wound environment of a Berkeley
musical number with one exception: the flying, biting, and annoying
gnats of Palm Desert. Buzz saw the crew that first day of location shooting with gnat nets on their faces and bodies. "What the hell are you all
made up for, Halloween or something?" asked the director. A crew member yelled that the gnats will get into your eyes and ears. Buzz wouldn't
heed advice from anyone. "You're a bunch of sissies. For God's sake who
needs a net?" The goddamned bugs drove the un-netted Buzz crazy! His
pride kept him from putting on covering that day, but he made sure to
wear top-to-bottom protection every shooting day thereafter.

One of Warner Brothers' up-and-comers was Ann Sheridan, an attractive redhead with about forty minor roles to her credit. Along with
the Dead End Kids, she, too, had made a splash in *Angels with Dirty
Faces* and was cast in Buzz's picture without dissent. She appears in
the early going as the disloyal girlfriend of Garfield's character. Keeping
things light, Ann and Buzz pulled a fast one on John Garfield. Buzz instructed his actress to kiss the leading man and "hold it until I say cut."
Impishly, Buzz decided not to say a thing. Garfield started to squirm;
they remained lip-locked. They rolled off the couch and onto the floor
and it wasn't until the crew and stars broke into infectious laughter that
Buzz mercifully yelled, "Cut!"

The boxing sequences were not preplanned to any great extent.
Buzz, as was his wont, made up his shots as he went along. This, he believed, made the scenes spontaneous and natural. In Burbank, the boxing scenes were filmed at Victory Boulevard and Buena Vista Avenue,

the site of the old Jeffries' Barn. Owned by boxing heavyweight James Jeffries, the barn was host to Thursday-night boxing matches for many years. The fight scenes made use of 250 extras. After a take, Buzz dismissed them, and they gathered outside the barn waiting for a callback when the director was ready. From a distance, a passerby mistook the situation outside of the barn and wrote a letter to the studio that was forwarded to Buzz:

> Dear Sirs:
>
> Last week I was with my real estate agent and we happened to pass by Jeffries' Barn as he was showing me some property in the vicinity. We saw a lot of Warner Brothers' trucks parked there and a crowd of people, so we stopped to see what was happening. There was a prize fight going on, and we went inside the building with the crowd and watched the fight. We thought it was wonderful and the director was such a perfectionist.
>
> We saw the extras after they were dismissed for a rest period, and they all seemed to huddle together in a conversation; and we thought they were pointing at us. We felt guilty being there and thought we might be intruding because we were outsiders, so we left. I am writing this to tell you that we are wondering how the fight came out. Who won it?

A misunderstanding to be sure, but the description of the director was quite accurate. Buzz said that the man and his real estate agent were made part of the final print without their knowledge, as both were present during an actual take.

In late September, Buzz was working on a long dramatic scene with Garfield and Gloria Dickson. It was another scorching Palm Desert day, but things had picked up, and a recent take had been progressing perfectly. Buzz, perched just below Howe's camera, stood without thinking and concentrated intently on the scene. "Cut! That was it! That was just what I wanted. Print it." James Wong Howe reluctantly spoiled Berkeley's exuberance. "Don't print it," said the cinematographer; "the last fifteen feet of that take was nothing but a shot of the back of your head."

A rough cut was screened for studio executives in October. The *Hollywood Reporter* said that several scenes were needed to boost the production values. These "fillers" consisted of inserts and footage used to bridge sequences (such as the United States map charting the character's westward journey). In a magnanimous gesture that same month, Buzz purchased 150 tickets and took his whole cast to the St. Mary's–Loyola football game.

They Made Me a Criminal was released to theaters on January 28, 1939. The film reveals a new maturation and assuredness in Buzz's direction. In addition to the superbly shot and edited boxing sequences, there are moments of pure art and wrenching emotion. In an almost unendurable ten-minute scene of suspense, Garfield and the Dead End Kids decide to swim in the town's open-air water tower. After a bit of splashing and frivolity, a nearby landowner opens his irrigation spigots, causing a dramatic reduction in the tank's water level. It goes unnoticed until it becomes too late to easily crawl out. Suddenly, the water stops its drainage, and everyone is left to tread water or drown as it now appears impossible to escape. With Garfield's help, he and the boys dive to the bottom of the tank (displaying Buzz's intriguing underwater shots) and release the valve that will drain the tank and prevent a disaster. Eventually, standing on one another's shoulders, one of the boys climbs over the top and sends down a ladder for the rest. Berkeley shot the sequence in two locations: an orange grove in Whittier and a tank on the Warner lot. The editing was timed decisively by Buzz with taut cuts and an elevating score that built the audience's dread viscerally through purely cinematic means.

Another example of the "pure cinema" that Buzz espoused is found in the scene when Garfield's character reads the newspaper that claims he died in a fiery crash. In close-up we scan the newspaper downward. When coming to the fold in the newspaper, most directors would have cut away, but not Buzz. The camera pans down and the newspaper slowly turns to reveal the next sentence below the fold, and the next as the music swells. Standing out boldly and directed impeccably, the sequence resembles the expository trickery seen in the pictures Alfred Hitchcock was making at the time.

There were two self-referential moments in *They Made Me a Criminal,* one professional, one personal. As he had done in *Comet over Broadway,* Buzz pulled a song out of his personal trunk. In the scene where Huntz Hall is up on a ladder supplying the water for Garfield's makeshift shower, the Dead End Kid whistles, then warbles, "By a waterfall, I'm calling you oo oo oo!"

It's impossible to know decisively, but interesting to speculate nonetheless, whether the film offers an oblique cinematic representation of Buzz's inner turmoil. In a scene that occurs early in the picture, Ann Sheridan and John Garfield's boxing manager (Robert Gleckler) are in a high-speed chase with the police in pursuit. Suddenly, *the left front tire* of the car explodes, leaving the driver unable to steer his careening vehicle off the road as it smashes headfirst into a tree. Was this Buzz's evidentiary proof to his accusers that accidents *can* happen this way?

Buzz regarded *They Made Me a Criminal* fondly. It was one of his favorites. It clearly shows him at a new level of self-confidence and directorial expertise. He'd been breaking free of the rigid categorization devices that defined his employ, first with *Garden of the Moon,* then *Comet over Broadway.* By the time of *They Made Me a Criminal*'s release, the contract that vaulted Busby Berkeley into the stratosphere of fame, fortune, and notoriety had run its course. In a chilly phone call from Palm Springs, Jack Warner told Buzz that his two-thousand-dollar-a-week salary would not be increased as promised, but that the contract would be extended for another year. "A contract is a contract," he told Warner. Buzz had done all manner of unpaid odds and ends and extras for his bosses with nary an iota of appreciation. The face-saving measure was to leave the contract unsigned. Around this time Buzz and manager Mike Levee had agreed that Buzz could (and should) freelance. Buzz paid Warner Brothers ten thousand dollars to close out his contract and, "in a friendly way without any hard feelings," he severed ties to the studio. Forty-eight hours later, Loew's Incorporated (parent company of MGM) signed him to work on *Broadway Serenade.* Jack Warner heard the news from Mervyn LeRoy. Warner Brothers had evidently lost faith in the golden boy whose work was so successful it single-handedly saved the studio from insolvency. To work on Leo the Lion's home turf wasn't just a phenomenal opportunity; it was Buzz's vindication.

8

Buzz's Babes

Buzz made the move to Metro-Goldwyn-Mayer with none of the grief he had suffered from Sam Goldwyn under similar circumstances. Mervyn LeRoy's May memo came to fruition with Buzz's first assignment. Bobby Connolly, Buzz's peer from Warner Brothers, had been hired to direct the musical numbers for *The Wizard of Oz* when Buzz was busy with *They Made Me a Criminal*. Arthur Freed allowed Buzz a free hand in directing the number "If I Only Had a Brain," sung by the scarecrow (Ray Bolger) to Dorothy (Judy Garland). Buzz employed reverse footage and undercranked his camera to an amusing effect. At his new studio he designed the number in much tighter physical space than his Warner Brothers soundstages allowed. The scarecrow flies, runs manically to and fro, and, like a dervish, spins merrily from fence post to fence post and back again. It was a great four-minute sample of Buzz's adaptive ability, and it allowed him the opportunity to work with the enormous three-strip Technicolor camera, its process much improved from the two-strip bleached hues of *Whoopee! Oz*'s director, Victor Fleming, was quite taken with what he saw and wrote to Buzz: "I've just run the Scarecrow number. It's simply great. You should have directed the whole picture."

The Wizard of Oz notwithstanding, Buzz's first true test at MGM was *Broadway Serenade*. The story of a musical couple (Jeanette Mac-Donald and Lew Ayres) who split when the wife's career trajectory eclipses her husband's (a similar story arc to *A Star Is Born*) was almost complete until producer and director Robert Z. Leonard decided a spectacular ending was needed. Time, unfortunately, was of the essence. Jeanette's availability was compromised with other commitments, and the picture had to wrap by early February 1939. The new director on the lot had his assignment: quickly create a ten-minute number. And so Buzz tweaked his imagination with little input on how to proceed. He followed the description in the film expressed by manager and impresario Cornelius Collier Jr. (Frank Morgan): "I'm going to treat the whole thing *impressionistically* with symbols and movement. It's never been done before." The boast sounded like Buzz's own.

He devised a surrealistic treatise on the birth, development, and maturation of a composition using Tchaikovsky's "None but the Lonely Heart" as its musical motif. Buzz contacted art director Cedric Gibbons and relayed his ideas. He needed a large set with various elevations, each level covered with black oilcloth. The cast would wear striking Benda masks (after Wladyslaw Theodor Benda), some of them meant to represent famous composers.

In the theater, the musicians play a short overture as the camera pans from stage lights to parting curtains. A shepherd in native garb is holding a shillelagh and playing an Irish flute; sheep are placed on various levels of the black-draped ersatz mountain. The camera pulls back to reveal a pianist (Tchaikovsky?) embellishing the flautist's melody. Out from the darkness steps Jeanette MacDonald as an ethereal choir sings. Buzz's camera is now fully maneuverable, swiftly panning to groups of grotesquely masked musicians—violinists, flautists, cellists, accordionists, kettle drummers, and singers. The dark lighting Buzz employs is especially effective, adding a sense of eeriness to the manic musicians. As the music, photography, and editing build to their shared climax, all illumination is removed, leaving Jeanette alone under a single spotlight. Buzz brings up another of his transitional devices, a tight shot of an Asian gong. The gong is lowered, and a new set is revealed, brightly lit and spectacular in dimension. Amid a busy stage of left and right risers—men in tuxedos and women in flowing white dresses—stands a pedestal, thirty feet high, on which Jeanette MacDonald is perched. From her vantage point she sees her true love (Lew Ayers) playing the piano. A quick nod from them both ties up a dramatic plot point from earlier on. The camera boom, high off the stage, pulls back from a final close-up of Jeanette as the orchestra stirringly crescendos, while the tall open curtains meet each other in the middle, and "The End" is superimposed on the screen.

Buzz's one-picture deal for *Broadway Serenade* paid dividends. His "audition" was lauded by studio chief Louis B. Mayer, who was quite impressed with the "None but the Lonely Heart" number. Buzz was offered a contract with MGM that stipulated his services "shall include, but not be limited to, devising, creating, staging, and/or directing dances and/or dance sequences." The contract's stated remuneration was five hundred dollars less per week than what Buzz had earned at Warner Brothers, but he wasn't concerned. He knew that Metro paid bonuses to directors who had box-office successes. He signed the contract with the foreknowledge that he'd be more than just a conceiver of dance numbers. He wanted to direct, and MGM was amenable. Soon after *Broadway Serenade* wrapped, Buzz got his first assignment: a job directing two of the biggest movie stars in the world.

Unexpectedly, Buzz received an invitation from Warner Brothers in March. The studio was pushing Ann Sheridan in what was called the "Oomph" campaign. They sent Ann's photo and measurements (five foot five, 122 pounds) to thirteen judges, Buzz among them. They were also given photos of other candidates for the "Oomph" prize: Carole Lombard, Alice Faye, and Hedy Lamarr. On March 16, the judges gathered at the Los Angeles Town House for a dinner of lobster supreme, Columbia salmon, and roasted squab. After dinner, Ann was officially crowned the Oomph Girl in a rigged election. Of course she won Buzz's vote (having worked for him in *They Made Me a Criminal*). Warner Brothers purposely used bad photographs of the other contestants (the back of their heads, according to Ann), and by default she was the most glamorous. Buzz didn't comment on what "Oomph" meant to him, but it's very likely he would have agreed with the Earl of Warwick's definition: "a feminine desirability which can be observed with pleasure, but cannot be discussed with respectability."

On April 8, the name Busby Berkeley was listed by the United States Treasury as recipient of one of the highest salaries paid in the nation for 1937. In that year his new boss, Mr. Mayer, earned $1,296,503. Directors by and large earned more than the stars they directed. At $73,750, Buzz was paid more than James Cagney and Bette Davis, but less than Joan Blondell ($84,799). The *New York Times* ran the story, whose data, most assuredly, were spread and shared throughout Hollywood. Soon after the salary exposé, it was announced that Carole Landis had finally won a divorce from the browbeaten Irving Wheeler, who, reports say, kept his mouth shut during the trial and contested nothing.

Arthur Freed saw *Babes in Arms,* the Richard Rodgers/Lorenz Hart musical on Broadway in 1937 and a year later thought it an ideal vehicle for reteaming Mickey Rooney and Judy Garland. Freed pitched his idea to Louis Mayer and told the boss the rights for the show were available for pennies. Freed wanted Buzz to direct. The story, dealing with the death of vaudeville and the staging, rehearsal, and opening night of a new production, was right up Buzz's alley. Mayer, much impressed with *Broadway Serenade,* agreed with Freed. On May 12, Buzz and cameraman Ray June begin shooting *Babes in Arms* with an initial budget of $664,000. The film had a shooting schedule of fifty days, ten for rehearsing, thirty-four for shooting, and six for recording. The first week was spent recording with music adaptor Roger Edens and rehearsing with Buzz.

Buzz started shooting the musical numbers on June 20. Unlike his daily routine at Warner Brothers, he had to contend with many interruptions from the front office. Last-minute conferences and unscheduled rehearsals were part of the MGM process. The day before shooting commenced, the studio's daily production report defined a usual morning:

9:00–10:05	Mr. Edens playing orchestration of Minstrel Number for Mr. Berkeley . . .
10:00–10:55	Mr. Berkeley, Mr. Edens, and Mr. Stoll [conductor] discuss presentation of number with Mr. Freed.
10:55–11:45	Mr. Berkeley outlining sequences in number and discussing wardrobe. . . .
11:45–12:20	Mr. Berkeley outlining requirements for number with Ray June. . . .
12:20–1:10	Mr. Freed and Mr. Berkeley discuss lyrics of "Babes in Arms"
1:10–2:10	Lunch

In 1921, vaudeville was king, and kings ruled in the palace—New York's Palace Theatre, that is. *Babes in Arms* begins at a time when motion pictures were still considered a "flash-in-the-pan." Two of its top performers, Joe and Florrie Moran (Charles Winninger and Grace Hayes) raised their children in the atmosphere where steady work for forty weeks was the ideal (summers were taken off to avoid theaters without cooling systems). Buzz paints the opening sequences in nostalgic colors, presenting an entertainment type descending into obsolescence. In a wink it's 1939, and newspaper headlines have been announcing vaudeville's death knell for years. The Moran kids, Mickey (Mickey Rooney) and Molly (Betty Jaynes) are talented performers in their own right, and along with another vaudeville babe, Patsy Barton (Judy Garland), the next generation is poised for success.

The generational divide is at the heart of *Babes in Arms*. When the vaudevillian parents decide to stage a comeback tour of sorts, local law threatens the children with life on a work farm. Mickey and all the performers' progeny defy the threat and plan to stage a show on their own. They aim to prove their worth and to prove that they're not just babes in arms. The first major number of the film, the titular song, is led by Don Brice (Douglas McPhail). In Buzz's brilliant direction, he tracks the dozens of performers through the town streets as stragglers join in carrying torches and boxes for kindling. The sequence climaxes in a spectacularly busy mise-en-scène where a center bonfire is encircled by dancers in one section of the screen, while in the periphery are smaller circles of dancers and swing-set riders. The stars (in the foreground) punctuate the final notes. Interestingly, Buzz adds no humor to the number, which plays out as a bit of juvenile anarchy. It packs a wallop, and it's the first sign that Busby Berkeley could create interestingly and effectively in a restrained environment far removed from swimming pools, top shots, and kaleidoscopic configurations.

By the 1940s, blackface sequences still hadn't come to be regarded as taboo or insulting. Minstrelsy was given new life in the Roger Edens number "Daddy Was a Minstrel Man." With placards that echoed "Goin' to Heaven on a Mule" ("Roll dem bones"), the minstrel show is treated as a fond memory of the days when dancers tapped to "Swanee River" while shuffling across the stage, tambourines slapping against their legs. Judy (as Mr. Tambo) sings "I'm Just Wild about Harry" when the entire outdoor production ends abruptly as inclement weather strikes.

Memories of *42nd Street* are found toward the end of the picture when the singer hired to perform the finale, "Baby" Rosalie Essex (kewpie-doll contortionist June Preisser), is abruptly removed from the production, leaving Patsy the understudy to take the reins. The final production number, the overtly patriotic "God's Country," is a rousing number thanks to Buzz's staging and camera setups. With lyrics that rang true to the 1939 public, "God's Country" compares Stateside values with those of warring Europe:

> Where smiles are broader,
> And Freedom's greater,
> Where every man
> Is his own dictator.

MGM's top stars also received a nod while fascists got the brush off:

> We've got no Duce
> We've got no Fuhrer.
> But we've got Gable
> And Norma Shearer.
> Hi there Yankee,
> Give out with a great big "thankee"
> You're in God's Country!

Production on *Babes in Arms* closed on July 18. The film was eleven days behind schedule and $82,000 over budget. Judy lost an entire day when she was called for retakes on *The Wizard of Oz*. Buzz scheduled the last two weeks of shooting for the "God's Country" and "Babes in Arms" numbers, and worked closely with Roger Edens while Arthur Freed consulted by phone. With time being of the essence, Judy's absence from a day of shooting the film's title number didn't dissuade Buzz from completing it. Judy's stand-in is easily identified in the number's final shot standing below Mickey and Douglas McPhail on the schoolyard slide.

"God's Country" was shot on stage 27 after five days of rehearsal. One day was needed to prerecord the number with a thirty-two-piece orchestra and twenty-five singers in the chorus. Buzz added ten men and women, nine kids, sixty-one dancers, and twenty musicians to his regular crew. He issued an unusual demand for this specific number. He wanted to make sure that every crew member who operated the camera boom had at least a fundamental musical education. Buzz reasoned that the action is so tricky that the boom needed to be moved on certain musical notes and phrases, from one angle to another as the song progressed. Buzz got his learned grips shortly thereafter. All fifteen who operated the boom had singing, piano, violin, or other musical training and could read music. Buzz handpicked each technician.

Mickey Rooney liked working for Buzz but called him "impossibly demanding." Buzz had "flashing eyes, huge expressive eyebrows, a smile that warmed everyone around him *and* had an alcoholic's perfectionism," said Mickey. He'd watch Buzz spend hours placing his camera just so. Then Buzz rehearsed his dancers for days, finally shooting take after take, each from a different angle. One day, Mickey was an eyewitness to Buzz almost falling from his high roost. Buzz wore a rope around his waist whenever he was up on the boom. Studio grip Harry Walden tossed the rope over a high strut and held the taught end with a strong grip. Buzz, camera finder in his hand, was setting up a shot. "This is going to make a wonderful shot and the camera will move back like this," said Buzz, and a moment later he fell off the boom while Harry held on for dear life. Buzz swung in midair, and the company looked up silently in disbelief. "Gosh, I'm sorry, Harry. I didn't mean to step off," yelled Buzz from up high. "Hang on Buzz," shouted Harry, "I've got ya!" He pulled the rope tight and up-righted Buzz, who returned to setting up his shot without missing a beat.

Buzz's "alcoholic's perfectionism," as Mickey called it, found the company sometimes working until 3:00 a.m. Other days, with cast and crew assembled in the early morning, Buzz wouldn't be ready until almost 6 p.m. One day, as everyone awaited Buzz's orders, the director couldn't help but overhear Mickey doing impressions of people on the lot. He did Clark Gable, Lionel Barrymore, Roger Edens, Louis B. Mayer, and himself. Buzz was so amused that he asked Mickey to try it in the picture. It worked, and the director kept a couple of impersonations in the final cut.

The night *Babes in Arms* finished shooting, the first preview of *The Wizard of Oz* was held at the Westwood Village Theatre. Buzz's scarecrow number was trimmed to the point of being unrecognizable. Different takes were used to assemble the final cut including Buzz's footage. Gone were the scarecrow's funny gyrations and gravity-defying leaps. What remained was a shortened, streamlined number with its charm intact but with Buzz's fancifulness all but eliminated.

The studio screening of *Babes in Arms* went well, and Louis B. Mayer was pleased. "Buzz, you have done a magnificent job with these two kids," said the complimentary studio boss. Three months later *Babes in Arms* premiered at Grauman's Chinese Theatre. Buzz, Mother, and his friends Etta and Leonard Judd were in attendance. Judy Garland had hoped the studio would clothe her in a mature dress by studio designer Adrian. "Too young!" said Mr. Mayer of his star. Actress and nascent gossip columnist (and budding rival to Louella Parsons) Hedda Hopper reminded Mayer that Judy wasn't too young to make $10 million for his company. At the premiere, Judy wore her designer original. Everyone associated with the film benefitted in some way. Arthur Freed was promoted as the number-one producer for MGM musicals.

Within the restrictions of a new studio, Buzz was able to adapt his singular style to numbers that flowed within the narrative, largely filmed on smaller stages. It was a challenge, but never did he complain on the record. He took his vocational changes in stride, merely stating that he was at the service of the story, and whatever it required, his workman's ethic would deliver the goods. A premature announcement had the college musical *Good News* identified as the next feature with the troika of Berkeley, Rooney, and Garland. But Louis B. Mayer had second thoughts on the project. It was just a hunch, Mayer said, but he urged Arthur Freed to go with *Strike up the Band* for their next collaboration. "It sounds so patriotic," said Mr. Mayer.

Before Buzz returned to the Judy/Mickey world, he first directed a nonmusical for the studio. The caper comedy *Fast and Furious* was actually the third in a series of similar productions. Patterned after the popular Thin Man films, *Fast Company, Fast and Loose,* and *Fast and Furious* were original screenplays by rookie writer-on-the-rise Harry Kurnitz. The casting of the married couple Joel and Garda Sloane, sellers of antique books by day and amateur sleuths the rest of the time, was never consistent. Melvyn Douglas, Florence Rice, Robert Montgomery, and Rosalind Russell played the lead roles in the previous two films. Urbane Franchot Tone and sharp-tongued Ann Sothern (who had a bit part in Buzz's "Shanghai Lil") played the bickering twosome on a murder case concurrent with a national bathing-beauty contest being staged at their hotel. Buzz's love, Claire James, the almost–Miss America, was (type)cast in a small role as Miss Grand Rapids.

Buzz shot the pageant scenes at the Rainbow Pier in Long Beach, California. According to reports, the pier was always crowded with the local fishermen and other onlookers hoping to get a glimpse of the beautiful extras (dressed in swimsuit and sash). With all the minutiae a director has to deal with in the production of a feature film, the last thing he needs is interference from the local police. Buzz's production crew was almost served a summons for "staging a contest or parade without suitable permit." Reminiscent of the boxing match incident from *They Made Me a Criminal,* here was Buzz's second picture where filming fiction was construed as recording reality. Buzz explained the situation to the police, and all was copacetic.

One tension-filled scene worth noting pins Joel and Garda in a room below the pageant stage. Someone above sets the stage elevator descending, leaving the couple in danger of being crushed. Buzz, editing the scene for maximum suspense, lets the couple squirm and scream until Joel cleverly shorts out the motor, stopping the stage elevator an instant before tragedy strikes. All in all, *Fast and Furious* is light and breezy, a yeoman's job from Buzz, who found the film "a joy to direct." Shot from August to September, it was released to theaters a month later.

Gertrude liked Claire James. She might not have objected to the age difference if Buzz avoided matrimony altogether. A pattern supported by years of reinforcement was getting the better of Buzz. He viewed his previous marriages with the kind of limited dissatisfaction that a shrug of the shoulders illustrates precisely. He had a dipsomaniacal bent, a job with the greatest pressures in the world, and a high-strung personality. Buzz just didn't have the time, maturity, or emotional stability to sustain a lifetime betrothal. For a relationship begun in the waning Warner Brothers years, it was a nice surprise for both Berkeleys that Claire and Buzz remained committed. One only had to see the couple in public to understand Walter Winchell's comment, in his column of October 17, 1939, that Buzz and Claire James were "in a coma." Through it all, Louella Parsons remained on friendly terms with Buzz despite the fact that *Hollywood Hotel* was not a hit at the box office. Things were said at the time, possibly misunderstood, but over the years an ongoing discourse between the two allowed Louella to remain Buzz's confidante. That same month, in an announcement clearer than Winchell's, she said that Buzz and Claire "are getting ready to announce the date."

Buzz liked to work with the same people from film to film. In the halcyon days at Warner Brothers, he brought his core Berkeley girls to each new project and worked with the same technical staff. He asked his bosses if he could keep the same crew for his next assignment, and they agreed. In a nice gesture, Buzz ingratiated himself with his new family when, at the conclusion of *Fast and Furious,* he personally handed a printed invitation to soundmen, grips, electricians, and cameraman to join him on his next film. They didn't forget, and when the film wrapped, they gave a party in Buzz's honor. The invitation Buzz received was designed by the crew to look similar to the one he gave them.

Buzz, a pioneer in more than monorails and revolving stages, was somehow credited for having been the first person in motion pictures to employ understudies that wound up in a film's final release. Nobody made reference to the conclusion of the "Babes in Arms" number (with the substitute Judy) when actress Nada Reynolds saw her name in print. Her role was "to take the place of players" in that film. It was Buzz who kept Nada on call, and in the tradition of the Broadway understudy (to say nothing of the major plot point of *42nd Street*), Buzz evidently became a pioneer filming the unknown Miss Reynolds in three scenes.

It's best to blame love for the foolishness that inspired Buzz to a take out a full-page ad in the *New York World-Telegram* of November 8. In a small island in a sea of white space was written, "It's been a lovely day here in the USA." That's all. Maybe the impetus was the news of an upcoming contract renewal. Whatever the reason behind paying the outrageous cost of an essentially blank newspaper page, Buzz, within the week, was awarded a one-year extension to his contract at an improved salary of $1,875 a week. On the day after Christmas, Buzz was to report to work on a new picture: a homespun comedy with maudlin overtones. Starring would be a friend from the past who, for professional reasons, had once taken sides against him. But as with Louella, Buzz held no grudge, even when he learned the lead role in his new film, *Forty Little Mothers,* would go to Eddie Cantor.

While in New York, Eddie and his wife, Ida, saw a foreign movie they liked. Eddie asked MGM if they could get the story for him. The film was *Le Mioche,* a 1936 French release about a schoolteacher who finds an abandoned baby and raises it as his own. He takes the baby with him to his new job, a teacher at an all-girls' school. The students at first don't like him and try to sabotage his career at the school by blackmailing him with the baby (whose presence is forbidden by strict rule).

Eventually the girls change their feelings as maternal instincts awaken, and they become a champion of the teacher and collective mother to the little infant.

The casting for the baby was not as easy as looking through a studio's extras list. There was never a formal announcement sent to agents with stage-mother clients. The studio used America's highly read gossip columns as their forum. MGM sent out word that a baby of a certain age was needed, and columnists like Louella Parsons obliged. Pictures were sent from all locations to Culver City. Buzz studied them and became deadlocked in decision. He could cast the greatest chorus lines since Ziegfeld, but was totally stymied by cute baby pictures. The pile eventually whittled down to two hundred babes-in-arms. They were interviewed, and one-tenth were professionally photographed. Six got a "screen test." Wallace Beery, whose second daughter had been recently adopted, submitted her baby picture and was rejected. Then, a stroke of luck: cute twin babies were found. Perfect! When one's sick, cranky, or in need of a wardrobe change, an identical spare is waiting in the wings. Barbara and Beverly Quintanilla, eight months old, naturals in front of the camera, with non-colicky temperaments, won the role. Who's who? Don't ask their mother, who confessed to barely being able to tell them apart. Who cares? We'll call 'em Baby A and Baby B if necessary. Buzz and producer Harry Rapf nodded in agreement. The twins were signed at one hundred dollars a week (more than the Berkeley girls who had soaked and suffered in "By a Waterfall"). Eventually things sorted out with Barbara being the lead thespian, and Beverly as her stand-in and subject for studio photographs. A doll was used in the place of the babies when Buzz set his shot with the lights and camera.

On January 19, 1940, the scenes with Eddie and "Chum" (baby Quintanilla's name in the film) were shot shortly after Eddie passed out cigars at the studio. This was the day he became a grandfather for the first time. His daughter had a girl.

In between takes that day, Eddie discussed a Broadway collaboration with Buzz for a new musical to be ready in the spring. Buzz liked the idea, contacted the studio, and asked for a leave of absence. He was denied. Advanced scheduling made it impossible to release him anytime in the early months of 1940.

One of the forty little mothers wore her hair in an interesting fashion that caught Buzz's attention. Constance Keane combed her blond hair so it rested right alongside her eye in a peek-a-boo style. Buzz liked it and encouraged her to keep it that way as it afforded a bit of variety from the other girls. She kept the coiffure and changed her name the next year to Veronica Lake.

Production ended on *Forty Little Mothers* on February 23. When looking back on the project, Buzz said that he just didn't want to do the film. He thought the public wouldn't buy Eddie Cantor in a straight role. The script didn't call for Eddie to roll his eyes after a punch line. Nonetheless, the results were admirable. Admittedly, there was an overall maudlin sheen to the film, and Buzz was guilty of too many close-ups of the cute Quintanilla babies, but the ending, where Eddie is forced to return Chum to its mother, was quite moving. The closing sequence featuring Eddie reprising "Little Curly Hair in a High Chair" with support from the college staff leads to a funny final shot of the girls' rowing team. At the head of the boat, holding a pint-sized megaphone, is baby Quintanilla, acting the role of the littlest coxswain.

The box office for *Forty Little Mothers* was tepid, somewhat confirming Buzz's initial forecast. *Variety,* in slamming both writer and director, said the film suffered from "dated scripting and erratic direction."

Strike up the Band, the patriotic title that Louis Mayer liked, wasn't a sequel to *Babes in Arms,* though the principals were the same. There were Judy, Mickey, a new story, old and new songs, and Buzz Berkeley with, hopefully, another miracle up his sleeve. And Buzz doesn't disappoint in the strikingly staged musical numbers. The film fails him in the book, where story resolutions are overly drawn out, with one patience-testing sequence that could have benefited from an editor's scissors.

Mickey, a drummer in a dreary high school band, dreams of his own orchestra. Sharing his dream is Judy. At her house one evening, Mickey envisions the orchestra by arranging pieces of fruit on her dining room table. Buzz defers to the special-effects department at Metro, who make the fruit come alive using stop-motion photography under the direction of new kid George Pal. A bunch of grapes forms the conductor's head, grapefruit halves are kettle drums, a sliced pineapple is an upright bass, and chocolate-cake slivers double as pianos. It's a great, crowd-pleasing effect underscored with one of Roger Edens and Arthur Freed's signature songs, "Our Love Affair."

At the Riverwood High School dance, Mickey leads his former band members (now a dance band) into a Buzz number of kinetic excitement, Roger Edens's "Do the La Conga." With the pulsating rhythms of the Caribbean, "La Conga" is one of the punchiest, audience-involving musical numbers of his career. One-two-three-kick, one-two-three-shift drives the conga beat, moving first to Judy and the band members beating bongo drums and shaking maracas, then to a Berkeley specialty: dancers on a mass scale. The second permutation, enhanced by tight editing on the beat, has Buzz filming at Dutch angles, left then right, then repeated in perfect symmetry as the number builds to a climaxed countdown of "One . . . Two . . . Three . . . BOOM." The excitement doesn't wane when Buzz shifts to the large ensemble moving in and out of line formations while his gliding camera effortlessly slides across the floor. In the third segment, Mickey and Judy conga their way through a gauntlet of clapping hands (another variation on a tried and tested Buzz trick) to an infectious dance for two. Surrounded by the whole gang, Mickey and Judy bounce the conga steps off each other while Buzz films them at floor level (perhaps to give the impression of equal height between the two). It's a comedic dance, both pretending to step on each other's toes while the driving beat keeps the momentum pulsating. A final ensemble snakelike formation and another Buzz trademark: two lines of conga dancers facing each other, the camera pulling far back to reveal the setup, as a crouching Mickey and Judy move quickly into close-up, shaking and smiling, looking directly into the camera singing, "CONGAAAAAAAAAA . . . . . . BOOM!"

Jazz king and orchestra leader Paul Whiteman soon becomes the center of attention when Mickey learns of a contest for the best high school band. It's Whiteman who's overseeing the contest, set for radio broadcast live from Chicago. June Preisser plays the new rich girl in town with eyes for Mickey. The story has Mickey thickheaded about romance, unable to translate Judy's unsubtle intentions in favor of June and her blithely bouncing blond hair. While Mickey succumbs, library-worker Judy broods. In sad reflection, she sings how she "ain't got nobody and nobody's got me." It's directed simply and empathetically by Buzz, who saves his final shot for a touching visual metaphor. At a high angle above an empty set, he emphasizes the emptiness of Judy's life as she exits the far end of the frame, turning the lights out while double doors slowly close behind her.

A seemingly endless fifteen-minute digression is awarded the "Nell of New Rochelle" sequence in *Strike up the Band*. A strained attempt at humor finds the cast playing Gay Nineties archetypes in the broad manner of the day, featuring a villain with a Simon Legree laugh (who provides overt asides to the audience), and a pitiful, poor heroine being taken advantage of. Looking more like a pastiche of the silent cinema (especially Chaplin's *The Gold Rush* in the third act), "Nell of New Rochelle" purposely leaves no cliché untouched. Despite the disruption of the film's momentum, there is some enlivenment in June Preisser's armless acrobatics where she somersaults without using her hands.

The "Drummer Boy" number affords Mickey his best turn hitting the skins and playing the vibraphone, and Buzz doesn't dampen the mood. Mickey's exuberance and rhythm on the floor tom, snare, and cymbals revealed a real lifelong passion that translated well in the printed take.

The plot machinations give Mickey and his band the whipsaw effect; first he's close to getting to Chicago and Paul Whiteman's contest, then a sick friend needs the money for an operation, and finally the contribution of a swell charters a train for the band all the way to the Windy City. The bombast is saved for last, and Buzz kicks his film into high gear.

A "battle of the bands" takes place (the winner is all but foretold), and Mickey, holding a baton half his size, gets to lead the full orchestra of all the competitors while the nation and the folks at home witness the proceedings by radio. Buzz arranges his musicians in complementary rows, shooting multiple pianos, harps, woodwinds, and brass with his single-file style, cutting in the camera, each shot defined and executed. First it's the booming "Strike up the Band" featuring a parade of faces and ensemble choreography where the men and women maneuver from opposite screen space to collect in the center. The welcomed reprise of "Do the La Conga" follows without missing a beat, and this time the abbreviated conga line is led by June Preisser, who (without much provocation apparently) doesn't exit until she performs a few more weightless tumblings. The scene shifts abruptly. "Our Love Affair" is refrained, this time introduced by four harps (recalling the human harps of "Spin a Little Web of Dreams"). It's very nicely staged by Buzz as Mickey and Judy sing alone under an imitation tree, supported by the background vocals of the supine cast spread among the leads. "The Drummer Boy"

takes off next, Mickey playing with vibrancy. His bass drum becomes
the transitional point to the final staging of the title number. Band members are facing each other separated by a clear runway. Buzz's camera
moves swiftly between the players as drum majorette June comes into
and out of view. Judy and Mickey (in the navy's dress whites) sing the
final notes, a flag is raised, our two stars are superimposed over Old
Glory, and "Columbia, the Gem of the Ocean" plays proudly as the
screen goes black.

The fruit coming to life in "Our Love Affair" might've been cut
and formed by the special-effects folks, but it was a new director from
Broadway who suggested the idea to Buzz. Vincente Minnelli was invited
to Hollywood by Arthur Freed. Buzz was rehearsing "Our Love Affair"
on stage 27 with Arthur in attendance. Arthur was notified by his secretary that Vincente was at the studio. Up until now, Minnelli had been
spending his days learning film technique, and spending lunches with
S. J. Perelman, Dorothy Parker, and Lillian Hellman. Arthur told Vincente that Buzz was having difficulty coming up with an idea for "Our
Love Affair." He asked Vincente to go to Buzz's set and be "inspired."
Buzz played the song back to Minnelli. A memory was ignited. He had
once seen a *Life* magazine article where pieces of fruit come to life as
musicians. He described the various roles for the pineapple, grapefruit,
and grapes. Buzz loved the idea and had it storyboarded and shot by
MGM's special effects crew.

Buzz worked well with Roger Edens. As a composer, arranger, and
producer, Edens was intimately involved in the studio's musical films and
was well liked by Arthur Freed and Louis Mayer. He gave Buzz credit
for the wonderful job he did for his song "Nobody." He admired the
way Buzz ended the number with the high camera shot. In a compliment
that sounded a bit backhanded, Edens said: "You had to watch Berkeley.
He was such a superb technician that a number could get totally lost in
images."

Buzz wanted to make "Do the La Conga" huge. He had taken Roger
Edens's arrangement and planned to film the number in every conceivable camera angle. For five days, Buzz and crew rehearsed. Buzz wanted
it shot complete, no breaks, in one take. Every camera movement was defined. Maracas, drums, and trumpets were photographed to be inserted
later. On the day of the shoot, Roger Edens found the set as tense as a

Broadway opening. Front office and other studio personnel were there to watch the filming. Everyone was keyed up, and great performances resulted. "Even now it has an unforgettable something extra about it," said Edens.

In September, Buzz was asked to lend his expertise to the finale of *Bitter Sweet,* a hybrid musical drama based on the play by Noel Coward. The story of a ne'er-do-well composer/singer (Nelson Eddy) and his talented operatic wife (Jeanette MacDonald) climaxes with the posthumous presentation of his operetta *Zigeuner* (The Gypsy). Buzz's complicated boom setups required so much rehearsal time that the film went over budget. Jeanette MacDonald, worn out following Buzz's orders, called in sick just as the number was finishing, citing "nervous indigestion." "I had to move down an incline," she said, "never watching where I put my feet, stopping at intervals for the camera to catch up with me . . . not stumbling or tripping—it was quite a steep slope—never getting out of focus with the camera, and singing all the while as though I had nothing else on my mind." Eventually Buzz placed blocks on the incline to help his star, but she occasionally missed them. The finished number, with its visually aligned dancers, fluid camera movements, and serenading violins bears Buzz's stamp, though he received no credit for the biggest number in the film.

After *Strike Up the Band,* MGM took advantage of Buzz's propensity for light comedy, so *Blonde Inspiration,* a marginal property with a second-tiered cast and a third-rate script, was his next assignment in that vein. A neophyte writer, Johnny Briggs (John Shelton, a Buzz alum in uncredited roles in *The Go Getter* and *The Singing Marine*), heads to the big city and gets involved with a pulp publisher of weekly western stories. Headed by Phil Hendricks (Albert Dekker) and his assistant "Bittsy" Conway (Charles Butterworth), he winds up ghostwriting the entire magazine when the usual writer, "Dusty" King (a funny lush played by Donald Meek), is away getting drunk at the local Turkish bath. Johnny is outraged that his byline wasn't used, so with the help of Angie (Virginia Grey, a former Berkeley/Goldwyn girl), he lands a publishing contract where his name is his own once again.

Blonde Inspiration died on the vine with so-so business in its February 1941 release. In fairness to Buzz, he wrung out as much humor as he could from the arid screenplay. The performances, especially from

Albert Dekker, are fine, and Virginia Grey sparkles in her close-ups. An incongruity nobody seemed to question was why the title of a film starring the brunette Miss Grey contained the word "Blonde." No matter, at seventy-two minutes, *Blonde Inspiration* doesn't overstay its welcome, but it's diluted Busby Berkeley by any measure.

Buzz's career path crossed again with Flo Ziegfeld in MGM's lush production of *Ziegfeld Girl,* a sequel of sorts to the best-picture Oscar winner *The Great Ziegfeld.* The story this time concentrated on three hopefuls (Judy Garland, Hedy Lamarr, and Lana Turner) who pursue their dream of one day walking down an ornate staircase as a Ziegfeld girl. Producer Pandro S. Berman didn't think twice about assigning Buzz to dance-direct the project. Who at the studio didn't know of his Broadway background and innate flair for spectacle? The first big number, the haunting "You Stepped out of a Dream," was given the Ziegfeldian treatment complete with girls in wildly elaborate costumes with accoutrements that hung from their heads, waists, and arms. Buzz, airborne again, was setting up a shot with his costumed dancers as they stood on different levels of a tall, winding set. At the very top stood one Berkeley girl wearing large papier-mâché balls affixed to her head and body. Buzz wanted her repositioned, and without thinking yelled out to all on the set, "Will the girl with the balls please step down two steps?" The cast broke into hysterics. When Buzz realized how it sounded, he enjoyed a good laugh at his own expense. The number, as Buzz filmed it, gives one a sense of what an audience might have experienced watching a Ziegfeld production in the 1920s. Music, singing, and rows of beautiful girls in extraordinary costumes elegantly descend the impossibly winding staircases of a production designer's imagination. It's all done with a surety of purpose as Buzz lovingly follows one girl after another while singer and actor Tony Martin belts out the vocals. The number's final shot is a real stunner as the camera pulls back in awe, revealing Martin flanked by Hedy Lamarr and Lana Turner, all dwarfed by the magnificence of the set décor. The take, as finally filmed, bore no resemblance to the rehearsed version. Buzz just came to the set one day after having a dream the night before, and the number was retooled to the specifications of his nocturnal imagination.

The "Caribbean Love Song" has Tony taking the lead vocal, singing to a stately, emotionless Hedy Lamarr. Soon the set magically transforms from a tranquil sea view to the Ziegfeld girls in underwater-themed costumes (each afforded its own bit of screen immortality). The number segues into a flamenco dance by the specialty team of Antonio and Rosario. Without missing a beat, the dancing ends, and the "Minnie from Trinidad" number begins with Judy Garland dressed in tropical garb in a faux Central American setting. Buzz really lets loose at the end of the number when Judy takes a seat in a large round basket while men holding ten-foot bamboo poles circle the star and lift her with the sticks, pointing them heavenward and back down again, and back up even higher. All the while, Buzz's restless camera is rapidly encroaching and retreating, and one could guess that the whole dizzying sequence must have terrified Judy.

The final numbers sung as a medley, "You Never Looked So Beautiful Before," "Ziegfeld Girls," and "You Gotta Pull Strings," nicely encapsulate the visual splendor of the Ziegfeld Follies with a montage of dance sequences of earlier times. The closing shot of a monstrous revolving wedding-cake staircase, decked out at every level with dancers, singers, and candelabra with Judy at the very top, reveals the perfect blending of two show business legends, each beloved for his own unique and spectacular vision: Florenz Ziegfeld and Busby Berkeley. The pressure or the strain or both worked to Buzz's detriment. When *Ziegfeld Girl* wrapped, he quickly checked into St. Vincent Medical Center to be treated for a painful case of piles.

Arthur Freed ended 1940 on an optimistic note when it was announced that Shirley Temple's debut film at MGM would be *Babes on Broadway*, costarring Judy and Mickey with Buzz directing. He divulged that one number would be a Topsy and Eva duet (recalling Buzz's involvement with the Duncan sisters in the early 1930s) with Judy as Topsy and Shirley as Eva. Shirley's mother, according to the agreement, would let MGM select stories and have the final word on casting. The contract, according to Louella Parsons in her column of December 31, 1940, hadn't been officially signed.

Warner Brothers owned the rights to the original George and Ira Gershwin Broadway show *Lady, Be Good!* In October 1940, MGM purchased the rights from Warner Brothers (who, as all of Hollywood knew, curtailed their musical output). Two songs from the original were kept ("Lady Be Good" and "Fascinating Rhythm"), and new songs were composed to complement a total rewrite of the story. Buzz was set to direct, but a nasty rumor arose that the contracted stars of the picture (Eleanor Powell and Ann Sothern) were against it and had complained to studio chiefs. If true, how could Powell's insistence be taken seriously? She had never worked in a Busby Berkeley picture before. Ann Sothern, however, a Goldwyn Girl from as far back as *Whoopee!* and the lead in *Fast and Furious,* could have grounds for her feelings (though there's no evidence that she and Buzz ever had a row). It's assumed that Buzz treated her no differently than any other star, yet it is telling that Buzz had this kind of push-back from talent just two years into his contract. This neither slowed nor dissuaded Buzz, who was eventually signed to handle the musical numbers alone, leaving the heavy directorial lifting to Norman Z. McLeod.

The new story of the on-again, off-again romance of a Tin Pan Alley songwriting team (Ann Sothern and Robert Young) and their rise to the top contained many opportunities for Berkeley-style numbers. The title song is performed a couple of times, most interestingly in a Buzz-devised montage where "Lady Be Good" is born, written, published, played, and sold. Soon phonograph records are made, the song is transposed to other keys and styles, and orchestra arrangements are written, all coinciding with its ascent to the top of the hit parade.

"The Last Time I Saw Paris" is a beautiful number tinged with sweet nostalgia by Oscar Hammerstein II and Jerome Kern. The Nazi occupation of France spurred Hammerstein to compose his ode to the city he loved. He doesn't hide his displeasure with the country's occupiers in the closing lines:

The last time I saw Paris, her heart was young and gay.
No matter how they change her, I'll remember her that way.

With respect and simplicity, Buzz photographed Ann Sothern singing the number in various medium shots. The reprise had Buzz superimposing footage of Paris with its street cafés, Eiffel Tower, and gendarmes into a moving testament that struck an emotional chord in audiences.

Eleanor Powell, the tap-dancing queen of the MGM lot in 1941, gets upstaged by a talented little dog named Buttons in their number together of the title song. The studio had tested several dogs, but none could perform the required movements on camera with any consistency. Powell made it her goal to find a suitable pooch, and as luck had it, a prop man on the set owned one who was receptive to instruction. Powell trained the dog herself, repeating steps, leg raises, and turns until Buttons was proficient enough to warrant a Buzz Berkeley take. The result was absolutely delightful. Eleanor taps around the living room while Buttons follows her lead, walking in and out from between her legs. Buttons stands on his points as Eleanor spins an arched leg around his head. She makes hoops out of her arms, and Buttons leaps through, never missing his mark. It's a terrific little number carried off with the apparent ease that only time-intensive rehearsals can produce.

"Fascinating Rhythm" is one of the great numbers in Buzz's MGM career. Split into three distinctive "movements," the number builds to a dance/music spectacle with the indelible mark of Buzz's creativity. The first movement features orchestra members in silhouette, flanking singer Connie Russell as she handles the lead. With a great effect that takes the shadows of the Berry Brothers (a talented dance trio) and makes them gigantic, the movement then shifts to the middle passage as the trio displays their intricate dance acrobatics. As they dance offstage, the action shifts to the third movement.

The final section of "Fascinating Rhythm" begins with a close-up of a pianist playing boogie-woogie runs up and down the keyboard. Cut to the tap shoes of Eleanor Powell as she dances across the stage, curtains opening to reveal a different pianist. The tall curtains swirl behind her, opening to a different piano, then another, as Powell continues her tap in a disorienting setting. It looks as if she is straddling three or more revolving sets, all turning in counterpoint to a great effect. How the trick was achieved is seen in the footage shot by a camera high up on the set that recorded the take in progress. The stage was made up of eight rectangular blocks, a piano on each one. As Powell dances across the stage, a stagehand using a movable cart (called a "mule") pulls a section away as soon as she moves to the next rectangle. Buzz is seen on the floor walking beside the camera as it's recording Powell's dance steps. Once all the rectangles are removed, the curtains open to reveal the final set. Buzz, still astride the boom, runs backward as the camera is raised to a new position.

The curtains part, and Powell finishes her number accompanied by one hundred tuxedoed male dancers, each sporting a black cane. They surround her as she spins under a spotlight. Then two rows of dancers, each facing the other, provide the "lift" as Powell is thrown like a pendulum nine separate times. She lands on her feet, projects a wide smile for her close-up as black canes complete the image, forming a circle around Powell's head and shoulders.

The entire "Fascinating Rhythm" number was approved with a budget of $81,000 by Arthur Freed. He was not about to give Buzz carte blanche when it came to expenditures. In discussing "Fascinating Rhythm," Buzz bandied a number of ideas before receiving an ultimatum from Freed: "You've got three days to rehearse and one day to shoot." From 9 a.m. to 10 p.m., Buzz worked on the number. At the thirteen-hour mark, cinematographer George Folsey was replaced with Oliver T. Marsh (he filmed *Broadway Serenade*) as shooting continued. As was his penchant when in creative mode, Buzz lost all track of time. By 2:30 a.m., the crew had had enough. Fortunately the final take met with Buzz's expectations, and he called it a wrap as the stagehands walked off the set.

"The Last Time I Saw Paris" won the Oscar as best song, but the selection was tainted a bit. Tony Martin recorded it in 1940, and it became a big hit. For *Lady, Be Good!* MGM bought the rights to use the song, but the fact remained that it was not written specifically for the film, and its selection was the subject of some controversy.

Eleanor Powell worked with Buzz on this film only, despite the admiration each held for the other (making the earlier report that she didn't want to work with Buzz somewhat dubious). When the picture previewed, she thanked her dance director for making her look good. "Eleanor was by far the finest female dancer we ever had in films, and a very hard-working perfectionist. . . . I've known very few women that talented and that gracious," said Buzz.

The next Berkeley/Rooney/Garland collaboration, *Babes on Broadway,* is the least of the three, built upon a more somber story line with diversions to overseas alliances and the stage stars of yesteryear. Buzz regrettably turns to minstrelsy in the final act, but it's saved from distastefulness through the exuberance of the direction and score.

"The Three Balls of Fire" are Rooney, Ray McDonald, and Richard Quine. Performing their slick dance steps for tips in a small restaurant, they're spotted by a talent scout, Jonesy (Fay Bainter), who might have a job for them. While celebrating their luck at a restaurant, Mickey meets Judy when he hears her sobbing at another booth. It's a meet-cute moment, purposeful in moving the story onto a different trajectory. She takes Mickey up to the apartment she shares with her piano-teacher father. The setting is quaint, realistic, and relatable for 1941, and when the two sing and dance to the delightful "How About You," it's Buzz Berkeley's manipulation of the camera and his stars within a cramped environment that reveals a mastery of ingenuity with limited space. All the furniture in the apartment is fodder for Buzz. He makes the number captivating when the two principals dance a soft-shoe together on a small, round table.

The big break didn't materialize, extinguishing the hopes of the Three Balls of Fire. Undaunted, Mickey devises a block party as a fundraiser to send needy kids to the country. While setting up initial rehearsals in a nearby gymnasium, another uniquely Buzz Berkeley moment in the Billy Barty vein occurs. Out of nowhere, unannounced and uncredited, a small boy of about four or five walks determinedly into view, taking a seat on the piano bench. Without so much as a hint of emotion, the prodigy adeptly plays Beethoven's Romance no. 2 in G Major, op. 40. After a few bars, he jumps off the bench, takes a few steps, turns, scowls, and walks out.

"Hoe Down" is another Buzz number pretending to be a rehearsal that's given the royal treatment. It's a square dance on the big scale with lively high-stepping. Guys in overalls and girls in farm dresses are paired off and rearranged in foursomes and in chorus lines, while Mickey sports some of his goofiest grins to the camera. Ray McDonald solos in the center, followed by another Berkeley specialty: the use of repeating props. For "Hoe Down," sections of white fence are used for their visual appeal. They part to introduce four cast members playing two made-up horses that wind up on two feet dancing with each other. The rousing "Hoe Down" concludes with a nice visual capturing Mickey and Judy in the center of the fences, pulling back as each piece is stacked behind another.

The block party is soon transformed into a short-wave broadcast where twenty refugees get to speak to their loved ones back in London. "Chin Up, Cheerio, Carry On" is reminiscent of Buzz's sensitive treatment of "The Last Time I Saw Paris." Sung by Judy and the refugees, Buzz superimposes images of England over the tearing faces of the youngsters. It's a diversion, of course, the sequence having no bearing on the balance of the film, but it works as a propagandistic acknowledgment of our battle-weary allies.

Mickey and the gang, thanks to Jonesy's help, are given a decrepit theater to refurbish, where they hope to perform in front of Broadway producer Thornton Reed (James Gleason). Some of the greats in history once performed at the theater, and in the film's second major diversion, Mickey and Judy don costumes and accents first as Cyrano, then as such luminaries as Harry Lauder, Blanche Ring, Sarah Bernhardt, and George M. Cohan. It's reverential nostalgia, not nearly as odious as "Nell of New Rochelle" in *Strike up the Band*.

The first number in the spruced-up theater, "Bombshell from Brazil," has Mickey in Carmen Miranda mode, dressed ostentatiously like the South American singer. It was an interesting choice, considering Miranda at the time was under contract at rival 20th Century Fox. Mickey sells the impersonation, accurately mimicking the "chika-chika-boom" style for which Miranda was making her name.

Eventually the cast wins over the crusty producer, and "Babes on Broadway" is presented at the "Amsterdam Theatre" (in this case the gargantuan set used in *Ziegfeld Girl* with its circular flowing curtains). It's blackface on an MGM budget with top hats, tails, and tambourines. Judy shuffles in as "Mr. Tambo," and Mickey is "Mr. Bones." Captured in spotlight is Ray McDonald's "Rufus Rastus Jefferson Davis Brown" tapping to "By the Light of the Silvery Moon." Judy goes into "Franklin D. Roosevelt Jones," and Buzz sets up a beautiful high shot where Judy is spot-lit in the center of the frame surrounded by the moving shadows of the other dancers. Mickey does an admirable job on the banjo to Stephen Foster's "Swanee River." The number increases in intensity before segueing to "Waiting for the Robert E. Lee," the liveliest number of the group. The dancing is rapid and athletic, and the orchestra blasts the toe-tapper as Buzz shifts our viewpoints from the stage to the rafters. A final "wave effect" as the minstrels remove their top hats and rest on one knee yields to the title song. Judy and Mickey, arm in arm and remarkably cleaned of their burnt cork, join with cast mates Anne Rooney, Virginia Weidler, Ray McDonald, and Richard Quine in a final march to the camera. Mickey pecks Judy's cheek, and the smiles on all are brimming wide as the picture ends.

The film previewed in Glendale, California, and to Roger Edens's chagrin the minstrel number unexpectedly fell completely flat. Why didn't it work? Was Buzz to blame? Edens and Arthur Freed came to the realization that there was no establishing shot showing Mickey and Judy applying the burnt cork, hence nobody knew it was them. A retake was ordered, shot, and shoehorned into the film, and Roger Edens learned a lesson on the basic nature of motion pictures and their audiences—don't assume anything. Lyricist Oscar Hammerstein was so moved by Buzz's work that he wrote to Arthur Freed: "I think Buzz shot the picture superbly and without straining too much, he built the numbers up to exciting peaks."

Buzz was high up on the set in one scene, some one hundred feet in the air. He had to scale that height eight times, climbing a ladder to a tiny aerialist platform with room only for himself, cameraman Les White, and the camera. One angle found the camera on an elevator coming down from the dizzying height to a close-up of Judy and then rising to the same spot. This was done nine times for rehearsals and takes, with two trips up for Buzz each time. Just before his last climb, Mickey Rooney appeared with a parachute borrowed from the prop dept. "If the scene looks too bad and you feel faint, jump, count three and pull the cord!" he advised Buzz.

A camera surreptitiously captured Buzz rehearsing the "Hoe Down" number in MGM's faux gymnasium. Wearing his white long-sleeve sweatshirt and white pants, he's standing on the top of a three-step ladder maneuvering this way and that for the sixty attentive dancers. Buzz is then seen peering through the camera's viewfinder studying the blocking. He moves off the boom and gestures to the dancers to take their places. He then walks to the front of the cast (Virginia Weidler and Ray McDonald among them) and demonstrates how to handle a spin-and-stop move. Buzz gives a gesture that says, "Watch me," and a microphone recorded his voice as he performed the little step: "Ho ho . . . ho ho . . . ho ho ho ho, de da da da da da boom." And he punctuated his move in that annoying register of his when he said, "Give it a little SPLASH!"

Buzz and Claire made a grand couple, and it seemed as if the demons plaguing Buzz had been relegated to the past. Friend Louella told her readers that the couple, spotted recently at the Copacabana, "reminds reporters that they will be married before Christmas."

In November, Buzz was assigned the musical finale for the B picture *Born to Sing*. With an enthusiastic cast (though B-leveled in MGM's hierarchy), the story of well-intentioned kids putting on a show could have been another Mickey/Judy vehicle, and critics at the time noted the similarities.

The song "Ballad for Americans" had an interesting history by the time Buzz was assigned to its filming. Originally titled "The Ballad for Uncle Sam" by Earl Robinson and John Latouche in 1939, it was composed as part of the WPA theater production *Sing for Your Supper*. The stirring anthem (it was described as a patriotic cantata) was performed by Paul Robeson on CBS national radio. He and Bing Crosby had successful recordings of the song. MGM purchased the screen rights soon after, and waited for the appropriate film for its inclusion.

Of all the patriotic numbers Berkeley had directed, "Ballad for Americans" is easily the most jingoistic of his prodigious output. The number (like his stacked finales at Warner Brothers) is self-contained and non-referential to the film it inhabits.

In the distance, conjuring the openings of "Lullaby of Broadway" and "All's Fair in Love and War," only a face is illuminated in the void. Buzz's monorailed camera moves steadily into a close-up of baritone Douglas McPhail (*Babes in Arms*) as he sings the opening verse. A tiered stage becomes illuminated with men and women positioned at various levels. They're dressed in outfits befitting their profession (the antithesis of the regimented singularity that Buzz demanded in costuming). McPhail sings of the Revolutionary War, the Declaration of Independence (where we read its preamble), and other American milestones. Then a shift in tone: McPhail turns to view above him four black Americans singing the spiritual "Let My People Go" as the main song returns with these remonstrative lyrics:

Men in white skin can never be free,
While his black brother is in slavery.

The camera lifts and turns around the cubist set as Buzz paints the visuals that correspond to the lyrics. When the ensemble asks McPhail for his identity and whether or not he is an American, he responds in the encompassing: "I'm just an Irish, Negro, Jewish, Italian, French and

English, Spanish, Russian, Chinese, Polish, Scotch, Hungarian, Litvak, Swedish, Finnish, Canadian, Greek and Turk and Czech and double-check American." In the verse following, he similarly claims all the possible religious affiliations. As the number reaches its conclusion, Buzz crafts an interesting shot as McPhail (standing on the camera boom) appears to float above the crowd as the camera rises to the top of the set. "Who are you?" asks the group. "An American!" replies McPhail. The camera pulls back to show McPhail on the top of a rapidly rotating set, arms outstretched, while the group below reaches toward him, as the ensemble of "Remember My Forgotten Man" extended their arms to Joan Blondell. *Born to Sing* ends as the song does, its patriotic didacticism made palatable by the combination of McPhail's stirring voice and Buzz's moving rendering of complementary images.

Someone (maybe Buzz) tipped off Louella Parsons in December with news that a new film *Babes in Hollywood* was on the drawing board as the sequel to *Babes on Broadway*. But juicier news, the kind that a gossiper salivates over, was withheld. Claire James had been sporting a diamond on her finger as far back as May 1941. Four months later, Louella reported that Claire and Buzz would wed by Christmas. She was only a few months off.

Busby Berkeley (forty-six) married Claire James (twenty-two) in Las Vegas on March 29, 1942. He had a short break from his schedule, and flew in from Hollywood. Claire didn't travel with him, as she was working on location in Phoenix. They eventually met in the quiet desert town and sought out Justice of the Peace Mahlon Brown to do the honors. Gertrude didn't attend, but listened to the ceremony via telephone from her Redlands house. Per Buzz, honeymoon plans were indefinite. Actually, the whole enterprise seemed indefinite for a couple that had been together for years. Despite her fiancé's two previous marriages, wouldn't the bride have preferred a planned wedding with the families and all the trimmings? Wouldn't romantic honeymoon plans be considered and discussed well beforehand? Would they be in separate cities rushing to legalize a wedding in Nevada if a modicum of planning had occurred? Whatever their plans, Claire's director husband was needed at the studio in April for a new type of film. Not a musical, not a drama, but a hybrid awaited Buzz in Culver City.

For Me and My Gal is a highly accomplished anomaly in the Busby

Berkeley canon. It's a film with musical numbers, yet Bobby Connolly (who came up through the Broadway ranks like Buzz) was assigned the dance direction. The script, the best one Buzz had worked with to this point in his career, was emotional and nostalgic, set in the years of the First World War. The film is dedicated to the tireless vaudeville performers who played a myriad of small towns while dreaming of headlining New York's Palace Theatre. Arthur Freed, knowing Buzz's army and stage history, suggested him for the director's job with only the slightest trepidation. "Since this was a story about vaudeville and the struggles of a young couple to reach the top, we needed someone who knew the route, someone who knew about the hard work and heartaches that went with that way of life," said Freed. "The obvious choice was Buzz, who had lived this kind of story himself—it was his own background. Our only reservation in choosing him was that this was not simply a musical but an emotional story with some pathos and drama. It also contained a great deal of music, and we [Freed and his writers] were a little afraid he might concentrate on that rather than the story." Undoubtedly, Freed made this clear to Buzz during the story conferences. No bombastic effects were considered, and Freed imposed his will by removing Buzz from handling the dancing chores.

Newcomer Gene Kelly played the wisecracking dancer/singer Harry Palmer. Arriving in town, he meets other performers on the vaudeville circuit, namely Jo Hayden (Judy Garland) and Red Metcalfe (George Murphy). Harry rubs both of them the wrong way, especially Jo, by demanding the perks only a seasoned veteran could enjoy. A light romance is hinted between Red and Jo, but Harry eventually wins Jo's heart, and Jo leaves Red to form a traveling duo with Harry. They plan to marry once they get their shot at the Palace. As soon as they learn that their dreams are about to come true, Harry receives a draft notice to join the army overseas. He purposely smashes his hand and fails the army physical. Meanwhile, Jo learns that her brother Danny (Richard Quine) has been killed in combat. When she sees the evident cowardice in Harry's action, they split. Harry regains his pride by enlisting in the YMCA's effort of producing entertainment for the troops. Circumstances find Harry on the battlefield acting the hero when he saves a convoy of Red Cross ambulances by tossing a hand grenade into an enemy stronghold.

Jo, performing for the troops, sees Harry (and his bravery medal) in the audience. They meet again, and the picture ends romantically.

Following *Babes on Broadway* and *Born to Sing,* the chance to direct straight drama must've been appealing to Buzz. Of course, there was the inherent nostalgia factor. In two montage sequences, Buzz elicited relevant stock footage of the war, newspaper headlines, and personages of the day (including Buzz's old commander General Pershing). Buzz filmed the picture without the slightest hint of flamboyance, and based upon this film and *They Made Me a Criminal,* it's quite apparent that Busby Berkeley could do it all: music, comedy, and drama. Except for scenes requiring a large audience, Buzz keeps his camera medium close for most of the picture. The stars get to shine, especially Judy Garland, who, after the Mickey Rooney films, matured as an actress with a dynamic range. Aiding her every step of the way was Buzz. "I had to sing before 1000 soldiers in a French canteen," said Judy. "If Buzz hadn't been in back of the camera, wildly gesticulating and singing right with me, I never would have maintained the emotional pitch needed for the song." To the reporters she mentioned the oft-told anecdote of Buzz's working habits: "Don't ever look for Buzz in a chair on the set. He'll usually be found hanging from a rafter, lining up an unusual angle." That quote certainly didn't apply to *For Me and My Gal,* a film whose austerity is as notable as Buzz's more outrageous endeavors. But there was no overstatement in this period of Judy's career when she said of Buzz, "I don't know what I'd do without him."

This was Gene Kelly's first film (he had been in the Broadway production of *Pal Joey*), and it almost didn't happen thanks to Gene's ego and inappropriate sense of entitlement. Arthur Freed was ready to cast Gene in a supporting part, but Gene's manager, Johnny Darrow, thought his client would pass on the role. Louis B. Mayer met Gene after a performance of *Pal Joey* and invited him to Hollywood with the promise that a screen test wouldn't be necessary. Soon after, an MGM representative called Gene and said a screen test was required. Gene told the rep to confirm with Mayer. The disappointing result was that Gene had to do a screen test. This so angered him that he rifled off a nasty letter to Mayer about the test. On top of that, he wasn't too thrilled to be working under the great Berkeley, who, he felt, had a heavy-handed technique that subjugated the performer to the camera. Johnny Darrow set him straight. On the evening before filming was to commence, he brought Gene up to speed with all he knew about Busby Berkeley anecdotally and from the whispering gossip of Hollywood. But Gene Kelly was luckier than he knew. His first feature was, in essence, a master class in acting for the camera taught by a perfectionist of the medium. "I taught him a great many things," said Gene's director; "I had to teach him the tricks of using his eyes to give expression and animation to his facial projections."

Filming *For Me and My Gal* took place between April and May 1942. Soon after, the first public screening was held near Louis B. Mayer's ranch at a Westwood Village theater. It was an emotional experience for all, especially Buzz. He shook and shook Gene's hand until it was almost embarrassing. Arthur Freed came up to them and broke the embrace. "You know Gene," said Freed, "when we cast you, Eddie Mannix [a high-ranking executive at MGM] told me he did not see any motion picture potential." "So I heard," said Gene. "Well, word does get around in this town," replied the producer. "But do you know what Mannix just told me? 'Arthur, remind me not to tell you how to make pictures.'"

The glad tidings on *For Me and My Gal* didn't last long. The preview audience in Westwood had a very negative reaction to the story line. The film, as it was sneaked, did not have any reference to Harry Palmer's redemption as a war hero. Also, Buzz had added a poignant scene in which Jo bids her brother farewell as he leaves for overseas combat. Palmer's cowardice, combined with the fact that he got the girl at the end of the picture, was particularly distasteful to the wartime audience. Eighty-five percent of them felt that the George Murphy character should have won the heart of Judy, according to the comment cards submitted after the screening. Mayer, who wore his patriotism on his sleeve, immediately intervened. "It's absolutely un-American! What the hell were we thinking? We've got to do a repair job," he told Arthur Freed. The whole cast was recalled for three weeks of reshoots. Combat footage was lifted from King Vidor's MGM film *The Big Parade,* and a montage featuring Harry advancing toward victory was added. The Kelly character was now a hero, and the entire finale was redone without George Murphy. The new inclusions went unidentified when the film finally opened on November 20. Grossing over $4.3 million (five times its production cost), *For Me and My Gal* was a critical and financial success. Arthur Freed thought his director "came up with a very warm and human picture." For Buzz, whose contract with the studio stipulated that he also direct nonmusical films, the success was especially gratifying. Reflectively, he said, "I think that of all the films I have directed, this is my top favorite."

Sometimes a lower-rung editor would take a director's raw footage and assemble a work print with scenes in the general order based on continuity and production notes. John Dunning was one of those editors, and he was assigned the first pass on *For Me and My Girl* before senior editor Ben Lewis. In the screening room, he showed his cut to Buzz, who looked at some of it. On his way out, Buzz said, "Nice work Jack. Now where is Bennie?"

In early June, Buzz heard a story over the radio that angered him. It was announced that he and Claire were soon parting. He called Louella Parsons and asked her to write "Claire and I are very happy and have never had any trouble." Does a secure, successful marriage need to be confirmed in print? Or was Buzz endeavoring to slap a pretty picture on a doomed relationship? Louella ran the story at her friend's request and closed with, "at Arrowhead where they are vacationing they seem completely happy." The next month, columnist Harrison Carroll denied separation rumors. He quoted Buzz saying that he and Claire had just purchased a new home in Westwood. Buzz then added this curious declaration: "I suppose the talk started because Claire sometimes spends the night at her mother's home, or I at my mother's. We do that just so they won't feel they are losing us." At face value, Buzz's comment reflects unusual behavior for a married couple. Were the mothers-in-law so bereft without their grown children that the truth of Buzz's statement was unchallengeable? Read between the lines, Buzz sounded like he was publicly offering excuses for a new marriage already beginning to unravel.

William Saroyan was in Hollywood when MGM was filming his story *The Human Comedy*. He met Buzz at the studio around the time the director was boasting of his marital bliss to the press. He walked alongside Buzz with the director's assistants and a female in whom Buzz was interested "beyond the call of duty." Buzz enjoyed cards and invited Saroyan to LA's Clover Club, a below-the-radar semi-private gambling house catering primarily to movie folk. Orson Welles played cards for two or three days at a time with Buzz until Welles or Buzz "became inspired."

Labor Day brought Buzz bad news. The *New York Times* ran a piece in early September reporting that income tax liens were recently filed against twenty-one members of the Hollywood film community. The largest sum of $43,576, based on earnings from 1941, belonged to none other than Busby Berkeley.

Vincente Minnelli had graduated from *Strike up the Band*'s animated fruit orchestra to a full directing assignment. In his first film, the all-black-cast *Cabin in the Sky,* he was unable to film one musical number due to illness. Buzz stepped up, and his contribution "Shine" (the old 1910 jazz tune) is a two-and-a-half-minute delight. John W. Sublett (Buzz had filmed him in the *Varsity Show* finale) with his twirling cane introduces his "Domino" character to nightclub patrons while Duke Ellington, in white suit and white tie, conducts in the background:

Just because my hair's curly,
And because my teeth are pearly,
And just because I always wear a smile,
And suits dressed up in the latest style.
'Cause I'm glad I'm livin'
Take troubles all with a smile
Just because my color shade
Is different maybe
That's why they call me "Shine."

And Sublett slickly glides across the floor, his cane spinning like a propeller. As he climbs the stairs to his exit, a visual clue to the director's identity is seen in the perfectly framed hand shadows on the wall over Sublett's shoulder, a Buzz Berkeley signature device that he used with effectiveness.

In September, Buzz was assigned *Swing Fever* to direct, but he dropped out of the film in early October because of a scheduling conflict with *Girl Crazy,* a reimagining of the popular Gershwin brothers musical that was completely unlike anything in the Wheeler and Woolsey version. Production on *Girl Crazy* was scheduled for the end of the year, but in mid-October the *Hollywood Reporter* announced that Buzz would codirect *Swing Fever* after all. It never materialized, and *Girl Crazy* was pushed back until January.

Early in 1943, before filming began on *Girl Crazy,* Buzz was reported to be without his characteristic white sweatshirt. In its place, he
received a gift of a beautiful long-sleeved garment embroidered with the
names of all forty showgirls who were to star in the film. In big letters
(also embroidered) it read, "Girl Crazy, Xmas, 1942." The gag gift came
from the girls.

The ingredients were perfect and the direction sound, but the souf-
flé that was *Girl Crazy* never rose, and Buzz was made the scapegoat.
Though Mickey Rooney always seemed to get along with Buzz, Judy
Garland was another story. She was tough, but extremely sensitive, and
Buzz's frequent raising of his voice in their previous collaborations af-
fected Judy more with each subsequent picture.

The first thing Buzz shot for *Girl Crazy* was the showstopper "I Got
Rhythm." Immediately there was friction from Roger Edens on Buzz's
planned presentation. Buzz had envisioned a huge, noisy rodeo-type
sequence with animals, pistols, and bullwhips. Edens violently disagreed
with Buzz's approach. "I'd written an arrangement of 'I Got Rhythm'
for Judy and we disagreed basically about its presentation. I wanted it
rhythmic and simply staged, but Berkeley got his big ensembles and trick
cameras into it again, plus a lot of girls in Western outfits with fringed
skirts and people cracking whips and firing guns all over my arrangement and Judy's voice. Well, we shouted at each other and I said there
wasn't enough room on the lot for both of us." Edens undoubtedly took
his concerns to the studio's highest authority, but there was no indica-
tion that Louis B. Mayer would remove Buzz from the film.

Nine days—four more than had been planned—were spent filming
"I Got Rhythm," putting *Girl Crazy* already $60,000 over budget. On
January 28, it was reported that Buzz was fighting pneumonia and trying to get well so he could resume his duties on *Girl Crazy.* That might
have been a bit of face-saving because Buzz had already been fired from
Girl Crazy by the time his illness was announced. According to sources,
it was Buzz's old champion Arthur Freed who had him dismissed, ostensibly for his continuing clashes with Judy Garland. Hedda Hopper
witnessed and reported Buzz's behavior toward Judy during "I've Got
Rhythm": "I saw him work her over. He watched from the floor with a
wild gleam in his eye, while in take after take he drove her toward the
perfection he demanded. She was close to hysteria. I was ready to scream

myself. But the order was repeated time and time again: "Cut. Let's try it again, Judy. Come on, move! Get the lead out!" Judy told Hedda, "I used to feel he had a big black bullwhip and he was lashing me with it."

It seemed as if a turning point had been reached with Busby Berkeley at MGM. After years of dishing out abuse, Buzz was now being held accountable for his bad behavior. B-actress Dona Massin painted a picture of Buzz in damning shades:

> Judy didn't like Buzz and neither did I! But I think the reason she didn't like him is that he made her nervous. He was always saying "Open your eyes! God, how big can you open your eyes?" He was a very strange, cruel man. . . . He'd work the hell out of his dancers and Judy and Mickey. I personally think he was terrible, and I think anybody that's honest would say that he was. No talent; all he had to do was pick up a kaleidoscope and he had his routine. I worked all the Judy/Mickey pictures with Buzz; the last one I worked on with her was *Girl Crazy* when she and Mickey were [being lifted] up and down, up and down. And she went out of her mind, she was so frightened. She was afraid of the gunshots.

When "I Got Rhythm" finished shooting, Judy's personal family physician, Dr. Marcus Rabwin, ordered her not to dance for three weeks. Judy was exhausted, and her weight had dropped to ninety-four pounds. With the number in the can, Arthur Freed replaced Buzz with Norman Taurog, and Charles Walters handled the rest of the musical numbers.

Buzz received his own title card: "I Got Rhythm Number Directed by Busby Berkeley." Tommy Dorsey and his orchestra introduce the number, and cowgirl Judy sings the opening lines to the members of the band. Dancers and instrumentalists mingle; as a group of four saxophonists move past the camera, a line of dancers walks in from the opposite direction. Soon the camera rises to take in the entire company, now sporting thin flags and long poles that drop sequentially to the floor and (thanks to reversing the film) fly back in the dancers' hands. Shots are fired repeatedly as Judy and Mickey are being hoisted off the ground. Finally, a field cannon is pulled into view. It fires, and in its wake are the two stars singing, "Who could ask for anything more?" as the film closes.

Whatever was said or written about Buzz, it is to his credit that he never, on the record, spoke deprecatingly about anyone. Even after his dismissal that may have been brought about by Judy Garland, he had nothing but nice things to say about her: "Judy called me 'Uncle Buzz' and always wanted me right there when the camera was photographing her. She would not do a scene unless I stood by the camera, and afterward she asked me how she looked and if she had done all right. She was the sweetest girl—so unspoiled and so cooperative. She and Mickey had great respect for each other's ability. I don't know any two kids who could be better than those two were. Over at Universal, they teamed a couple of very talented kids, Donald O'Connor and Peggy Ryan. And they had Deanna Durbin. But nobody ever topped Judy and Mickey."

The news got worse for Buzz. Despite the numerous comments on the record about his marital tranquility, Claire James-Berkeley instructed her lawyer to file divorce papers just weeks after Buzz's dismissal from *Girl Crazy*. She told newsmen she didn't want any alimony from her husband. "All I want," she said, "is for him to finish paying for the mink coat and the auto he gave me." A couple of weeks later, Louella Parsons publicly announced that Claire refused to listen to any talk of reconciliation.

9

Art and Audacity

Buzz requested a respite. He hadn't taken a real vacation in years. He wedged in his weddings and his honeymoons whenever there was a free day or two in his schedule. His work on *Girl Crazy* ended far too precipitously, and his marriage was no longer tenable, so Buzz found himself with enough free time for a holiday. Louis B. Mayer, knowing full well the histrionics that had occurred between Arthur Freed, Roger Edens, and Buzz, gave him a month off. He decided to take an ambitious cross-country automobile trip with Mother. They would wind up in New York, see old friends and colleagues, and take in a Broadway show or two. Buzz might even do a little unpaid scouting for the next Berkeley girl.

Buzz and Mother rode in a limousine chaperoned by a man identified as "Gene." They wheeled through Arizona, New Mexico, and Texas as Gertrude took in the sights from the right side of the backseat. In Oklahoma, a deep dip in the road caused the vehicle to bounce severely, forcing Gertrude off her seat and onto the limo's hard floor. She was in pain, and her son brought her to the closest Oklahoma hospital he could find. Gertrude had torn the ligaments in one leg and needed a week's hospitalization. Buzz was fraught with anxiety and need. He called Etta Judd and asked his kindly friend to come to the hospital and assist him with his mother, and she did so without a qualm. Though the automobile part of the trip was now canceled (Buzz asked Gene to return to Los Angeles), they planned to travel to New York by train. Gertrude looked at real estate advertisements during her convalescence. With her spendthrift son's future in mind, she found a house in Oklahoma City and a cattle ranch in Shawnee on the market for a steal. Before Buzz and Gertrude boarded a train to points east, he had purchased the properties in his mother's name per her request. The ride to New York could not have been comfortable for Gertrude. She was carried onto the train by stretcher (the second Berkeley to make such a public appearance). Approaching eighty, Gertrude was now permanently wheelchair bound. When the two arrived at their destination, the dutiful son kept at his mother's side around the clock. During a day trip to Dover, New Hampshire, Buzz and Gertrude revisited the twenty-four-room mansion she loved. When they returned to California, one of the first things Buzz did was install wheelchair ramps in the Adams Street mansion.

In April, Claire James instructed her lawyer to cancel the divorce action she had filed just two months before. She told reporters that despite the cancellation, "there's no reconciliation in sight. Just say I'm canceling it for the time being. I may have something to announce later." Buzz said it was news to him that his wife's suit had been withdrawn. His ignorance of the postponement could explain why he was seen with a San Francisco showgirl named Sally Wickman around this time. He and Sally were also seen at Slapsy Maxie's. Columnist Dorothy Kilgallen said Buzz was "daffy" about Ms. Wickman, but neither the romance nor the showgirl's career advanced very far.

That same month, Buzz went to work for 20th Century Fox after they made an offer to MGM to "borrow him" for a one-picture deal. The studio was not selfish with Berkeley (certainly not in the way Warner Brothers had been) once the *Girl Crazy* fiasco had played out. For Buzz, it was a chance to work again under studio chief Darryl F. Zanuck, his mentor and champion in his early Warner Brothers films. The picture's working title was "The Girls He Left Behind," and it was intended as Fox's Christmas release of 1943. It was a wartime Technicolor homefront musical filled with specialty acts, spirited songs, and outrageous dance numbers. Its subject was certainly within Buzz's artistic means and temperament. Composer Harry Warren (who hadn't worked with Buzz since *Garden of the Moon*) was to collaborate with lyricist Mack Gordon, but by the time Buzz became attached to the film, Gordon had left the project and Leo Robin was assigned the lyrics.

America's entry into World War II, following the 1941 Japanese attack on Pearl Harbor, signaled an end to Hollywood's profitable relationships with the Far East markets. At Fox, their continental and Japan-based operations were shut down. The studio looked to other markets for film distribution and found the Latin American countries of South America very receptive. With films such as *Down Argentine*

Way, Week-end in Havana, and *That Night in Rio,* Fox cemented itself as the studio most willing to cater to this emerging market. A number of other factors contributed to the prevalence of Latin-themed films, namely FDR's "Good Neighbor Policy," North and South America's hemispheric partnership against fascism, and the Office of Coordination of Inter-American Affairs, which had its own motion picture division. Even the Hays office appointed an expert in Latin America, but there was another factor besides the political that helped support this new emerging market; the songs and dances south of the border were extremely popular with American moviegoers. Buzz capitalized on the craze with the "Do the La Conga" number in *Strike up the Band,* but it was 20th Century Fox, above all other studios, that reaped the greatest rewards from its Latin-themed pictures in the early and mid-1940s.

The Gang's All Here, as the film was now officially known, began production in April. Its cast included Fox's contracted "ambassador" to the Spanish world, Carmen Miranda (who, by this time, had a couple of successful Fox musicals under her belt); Alice Faye, the contralto-voiced singer/actress who previously starred with Miranda; Charlotte Greenwood (working again with Buzz some twelve years after *Palmy Days* and *Flying High*); and radio host Phil Baker. Strong supporting character actors included Eugene Pallette and Edward Everett Horton as wealthy businessmen friends. Linda Darnell was to play Horton's daughter, but her involvement in the film didn't last long. A sprained ankle during rehearsals (Darnell had plans to dance for the first time in *The Gang's All Here*) kept her sidelined. After her recovery, she eloped with famed cinematographer J. Peverell Marley and asked Fox for an indefinite leave of absence. Actress Sheila Ryan, under contract to Fox with about twenty film roles to date, replaced her.

Buzz learned that Darryl Zanuck would not be overseeing the production. Fox's studio head was in Europe on behalf of the war effort, leaving the chore to William LeBaron. LeBaron was a producer and songwriter who had worked at other studios before coming to Fox. Under Zanuck, he set up an independent unit at the studio, mostly making musicals. He and Buzz got along well at first, but the relationship was soon strained as the showman in Berkeley wouldn't yield to the budget-trimming mandates of LeBaron (who, in turn, was forced to trim expenses due to the demands of the War Production Board, which sought cost cutting in all aspects of businesses during the war). In spite of the producer/director set-tos that took place during shooting, the film turned out to be an outrageously conceived work of art, blending with subtlety the politics of alliances while overtly disarming the viewing public with surrealism and spectacle.

The motivations of Claire James were unknown to those who worked with Buzz. Claire was often seen driving him home from the studio, "despite reports that they're kaput." In early June (two months after filming began on *The Gang's All Here*), she filed suit to annul the marriage. She said that at their ceremony, Buzz had expressed his willingness to be her husband, but that afterward he had refused to live with her and had been a husband in name only. The final straw came when Claire went to visit Buzz on his set. He had her thrown off by her own father, who worked as a studio watchman.

By midmonth she had received her annulment; she had requested no money from Buzz. Claire's cryptic remark to reporters in April ("I may have something to announce later") came true less than one week after the annulment. Her photograph was featured on the syndicated wedding announcements page with the news that she was to become the bride of twenty-four-year-old Lt. Ray Dorsey as soon as he could get leave from his duties at March Field, California. Evidently, the lieutenant received his leave sooner than expected; he and Claire were married before the month was over.

The Gang's All Here begins in motion, and for the first seven-plus minutes it thrills, disorients, and confounds the nature of space and place through purely cinematic means. Far in the upper left corner of the screen, we hear and see a man (Aloysio De Oliveira) sing the popular song "Brazil." In a shot reminiscent of the opening moments of "Lullaby of Broadway," Berkeley's movable camera slowly closes in on the singer (whose face is half-hidden), and just as quickly moves away from him as a new, undefined image appears: a group of thin strips of bamboo, angled left, giving way to the marking on the docked ship SS *Brazil*. The camera flies weightlessly as it follows embarking passengers and the ship's crew and cargo, when, in a clever transitional shot (a roped fruit basket blending into a fruit-filled hat), Carmen Miranda is introduced. A few seconds later Buzz allows the audience to regain its bearings by dollying back, revealing the locale as a nightclub with an audience and a small stage. As in previous films, his flights of fancy disregarded any physical limitations imposed by reality. Here, the stage is quite small, making the opening number a supreme example of the director's art meeting visual trickery. Miranda yields her singing to the audience as the heretofore unknown showgirls are seen, one at a time, in close-up. The camera moves from one face to the next accompanied in the shot by small musical instruments used in the show. The last of the showgirls (played by Alice Faye) remains unidentified until the number ends, and we're finally introduced to the film's supporting players.

The "book" of *The Gang's All Here* is fairly simplistic, as insubstantial as the Mickey/Judy "Babes" pictures. On the record, Buzz had mentioned his disinterest in or outright disdain for the expository passages of his musicals. Here, especially, the dialogue sequences are generally insignificant relative to the total sheen that Buzz, the preeminent showman, provides. Dialogue-driven scenes are played mostly in a fast, clipped manner where one sentence has barely enough breathing room before a reply is uttered. It's an interesting way to direct his actors (one thinks of Buzz's similarly rapid-fire *Fast and Furious*), as if he hadn't the patience to slowly maneuver nonmusical moments. In light of the fact that Buzz almost always directed a picture's musical numbers first and concentrated on the story afterward, it isn't a stretch to imagine him picking up the dialogue's tempo in an effort to wrap the picture on time and under budget.

Of the half-dozen songs in *The Gang's All Here,* certainly the one most playful to both ear and eye is "The Lady in the Tutti Frutti Hat," written especially for Carmen Miranda per Buzz's request to Harry Warren and Leo Robin. It has all the earmarks of classic Berkeley: a self-contained story without reference to the "book"; sets that can exist only on an expansive soundstage; and unworldly (if not unwieldy) large props unfamiliar in scope to anything found in nature. As the number begins, an organ grinder and monkey make their way toward the stage, where we see a number of ersatz banana trees, each with its own monkey. We're carried along on Buzz's buoyant camera as it surveys an imaginative set evoking a South Seas atoll. On this idyllic islet reside dozens of Buzz's beauties, all sporting yellow kerchiefs, black, flaring midriff tops, and canary yellow short shorts cut high above the thigh. There they dally and rest under imaginary sunshine, their legs bent in suggestive poses.

Suddenly they hear someone approach, which causes them to line up in two rows, single file, and wave to the visitor. This action keeps Buzz's camera moving up to the outrageous image of the Brazilian Bombshell herself being pulled on a banana cart by two gold-painted oxen, supported by two muscle-bound manservants and a half-dozen musicians! "The Lady in the Tutti Frutti Hat" immediately establishes itself as a self-affirming and presence-establishing number for Miranda. From the first line, in which she asks naively, "I wonder why does everybody look at me?" and follows up later with an interesting declarative: "Some people say I dress too gay, but ev'ry day I feel so gay, and when I'm gay I dress that way, is something wrong with that?" the song revels in the excess of her character, giving Buzz ample opportunity for unbridled impressionistic creativity. The action shifts to the girls formed in a circle holding portable xylophones made of small bananas while Carmen pretends to play. The scene blends into shots of the girls' legs and feet as they line up in formation, now holding five-foot plastic (and unashamedly phallic) bananas over their heads. This allowed Buzz to pursue the folly of his imagination as his dancers raise and lower their bananas in patterned sequences, while he overcranks the camera for a slow motion effect. Buzz's camera rises, dips, and tilts in glorious abandon like a drunkard on ice. The girls eventually return to their original positions, and the camera pulls away to reveal a dozen organ grinders with their monkeys. Buzz tracks past the last one to reveal Miranda again in a surrealistic final shot. As she finishes her number, the camera pulls back, revealing the allusion that her banana hat is the largest one in the world, extending to infinity (thanks to the terrific matte painting and production design of James Basevi and Joseph C. Wright). Buzz surreptitiously winks to the audience as he closes the song and the stage curtains drop.

Buzz boasted of his one-take acumen when the camera rolled, but it seems he forgot about the problems he encountered in the "Tutti Frutti" number. Cinematographer Edward Cronjager was a well-respected professional, and by 1943 he had photographed some one hundred pictures, including *Western Union* for the demanding Fritz Lang and *Heaven Can Wait* for Ernst Lubitsch. He also worked with Buzz back in 1932 for the numbers in *Bird of Paradise*. In all those films, he couldn't recall working on a picture that demanded he ride the boom as aggressively as he did in *The Gang's All Here*. That aggressiveness almost caused a serious accident. Reporter Harold Heffernan of the *Detroit News* was on the set during the "Tutti Frutti" number and noticed how happy Buzz was riding shotgun on the boom as Cronjager manned the camera. All the while the camera boom darted and swooped and raised and tilted mere inches past the faces of the lovely Berkeley girls. In one near-tragic take (what Heffernan called "Berkeley's frantic gesticulations"), the boom overshot its mark and came uncomfortably close to Carmen Miranda's head, knocking off the top layers of flowers and fruit leaves from her hat. As Buzz and Cronjager reset their position at the top of the stage, Miranda let off steam to the reporter saying, "Dat man ees crazy." She went on a bit louder so Buzz could hear: "What you theenk you are anyhow, a head hunter? If you want to keel me why you don' use a gun?" According to Heffernan, Buzz pleaded nicely with Carmen from his position high above her. "Hookay. Thees time make with the careful! Knock one banana off my head and I will make of you de flat pancake," threatened the malapropist. According to another reporter visiting the set when "The Lady in the Tutti Frutti Hat" was filming, Buzz was up on the boom and yelling at the dancers below, his rasping voice pleading, "Girls, girls, can't you see?" He explained his method to the reporter: "We've got a camera that can go anywhere. Why not use it? Sure a theater audience couldn't look down on a stage full of dancers, but that's no sign it wouldn't like to. If the camera can let 'em why not?" After a day's filming, the more amiable director took his girls to the projection room to watch the dailies. "They're usually surprised," said Buzz, who, according to the report, seemed anything but.

Buzz again displayed a director's maturation in his sensitive and restrained touch with the two main numbers sung by Alice Faye. The melodic "A Journey to a Star" is repeated throughout the picture, but in its first incarnation it's sung as an audition of sorts on board a ferryboat with the moon as its sole light source. Alice "cues" an unseen orchestra (the film is all about the suspension of disbelief) and sings to B-actor James Ellison while Buzz holds a steady shot of his principals bathed in beautiful, artificial moonlight. At one point during the song's reprise, both actors turn to face the water, leaving their backs to the camera (and audience) in a complete disregard for propriety (one wonders how the MGM brass would have reacted). Yet Buzz made the right directorial decision, keeping the number fresh by the simple act of pivoting his leads within their confined space. (Such is the unimportance of narrative that, although James Ellison's role is the romantic lead, he's billed ninth in the credits.) "No Love, No Nothing" is sung by Faye onstage at the club New Yorker using the show's rehearsal time as a pretense for the performance. In the number, she plays a woman missing her man who is fighting in the war. She meanders about her small apartment; runs to the door in vain when someone approaches; lovingly picks up her man's pipe and his slippers; and in tears she turns off her lamp, finishing the song as a sliver of light illuminates her sadness. The number (as meant for the live audience) is an undisguised metaphor to the ongoing story line (the James Ellison character has gone overseas, leaving Alice bereft). Buzz accomplishes a wonderful sleight of hand. At the song's conclusion, not only is its veiled reference to the narrative made obvious, it becomes warmed with emotion, leaving the reason for performing the number in the first place (it was a dress rehearsal) completely forgotten.

Not since his films at Warner Brothers had the stacking approach to Berkeley's musical numbers been given. The ganging up of big production numbers, as already mentioned, left only those numbers in memory while a film's preceding one hundred minutes were all but dismissed. In *The Gang's All Here,* the over-the-top combination of Berkeley's fertile imagination painted with three-strip Technicolor swatches kept even the early numbers (including the bravura opening) still vivid in recollection. The final ten minutes of the film is a type of number stacking that leads to an explosively surreal climax in which the kaleidoscopic and expressionistic vision of Busby Berkeley is fully realized.

As originally designed, Buzz regarded the finale with little enthusiasm. It didn't seem big enough. It wasn't "spectacular." Production notes point to a patriotic ending featuring a military wedding (James Ellison and Alice Faye), costumed in red, white, and blue. How this potentially bombastic number (military marching bands, explosions, and song; all de rigueur for a Berkeley ending) was deferred for the visual splendor of the avant-garde finale isn't known. But the authorial stamp of *The Gang's All Here* is Buzz's in the two credits given him ("Dances created and directed by," and the full director's credit), so his final word for the final number was final.

The film ties up all its narrative strings as the action turns to a war-bond garden party to be given outdoors on the well-manicured grounds of the Edward Everett Horton character's Westchester County estate. The finale begins with a close-up of the invitation, a five-thousand-dollar bill strategically placed below it (the price of an invitee's war-bond purchase) and two polished fingernails holding both. Chopin's Nocturne plays as the Berkeley camera surveys the grounds, stopping at a tastefully nude statue as the action and tempo change. A pink-lit, circular, colored waterfall drops to reveal Benny Goodman and His Orchestra as the scene shifts in focus. (Buzz's use of the waterfall as a transitional device is highly effective in a reverse-curtain way. Here the waterfall descends as a sequence begins in contrast to a theater's curtains that rise.) "Paducah" ("If you wanna, you can rhyme it with bazooka") is Benny Goodman's at the start, as Buzz's boom follows him from one musician to the next up a U-shaped bandstand with Goodman at the center (instead of out front) of his band. It should be mentioned that, in this elegant outdoor setting, over his left shoulder is the earthly impossibility of a grand chandelier! What is it hanging from and who is holding it? Is it tethered to the moon? But these are retrospective musings for the literalist only, as Buzz and his production designers forswore physical reality from the film's first frame. Carmen Miranda takes over the vocals, and the number shifts to a dance with Tony De Marco, once again, playing to the South American market. The vertical waters, now tinged blue, drop to reveal Berkeley's girls positioned in ascending order for a reprise of "A Journey to a Star." A close-up of each face passes the camera, resting on Alice Faye. As she finishes, Buzz's camera-in-motion turns left to a pink-shaded water curtain. As it drops, we watch De Marco and Sheila Ryan in a pas de deux. Their number ends, and the camera repeats it movement, closing on Alice Faye as she finishes while a blue fountain rises. A small pause is taken to wind up the narrative (the course of true love is set on its proper path and wrong suppositions are righted—as if Buzz [and we] cared a hoot) before the grandest of grand finales unfolds.

The circle is the shape on which "The Polka Dot Polka" number is designed. In the cinematic world of Busby Berkeley, an object or a geometrical pattern is given uncommon significance as seen as far back as the Gold Diggers films. Here, the song's title (lyrics be damned) enmeshes with the director's vision of circularity. The number begins with two dozen girls dressed in polka-dot outfits dancing with boys wearing polka-dotted bow ties. Alice Faye (in a dress of blue polka dots) walks in gracefully, singing as she maneuvers between the children. "The Polka Dot lives on," sings Alice, and from this point to the end of the film, any relation to spatial reality is strictly coincidental.

A shot of a girl's hand and forearm with interlaced circles amid a white sleeve transforms to a larger version of the arm as the red circles change to round, red neon tubes and position themselves in a long string, barely touching. The neon tubes then drop into the waiting arms of the Berkeley girls (dressed in outlandish full-body costumes reminiscent of those in the Flash Gordon serials). The girls, now spread out on a five-tiered set, take the neon circles and rotate them (the ubiquitous Berkeley shadow of a dancer doing the same moves can be seen in the background). The neon has been be replaced by flat circles that are rolled to the floor. In a terrific shot that was projected in reverse, the circles lift off the ground into the arms of the girls. They, in turn, pivot around and send the flat circles to the girls in the lower tier. A large gold circle fills the frame as a transitional device, and now Alice Faye can be seen in a high shot, swirling in a large blue dress. The image changes again to a full kaleidoscopic view of her in eight mirrored representations. At this point, thirteen years in development, the Berkeley aesthetic has reached the apex of maturation in the loftiest cinematic affirmation of his singular talent. Buzz's dominating acumen is presented in arresting, color-flushed images supplemented by an ascending musical score that blends to a fever pitch of unrestrained frenzy as the kaleidoscope turns and turns, every two seconds, at every manifestation a repainting of the screen with hypnotizing hues until the number ends breathtakingly and satisfyingly in complete and total exhaustiveness. With a start and a laugh, the number abruptly transitions to a circular-framed shot of Eugene Pallette's disembodied head zooming toward the camera as he warbles the first line of "A Journey to a Star." Joining him, one by one, are the rest of the cast, each filmed as a headshot against a different-colored background until the whole gang (including the Berkeley girls) is seen in a single shot with heads in (and bordering) the frame (a fine special effect for its day). The pink-tinged water fountain rises for its final time and gives way to the end card, which, in its lower right corner, reads: "For Victory, U.S. War Bonds and Stamps. Buy yours in this theatre." The not-so-subtle solicitation worked (that is, you in your seats can help our servicemen just as the happy singing folks you witnessed did), and audiences of the day responded enthusiastically.

Buzz worked longer on "The Polka Dot Polka" finale than any number he had done. At first, he couldn't envision the closing sequence. One day, by chance, he stared intently at a topaz ring he had recently purchased for Gertrude. The stone acted like a prism, bending the light in interesting ways. "If only I could shoot through this," mused Buzz. His secretary, Helen McSweeney, came up with the idea of a kaleidoscope. She said she knew of a kid who had one nearby. Buzz looked into the toy and began a "mental victory dance." Always the idea man, he came up with a contraption costing roughly eight thousand dollars. It was a vertical shaft with two sides supporting hinged mirrors at 45-degree angles from each other. Buzz and his boom were placed high above the device, looking downward while the stage revolved like a turntable. As it spun, a section of the moving floor came into camera range and the mirrors reflected the multiple images of whatever was on the stage. So Buzz placed Alice Faye, his girls, and the color combination that suited his fancy, and created an amazing collage in the final edit.

In July, Jack Warner was back in Buzz's life. Although still employed at MGM, Buzz had heard word from Warner Brothers that they were again interested in his services if he could somehow be released from his contract. MGM packaged Buzz with studio stalwart Joan Crawford, and made a double deal with Warner Brothers. They could have him if Joan was included. Jack promised Buzz a five-year contract at better terms than what he was getting. "He's back on the Warner lot to stay," announced Louella Parsons.

Lorraine Breacher, a native Chicagoan, was an extra in *The Gang's All Here*. Buzz found her attractive, and soon she was seen on his arm. With the rapidity of the grand emotional gestures that had plagued Buzz, he placed a "sparkler" on Lorraine's proper finger. On August 10, it was announced they intend to wed in 1944. There was a twenty-one-year age difference between them.

In September, Jack Warner learned that 20th Century Fox recently had ceased to pay Buzz for any additional work. There was a small problem. Buzz needed to return to Fox for a day's pickup shots for *The Gang's All Here*. Jack gave his OK, but he made sure that

Fox paid the studio for the day. The next month, producer Alex Gottlieb complained to Jack that Buzz had requested a couple of days off. Buzz flew to Chicago with Lorraine to see her ill mother. In a memo to Warner, Gottlieb wrote, "I felt this was entirely out of line." *Girl Crazy* was finally released in November, the same month that Buzz learned of new IRS troubles. A $26,947 income tax lien had been filed against him on November 25.

Buzz was working on the budget for his next project, his first film at Warner Brothers as full director since *They Made Me a Criminal.* But things had changed in the four intervening years. One of these changes was Jack Warner's temper regarding Buzz. Though famous directors basked in the public spotlight, they were often castigated in private. To the heads of the studios, directors were regarded as overhead. They were employees, subject to verbal assault from their bosses. When Buzz missed a scheduled budget meeting, Jack Warner, in a rage, fired off a memo stating that he had called Buzz and asked him why he hadn't come to work. Buzz answered that the battery in his car would not start. Quote Jack: "I told him off plenty and he started to apologize and I then virtually insulted him. In case we need evidence against him in the future you can hold this on file as well as the trip to Chicago he made several weeks previous to today."

In mid-December, initial work had begun at Warner Brothers on the tentatively titled "Judy Adjudicates," set to star Faye Emerson and Dennis Morgan. Emerson was to replace the previously cast Jane Wyman, but ultimately Emerson was dropped in favor of Joan Leslie. Robert Alda was assigned Dennis Morgan's lead role. The title was changed to *Cinderella Jones,* and it was announced as Busby Berkeley's new picture at his "alma mater." Things started off precipitously; two days before Christmas, Buzz threw a party at his Adams Street home. The host's sobriety might have been at issue, for Buzz slipped on a piece of spaghetti on his kitchen floor and broke his right wrist. One of the guests, a doctor, rushed Buzz to his office and placed his arm in a plaster cast. Later, after the plaster hardened, a hole had to be cut out so that the face of his watch (which the doctor forgot to remove) would show through. It was a disappointed Busby Berkeley that never made it to the premiere of *The Gang's All Here,* his magnum opus of art and audacity.

The Gang's All Here opened Christmas 1943 at the Fox-owned

Roxy Theatre in New York. Most of the reviews were positive with the exception of the one appearing in the *New York Times,* which noted a Freudian slant to Berkeley's giant bananas: "But in the main, *The Gang's All Here* is a series of lengthy and lavish production numbers all arranged by Busby Berkeley as if money was no object but titillation was. Mr. Berkeley has some sly notions under his busby. One or two of his dance spectacles seem to stem straight from Freud and, if interpreted, might bring a rosy blush to several cheeks in the Hays office."

The American Motion Picture Arts and Sciences library offered no confirmation to the rumor that *The Gang's All Here* was banned in Brazil because of the way the giant bananas were used in "The Lady in the Tutti Frutti Hat" number. The picture was approved for export to South American countries soon after its New York release.

Buzz convalesced as well as his short temper would allow (he was anything but a subdued patient). On December 30, with his arm in a sling, he "directed" his *Cinderella Jones* stars in a radio truncation of the film's story. Douglas Drake, a new young actor in the cast, joined Robert Alda and Joan Leslie. During the radio play Drake made a tentative upraised gesture with his hand. Why he did it was a mystery (who would see it?), but evidently stage directions prompted him. Buzz didn't like it a bit. In a voice that could be heard from every corner of the stage he yelled, "Drake! Stop raising your hand so high! The way you're doing it looks like 'Teacher, I want to go!'"

10

The Stage Debacle

Buzz was still sporting a sling when he was seen again at Slapsie Max-ies's with his good arm around Lorraine. The two were close, and Buzz gave Lorraine a small no-credit role in *Cinderella Jones*. Divergent an-nouncements of Warner Brothers' plans for Buzz were issued in January. First, Buzz was to direct *and* appear in "Star Spangled Banner Girls" followed by a biography of Marilyn Miller, Florenz Ziegfeld's talented singing and dancing star.

Cinderella Jones was a tepid comedy with a couple of songs. Saddled with a basic premise that was somewhat dated in 1943, Judy Jones (Joan Leslie), an adorable dimwit, stands to earn a $10 million inheritance if she gets married within the next forty-eight hours. She decides to en-roll in the local all-men's college, hoping to meet a suitably intelligent marriage-minded fellow (a promise of largesse to the college eases her entry). All the while there's Tommy (Robert Alda), the guy who really loves Judy (if she could only take a hint). By the end of the picture it's revealed, not surprisingly, that he graduated college cum laude with an IQ of more than 200. As Judy and Tommy try to beat the deadline to marry, they're stopped by an army transport rumbling through town. They hop a ride on board a tank and sing a final number, allowing Buzz a few girlie close-ups, some robust singing soldiers, and a happy ending.

Despite Buzz's usual flair for fast comedy and snappy repartee, he was restrained with the limitations of a telegraphed script, causing him to default to broad physical comedy. As Judy absentmindedly substitutes a bar of soap in a cheese sandwich, the eater spews out bubble burps, à la the Three Stooges, and the gag gets repeated at least three more times. Hungarian character actor S. Z. ("Call me Cuddles") Sakall, playing the role of the chemistry professor, fares a bit better. He sings, dances, and plays the jowly jailbird accused of hanky-panky near the girls' dormi-tory. An in-joke (a form of which was seen in *They Made Me a Criminal*) has a hardened convict happy at last to have a cell all to himself. As he lies in his bunk, he sings the opening bars of a song suggested by his director, used here for the second time since 1933: "By a waterfall, I'm calling you oo oo oo."

Buzz wrapped *Cinderella Jones* in May 1944. A release date two to three months thereafter wouldn't have been out of the ordinary, but Buzz wasn't privy to the behind-the-scenes manipulations of the studio. Robert Alda was Warner Brothers' new star on the lot, and the studio wanted to introduce him to the moviegoing public in a film more prominent than *Cinderella Jones*. Alda's next role, as George Gershwin in *Rhapsody in Blue,* certainly filled the bill. So while that picture was filmed, edited, released, and reviewed, *Cinderella Jones* languished on Warner Brothers' shelf with no opening date in sight.

"Star Spangled Banner Girls" never materialized, and the more promising bio of Marilyn Miller was mired in legalities. The estate of the late singer-dancer refused to give the studio permission to film her life. Buzz and producer Jerry Wald hadn't even thought of a leading lady for the role, so the life of Marilyn Miller was a dead project. Buzz was now in the position he hadn't been in since *Kiki:* he had nothing on the drawing board and was technically unemployed. To make matters worse, Jack Warner wasn't returning his calls.

Lorraine Breacher and her "sparkler" never made it to the altar. The relationship chilled in early summer. By this time, Buzz was spending more time looking after Gertrude, and it's certainly possible that Lorraine was in no mood to compete for his attention. On June 2, the house maid drove Gertrude on an errand. They took the new large station wagon Buzz had purchased that allowed his mother easy access for her wheelchair. At the corner of Melrose Avenue and North Wilton Place, the maid suddenly and without warning slammed hard on the brakes, trying to avoid hitting a car that had stopped short. Without a belt to hold her in place, Gertrude was thrown forward, and she hit her head hard against the unyielding front seat. She was rushed to the hospital. The doctors told Buzz it might be a skull fracture.

The pressures were beginning to mount. No work meant no income in the face of Gertrude's mounting medical bills. She was in miserable shape, and a fully positive prognosis wasn't forthcoming. Buzz carried the weight of jumbo mortgages, property taxes, and alimony. And he still couldn't get Jack Warner's ear. Jack was in conference; Jack wasn't in his office; Jack wasn't on the lot. Buzz gave a message to Jack's assistant: Either Jack sees me soon or I want to be released from my contract. The bluff, fueled by nagging anxiety and impatience, backfired. Less than a week after Gertrude was admitted to the hospital, Buzz received a telegram from Jack Warner that stated his contract with the studio had been terminated.

After what must have seemed an interminable wait, Buzz was contacted with a job offer that piqued him. Jule Styne and Sammy Cahn (the composers for *Cinderella Jones*) were writing a new show back East called *Glad to See You,* and they and producer David Wolper wanted Buzz to stage and direct it. There would be out-of-town tryouts before coming to Broadway. By this time Mother was mending well, so Buzz took the job, his first stage show in fourteen years. He brought Gertrude and his secretary, and the three of them checked into New York's Savoy Plaza Hotel in September. Before casting began, columnist Dorothy Kilgallen got word that Buzz had gone to Atlantic City one weekend "out of sheer nostalgia." She didn't need to mention that Buzz used to be married to a "Miss America" and that this year he couldn't even get a date.

From almost the very beginning, *Glad to See You* was cursed. Rumors of financial problems surfaced. Buzz had made it past the casting stage when his leading lady, Hollywood actress Lupe Velez, had a snit over the unstarlike treatment she was receiving. She abruptly quit the show. Nightclub proprietor Eddie Davis (part owner of Leon and Eddie's on New York's Fifty-second Street) fancied himself an actor. Soon after winning his role, he was in a taxi accident and broke his collarbone. A showgirl in the cast took advantage of her day off and went to New York, where she had an accident and fractured her skull. One of the play's authors, Eddie Davis (not the sidelined actor), came down with pneumonia while he was furiously rewriting the show.

The casting process was more like casting and replacing. One can imagine Buzz rehearsing his troupe like *42nd Street*'s Julian Marsh: loud, irascible, and demanding. Both men had a lot riding on their shows. Both had financial troubles. The producers sought out the help of comic actor Eddie Foy Jr. in Hollywood to find West Coast replacements for his East Coast defections. For Buzz it was his chance to exploit his position and seek out the company of a pretty actress or two on the road. On November 20, Dorothy Kilgallen made a surprising announcement that Busby Berkeley would wed Marge Pemberton, a *Glad to See You* showgirl. Dorothy was only half right. While in Philadelphia, Buzz married former high-fashion model Myra Steffens. It was her second marriage and his fourth. Known as "the girl with the velvet skin," Myra auditioned for *Glad to See You,* and Buzz took it from there. The courtship lasted less than two months. Gertrude must have been beside herself.

When *Glad to See You* opened on November 13 at Philadelphia's Shubert Theatre, Gertrude was there. She insisted on going, saying to whomever would listen that she never missed Busby's openings and she didn't intend to start now. Hopefully her opinion of the show was brighter than the critics', for the next-day reviews were perfectly awful. They lauded the production design and hated the production. In the theater program (*The Playgoer*), Buzz was given the bloviated credit "Entire production staged and directed under the personal direction of Busby Berkeley." The one expected credit Buzz didn't take was for "dances and ensembles." They were handled by Valerie Bettis. *Billboard* magazine complimented Buzz and compared him to Flo Ziegfeld. David Wolper, the chief backer and victim, was similarly praised for the lavish sets and costumes ("he took the rubber band off the roll of bills"). Though Bettis's dance direction was described as "optic-pleasing" and the sets called "breathtaking" for the around-the-globe settings the story demanded, the show had a terminal problem at its core: the book. "Sorely in need of mirth and merriment throughout," "Radio's soap operas pack better situations than are found in this trivia," and "The book is threadbare and shallow" were some of its critiqued shortcomings. Buzz never met an obstacle that was as insurmountable as the bad script he was dealt. "Dr. Buzz The Show Fixer" had been unable to resurrect a production that was dead on arrival. When the show dragged its feet to the Opera House in Boston, it was described most accurately as "the worst hard-luck show in years." Closing on January 9, 1945, the $240,000 flop never made it to Broadway.

There came a point during rehearsals when Buzz had a sinking feeling that there was no future in *Glad to See You*. The advance ticket sales were weak, and he was made aware that producer Wolper was running short of funds. Buzz contacted an attorney and weighed his options before finally canceling his contract in December. Buzz, Myra, Gertrude, and his secretary returned to Los Angeles to sad news. On December 20, it was reported that Merna Kennedy had died of a heart attack at the age of thirty-five.

The late autumn/early winter chill in Philadelphia contrasted sharply with the weather back home, and when Gertrude returned to Los Angeles, a virus got the better of her compromised immune system. At the age of eighty she was diagnosed with pneumonia. Buzz searched in vain for a specialist. Gertrude recommended a doctor from the hospital in Oklahoma City where she stayed after the road trip accident. At his own expense, Buzz flew in the Sooner pulmonologist. Gertrude responded to treatment and was subsequently admitted for extended care at the Garden Grove sanitarium in Orange County.

Buzz was just too distracted with Mother to make a go of his sham marriage. Myra admitted honestly "the marriage was a big mistake. We will be better off apart." She sought an annulment. Buzz agreed, and his fourth "marriage" ended with nary a whimper.

Frank Honda, a genial man of Japanese ancestry, worked as Buzz's "houseboy," a combination butler, maid, and social secretary. More than a mere employee, Buzz respected Frank and regarded him as a friend. Around the time of Gertrude's sanitarium stay, Frank developed a urinary obstruction that almost proved fatal. He was rushed to the hospital and underwent emergency surgery. Buzz paid for the operation. For the first time in many years, he was completely alone while Frank and Gertrude were recuperating. On May 7, a few days into his solitude, the doorbell rang. It was Marge Pemberton, the showgirl mentioned in Dorothy Kilgallen's partially correct report. Buzz's spirits were instantly lifted, and he invited her in. They talked about many things, and Marge suggested they take up where they left off.

The very next day Buzz and Marge drove to Tijuana and were married.

Gertrude didn't like her surroundings, and she pleaded with her son, who brought her home and hired round-the-clock live-in nurses. Buzz lamented, "One of the bad things about Los Angeles is that there are two sets of prices, one for ordinary citizens and one for those in the picture business." Indeed, his expenses were weighing heavily on his mind; the stage debacle and an unreleased film left him with less and less to draw upon. Mother's health, once on the rebound, had now taken a precipitous decline. Around September 1945, Gertrude received a wrenching prognosis from her physician. She had terminal cancer. For Buzz, it was a bombshell. He couldn't be a devoted husband with this news hanging over his head. Buzz needed to be at Mother's beck and call, and he asked his wife of four months to move back with her parents, at least for the meantime. Marge sympathetically obliged.

Buzz kept a constant watch at Gertrude's side and left her for only brief periods during her cancer battle. Circumstances had found him married and separated, and due to his fragile emotional state (buttressed by the bottle) he was bound to make injurious moves, one of which was trying to reconnect with Claire James. On October 8, Harrison Carroll's column "Behind the Scenes in Hollywood" described Buzz calling his ex-wife, but, according to the director, "she isn't answering the phone."

Did Marge read Carroll's column? Two days after its publication, as Buzz finished a late-night vigil with Mother, he reportedly had a "family argument." Whether it was with Marge or Mother isn't clear, but a heavily liquored Busby Berkeley went for a late-night drive to cool off. He left the Adams Street mansion without thinking, dressed in pajama top, slacks, and hat. He drove about six miles when, near the corner of San Pedro Street and Vernon Avenue, his car stalled. Four black men saw the distraught director outside his vehicle and helped him push it down the road a short distance. When the engine started, all five got in the car. A few minutes later, a squad car pulled up behind them, and Buzz stopped at the side of the road. He explained that the men were just trying to help him and that he'd been up all night with his dying mother, but the police officer would hear none of it. Buzz was arrested for drunk driving and booked at the Lincoln Heights jail, where he gave his name as Busby Berkeley Enos and posted one hundred dollars bail.

Two days after the arrest, more grist for the mill: Dorothy Kilgallen claimed that Claire James (currently divorcing Ray Dorsey) might re-wed Buzz. Marge was again humiliated in the press. The source of the story remained anonymous.

On October 24, Municipal Judge Ben Rosenthal ordered Buzz's bail forfeited when he failed to appear in court for his hearing. The repercussions went further than a simple forfeiture of one hundred dollars. MGM was in the planning stages for a new film, *Till the Clouds Roll By*, a biographical musical of songwriter Jerome Kern. They wanted Buzz to reclaim the director's chair, but the drunkenness charge (reported in the local papers) had eliminated him from consideration. For the balance of the year, Buzz claimed only one film credit. A slapped-together Warner Brothers featurette titled *All Star Musical Review* contained nothing but archived musical sequences, but because Buzz had directed some of them, he received credit. By the end of 1945, he was still separated from Marge. During his extended unemployment, Buzz remained at Gertrude's side for the duration of her illness, which lingered well into the following year.

11

Inconsolable

There was no Hollywood red-carpet premiere for *Cinderella Jones* when it was finally released on March 9, 1946. By this time, the film had been recut and repackaged into a studio afterthought that garnered little praise. The gamble of waiting until Robert Alda had struck it big with *Rhapsody in Blue* didn't pay off. Alda never reached the studio's idea of his potential, and *Cinderella Jones* suffered because of it. The comedy with pertinent references to 1944 was dated and irrelevant two years later, and many of its war references were deleted by the studio.

Buzz's twenty-two-year-old bride separated from her husband less than a week after *Cinderella Jones* opened, and she sought a divorce on the grounds of cruelty soon thereafter. On April 1, in front of Judge Kenneth Chantry, the plaintiff spoke disparagingly about her husband: "He constantly accused me of being with another man—things like that." Newspapers reported the demise of Buzz's fifth marriage. Weeks later, a crazy coda was appended to the story. By the end of the month, there were rumors that Marge was thinking of marriage again—to Busby Berkeley!

If Buzz courted the idea of remarriage, the timing couldn't have been worse. Gertrude was declining rapidly, and Buzz admitted the whole situation "almost deranged me." He held hope and maintained a vigil, but by early summer life's spiraling senescence had Mother in its grip. A day nurse and a night nurse were on hand and kept a round-the-clock watch over Gertrude as Buzz dozed fitfully. On the evening of June 14, 1946, the night nurse exited Gertrude's room and approached Buzz, relaying the following: "Mr. Berkeley, your mother has gone." Moments before the pronouncement, Nellie Gertrude Berkeley Enos had silently died from cancer at the age of eighty-one.

Theirs was a co-dependency in the truest meaning of the word; their existences depended on each other. Buzz was overwhelmingly bereaved, for no mother and son had been closer in life. Her death enveloped Buzz like a tsunami wave. At low tide he could distract himself with the minutiae of gathering her things and making plans for her interment. Then suddenly the tremendous loss of his greatest champion in life profoundly saddened him and the cycle repeated itself. To the front of the line came a most pressing issue: the burial. A plot was never purchased in California, though a service was held at Forest Lawn Memorial Park. At the end of the service, Buzz placed both hands on the casket. With copious tears that blurred his vision, he bent down and for a final time he whispered the valediction he had given Gertrude every morning on his way to the studio: "I'll be right back, Mother . . . just as soon as I finish shooting."

Buzz sent his mother's casket to Mansfield, Ohio, where she was buried in the Mansfield cemetery alongside her beloved Frank. It isn't known whether this was Gertrude's request or the act of an idealistic son bringing his parents together in perpetuity.

Frank Honda welcomed his grieving employer upon his return from the Ohio funeral. There was little in the way of distraction as Buzz did not have work to ease his troubled mind. Mountainous debt was psychologically debilitating under the best circumstances; with Buzz in a veritable fog, his emotional and financial states were precarious. Gertrude's will named him her sole heir for everything including her real estate holdings and antiques. Buzz often made major decisions, like his ill-conceived marriages, without the least bit of reflection. In his bleak state, he moved to liquidate Gertrude's assets to raise the needed capital for bills that appeared beyond his means. The antiques were first to go to the auction block. The magnificent Beaux-Arts mansion on Adams Street was sold for pennies on the dollar; his $200,000 investment netted him a measly $35,000. The Redlands and Oklahoma properties were put on the market. Unfortunately, Gertrude's beloved twenty-four-room mansion in Dover, New Hampshire, was no longer Buzz's to sell. He had lost the property in a tax foreclosure while Gertrude was still alive. The nightmare of the liquidations was compounded by the federal government, which went after Buzz with a vengeance. He owed them $120,000 in back taxes. With the debts mounting and years of unemployment, it's no great surprise that Buzz's exorbitant cash-flow requirements made the payment of federal and property taxes a secondary consideration.

Buzz asked Frank to continue in his employ, and as soon as it was possible, he turned over the keys to the Adams Street mansion and, along with Frank, moved to a very small place in the much-less-desirable neighborhood of Echo Park on a street called Altivo Way. For a few weeks after Gertrude's burial, Buzz found himself in the dusty taverns located in the perimeter of his new home. According to a police report, Buzz was charged with public intoxication and brandishing a gun. The judge fined him only ten dollars because he was told that was all the money Buzz had.

An all-encompassing lachrymosity weighed heavily on Buzz's shoulders. It was an emotional burden of immeasurable depth, anxiety, and melancholy. A severe depression haunted his waking hours while fretful sleep came only at the hands of a prescription pill and a liquor chaser. His telephone remained mute. No studio wanted him. Tomorrow held nothing in the way of opportunity. Mother was gone, and he needed her and missed her so much. And so it repeated from sun to sun until July 17, when Buzz crossed the invisible line of madness.

He had been drinking heavily the night before and had later visited a physician for some sleeping pills. The doctor gave Buzz the medication and drove him home. The next morning his tortured mind lost all abandon. He leapt out of bed as if in a panic and went to the telephone, calling the city desk at the *Los Angeles Times*. He identified himself and said, "If you come out here, you'll find what's left of me." In his small bathroom, he quickly, without entertaining a counter thought, picked up a razor blade and slashed his left wrist and throat. Frank heard a yell and a thump, and he ran into the bathroom, finding Buzz on the floor in a blood pool. He thought fast and ripped a bed sheet to use as a tourniquet and then called for an ambulance. Reporters arrived at Altivo Way riding behind the sirens. They entered the property and found press clippings and autographed pictures of Judy Garland and Mickey Rooney strewn across a crimson-splattered floor. A reporter's photograph taken at the scene showed Buzz with two policemen and an ambulance attendant, his face in a horrible grimace as he's being forcibly restrained. He was rushed to the Georgia Street Receiving Hospital.

A calmed Frank Honda later told patrolmen J. B. Jameson and V. R. Bohl that he found Berkeley near collapse, gasping: "I'm going. No one cares about me anymore but you. I'm going to Mother." The razor wounds were superficial, and Buzz was bandaged. The psychological wounds were still on display when Buzz said: "I'm a has-been and know it. There is no comeback trail for a has-been. I can't seem to get myself straightened out for any length of time. Each time I get married it seems to turn out wrong. I'm broke. When my mother died, everything seemed to go with her."

Sober and detoxed, Buzz was taken to Los Angeles General Hospital and placed in the psychiatric ward. Since the hospital lacked space, he was denied a private room and was placed in the corridor, where a mixture of disturbed patients walked past in a never-ending horror parade. Buzz was moved to a room the next day; its previous occupant had died. A thick iron bolt on the door prevented escape. An AP wire photo taken the day after the suicide attempt and titled "Berkeley and Ex-Wife No. 5" showed Buzz on his hospital bed while, at his bedside, Marge Pemberton talked on the telephone. The caption specifically mentioned an overdose of sleeping pills and that the couple had divorced three months earlier.

In order to gain his release, Buzz had to come up with a convincing argument to a judge who made the hospital rounds on a weekly basis. The judge moved from room to room and listened to patients pleading their cases. Buzz told the judge the circumstances that had brought him here and that he would seek out the services of a private sanitarium upon his release. The judge agreed, and Buzz was discharged. He followed through with his promise and admitted himself into a sanitarium. He pleaded with his doctors not to administer shock treatments. He said he just wanted to rest. Six weeks later, after shedding more than 60 pounds from his already thin 170-pound frame, Buzz, looking extremely gaunt, was released. He returned to his Echo Park residence with Frank Honda, and was, in a strange way, happy to learn that when his and his mother's bills were finally paid and accounted for, he was left with seven hundred fifty dollars. "After all I had been through," said Buzz, "I was grateful to get that."

The pining for Claire James was over. Buzz, in a weak moment, had tried to regain contact during Gertrude's final days, but nothing came of it. In February 1947, Claire married movie producer William Girard.

Buzz wanted and needed work. He was willing to swallow his pride, to grovel if necessary. He phoned longtime colleague and friend George Amy and told him of his readiness to return. George, who went back with Buzz to when they codirected *She Had to Say Yes,* and most recently had edited *Cinderella Jones,* had not contacted Buzz during his recent dark days. Amy was, nonetheless, glad to hear from Buzz. Over lunch, George and Buzz talked shop and about Mother, and Buzz learned the latest Hollywood developments. The prolific Warner Brothers director Michael Curtiz had his own production company with the studio, and George was its vice president. He described their first project for Buzz, a musical titled "Romance in High C." Of course, he'd like Buzz to come on board, but Curtiz Productions was not autonomous. Buzz would first have to be the recipient of Jack L. Warner's forgiveness and approval.

Buzz entered Jack Warner's office hat in hand. He had no appointment, but he conned Warner's secretary into believing he did. She knew Buzz and believed there was an oversight on her part. Warner wasn't in, so Buzz took a seat and waited. When the boss returned, he was friendly and kind to Buzz, and Buzz reciprocated. Buzz offered a sincere apology for the rashness of his demand of years earlier and described for Jack the hell he had been through, offering a final anecdote or two about Mother. Buzz mentioned George Amy and the Michael Curtiz picture and humbly asked for a job. Warner was sympathetic and willing to let bygones be bygones. In a June 4, 1947, studio memo from Eric Stacey to T. C. Wright, Jack Warner's influence was implicitly stated: "Curtiz is thinking of employing Busby Berkeley to do the work now being handled by Bob Sidney. This suggestion came from J. L. Warner 'that Busby be given a chance to do some work.'"

And Buzz was hired that very day. An announcement that "The Curtiz Company has engaged Busby Berkeley to do the song routines for *Romance in High C*" was immediately released. The following week Michael Curtiz went one step further and announced in a trade article that he was keeping Buzz on as full-fledged director for some of his independent movies. The article described Buzz as "completely straightened out."

The film was already in production with Curtiz as director, but no lead actress had been signed. The producers failed to get Mary Martin or Betty Hutton. As their third choice, they signed twenty-five-year-old singer Doris Day, who had had a hit record with "Sentimental Journey" two years prior. In her first film, Doris spent her mornings working with Buzz and afternoons with Curtiz.

"The [girls on the set] are better than ever. Their legs are prettier, their faces are fresher, their posture is better, and I think they even dance better!" exclaimed an enthusiastic Busby Berkeley to the United Press. "One thing I'm sure of, these girls are ambitious. There's the gleam of stardom in every eye. Too bad they won't all make it." On the subject of gold diggers, Buzz said: "I always feel a little remorseful when I think that maybe it was my fault that everybody used to think all chorus girls were gold diggers. It isn't true. Only some of them are." The complimentary piece went on to quote a studio policeman who was having a hard time keeping prying eyes off the set. "You'd think they had free beer in there. I have never seen such a crowd in 10 years."

Jack Warner didn't like the title "Romance in High C," and it was per his edict that the title was changed to *Romance on the High Seas*. In the colorful picture, Buzz is given the generous "Musical numbers created and directed by" credit. He also directed the film's trailer under the supervision of Arthur Silver. George Amy was on board as associate producer. This assignment was, in no small way, the antidote to Buzz's despondency. Here he was, back at the old studio of his ascendancy for the first time since he wrapped the ephemeral *Cinderella Jones*.

The number "The Tourist Trade" is a bright tune performed by former Cotton Club singer Avon Long and danced in Warner Brothers' version of a Havana marketplace. Buzz's breezy camera floats effortlessly through the confining stage, ending in a perfectly framed shot of a birdcage in the foreground while Long dances away from the camera merrily singing the melody. The film's only hit song, "It's Magic," is performed a few times, the first when Doris Day sings it to Jack Carson at tableside. Buzz doesn't add his stamp of originality here, and the number is filmed without any visual excitement. The same could be said for the lackluster "Put 'em in a Box, Tie 'em with a Ribbon and Throw 'em in the Deep Blue Sea," shot with little flourish. Jack Carson gets in a calypso song ("Run, Run, Run") in artificial Trinidad Creole English, but the number also lacks a strong directorial imprint. Fortunately, the Berkeley touch is recognized strongly in the final sequence, a brilliant bout of direction reminiscent of *Wonder Bar*'s "Don't Say Goodnight" on a smaller scale. As the scene opens, colorful balloons fill the screen. The balloons are removed, revealing a twirling dancer. She moves backward and turns the hinged wall, which now displays a mirror. Then three more walls turn into mirrors reflecting a complexity of images as Buzz's brilliant camera remains incognito. The camera turns away from the mirrors as the procession of dancers and multihued balloons dance out of the scene. It's a redemption of only two minutes length, but Buzz proved again that he was still viable, still creative, and could direct with his artistic integrity intact. The film wrapped production on August 5, its fifty-third shooting day, placing the production seven days ahead of schedule. On August 18, it was reported that Buzz's next project would be directing "Forever and Always."

That "next project" from the Curtiz group never materialized. The studio offered nothing either. Buzz was understandably concerned as promises were seemingly broken. But promises without contractual muscle were weightless. In November, a throwaway line from a Louella Parsons column brought to light a situation that the studio would have rather kept private. She reported that Buzz and Jack Warner had had a row of such proportions that he had been banned from the studio lot. "Jack gave him a job when he was down and out and needed a hand," wrote Louella. For the third time, Buzz left Warner Brothers; this time, though, he could smell the fire of the bridge that was burning behind him.

12

One Last at Bat

The trades in May revealed that Esther Williams was named by MGM to play the leading role in its newest film, *Take Me Out to the Ball Game,* which was to begin filming the following month.

Whatever instigated the ugly argument that sealed his fate with Warner Brothers mattered little to Buzz now. *Romance on the High Seas* had garnered positive reviews and turned a tidy profit. Buzz proved to himself he could still direct with imagination and authority. Over the Fourth of July holiday, he undoubtedly was a recipient of some very troubling news concerning Carole Landis. She was found facedown dead by her lover, actor Rex Harrison, who was married at the time to actress Lilli Palmer. In Carole's clenched hand was an envelope containing a single Seconal, the only one of a bunch she didn't ingest. If Gertrude hadn't interfered, the shapely and beautiful Carole would have been a sure bet to take the role that Claire James later won. Carole never saw thirty.

Take Me Out to the Ball Game originated with Gene Kelly and his friend, choreographer Stanley Donen, in the summer of 1946. Its inception came after Kelly had refused an idea from MGM producer Joe Pasternak. *Anchors Aweigh* had been a solid hit a few years earlier, and Pasternak wanted a reteaming of Kelly and Frank Sinatra. Gene listened to Pasternak's idea of two sailors (again) caught up in wacky nonsense as they unexpectedly end up owning a government surplus aircraft carrier. A short time later, they transform the carrier into a swinging nightclub. Kelly balked, so to speak, and began developing his and Donen's story of three baseball players in the early days of the twentieth century. In 1946, MGM bought the rights for twenty-five thousand dollars.

Arthur Freed was the producer of *Take Me Out to the Ballgame.* Despite the fallout suffered during *Girl Crazy,* Buzz contacted Freed and told him he wanted to direct again. "I wanted to help him," said Freed, "but it was a case of getting the right property for him. His was a very special talent and at this time in his life he couldn't afford to fail." The story's themes of vaudevillians and ballplayers before the First World War seemed a nice fit for Buzz. He and Kelly were amiable going back to *For Me and My Gal,* and Freed thought their working relationship could be harmonious. They both agreed on Buzz.

Unfortunately, Arthur didn't have the final word on the choice of directors. Buzz would first have to pass muster with his old boss, Louis B. Mayer. He and Arthur arranged a meeting with the studio chief. Buzz expressed contritely that he was capable and cured and ready again to take the director's chair. He told Mayer that he considered himself as good a director as he was in the past. "What makes you think so?" asked Mayer. From his jacket pocket Buzz pulled out a small notebook. "It's a little saying I had in my notebook which I carried close to my heart all through the first World War and today that saying applies to me more than anything else, and this is it: 'I have traveled a long way over sea and sod and I have found nothing as small as me and nothing as great as God.'" This made a strong impression on the pious Mr. Mayer. He was silent for a few moments. Then, in a quiet voice, he said, "God bless you, Buzz. God bless you." He turned his attention to Arthur Freed and gave the order: "Buzz will direct *Take Me Out to the Ball Game,*" and the meeting was adjourned.

When Buzz signed on to *Ball Game,* it was understood that Kelly and Donen would conceive and direct the musical numbers while he would direct the book. Freed said this arrangement took the strain off Buzz. There is evidence, however, that Buzz would have contributed to the film in a spectacular fashion had he not been overruled by his leading actor. But trouble of another sort was percolating.

Buzz was asked to mediate an increasingly sour situation between Gene Kelly and Esther Williams. She was, simply put, a swimmer, not a dancer. She had a swimmer's broad shoulders, long legs, and long waistline. But it was obvious she was not what the perfectionist Gene Kelly had in mind. He was, according to Williams, "a tyrant behind the camera." Esther's inability to hoof as well as her costar wasn't the only thing that irked Kelly. An organic difference also raised his ire; she was at least half a head taller than him. In a musical scene where they sat together on a bench, Kelly was forced to look up to see his costar's face. "You know something? This sonofabitch even *sits* tall!" quipped Kelly to Stanley Donen (who was manning the camera).

Esther was the constant butt of jokes and sarcastic remarks from Kelly and Donen. She sought Buzz's sympathy in the hope that he could ease the tensions developing on the set. A meeting was scheduled with producer Freed in attendance. Buzz played ombudsman. As a diversionary tactic, he presented a remarkable idea designed to tamp down the flare-ups between his stars: he would direct a musical number for the picture. He had it all planned out in his mind, like every super-production he had ever conceived. It was to be his forte—a water number. A dream sequence would feature Esther swimming in a strong current while Gene, in a futile stretch, would reach out to grab hold of her, missing by inches. The theme of barely touching and losing would be repeated again and again. Esther called the idea very sexy and very pretty. Arthur Freed loved it. He instructed Buzz to transfer the number from his mind's eye to storyboards and have them ready for a follow-up meeting.

Esther saw the storyboards and was wildly enthusiastic. To her, this man had a sense of showmanship. She could envision Busby Berkeley directing all her films from now on. Despite the fact that in some circles Buzz was "still known to drink a drop or two," it was very obvious that he was bubbling with inspiration and far from being burned out.

As Esther explained, "Other writers and producers were coming up with only the most contrived excuses to get me into the pool, but Buzz had all kinds of marvelous ideas, not just for this film, but for others as well." Alas, the number Buzz had in mind for *Ball Game* never advanced beyond the storyboard. Kelly vetoed it as soon as he saw the drawings. The director couldn't pull rank as Arthur Freed gave Gene the final say-so. Esther insinuated that he hated the number because he couldn't swim. "I know how to swim, smartass," replied Kelly through squinted dagger-eyes.

Filmed in its place was an ill-conceived number called "Baby Doll." Esther and Gene played adult babies taking stutter steps around a park's water fountain. The "choreography" makes the stars look like robots badly in need of repair. The end of the number was to have both of them fall into the fountain. Fortunately, the camera operator failed to catch every nuance of their performance and fumbled his cues. The stars were soaked from the fountain, and rather than waiting to have them dry off, production was halted and the number was never reshot.

With his water ballet discarded, Buzz became nothing more than a director for hire. A coworker remarked that Buzz simply shot his scenes and went home. His career had turned on its ear. At one time it was *he* who had worked autonomously. In the golden Gold Digger days, Buzz banished meddling producers from his set. Now it was Buzz who was kept from meddling in the musical numbers of others.

The film's trailer proudly announced "Those *Anchors Aweigh* Boys Are Back . . . With a Gorgeous New Playmate!" followed by this comparison: "In the Spectacular Entertainment Tradition of *Anchors Aweigh, Easter Parade, A Date with Judy, Words and Music*." The name Busby Berkeley, once a ticket-selling motivator, was nowhere to be seen.

It's 1906 as two vaudeville stars, Eddie O'Brien (Gene Kelly) and Dennis Ryan (Frank Sinatra), travel by train from Pottstown, Illinois, to Sarasota, Florida. Both are ballplayers for the world-champion Wolves, shortstop and second baseman respectively, and they're meeting up with their team already in spring training. Eddie's heart belongs to the stage, not the baseball diamond, and in a wistful moment he expresses a deep desire that could have come from Buzz himself: "Give me Vaudeville anytime . . . and maybe a musical show. Fifty girls, fifty! Maybe even a hundred girls, a hundred! Oh boy."

Upon arrival in Florida, the boys sing a rollicking number describing their days on the vaudeville circuit. "Yes, Indeedy" is clever and witty with lyrics that are just bawdy enough to risk a violation of the Hollywood Production Code. News that the team would have a new owner by the name of K. C. Higgins (Esther Williams) is met with trepidation. They've never heard of this "Mr." Higgins before, and what did he know about baseball anyway? The complications are soon rectified as it's revealed that, improbably, K. C. is short for Katherine Catherine. Both Kelly and Sinatra are smitten and misguided, especially Sinatra, who's oblivious that a gambler's moll (played with wide-eyed gumption by Betty Garrett) has her sights set on him.

Balancing the picture was actor Edward Arnold, playing a high-stakes gambler who enjoys wagering on baseball. It's his plotting to keep star player Kelly on the field during the day and on the stage at night that keeps the flimsy plot afloat. The film wrapped on a rousing self-congratulatory note. In a vaudevillian setting, Frank and Gene, blue-vested and top-hatted, inform us in song that "Sinatra Gets Garrett" and "Kelly Gets Williams."

Buzz still managed to add a bit of directorial pizzazz even in the most mundane scenes. One simple, yet beautifully directed, sequence takes place as Kelly and Sinatra watch Esther Williams swimming privately in the team's hotel pool. As she sings the title song, Berkeley's camera follows the swimmer through her paces, slowly and elegantly, artfully illuminated by strategically submerged pool lights.

By this time, Gene was already an established star with his own ideas on filming a musical number, and one day during shooting Betty Garrett overheard a snickering remark from her costar. Buzz, high up in his perch, was setting up a panoramic shot and wasn't happy with the perspective. Cinematographer George Folsey caught the fury of Buzz's lacerating voice, "Back . . . back . . . take the camera back, Folsey!" In a volume louder than a whisper, Gene said, "Yeah, back to 1930." An equally interesting mischaracterization came from Frank Sinatra, who found Buzz "too epicene and flamboyant to take seriously."

With such rancor in the ranks, it was somewhat merciful that *Take Me Out to the Ball Game* wrapped in late September 1948. Buzz proved himself again and did a yeoman's job for his producer. The most accurate assessment of the misunderstood director came from Arthur Freed: "He was probably the most remarkable talent we had in the early days of movie musicals. He had an inborn camera sense, a fantastic eye. His creations are like dreams of the imagination. I consider him an instinctive surrealist, although I doubt if he himself has ever realized it. Like 'beauty is what beauty does,' Buzz just is."

On October 1, Buzz was paying off a one thousand dollar loan to his producer/mentor. He authorized Loew's Incorporated to deduct the amount from his pay and issue Arthur Freed a check in its stead. Less than a fortnight later, in the wee hours of the morning, Buzz was arrested on a suspicion of drunk driving.

Four motorcycle officers with screaming sirens chased him for a half mile. They brought him to the Culver City Jail. There, to newsmen, Buzz rambled drunkenly: "I was on my way back from the beach alone. I only had one cocktail and I was cold sober. I just finished a picture at

MGM. The last time I got into trouble I was out of a job for three years. It takes courage to pick up the pieces and start again." Coast to coast, his transgressions with the bottle provided fodder for the press. On October 13, Buzz pleaded innocent in front of Judge A. A. Randall and told him that his attorney (Jerry Giesler) couldn't come to court. The judge rescheduled, and on October 19, Buzz changed his plea to guilty. He walked away with only a $250 fine.

Buzz lay low following this humiliation. His groveling to Louis B. Mayer before *Take Me Out to the Ball Game* must have seemed disingenuous in light of his weakness and arrest. No assignment came his way in November, but a fortuitous bit of good news the following month had him poised as director for MGM's production of Broadway's hottest musical of 1946, Irving Berlin's *Annie Get Your Gun*. There was a snag, though. An impenetrable rift had been established when the actress cast in the lead role of Annie Oakley was told the director was to be the whip-cracking, gun-shooting Busby Berkeley. She went into a "weeping rage" and refused to work with the man ever again. But that's exactly how Judy Garland felt.

An anomaly in Buzz's public record is an unexplained photograph by Peter Stackpole taken on New Year's Eve 1948. The setting is a party at the home of producer Sam Spiegel; the interior: a staircase with a white runner and decorative white S-shaped balusters. In the background is Spiegel, bald and bespectacled. Leaning over the banister is an attractive brunette in a strapless evening dress. She's made up and accessorized in the Hollywood style. Between her first two nail-polished fingers is a lit cigarette. The official title of the image identifies her as "Mrs. Busby Berkeley." It was Marge Pemberton—the same Marge Pemberton who was labeled "the ex–Mrs. Berkeley" in the wire service reports issued after Buzz's suicide attempt.

Annie Get Your Gun was being honed, the tempers of Judy and Buzz were tamped, and only costume tests were being done, with no real shooting scheduled for months. Judy was talked into staying with the project, and it isn't unreasonable to believe that Buzz got a nod and a wink from Arthur Freed persuading him to treat his star with kid gloves.

Buzz played nice. He had to. The Internal Revenue Service was after him again, and he needed cash now; otherwise a near-$100,000 liability would be due in full. In a letter dated March 30, 1949 (on

Metro-Goldwyn-Mayer Pictures letterhead), the officers of the studio agreed to a cash advance for Buzz. In part, it read: "Under the terms of a Tax Settlement Agreement, Mr. Berkeley was required to pay the Treasury Department $6,500.00 not later than March 11, 1949. Otherwise he would be in default under the agreement and in the absence of making payment as aforesaid there would become immediately due $96,000.00 in back taxes. I explained the above circumstances to Mr. Moskowitz who, after due deliberation, telegraphed approval to advance $6,500.00 to Mr. Berkeley as a loan." Louis B. Mayer signed off on the loan along with executives Eddie Mannix, Benjamin Thau, and vice president L. K. Sidney. Buzz agreed to pay the studio back at the rate of six hundred dollars per week.

Take Me Out to the Ball Game opened in April in New York and Los Angeles. When it played in the United Kingdom, the strictly American title was changed to the bland *Everybody's Cheering*. *Variety* accurately described the picture: "short on story, but has amusing moments. It doesn't add up to much in the end but it's a constant joy to watch under Berkeley's expert guidance." The *Hollywood Reporter* praised the director when it said, "Berkeley takes these tried and true elements and fashions them into a directorial job that abounds in good humor, deft touches of business and sly sauciness." The *Los Angeles Examiner,* in an overly effusive vein, asked its readers to "pay a happy tribute to Busby Berkeley who directed all this giddy froth with such a sure touch that it kept it from blowing straight away, even while it bubbled up like a fresh strawberry soda on a hot summer day." Howard Barnes of the *Herald Tribune* wasn't nearly as amused: "Busby Berkeley directed the book as though he were trying to drive home jokes with the nearest thing at hand—a baseball bat."

Regardless, the profits Arthur Freed had envisioned were met and surpassed. On a budget of roughly $1.75 million, *Take Me Out to the Ball Game* earned worldwide a respectable $4 million.

For its stars, the film proved to the producer that the team of Kelly and Donen could handle musical sequences for film. They wanted a promotion to the director's chair, and Freed agreed. Almost immediately after *Ball Game* was released, work began on *On the Town*. In December of that year, the film premiered in the city of its opening number, "New York, New York." One would suppose the film's trailer would make

mention of *Take Me Out to the Ball Game*. After all, four of its principals were reteamed. Instead, the studio decided to reference a previous
success in the rhymed exclamation: "Twice as gay as 'Anchors Aweigh!'"

Unexpectedly, the Writer's Guild saw fit to nominate Harry Tugend
and George Wells for their script of *Take Me Out to the Ball Game*. A
plagiarism suit was later filed against the studio, but nothing came of it.

Buzz won *Photoplay*'s Blue Ribbon Award for the film. The award
read: "The Best Picture of the Month for the Whole Family. Box Office
Blue Ribbon Award April 1949 Busby Berkeley Director *Take Me Out
to the Ball Game*." He also received the industry's Laurel Award. It was
an engraved wooden and brass plaque that read "Exhibitor 1949 Voted
by the Film Buyers of the Motion Picture Industry Laurel Awards "Take
Me Out to the Ball Game" Directed by Busby Berkeley, A Laurel Award
Winner."

Esther Williams placed an inspirational bug in Buzz's ear with vi-
sions of water ballets yet unfilmed. They left the project with a promise
of another director/star collaboration. But at MGM in the late 1940s
budgets were tight, and a man with Buzz's extravagant directorial style
was not awarded a blank check. "Anyone who gave Berkeley an unlimited budget would be out of his mind," said an unidentified producer.
After a few months of inactivity, Buzz was focused on two fronts: bringing *Annie Get Your Gun* to the screen and the troubled Judy Garland
into the fold.

On April 4, 1949, production began. Judy and the cast had recorded
the entire score. She took accent lessons and was fitted for costumes.
Photos of her wardrobe tests (the identification placard reads "Berkeley,
Indian Village, Scene 53, Change #6") show her standing, purse-lipped,
in headband, single feather, and full-length Indian dress. Judy's festering
drug abuse was a secret only to the public. Soon after finally accepting
the lead, she noticed her hair was falling out. The drugs exacerbated her
condition.

The lead actor, Howard Keel, was new to motion pictures but had
had a recent success in London with *Oklahoma!* A few days into the
shooting, Buzz put him in the hospital. Keel was supposed to ride a
horse slowly on the soundstage. Buzz wanted the horse to pick up the
pace. He directed Keel to up the horse's speed to a gallop. On take seven,
across a shiny floor, the horse slipped. Keel's ankle broke when his spurs

caught into the ground. Of his director, Keel remarked: "Buzz was a bad drunk. He didn't drink when I was there, but he was a wild man when he worked. He didn't care what the actor was doing. All he thought of was the camera."

On April 6, while Keel recovered, Buzz shot the number "Doin' What Comes Natur'lly." Judy, in a ripped brown dress, and four children sing the number to actor Clinton Sundberg on a cheap-looking set whose frugality called attention to itself. The number came off embarrassingly flat for both Buzz and Judy. Her backwoods accent wasn't the one required. She appeared distracted while mouthing her singing track. As Sundberg exited, the scene ended as Annie was talking to her rifle. Before she finished, Buzz interrupted and yelled, "That's it!" which visibly angered Judy. "Hey you cut before I got my line out," she said irately.

The clapboard for the "I'm an Indian Too" number clearly shows John Alton's name and the date (4–28), yet the look and style of what was saved feels like Buzz had a controlling hand. The costumes and setting are colorful in flaring reds, maroons, and oranges. The sunset backdrop on the obvious set is reminiscent of the stage-bound *Whoopee!* Judy looks haggard as she bounces between the tribe of tom-tom players. When she receives her answer to "am I an Indian yet?" she dons a single feather and is hoisted up and down. For a moment, a balding patch can be seen on her head. The number ends with Judy running backward beneath a bridge of connecting arms, then reversing herself moving right up to the camera in a shot that, if not credited to Buzz, certainly feels like his handiwork.

On May 3, Arthur Freed looked at Buzz's footage. "Buzz had no conception of what this was all about," said Freed. "He was shooting the whole thing like a stage show. Everyone would come out of the wings, say their lines, and back away upstage for their exits." He took Buzz off the picture and replaced him with Charles Walters. Walters was "appalled" with the footage already in the can, and together he and Arthur Freed decided that none of it could be saved. The *New York Times* announced Buzz's separation from the picture with news that his next assignment would be *Summer Stock*, set to begin filming in June.

On May 6, *Annie Get Your Gun* shut down for a few days. On May 10, Judy had a very bad day. Buzz had already been removed from the picture, so he couldn't be blamed for Judy showing up on the set hours late and not in wardrobe. After a two-hour lunch break, Judy received a letter from studio vice president L. K. Sidney. In it, Judy was reprimanded for her many delays. The studio had had enough. Judy was placed on suspension, and the film was shut down from May 11 to May 21. *Annie Get Your Gun* would not roll before the cameras until the end of September, when Betty Hutton was signed for the lead. The film marked a chilling of the working relationship between Buzz and Arthur Freed. Though Buzz remained contracted to MGM, Freed never again used his services as director either in full or for a picture's musical numbers. A career non sequitur was announced in the papers on August 2. Mickey Rooney was now independently producing films, and he was planning to go to Argentina to make a picture with his old pal Buzz Berkeley. Neither his helming of *Summer Stock* nor his South American sojourn would come to pass.

13

Jumping, Tapping, Diving

For ten months, from the *Annie* dismissal of May 1949 to the last day of February 1950, Buzz remained unemployed. An agreement dated February 28, 1950, between Buzz and Loew's Incorporated was signed. Buzz was to act as a dance director for an untitled film for a period of at least seven days and possibly more, at a salary of five hundred dollars per week. On March 23, the untitled film was revealed to be *Two Weeks with Love,* and production officially began.

If you were in your fifties in 1950, the nostalgia of fin-de-siècle America, as wistfully portrayed in *Two Weeks with Love,* would've elucidated a warm memory or two. It was an era when a corset bridged the gap from young miss to lady, and knickers separated the boys from the men. Buzz, always making the most of what little was given, staged his numbers on smallish sets with verve and creativity. In the lovable nonsense number about love between a chimpanzee and monkey, "Aba Daba Honeymoon," fresh-faced Debbie Reynolds and long-legged beanpole Carleton Carpenter dance, sing, and cavort under Buzz's direction. In close-ups of his leads, you can almost hear the demanding boss urging them to "open your eyes . . . be expressive" in that razor tone he used on Judy Garland so many times. For their part, Reynolds and Carpenter were totally compliant (and utterly charming). In the downtime between camera setups, Debbie and Carleton marveled at the sight of Buzz being lifted at odd levels and angles, and together they jokingly sang the following to the tune of "How High the Moon":

> Somewhere there's Busby,
> How high the boom!

Jane Powell ("Janie" to Buzz) in the lead role uses her trained soprano voice in the fantasy number "My Hero." With his eye for lighting and

blocking, Buzz mixes sword fighting and romantic dance in the guise of
a mini operetta. His ascending and descending boom follows Janie and
Latin heartthrob Ricardo Montalban as they pirouette and spin in graceful, complementary movements. Montalban gallantly raises Janie on his
shoulder as the music reaches its peak. He then takes his partner's gloved
hand, slowly spins her around, and they end the number in a caressing
embrace. It's another of those great Berkeley routines, isolated and im-
pervious to everything that precedes it. Carleton Carpenter and Debbie
Reynolds return for the athletically performed "Row, Row, Row" while
Jane Powell and Ricardo Montalban dance the tango. Both numbers
were stage-bound and filmed perfunctorily without much of Buzz's zip.
Buzz's legacy on *Two Weeks with Love* was his little number that turned
out to be a million-selling record. A recording was made at the time of the
film's release, and in 1950 you couldn't pass a radio or groups of singing
teenagers without hearing the revived 1914 vaudevillian tune: "Aba daba
daba daba daba daba daba said the monkey to the chimp . . ."

With Broadway still in his marrow, Buzz announced to the world
that he was returning to the stage after Labor Day to assume the role as
"producing director" of the musical once known as *The Bowl of Brass*
(from the 1944 novel of the same name by Paul Wellman). The official
producer was Broadway veteran Arch Selwyn, and the show was now
temporarily referred to as "It's an Old Kansas Custom." John Raitt
(*Oklahoma!* and *Carousel*) had been signed, and if Buzz persuades her,
high-kicking Charlotte Greenwood might make a return to the theater.
Financing to the tune of $150,000 had been secured, and, reportedly, a
"mammoth" square dance was set for the finale.

On June 5, it was announced that October would be the month when
"An Old Kansas Custom" (its final title) would play road engagements
prior to Broadway. The scheduled cities were Pasadena, San Francisco,
and, naturally, Kansas City. Two days later, Buzz received a pat on the
back from MGM in the form of a letter and enclosure. "In appreciation
of your cooperation and of the excellent services rendered by you we
take pleasure in handing you herewith our check representing payment
to you of the sum of Two Thousand Five Hundred dollars (less proper
deductions)." The letter reaffirmed that the payment did not alter the
contract of February 28.

Buzz's planned return to Broadway, his first since 1930's *Sweet and Low*, came to a screeching halt sooner than the *Glad to See You* failure of the 1940s. Producer Arch Selwyn hadn't brought a show to Broadway since 1939. Something always intervened. When a new Selwyn production was announced, it was taken with a grain of salt by the press. "An Old Kansas Custom" never made it out of rehearsals, and Buzz forever remained mute about the project.

Just two months before, the *New York Times* had announced that Fox Studios had engaged Buzz's services for the musical sequences in *Call Me Mister*. For Buzz it was a double reunion. Director Lloyd Bacon collaborated last with Buzz in *Gold Diggers of 1937*. The leading lady, a star for a decade and the pin-up icon of World War II, was Betty Grable, now mature and worldly, but just as perky and cute as the anonymous teenage cowgirl in *Whoopee!*

The following month, the Technicolor cameras rolled on *Call Me Mister*. It was based on the Broadway musical of the same name, but this version contained eight songs, only three of which were carried over from the original production.

It's the end of World War II, and with the announcement that the Japanese have surrendered, the soldiers stationed in Japan are itching to get home. Shep Dooley (Dan Dailey), a GI for the entertainment services, runs into his estranged wife, Kay (Betty Grable), while on a final leave in Tokyo. She's part of C.A.T.S. (Civilian Actress Technicians Service) doing stage shows for the troops and, supposedly, wants nothing to do with her "ex." Shep arranges for Kay to put on a stage show at which time he feels he could win her back. The outcome is fairly obvious, but the stars, Lloyd Bacon's crisp-as-ever direction, and Buzz's color-infused musical numbers make for an enjoyable ninety-six minutes.

Buzz's first number, the stage-bound "Japanese Girl Like 'Merican Boy," is a love letter to the American soldier. It features a couple dozen Geisha girls in brightly hued kimonos, who flap their hand fans and sing of awe and respect to a giant painting of a GI. Grable sings the lead vocal (with lyrics as corny as, "Gee I wish I had a G.I.") in Asian-style makeup. The Buzz imprints are all there: the hand fans surrounding the lead singer, the interesting blocking of the dancers, the gauntlet effect (two rows facing each other moving apart as the camera passes through them) that leads to a circumstantial change. Now it's Grable in white navy garb, synchronously rapid tapping with three other sailors.

"Going Home Train" is, like so many other Berkeley numbers, performed as a dress rehearsal and presented as a masterful miniature of cinema. The effects (train whistle, panoramic moving backdrop) are revealed before the number commences, but Buzz's filmic eye takes the limited ingredients and makes the train a viable entity. His camera moves from engine to caboose, seemingly through walls, as an unbilled Bobby Short sings-guides the viewer through the various cars. Only the closing of the stage curtains returns the viewer to familiar territory.

"Love Is Back in Business" finalizes *Call Me Mister* in the great tradition of the Busby Berkeley closers, with most of Buzz's panache intact. A newsstand illuminated by a single light in the vacuum of Berkeley-black announces the song by revealing its name in the headline. Betty Grable sings on the barren stage, a black scrim separating her from Dan Dailey. It spins, she disappears, and Dailey gets the vocal. The leads are photographed in close-up, spinning from face to face. They're actually lying on their backs staring upward toward the camera, an old Warner Brothers effect. The camera ascends, a spotlight falls on the group, and the shadows of other dancers surround them. The setting changes again as the principals do a dance on a rising platform while fountains spew colored water. The end credits display intrusively during the singing, and the number ends without a fitting final image. Regardless, the Berkeley imprimatur is quite evident in Buzz's final assignment for 20th Century Fox.

Buzz fielded all offers, and the most flattering came in November from two writers now producing at RKO studios, Jerry Wald and Norman Krasna. Buzz would direct *All the Beautiful Girls,* a story based on his own career. He and Jerry had worked together decades earlier in *In Caliente.*

A post–Thanksgiving Day leftover was syndicated in the press on November 29 wherein Buzz named the twelve cities with the most attractive females. He thought Baltimore had more beautiful women than any other city in the country. In no certain order, he rifled off the other eleven: Louisville; San Antonio; Dallas; Houston; Philadelphia, Grand Rapids, Michigan; Richmond and Norfolk, Virginia; San Francisco; Portland, Oregon; and Miami. "Don't ask me why there are so many beautiful women in these towns," said Buzz, "because I don't know why.

I only know there are. I've been in most of the leading cities of the U.S. and I keep my eyes open. I'm not saying there aren't beautiful specimens outside these 12 cities. The most gorgeous woman in all America might be found on a farm. I'm just saying these cities have a bigger ratio of beauty than any others." On the subject of Hollywood and New York, he was a bit derisive: "Their beauties are mostly imports. These towns are loaded with glamour—but it comes from somewhere else. [Those girls] don't begin to stack up with the babes from Baltimore."

Buzz's life story, *All the Beautiful Girls,* remained in a holding pattern while other work was presented. In early 1951, it was announced that Buzz, along with director Josef von Sternberg and director/actress Ida Lupino, had been added to RKO's list of directors. Buzz's first movie at the studio would be *Two Tickets to Broadway,* produced by millionaire-eccentric Howard Hughes.

In the lavish color production *Two Tickets to Broadway,* the credit "Musical numbers created and directed by Busby Berkeley" is followed by a list of eleven songs, seven by Jule Styne and Leo Robin. A trifle of a story thickly padded with music features naïf Nancy Peterson (Janet Leigh) leaving small-town America to follow her dream of Broadway stardom. She hooks up with sadder-but-wiser girls Joyce (Ann Miller), Hannah (Gloria DeHaven), and S. F. (Barbara Lawrence). Along with an aspiring singer Dan Carter (Tony Martin), they all converge in Manhattan with a stop to perform on Bob Crosby's television show. Stan Laurel and Oliver Hardy were originally signed, but when Laurel took ill, the legendary vaudevillian comedy team of Joe Smith and Charles Dale was brought in as Harry and Leo, delicatessen proprietors and part-time angels to aspiring actors.

The director, James V. Kern, had been directed by Buzz back in 1936. In those days he had been a member of the Yacht Club Boys, and an unheralded Buzz directed Kern and his three comrades for the "My How This Town Has Changed" number in *The Singing Kid,* and in the film *Stage Struck.* James had a few pictures under his belt by 1950 but not many, certainly not enough to handle the strain of almost a dozen musical numbers. He remained unobtrusive while Buzz, creative juices flowing, devised colorful and uniquely creative musical interludes.

"Pelican Falls," a spirited march, opens the picture as a sendoff to Nancy. It's all filmed quickly, with Buzz giving a nice overview of the town from a third-story vantage and Janet Leigh showing off her prowess with a baton.

Buzz introduces Tony Martin through the eyes of children. They're captivated as he sings "There's No Tomorrow" (the Englished "O Solo Mio") while pulling his laundry from the line. It's shot simply and effectively on a three-walled set with the kids nicely lit and poised on the fire escape beyond the open window.

One of the best examples of the mastery by which Busby Berkeley elevated musical numbers set in confined spaces is found in the "Manhattan" number by Rodgers and Hart, sung by Martin and Leigh. The setting is the small sitting room at Leigh's boardinghouse. There is dancing and a dozen girls in formation, and his camera darts in and out like a snake's tongue. Buzz's closing shot is a classic of personal style. The roommates gather on the narrow staircase to sing the final line, and Buzz moves in tight to show us their pretty faces; it was the cinematic invention of which he was most proud. And it's just as impressive and viscerally impacting as it was in *Whoopee!*

"Baby, You'll Never Be Sorry," a comic number, has Eddie Bracken and Gloria DeHaven in a battle of the sexes inexplicably staged on the set that was previously used as Tony Martin's apartment. The principals engage in witty repartee, and Buzz tosses in a nice punctuating gag. Eddie, on one knee, surreptitiously steals a bracelet off Gloria's wrist. As they leave the apartment, in a move of one-upmanship, we see Gloria dangling the pilfered bangle behind her back.

Atmosphere is everything in the rainy "The Closer You Are." Tony sings his new composition to Janet outdoors behind Harry and Leo's place. The rain lets up enough for a sprightly dance for two between candlelit tables. Buzz raises his camera just high enough to allow an appealing view of his stars maneuvering on a wetted porch. The number closes with a kiss and a thunderclap beneath an open umbrella, the candlelit tables an extinguished memory.

The four gals and Buzz have fun with "The Worry Bird," a totally nonsensical number where a colorful toucan (an Australian worry bird) is given tribute for his empathetic characteristics. "Let the worry bird worry for you" is the repeating line in Buzz's bouncy number. Ann Miller takes center stage, and she taps and spins with such velocity that her skirt looks like an open parachute. In a self-plagiaristic vein, Buzz closes the number on the toucan's nest as her four chicks open their little mouths in sequence, reflecting back to the idyll by a waterfall.

The definition of "value-added" applies to the Charlivels, a French acrobatic troupe. Of course, Buzz knew all about value-added digressions at both MGM and Fox when he filmed popular bandleaders playing themselves. What makes the Charlivels' routine stand out is the rarely used effect of overcranking the camera to create a sequence in slow motion. It's quite dreamy as one flyer spins in midair and is caught by his partner. There isn't a song attributed to the Charlivels' number ("The Worry Bird" returns instrumentally), but the manner in which the number is photographed and cut reveals Buzz's authorship.

For the first time in his career, Busby Berkeley worked alongside the biggest emerging threat to his industry: television. But as a true artist, his visionary musical numbers rose above their environment. As he made the proscenium vanish from a theatrical setting, so it was with a television shoot. Buzz's technique usurped and upstaged the limited lumbering television camera. The numbers that close *Two Tickets to Broadway* are purported to be taking place on live television, but artistic license gave Buzz the wherewithal to cast off television's trappings.

Bob Crosby makes fun of older brother Bing in the static "Let's Make Comparisons." A wax statue of Bing (complete with golf club and smoking pipe) is wheeled onstage for cheap laughs. The final shot is amusing as the "statue" walks off under his own power, tossing a little wave to the audience on his way to the wings.

Buzz's use of gigantism with stage props goes back to his Broadway days. "We're in the Money" had human-sized coins; their appearance accentuated the optimism of the lyrics. He uses giant props again in Tony Martin's version of Leoncavallo's "Pagliacci." Huge 78-rpm records dress the stage as Martin makes his entrance rising through a hole in one of the disks (similar to Ruby Keeler popping up through her own gigantic eye). Buzz keeps Tony centered in the frame, maneuvering in and around him while colored lights enhance the image, building to Martin's crescendo filmed as the camera rapidly pulls back to a dramatic high shot and the curtain closes to enthusiastic applause.

Nobody could accuse Busby Berkeley of sensitivity toward minority groups. His blackface routines and especially, "Goin' to Heaven on a Mule" bear that out. The number "Big Chief Hole-in-the-Ground" of-

Buzz

fers another example of his cavalier treatment of minorities. It portends to be a humorous number about an Indian (Tony Martin) who realizes wealth after he strikes oil. Four materialistic "squaws" follow Big Chief around, and their spoof of Native American dancing and customs is hardly complimentary. They enter Big Chief's teepee and exit wearing jewelry, furs, and bedazzled headdresses, sashaying around like nouveaux riche vulgarians. A final insult has the girls spinning around to reveal four cradleboards, a baby in each. In context, 1951 audiences that had been nurtured on a diet of westerns were well aware of the conventional cinematic treatment of Native Americans, and any perceived contempt fell below the radar (if not assumed to be hypocritical).

In *Two Tickets to Broadway,* a film prolific with musical numbers, the most visually exciting is the finale. "Are You a Beautiful Dream?" is beautiful and austere, with minimalist props on a bare stage. What makes the number so pleasing is the unusual manner in which it's filmed. A medium close-up of Tony Martin starts the number, but as the camera descends, Martin moves along with it and stays in the foreground. The trick is easy, the effect, magical. Martin is actually poised on the boom, so wherever it's pointed and moved he remains within the frame. First it's past Janet Leigh, who is lounging enticingly on a four-poster bed. Then we (the audience and Tony) follow her as she glides past a floor-standing candelabra and other props on a largely bare stage. The camera tracks her flowing movements back to the bed where the number began. It's all highly accomplished by Buzz, containing the building blocks upon which many of his best numbers depended: the unusually lit stage, the weightless camera, a disarming point of view, and a 360-degree narrative that concludes where it began. Tony was strapped on a camera boom thirty-five feet high, and was thoroughly relieved when shooting was finished.

Needless overhead expense came from Howard Hughes. He spent a good deal of his time at the Goldwyn Studios. Instead of viewing the film's sets at RKO-Pathé Studios in Culver City, where the picture was shot, Hughes ordered that they be torn down and reassembled at Goldwyn. Once approved, the sets were broken down and sent back to RKO. Buzz claimed that none of his pictures lost money, but sources have noted that *Two Tickets to Broadway* lost $1,150,000. Hughes was no Jack Warner (or Sam Goldwyn for that matter) when adhering to a lean budget.

On January 16, 1951, it was announced that RKO was producing *The U.S.O. Story*, a Jerry Wald/Norman Krasna production. Buzz was attached, and Tony Martin signed for the role intended for Al Jolson. According to the reports, Tony would sing Jolson's songs, and singer Dinah Shore would play a major role.

In between projects, Buzz accepted a brief assignment in April as dance director for RKO's episodic melodrama *The Blue Veil*. The film starred Jane Wyman as a grieving mother whose newborn child has just died. She reluctantly takes a job as a nanny, and over the course of the film winds up working at a number of households, each with its own characteristic quirkiness. The producers were Jerry Wald and Norman Krasna, the editor was his friend and first-time-director/collaborator George Amy, and playing the role of one of the mothers whose daughter is in Jane Wyman's care was none other than Joan Blondell. It was a happy reunion for Joan and her famous dance director, who had worked together last in the "All's Fair in Love and War" number from *Gold Diggers of 1937*. Sources credit Buzz with directing the inconsequential musical number "Daddy," sung by Blondell on a small stage in front of closed curtains. The number begins with a tight close-up of Joan's face, the camera slowly pulls back revealing her showgirl outfit (boa, feathered headdress, dress cut up to the thigh) as she dances across the stage under a single spotlight. The camera continues backing up and away from the stage until a nicely composed shot of Blondell on the left of the screen and patrons sitting in loge seats on the right is held for a few seconds. The rest of the number has no other noticeable directing attributes from Buzz, and following the audience's applause, his two-minute contribution to *The Blue Veil* ends.

All the Beautiful Girls and *The U.S.O. Story* had stalled in preproduction. Buzz's involvement with the team of Jerry Wald and Norman Krasna extended only to *Two Tickets to Broadway* and *The Blue Veil*. A new contract from MGM in September brightened a lackluster summer. Buzz was hired as dance director for the tentatively titled "One Piece Bathing Suit." In November, the *Hollywood Reporter* ran an item stating Buzz was to direct the "Girls Girls Girls" number from MGM's upcoming *The Merry Widow* and that Buzz had signed a studio contract on November 29, 1951.

Buzz and Esther Williams were collaborating again. In the intervening years since *Take Me Out to the Ball Game,* Esther had made five films for MGM, including the aquatic *Neptune's Daughter.* The new project, "One Piece Bathing Suit," was retitled *Million Dollar Mermaid,* and Buzz was ready to flex his creative muscles.

She went by many names. The Australian Mermaid, Neptune's Daughter, Divine Venus, and Queen of the Mermaids were titles bestowed on Annette Kellerman, Australia's first superstar. She was a champion swimmer, diver, Hippodrome performer, and actress in a dozen silent films. Her scandalous effrontery in her home continent by wearing a one-piece bathing suit in public made the newspapers. Her story was eminently filmable, and in 1952 Annette Kellerman was alive to see her biography strained through the glossiness of an MGM musical.

The casting of Esther Williams was obvious. By this time, the statuesque beauty had appeared in eighteen films (a few on dry land), and MGM so believed in her that they built a swimming pool on the studio grounds in her honor. The director was the old stalwart Mervyn LeRoy. Esther, who made a plea for Buzz, knew that he could make the water scenes "spectacular," and, truth be told, Mervyn had no idea how to stage a water number. So it was to be Berkeley and LeRoy, their first film together since their alchemic collaboration in *Gold Diggers of 1933.*

There's an anticipatory thrill in the opening credits of *Million Dollar Mermaid* that read, "Fountain and smoke numbers staged by Busby Berkeley." What they were and what they referred to was well worth the wait.

The story gave a nod to reality, but, as told in MGM's extravagant style, the embellishments couldn't be quibbled with. We follow Annette Kellerman's life from a young girl in leg braces to the swimmer who dared to swim twenty-six miles for three-and-a-half hours down the Thames River from Putney Bridge to Blackwall. Her stunt diving, performed at small sideshows, caught the eye of a Ziegfeldian-type impresario. Her career eventually brought her billing at New York's famed Hippodrome Theatre (located at Sixth and Forty-third), where she performed amazing aquatic numbers in a giant glass tank.

Buzz's "fountain" number begins where the finale of *The Gang's All Here* ends, with a descending color curtain of water revealing Esther illuminated among the blackness. Wearing a crown and a gold lamé swimsuit of thousands of sequins, she swims through and under cascading water curtains in a royal blue setting. A high dive follows. She emerges from the water surround by eight gold water nymphs, and as the camera retreats, the water curtain rises. In a long shot, we see the physically impossible water curtains spraying the stage while the appreciative audience applauds.

Nobody (not even Buzz) at first realized that a life-threatening tragedy had occurred during the filming of the fountain number. Esther Williams's swimsuit (designed by Helen Rose and Walter Plunkett) was already quite heavy from all the sewed-on sequins. For her headdress, Esther wore a gold turban that supported an aluminum crown. She was raised out of the water by a hidden-from-view hydraulic lift fitted with a Lucite disk. As she reached the fifty-foot mark, she prepared to dive. Buzz shouted, "Okay. Let's do it, Esther." She stood there for a moment, then another. She became a bit dizzy (her eardrum had been previously broken seven times from all her water work). Short-tempered Buzz yelled again, "We're waiting Esther." Then he gave the order "JUMP!" Somewhere between swan dive and splash, Esther Williams came to a horrifying conclusion. The immovable crown on her head was stronger, heavier, and less flexible than her neck. At the point of maximum impact with the water, her head snapped back, fracturing three vertebrae. LeRoy, on the soundstage with Buzz, yelled, "Great . . . time for lunch." Shooting stopped, and Buzz and Mervyn left the set. Nobody knew Esther was in trouble. Flossie Hackett, Williams's wardrobe woman, remained. Esther called out to her in extreme agony. She was able to kick her legs, but her arms were paralyzed. Some men rushed to the pool on Flossie's urging. They tossed off their shoes, dove in, and pulled the star out of the pool. Esther cried from the intense pain. She was rushed to the hospital, and doctors put her head in a brace; the rest of her body was placed in a body cast from neck to knees. Most of *Million Dollar Mermaid* was already "in the can," including Buzz's "smoke" number, so replacing Esther Williams at this stage was not an option. She remained out of work for six months while LeRoy shot the balance of the picture around her. Buzz went to Esther's home for a visit, and she was thankful, but she had mentioned to others that Buzz just didn't give much thought to her safety. He expected her to do whatever his imagination dreamed up. He told Esther that because she was the star, she had to do the numbers better than anyone else. Her three vertebrae eventually fused together; the side effect was a constant headache from the solid mass of bone in her neck.

Filmed before the "fountain" number, but shown afterward was the "smoke" number. Red water curtains drop to a stage with two water slides facing each other. Between the slides at the rear of the "stage" are billowing smoke plumes coming from four hundred electrically controlled smoke pots. Swimmers slide down on their stomach between the legs of men holding red flags. Eventually Esther makes her appearance at the top of slide, coming out from behind red and yellow smoke. Standing, she maneuvers down the waterslide, grabbing a hidden tether that pulls her toward the camera at quick speed. Soon six girls standing on swings high above the water appear. In counterpoint, six guys standing on *their* swings come into view. The girls dive in; the men join them, and repeat. The star of the show comes into view on her own swing smiling as a swan dive awaits. Back in the pool, Esther grabs a white ring that lifts her up up up and almost through that proverbial roof that in the old days couldn't constrain Buzz. She dangles high in the air. Below are the Berkeley girls and their handlers in a symmetric circle moving in the synchronized patterns that characterized Busby Berkeley to the world. In the center of the formation is an eye into which Esther aims. The pattern is alluring and hypnotic from Buzz's vantage. Esther, on cue, releases her hold on the ring and torpedoes down, just left of center, into the crowded pool. The circle expands to the lovely star patterns that Buzz first conceived in *The Kid from Spain*. Then there's a bit of magic to close the number. Esther, submerged, rises on her platform; behind her are five hundred sparklers that light *as they are coming up from the water!* She waves and smiles and descends again below the surface as the sparklers extinguish. The projected-in-reverse effect is quite dazzling.

Buzz's crassness to his performers was often manifested while actively shooting. At the same time (often within the same take), he would laud his technical team. Musical arranger André Previn saw Buzz in action during the "smoke" number and described the scene: "He sat behind his camera, eyes blazing, shouting directions and exhortations while the music playback added to the atmosphere of panic. 'Great, great' Buzz yelled, 'the green smoke is perfect, let's have more . . . yes, that's lovely. Now, whip the mirrors around . . . wonderful, just right, get those prisms ready for the waterfall. Oh boy that's perfect.' Suddenly Buzz's head swerved and he screamed in anguish, 'Goddammit you silly bitch, can't you dance any faster?'"

The trades' prediction of a hit for MGM was accurate. Box-office grosses made *Million Dollar Mermaid* one of the top earners of the year, and cinematographer George Folsey was nominated for an Academy Award in the "Color" category. Buzz's contribution didn't go unnoticed: Bosley Crowther, in his December 5, 1952, review, referred to the new ultra-wide-screen, three-projector presentation format when he wrote, "The smoke and fire number approaches Cinerama."

During the making of *Million Dollar Mermaid*, it was again reported that Jerry Wald was attached to *All the Beautiful Girls*. Wald was to reproduce the Aqua Show at Flushing Meadows, New York, for the musical to be filmed at RKO. According to a *New York Times* report, Wald was negotiating with Buzz to direct the picture.

While Buzz was shooting *Million Dollar Mermaid*, a script titled "Small Town Girl," dated March 12, 1952, was stamped "Temporary Incomplete" with the producer listed as "Mr. Pasternak." Three months later, the picture went into production at MGM under the Joe Pasternak unit. The list of assignees to the project sounded positively nepotistic. Directing was assigned to Budapestian László (aka Leslie) Kardos, a director of little acclaim back in his native Hungary and of equal repute in the States. His most recent low-wattage flop, *The Strip* starring Mickey Rooney, was a Joe Pasternak production that didn't even merit a review from the *New York Times*. The fact that Kardos and Pasternak shared a homeland in Austria-Hungary, and that Kardos was married to Pasternak's sister Lenka, assured him a top slot on a short list of brothers-in-law for consideration. The familial goulash expanded with the casting of Hungarian actor S. Z. Sakall ("Cuddles" in *Cinderella Jones*). Anne, his second wife, was Leslie Kardos's sister.

Small Town Girl shares only its name with the 1936 film starring Janet Gaynor and Robert Taylor. Jane Powell and Farley Granger took the leads while dancers Ann Miller and Bobby Van (in his third film) moved to Buzz's beat. A story as quaint as a lunch-box social finds millionaire playboy Rick Livingston (Granger) in trouble with the law for speeding 80 mph through the somnambulistic town of Duck Creek, Connecticut. The town's judge (irascible Robert Keith) orders a sentence of thirty days for Livingston, who captures the eye of the judge's small-town girl Cindy (Powell). Rick's girlfriend, the glamorous Lisa Bellmount (Miller), is a Broadway singer and dancer. She leaves her boyfriend in the one-horse town and heads back to New York, but not before she's accosted by Ludwig Schlemmer (Van), the son of haberdasher Eric Schlemmer (Sakall). Ludwig has show business aspirations (and the talent to back them up), but both his father and Lisa try their best to dissuade him. Ludwig has been "promised" to Cindy, but neither seems all that interested. At the picture's end, the couplings have been all but telegraphed, Broadway dreams are being realized, and Duck Creek can once again bear the motto of a "small town that's a smile town."

In the short preparation phase of the film, Buzz had some interesting ideas, one of which he shared with musical director André Previn in their first meeting. Previn wanted to discuss some orchestrations with Buzz prior to filming and went to his office. He remembered the exchange vividly: "He sat behind his desk, shuffling storyboard cards—individual drawings of each proposed camera setup—and he looked up briefly to wave me closer. He was not an imposing figure, and the features of his face didn't really match, like a toy that has been mended hastily. 'Look at this. I'd like Janie Powell to make an entrance in a small buggy drawn by forty eagles. Do you think Joe Pasternak will okay that? It's likely to be pretty expensive." Previn didn't say anything. The nonreaction made Buzz smile. "By God you didn't even flinch," said Buzz.

According to Buzz, an ox would be cheaper than forty eagles. The animal was brought in for inspection. Buzz scrutinized the ox and decreed it should be painted gold. The assistant director ran around the set directionless yelling, "Paint the ox gold!" After lunch, a golden ox was walked to the set. Buzz thought the paint job was a rush job, and he got on his knees to check the ox's nether regions. Timing is everything in show business, and the ox's sense of it couldn't have been more piquant. As the director knelt, the animal began emptying his bladder on the tidy white outfit of Mr. Berkeley, drenching him in a yellow cascade. Buzz was given towels as he was escorted off the set to a private dressing room. The ox blew his audition. He never made it to the screen test phase, and the whole idea was scrapped.

What remained were some of Buzz's sharpest numbers, one of which, a surrealist masterpiece, was indicative of the continuing experimentation and inventiveness he brought to every assigned project.

"Fine, Fine, Fine," "Small Towns are Smile Towns," and "The Fellow I Follow" numbers contained none of the spectacle nature of Buzz's art, but three others are worthy additions to his canon. The first, "Take Me to Broadway," was sung and danced by Bobby Van in the setting of the family store after closing. Buzz used the set marvelously, following Van as he danced athletically up and down stairs, chairs, display cases, banisters, and tabletops.

In Van's other big number, he learns the great news that he needn't get married since his betrothed isn't interested. The physical manifestation of his happiness makes him jump, jump, jump like a human pogo stick all through the town. In what appears to be a single take (actually a few takes seamlessly melded), Van continues his kangaroo hopping mingling with the denizens, dodging cars, jumping through jump ropes, bouncing on hedges, sniffing flowers, passing bananas to the children in a school bus, and stealing a dance or two, all without missing a beat. Buzz's camera work is absolutely astounding as it follows Van on his trip through town. One can imagine the preparation time needed to make a success of a number of this complexity since the extras and props must take their cues at the precise moment. Buzz's career-length espousal of the need for exacting rehearsals (akin to "measure twice and drill once") paid off beautifully in a sequence quite like no other.

The originality of *Small Town Girl*'s numbers extends to Ann Miller in the brilliant "I Gotta Hear That Beat." Buzz, along with various art directors, discussed the kind of set he required. Buzz disliked the song (by Nicholas Brodszky and Leo Robin). He saw nothing spectacular in it. While Buzz was filming his numbers with Bobby Van, producer Pasternak came up and asked him what kind of set he had in mind for the Ann Miller number. Buzz replied that he hadn't had much of a chance to think about it. Pasternak (like so many other producers before him) gave him the order, "Well, hurry up, we haven't got much time." In the midst of filming Van's bouncy number, Buzz came up with an idea for a most unusual set. From the art director he requested a five-foot-high stage with a small platform in the back and steps coming down on either side. In the floor and through the steps, round holes would be bored to Buzz's precise specifications, 172 in total, through which 86 pairs of disembodied arms (black tuxedoed with white cuffs) would be sticking out, "playing" musical instruments. Buzz worked late into the evening, preparing the graph drawings that were turned over to the stage crew. He visualized camera placement and movement and how he would follow Miller as she tapped her way past the limbs. When he told Pasternak of his idea, Buzz saw the producer turn pale. "I hope to hell you know what you're doing because I don't," remarked Pasternak. According to Buzz, word spread around the lot that he "probably flipped out this time," but that was old news to the dance director, who had probably heard the same thing from Sam Goldwyn. With the holes drilled, men below the stage took their positions. Each wore a tuxedo jacket and stood on a small table, giving them enough height to stick their arms out through the borings. The players were arranged in groups of five or six, each man holding an instrument. Buzz wasn't interested in the type of dance Miller was going to do. For that, MGM brought in Willie Covan, a professional dancer for some fifty years, to go through the steps with Ann. Buzz busied himself with camera angles and turns, knowing full well that he couldn't maneuver the musicians once their arms popped up through the floor. When Buzz mounted the boom in rehearsal, everything he envisioned was realized to perfection. No new holes would be drilled—none were needed. The electric fans on the soundstage had to be turned off once filming commenced, and this made the men below the floor extremely uncomfortable. One fainted and was carried out. Ann Miller had a nagging problem of her own. A painful bloody blister had developed on her heel, and she asked Buzz to please pause for a moment while she applied a bandage on her foot. "NO!" barked Mr. Sympathy. "We're not stopping. That would mean you have to take your stockings off. No, we're not stopping. You can do it . . . just think of something else. I don't care about you and I don't care about your blister. I care about the studio and I have to bring this thing in tonight and if you don't like it, it's too bad, but you're doing it!" She thought it so unusual that a man who, in her words, was "such a genius" lacked compassion.

Buzz begins "I Gotta Hear That Beat" with large tom-toms in the foreground while Ann Miller is spot-lit between them in the distance.

The light over her changes to yellow, matching the floor and walls, and it leads her to the surrealistic stage of Buzz's imagination. Miller taps her way past the disconcerting sight of dozens of disembodied arms sticking out through the floor "playing" musical instruments. She taps and spins around the uniformly clad bongo players, trumpeters, clarinetists, violinists, and cellists. Buzz's timing is exact, matching the visual with the audible as Miller's movements precisely correspond to the instruments featured in the song. Adding to the complexity of the mise-en-scène are the ubiquitous wall shadows of a drummer drumming and a violinist playing. Miller moves up and down the dual-entry staircase while new sets of arms get camera time. The entire sequence is outré surrealistic, if not a bit unseemly. The number ends thrillingly as Miller resumes her first spot-lit position as two dozen beating tom-toms surround the frame. The camera moves in to reveal an empty stage where Miller rapidly spins and abruptly stops, ending the most bizarrely conceived number of Buzz's career.

Easy to Love, a misnomer of a title, takes place at Cypress Gardens in Winterhaven, Florida, and never lets you forget it. It does succumb now and then to the level of travelogue when it isn't spooling the artificial complications of a singer, swimmer, actor, and manager. Julie (Esther Williams), a model and disgruntled aquatic performer, loathes and loves her successful advertising boss, Ray (Van Johnson). But she's also linked romantically to her chiseled costar Hank (John Bromfield). On a working trip to New York, she meets the lips of singer Barry Gordon (Tony Martin). Amid the dramatic interludes are the Busby Berkeley water inventions, "love in a natural setting" as Dick Powell sang it by a waterfall. MGM owned the rights to Cole Porter's song, and since it made a reasonably good title for a feature film, it stuck. Buzz at fifty-seven was full of ideas, and he allowed the most outrageous ones unrestrained rein. Positioned high in the sky over Florida's Lake Eloise, he was once again 2nd Lt. Busby Enos flying aerial spotting missions *over there.*

The title card lists five songs in *Easy to Love,* but Buzz (credited as "Musical numbers created and directed by) also contributed to three nonsinging water numbers, the first of which takes place in an impressively designed moonlight cove. Gypsy musicians play their instruments standing at the base of water-planted cypress trees as Esther and John Bromfield dive in from a high ledge and swim synchronistically. In one beautifully composed shot, Buzz's camera is medium-high above the water that's covered with yellow, red, and white gardenias. The swimmers pop their heads up and spin slowly on submerged platforms. Buzz takes it one step further by killing all the lights save for two spotlights aimed at his rotating stars.

"Didja Ever" takes place in that often-used Busby Berkeley setting of the nightclub. Tony Martin sings past candlelit tables, pulling pretty girls he finds onto the stage. The girls mount a piano, and, in a bit of trickery, Buzz has the piano rotate a quarter turn at a time and pause, allowing the audience to admire each and every member of his attractive parade of faces.

Two brief numbers, the minimalist "Look Out! I'm Romantic" and "Coquette," looked promising (the latter with defined lines of girls and legs on display), but both fizzled when the story interceded.

Esther in clown makeup has fun in the second water number of the film. Her chair moves comically through the water to the glee of the kids in the audience. She dives off the high board through two large paper hoops and later bounces on a trampoline while seals, alligators, and a chimp play supporting roles.

There's a melancholy undertone to "That's What a Rainy Day Is For" as sung by Tony Martin at the piano in his hotel lobby. Listening attentively are not Buzz's beauties, but elderly white-haired women. They join Tony in song, and at one point he romantically dances with one. It's all shot perfunctorily, yet one ponders Buzz's casting. The number would work just fine with younger women, yet it's an unexpected delight that results from deliberately allowing maturity on display. It was as if Buzz were saying, "Here are my gold diggers from decades ago and we've all aged together. We still sing and we still dance and in this number the evidence is clear; we're still *viable*."

The titular song is Tony and Esther's. He sings to her as they float on a river, and Esther (dressed in Indian goddess garb) looks on and smiles. Later it's reprised in a different setting, as Buzz follows Esther elegantly swimming past her singing costar while a marvelous high shot captures the enormous dimensions of the pool.

The finale of *Easy to Love* is about as unique and spectacular as anything to emanate from three decades of Busby Berkeley. It's a number on water skis with more than seventy water-skiers in support. Esther is pulled through an archway of water jets through a makeshift proscenium and on to Lake Eloise, where more than a half-dozen speedboats, each pulling six skiers, ride alongside in a birdlike "V" formation. The number moves at an alarming rate as Buzz films his star from passing motorboats, quickly cutting to camera placements so high that no roof-cutting at Warner Brothers could ever duplicate them. Shooting from a hovering helicopter, Buzz brings an unforeseen excitement to the action's breathtaking point of view. This vantage point offers a view of the longest line of water-skiers ever filmed. The editing is rapid and kinetic; traveling shots commingle with airborne ones; skiers traverse ramps; geysers sixty feet high erupt as Esther passes them. She (or more accurately, her double) grabs a hanging bar from the helicopter that pulls her up to a dramatic height, at which point she dives in. She's pulled out of the water by her tether and skis some more while being flanked by flag-waving supporters. Moving between the cypress trees, Esther eventually ends where she started, moving through the sprinkler arch to a tall podium where wind and water work together in creating a brilliantly and spectacularly realized final shot.

For the second time, Buzz came close to disabling his star. Few people knew that Esther Williams was pregnant while filming. She hid her condition throughout the shoot (camouflaging her growing midsection under the gardenias in her duet with John Bromfield), but Buzz, as oblivious as ever to the safety of others, put her through a rigorous sequence that almost ended in disaster. The geysers that Esther had to water-ski around had their heads some six inches above the water's surface. Striking them at 35 mph could be painfully injurious. Buzz and whomever he wanted to impress were on a small boat ready to film Esther as she maneuvered her way around the geysers. Buzz yelled "Action," and his weighted boat carefully tracked his star. At every key moment, he shot a gun in the air to cue the technical staff manning the geysers. Like a general making a beach landing, Buzz yelled through a bullhorn, giving Esther directions. As the scene progressed, he didn't realize that his boat was coming uncomfortably close to Esther's left side while she, nearsighted as she was, did her best to avoid the geyser heads to her right. The overloaded boat was closing in on her, and she realized the space available to avoid the geyser heads was slimming. "Esther! Esther!" yelled Buzz, "Turn to me! Turn to me!" She shouted back, "Buzz, you're too close!" The boat was less than a foot from Esther, and she saw its propeller. She figured that either the geyser heads or the propeller would impale her, so she let go of her tether and fell into the water, and Buzz had no other option than to yell, "Cut." Esther was furious. "If I'd seen Busby's damned starter's pistol I'd have shot him with it," she later confessed. She swam to shore and stormed into her little cottage. After an hour or so, Buzz sent a production assistant to request that Miss Williams return to the set. She sent the assistant on his way with a message: she was done for the day. Later, a clueless Buzz asked her, "Why did you go home? We were having a great day!" "Shut up, you goddamn fool!" she snapped. "Don't you know how close that boat came to me? Did it ever cross your mind that my life was in your hands?" Esther saw her words registering. "God, Esther," said Buzz pliantly, "I didn't know all that was going on."

She told Buzz to shoot around her for a couple of days while she waited to see if her fall had caused any real damage. He agreed and contacted her once, by phone, a few days later—at two thirty in the morning. Esther woke out of a sound sleep. "Where are you?" she asked Buzz. "I'm in the tub." And he wasn't alone. A martini was propped up on the ledge. He told his star that he had another great idea. She yawned but was curious. Along with many in Hollywood, Esther knew that bathtubs and booze inspired Buzz. He asked her about her willingness to hang from a trapeze hooked to a helicopter and drop into a "V" formation of eight motorboats pulling skiers. When Buzz told her that she'd be eighty feet in the air, she hesitated. Esther suggested that her friend Helen Crelinkovich act as her stunt double, but Buzz didn't like using doubles (though he had on several occasions). Esther pushed the point, using her condition as her excuse, and he reluctantly agreed. She arranged for her friend to get paid each time Buzz yelled, "action." At three thousand dollars per jump, Helen cleared a cool nine thousand with three eighty-foot dives. It is she who is onscreen after the cutaway where Esther grabs a trapeze and is hoisted out of camera range.

It was a good shoot for Buzz, who flew as high as gravity allowed. Photographs taken on the set show him up on a ladder barking his orders. Magazine articles and promotional brochures never failed to feature Esther Williams carrying a leatherette case stamped "Beautiful Cypress Gardens." The lovely locale received an influx of tourist dollars thanks to Busby Berkeley's breathtaking images that no tour book or flyer could ever match.

In September 1953, film exhibition changed forever when 20th Century Fox released *The Robe* in the brand-new widescreen format called CinemaScope. The anamorphic process was Hollywood's proprietary weapon against the mounting sales of television sets that were resulting in steady declines in box-office revenue. Just prior to *The Robe*'s release, MGM made the decision to employ CinemaScope for its first widescreen musical. Mervyn LeRoy was brought on to direct the third version of the Broadway operetta *Rose Marie*. The irresistible combination of the shooting locations (the Canadian Rockies and the California Sierras) and a new process to record the grandeur of both gave MGM the impetus to green-light the project. Audibly complementing the CinemaScope process was a technology invented by Western Electric Sound System. *Rose Marie* would be recorded in four-track stereo (and played back from 35mm magnetic prints).

Ann Blyth (with an unconvincing French accent only a *oui*-bit more authentic than *Kiki*'s Mary Pickford) was cast in the title role played previously by Joan Crawford and Jeanette MacDonald. The male leads (Howard Keel and Fernando Lamas) play a Canadian Mountie and rogue fur trapper respectively. Buzz was hired to stage a mock ceremonial dance number and a couple of others too. Throughout his career Buzz had composed his numbers in what is commonly known as the "academy ratio" of 1.375:1 (the ratio of image width to height). For *Rose Marie* Buzz had to adapt his unique vision from the academy ratio to the radically rectangular aspect ratio of 2.55 inches wide for every 1 inch high. The results of this reenvisioning are quite rewarding, and are evidentiary that Busby Berkeley, in his late fifties, could rapidly embrace and master new technology.

Buzz's initial exploitation of the wide screen is noticeable in the early "Mounties" number. Howard Keel (his spurs/ankle incident with Buzz unforgotten) sings and leads his regiment through the Canadian forest. With dozens of flag-bearing Mounties on horseback, two astride are shot from advantageous angles that reveal the entire snakelike regiment as Keel is placed front and center. Ann Blyth, in her number "Free to Be Free" ("Free as zee air . . .") leads Buzz's camera through the corral area of the camp, stopping along the way as she sings to a penned horse and a squirrel in the tree (recounting again the final image of "By a Waterfall").

"I'm a Mountie Who Never Got His Man" reunited Buzz with

Bert Lahr for the first time since *Flying High* back in 1931. It's a funny number, with Lahr singing of his career's missed opportunities in his endearing vibrato vocal style. Buzz packed the number with end-to-end extras as he followed Lahr's routine, leaving not a trace of wasted space on the periphery of the CinemaScope canvas.

"Indian Love Call," one of the four carryover songs from the 1924 Broadway show, is shot very simply on a soundstage, as Ann Blyth and Fernando Lamas lend operatic fervor to Rudolf Friml's beautiful melody.

The big spectacular number in *Rose Marie* is Buzz's rendition of "Totem Tom-Tom." Shot on MGM's largest soundstage, it's an expensively filmed, erotically charged, tribal/pagan piece (and about as nonauthentic as the Native dances he staged in *Bird of Paradise* and Broadway's *The White Eagle*). A large multitiered set resembling a "mountain stronghold" (Buzz's term) features Black Eagle (Chief Yowlachie) singing to the tall totem pole in the middle of the set. Then actress Joan Taylor (as the chief's daughter) descends the different levels of the set, down cliffs and runners, and drops to the ground. Immediately the rest of the tribe (some three dozen extras) fill the screen and surround her. The Native Americans sit together in a tight circle as Taylor, in the middle, dances among them. She eventually climbs back up the set and, from a height of fifty feet, gets thrown into the outstretched arms of the men below. She's carried back to the totem pole, and the Natives tie her up. The camera ascends to reveal the totem pole, Joan Taylor, and all the dancers spinning in frenzied circles swinging feather sticks. The final shot, a closure in the manner of many Berkeley numbers where the first and last image are of identical object, again centers on the face of the giant totem pole. "We rehearsed this number for a month and it ended up costing two hundred thousand dollars," reflected Buzz. "It was an exciting routine to stage, and people seemed to be very impressed with it."

Collectively, Buzz's work in the 1950s was a splendid reaffirmation of his skills, reflecting the creativity and enthusiasm of his younger years. He worked tirelessly, and there was no hint of declined capacity or diminished inventiveness. After *Rose Marie* finished shooting in late 1953, he waited for his phone to ring. Strangely, waiting devolved to languishment; nothing at all was either offered or forthcoming.

14

Out of Sight

"Busby Berkeley will make a comeback," wrote the *Daily Review* in September 1954. It reported that Buzz would be directing singer and actor Harry Richman for his show on a local Hollywood TV station. Although Harry had worked with Buzz back in 1930 for *Lew Leslie's International Revue,* there was no reteaming despite the announcement.

The following month, producers Jack J. Gross and Philip N. Krasne of Gross-Krasne, Inc. signed Buzz to direct three new "telefilms" for their series *Big Town.* The offer was real, and there was no question of the show's viability since it had been around since radio. The show bounced around to different networks by the time of Buzz's involvement. For its fifth season, NBC picked up *Big Town,* and the show was sponsored by AC Spark Plug. The lead role of Steve Wilson had been played by a few actors, Patrick McVey the most notable. In NBC's version, Mark Stevens, a B-level actor whose biggest role to date was playing Olivia de Havilland's husband in 1948's *The Snake Pit,* was cast as Wilson. The setting was the newsroom of the fictional "Illustrated Press." There, like Clark Kent at the *Daily Planet,* Steve Wilson could be privy to breaking stories of unscrupulous lawbreakers. The established tone was akin to Jack Webb's *Dragnet,* with voice-over narration time-stamped to the minute. In the episode "The Lovers," Buzz's direction is interesting and erratic. A woman's murder opens the drama, the weapon seen only in shadow. The assailant smashes it on her head, drops what appears to be a silver candlestick, and exits without being revealed. The de rigueur solving of the murder with false leads and red herrings left Buzz little to do. There was, however, something quite interesting in Buzz's approach to filming dialogue, as can be seen in three short segments. Each was shot in extremely tight close-up which, after a while, conveys a claustrophobic feeling to the viewer. In one escalating dialogue passage, three actors are filmed this way, and the cutting between the faces makes them almost indistinguishable as their tempers flare. In all, Buzz worked on four episodes of *Big Town* that aired in late 1954 and early 1955.

About two weeks prior to the airing of Buzz's first episode of *Big Town,* he was arrested again on a charge of drunkenness. On Sunday, December 12, police found him sleeping on the doorstep of a retail store. They had answered an anonymous complaint about a prowler. The police stated that Buzz was in an "intoxicated condition." The public report said that the director had $515 in his pockets, $20 of which was used to pay his bail. The next day Buzz received a continuance until the end of the week to answer the charge. He pleaded guilty on December 17 and was fined $50. Ten days later, his episode of *Big Town* titled "Boys Week" premiered.

Either Marjorie Mae Pemberton Berkeley was divorced from her husband in April 1946, as numerous wire stories reported, or she wasn't. She might have divorced Buzz and remarried him as rumors hinted. Perhaps the divorce proceedings were retracted when the couple had a change of heart. In any event, history repeated itself when, in the February 15, 1956, edition of the *New York Times,* a story broke with the headline "Film Director Sues 5th Wife for Divorce." The complaint mentioned "cruelty" but offered no specifics other than that a property settlement had been reached. Their Tijuana wedding date of May 8, 1945, was listed, as was the fact that they had been living apart for a year and a month. The attorney for the plaintiff was Jerry Giesler.

On January 21, 1957, Buzz was granted an interlocutory judgment indicating he was *entitled* to divorce Marge Pemberton. At the trial, he blamed the breakup on three things: the lack of real love, his mother-in-law, and Kelly, a fox terrier. Buzz told the court that Marge didn't love him and married him only "out of respect for my professional ability." In a complaint that flew hypocritically in the face of his own devotion to Gertrude, Buzz charged that Marge constantly kept company with her mother. Marge's mother also lived at their home part of the time. The damn dog, owned by Buzz's mother-in-law, had caused seven thousand dollars in damages romping through the house. According to California law, unless there was an appeal, the divorce would be finalized one year hence.

Hollywood hadn't rung up Buzz for quite a while, but that didn't prevent him from seeking any kind of work, even if it were marginally linked to show business. Such was the case when one of his earliest career successes was about to be restaged. In Albuquerque, New Mexico, under the sponsorship of the College of St. Joseph Alumni Association, *Irene* was presented July 3 through 7. Buzz's involvement with the production came by way of a producing company he had recently formed called "Spectaculars, Inc." The company was engaged for the production, and Buzz was to direct. On May 20, he arrived in New Mexico and began holding auditions at the local USO during the week. The excitement of a Hollywood director landing in a relatively small town was infectious. Almost daily reports were featured in the local papers. The part of Madame Lucy was won by local boy Ron Kennie. His sister was Miss New Mexico of 1955. St. Louis was mentioned as the next city where the director would take *Irene*. The whole town was abuzz on Wednesday, July 3, when the curtain rose at the Civic Auditorium for the premiere performance. In its own modest way, the show was a success. No record of its St. Louis run exists.

Throughout his tumultuous life, Buzz had few intimates to whom he could turn for advice and counsel. Merna Kennedy, regardless of the outcome of their volatile marriage, deserved Buzz's gratitude for introducing him to her friends Leonard and Etta Judd. The Judds were Buzz's stalwart supporters. By the late 1950s, Etta had been a widow for several years, but she remained Buzz's confidante. Reciprocating romance crept in only upon reflection. "I realized she had been my closest friend and I had always been fond of her," said Buzz. "I told her we would do what we should have done years before—get married." On January 23, 1958, the final judgment of divorce between Buzz and Marge Pemberton was granted and filed in California Superior Court. That same day, Buzz and Etta Judd took out a marriage license in the clerk's office of Ventura County and then walked across the hall to Judge Richard Heaton's courtroom, where they said their vows. For the fifty-five-year-old bride it was her second marriage; it was her betrothed's sixth. For the first time in his life, Busby Berkeley married a woman without show business aspirations. Etta was broad-shouldered and big-boned and didn't resemble any of her predecessors. She was practical, protective, and, as Buzz could vouch, devoted.

One of the newspapers reporting the marriage had Buzz quoted as saying he was now a television writer. The term was rather exaggerated, but Buzz did get involved with the creation of a television show that crumbled in the wake of a national scandal. *Money from Home* was a new game show that would be contacting servicemen stationed overseas. Buzz lent his name to the overall production when it was learned that the government had approved the show idea. The Alcoa Aluminum Company was signed as the sponsor. Buzz had numerous plans for the show, and he went to Washington, D.C., to engage some of the high-powered brass in discussions. *Money from Home* was in its early stages of production when, in October 1958, a New York grand jury convened to investigate the charges that the game shows *The $64,000 Question* and *Twenty One* were rigged. The ratings for all game shows plummeted. *Money from Home* didn't stand a chance and was canceled before a single episode aired.

The famous comic strip *The Phantom* was to be a weekly television series, and Buzz was brought on to direct the pilot on location in the northern Yucatán. He brought Etta along, and together they scouted locations around the Chichén Itzá ruins. It was a pleasant vacation, but an aborted effort as *The Phantom* joined *Money from Home* in being canceled without so much as a premiere episode.

Buzz's name was bandied about in early 1959 in an interview with Dick Powell. Powell was promoting his *Zane Grey Theater* television show and briefly mentioned that he had worked with Buzz on the coast. Whatever the project was, and whatever the extent of Buzz's involvement, it can only be accurately assessed as another in a series of false starts and premature endings.

In August, Buzz was linked to a new musical titled *The Count of Ten* by William L. Penzner. The title refers to a nightclub owned by a heavyweight boxing champion nicknamed "The Count" due to his stylish way of dressing. Buzz would direct the production, and Hermes Pan would handle the dance direction. Buzz made offers to two of the up-and-coming stage stars of the late 1950s, Fran Jeffries and Juliet Prowse. He worked with Penzner on multiple drafts of the script in addition to jotting down ideas for the promotion of the show. All was for naught, as Penzner's first stage production (after producing a string of low-budget movies), destined to open in February 1961, "closed before it opened," a description reminiscent of Aline MacMahon's in *Gold Diggers of 1933*: "they close before they open."

Hedda Hopper gave some ink in her column to Buzz and singer Molly Bee ("I Saw Mommy Kissing Santa Claus") on September 21. She announced that Molly would be filming a new picture called *Chartroose Caboose* in Eugene, Oregon, with Buzz directing.

The production charts featured in *Daily Variety* magazine do list Buzz's name as director, but by the time of the film's release in 1960, William "Red" Reynolds received the director's credit. How much and in what form Buzz contributed to the film has never been positively determined.

A major disappointment, one which Buzz ranked at the top of his list, occurred when an actor he once worked with came to him with a proposal that sounded too good to be true. In 1941, John Shelton was the lead in Buzz's *Blonde Inspiration*. Now, twenty years later, he was a businessman. The government of Egypt had contacted Shelton to make a musical on location with the title *Only the Poor Dream Rich*. Shelton, acting as producer, wanted Buzz to direct at a salary of $100,000. The songs were to be written by Ralph Blane and Buzz's old colleague Harry Warren. Etta and Buzz flew to Egypt and stayed at the Nile Hilton. The Berkeleys scouted locations while the score was being composed. Buzz devised some interesting numbers using Egypt's great landmarks. John Shelton was busy with the financing. A Swiss bank account in which the film's production funds were to be kept was later revealed not to exist. Shelton couldn't pay anybody, but like every clichéd producer, he told his crew not to worry. Three weeks passed, and no money changed hands. Shelton told his people that the Egyptian government would come through with the financing. Weary and wise to shows that started strong and fizzled fast, Buzz left the production before its debut (as he did with *Glad to See You*). He could no longer allow himself to be subjected to another producer's empty promises.

15

The Ringmaster

For a while the Berkeleys lived at 11968 Wilshire Boulevard in Los Angeles, but Buzz became increasingly disillusioned with the industry that was reluctant to offer new opportunities to a sexagenarian with his singular talent. In a momentous decision, Etta and Buzz picked up stakes and moved to Palm Desert, 140 miles east of Hollywood, and one mile from the date groves where *They Made Me a Criminal* was filmed. They purchased what real estate agents might term a "modest" residence on a street named "Peppergrass." The house, a one-floor unit with a sloping roof, minuscule front yard, and covered breezeway, blended anonymously with those of his nearby neighbors. The Beaux-Arts mansion at 3500 West Adams was, in every way, the antithesis of the Peppergrass house, but that grand residence had never made Buzz happy. It was purchased for Gertrude and sold in despondency. In Palm Desert, Buzz and Etta settled for a quieter life, less demanding, in a climate that suited them both. "The winters are delightful," said Buzz. "As for the extremes of afternoon heat in the summer—thank God for air conditioning." Weather notwithstanding, the fact was that the Palm Desert abode made Buzz happy. "Of all the beautiful homes and mansions, this little home surpasses them all," said Buzz. "Now for the first time in my life I know what a home really means. I never had one before until now." Such was Buzz's not-so-veiled compliment to Etta.

Despite years of inactivity, Buzz retained his membership in the Directors Guild of America. Annually he received a confidential form on which he was required to list past earnings and estimate future ones so that his dues, based on income, could be calculated. Buzz wrote he had "No earnings for the year 1960," and $3,500 for all of 1961. For the fill-in sentence that read, "I estimate my earnings for 1962 to be," Buzz truthfully entered a question mark and signed the form dated January 8, 1962.

Jumbo, or, as it's also known, *Billy Rose's Jumbo,* had a choppy history. Impresario Rose brought the Rodgers and Hart circus musical to New York's Hippodrome Theatre in 1935. The show received favorable reviews, but the Great Depression forced its closing after five months. In the 1940s, MGM bought the film rights for around $100,000. It was planned that Arthur Freed would produce the picture with a cast that was to include Frank Morgan, Mickey Rooney, and Wallace Beery. By 1945, the project had been dropped, not to be revived again until 1952, when it was abandoned again until 1961, when MGM finally green-lit the project. Doris Day was cast as the lead, accompanied by the nonsinging Stephen Boyd, Martha Raye, and Jimmy Durante (reprising his stage role). Joe Pasternak and Day's husband, Martin Melcher, produced, and MGM's choreographer-turned-director Charles Walters helmed the production. Walters didn't feel he could do justice to the musical numbers. Soon after production began, a telephone rang in Palm Desert and an offer to return to Hollywood was made to the new owner of the modest house on Peppergrass.

For this film, Buzz's first in almost eight years, his credit was to be "second unit director." The title was really a misnomer (if not a downright demotion), and not the least bit descriptive of his contributions. Normally, the second unit on a feature film is assigned "pickup" shots, establishing shots, stunt work sequences, and inserts. More accurately, the screen credit should have read "Musical numbers created and staged by Busby Berkeley."

Exteriors were to be shot on MGM's lot 3, the site of the studio's brand-new oil well. There was a main tent (capable of holding two thousand people), a midway with sideshows, antique circus wagons, and a carousel. Everything was in place to look like a real traveling circus. The animals (including the elephants and horses) were kept on another lot. Two soundstages were assigned for the interiors.

Casting was pretty much in place when Buzz came to the project. He and Doris Day spoke fondly of their past collaboration, *Romance on the High Seas.* Billy Barty, the littlest letch from the "Pettin' in the Park" and "Honeymoon Hotel" numbers, surprised his old director on one of the soundstages. Barty had been filming a television commercial at MGM when he heard that Buzz was attached to *Jumbo.* He went to the soundstage, but was refused admittance by the young guard. "Would you please tell Mr. Berkeley that Billy Barty is here?" The guard relented and left his post. A short time later, Barty heard a booming voice yelling, "Billy! Get in here!" Buzz introduced Billy all around. They reminisced over *Gold Diggers of 1933* and *Footlight Parade*. Just as Billy was about to leave, Buzz asked him if he'd like a part in the picture. Billy said he would. Buzz turned to screenwriter Sidney Sheldon and said, "Write Billy a part." And *Jumbo*'s list of actors was appended with one of Hollywood's favorite diminutives, credited as Billy Barton.

Stephen Boyd introduces the picture from, ostensibly, a stage in a theater. The proscenium is soon abandoned, opening the action to the outdoors as the circus's riggers drive spikes, hoist tent poles, and corral the animals. This early "circus on parade" number is identifiably Buzz's from the top shots of anvils striking the spikes, to the two distinct lines of circus workers moving in tandem to bring up the "big top."

The biggest number, the very ideal of spectacle, is the impressive "Over and Over Again" number sung by Doris Day. Buzz begins the piece slowly, isolating Day in solo voce, as he slowly increases the setting's complexity by bringing in the trapeze artists, trampoline performers, unicyclists, and acrobats. By the end of the sequence, all the acts are performing simultaneously; it is a marvelous visual cornucopia in which Buzz's single camera is placed at the optimum viewing distance and angle to take in the full, colorful splendor.

"Circus on Parade" is reprised, this time more impressive, as the circus acts parade through the center of town. Buzz wisely uses the widescreen frame, filming the caged animals (one of them Martha Raye in a faux-lion outfit) as they maneuver left to right through the screen's rectangular format. In what appears to be a Buzz invention (harkening back to his days of unusual animal-costuming requests), Doris Day is being pulled by a half-dozen white horses. Like Pegasus, each horse is outfitted with white wings.

The combination of a half-dozen horses and almost as many stunt people brings to life "This Can't Be Love," filmed dizzyingly by Buzz. His overhead camera is constantly on the move, tracking and circling Doris Day as she stands on a horse as it jumps over ribbons and through hoops. "I had all types of shots in it and even carried a camera on a trapeze," said Buzz; "I changed doubles in that four times and I changed horses five times, but you'd never notice it." Indeed, his precise cutting never reveals the stunt women. In the melodic "The Most Beautiful Girl in the World," Buzz defers to the music as he follows a lip-synching Stephen Boyd singing to Doris on a spinning carousel, his most subdued staging in the film.

Buzz had nothing to do with *Jumbo*'s ultimately disappointing finale, "Sawdust and Spangles and Dreams." It was dreamed up by Charles Walters and associate producer Roger Edens. Buzz's idea of ending the picture was something quite spectacular, but Charles Walters (feeling obligated to accept the number) brought little imagination to the song. It's obviously stage-bound, perhaps designed as a book-ending device to the film. Its phony appearance (contrasting to all the outdoor shots) is as ill-fitting as Buzz's stacked numbers for Warner Brothers, but without the verve and aplomb of those routines. Buzz knew the number was wrong for a finale and had his own ideas on how the film should have ended: "I would have shown the main characters gradually building up into a spectacular three-ring circus. You have to hit the audiences hard with a spectacular finish. A Barnum & Bailey 'Greatest Show on Earth' routine would have been terrific." Buzz was correct in his assessment. The film opened in December 1962 to middling reviews and seriously underperforming ticket sales.

Buzz returned to the desert and kept himself busy dictating new story ideas to a professional secretary. "There's Gonna Be a Great Day," "It Came Too Late for Me," and "Four Characters in Search of an Author" were three titles that never found a publisher, if publication was ever pursued.

16

Remember My Forgotten Director

Buzz's 1963 Director's Guild dues form showed earnings of $16,000 (*Jumbo* money and little else). As before, Buzz couldn't venture a guess to the coming year's financial potential, so he left the "future earnings" field blank.

In March, Buzz took another job at MGM. He was again credited as the second unit director, but this time the title was more appropriate than it was in *Jumbo*. He was assigned the stunt work for the tentatively titled "Moonwatch." Buzz directed helicopters and navy craft and supervised a colossal automobile wreck on a California freeway. "I had the time of my life cracking up 12 cars," he said. His work was appreciated, but by the time the renamed *A Ticklish Affair* was released, Buzz's contribution went without credit.

Around this time there was talk of a lavish stage musical in the works based on George du Maurier's novel *Trilby*. The story, featuring the irresistible character Svengali the hypnotist, revolves around the tone-deaf Trilby O'Ferrall. In her sessions with Svengali, she's made into a grand diva. When the hypnotist falls ill, Trilby loses her talent and caterwauls her way through an important performance. Buzz was approached to stage the whole thing, and of his plans he boasted, "I'm going to combine stage and film technique with some wild things that have never been seen before." Screen actor Paul Henreid was signed as Svengali, but he never played the role. One can't help but wonder about the "wild" combination of techniques Buzz devised for the ultimately aborted project. Expressionistic lighting, chorus girls, mirrors, dancing, and unique celluloid effects might have revived Buzz's career. Now in his late sixties, he was not idle by choice. Although it appeared he would take any project that crossed his desk (no matter how dubious the prospects), he remained optimistic, answering personal and fan letters, devising new musical numbers in his mind, and hopeful that an offer was only a phone call away.

On his personal letterhead, dated November 27, 1963, Buzz wrote to a person only identified as "Gen" with casting ideas for an undisclosed project. In part, it read:

> What news from Curt Jurgens? Have been holding off from this end before I make any contacts from his end. Here are some of the possibilities I have thought of . . . what do you think? Alfred Drake, Anthony Quinn, Jason Robards Jr., Fernando Lamas, Caesar Romero, Lawrence Harvey. And I still think with a little wheeling and dealing we could get Paul Henreid. I have a big article coming out about me the end of the week by Hal Humphries [sic], the nationally known syndicated T.V. columnist. Tune in on NBC this Monday night Dec. 2nd. A Wolper Documentary Production on the 'Fabulous Age of Hollywood Musicals.' Joseph Cotton [sic] is the narrator, and they feature clips from many of my musicals and also feature me—(look quick and you will see me in one or two of the shots). Boy—they sure gave me a terrific plug!

The name "Wolper" referred to the same David Wolper who apparently held no grudge or ill feeling toward Buzz despite the *Glad to See You* collaborative failure of the 1940s.

Hal Humphrey wrote a laudatory column and featured a couple of quotes from Buzz on how things were done in the old days. The waltzing pianos from *Gold Diggers of 1935* were discussed. "I had a boy dressed in black under each piano. That's how I moved them in unison. It was a real problem in geometry," said Buzz, the poor math student. Hal identified *Fashions of 1934* as "Fashion's Follies" when he referred to an incident relating to the "Spin a Little Web of Dreams" number. Apparently some irate mother had come charging onto the set and screamed at Buzz, "I didn't bring my daughter up to be a harp!" At the end of the piece, Buzz let the world know he was still up for a challenge: "They think because of that small screen it can't be done, but I know it can. I've got a great idea for a number with 60 dancing copper cuspidors—you know those things they used in the old West—and they'd be manipulated by 120 hands in black gloves." The image of this can only be guessed, but one imagines that faces would be in shadow, and only black gloves and copper spittoons would be arranged in mesmerizing patterns not lost on small black-and-white television sets. But Christmas and New Year's intervened, and it wasn't until mid-1964 when a story surfaced about Buzz's involvement in the planning of a film tentatively titled *Project 22.* Rumored to star George Hamilton and Geraldine Chaplin, it was to have been shot on location in Yugoslavia. It was never made.

Buzz's name became attached to Noel Langley, the screenwriter who burst to fame with his adaptation of *The Wizard of Oz.* Langley's new script, *Only the Poor Have Rich Dreams* (not to be confused with John Shelton's aborted *Only the Poor Dream Rich*), was based on the book by Gene Fowler. Buzz was to direct the film cofinanced by the United Arab Republic and an unnamed American company. The Fitzroy Films production never got off the ground.

In forced semi-retirement, Buzz and Etta left the desert in October 1965 to attend a tribute to him at the San Francisco International Film Festival. It was a star-packed event in which Shirley Temple, Ray Bolger, Elia Kazan, and George Cukor were also honored. Ruby Keeler, long retired herself, came up for the event and told reporters: "I know my pictures were corny, but they were wonderful in a way too—especially when you remember some of the things we did and how long ago it was. And they're still fun to see. . . . I understand that I'm camp now, and I'm really very flattered by the whole thing." The festival showed an hour's clips from the heyday at Warner Brothers. Seated alongside Buzz, Ruby whispered in his ear, "Buzz, you know I never really appreciated what it was you were trying to do in your pictures." During the presentation, Buzz turned in his seat and remarked to *New York Times* writer Howard Thompson, "Takes you back all right, doesn't it?" Buzz was asked by the festival staff which feature of his he would like screened after his tribute. Would it be his monumental *Gold Diggers of 1935,* or perhaps the colorful and crazy *The Gang's All Here*? During Buzz's fruitful years when he proved he could direct comedies, musicals, or dramas with equal adeptness, he was most proud of one drama with music that, despite its last-minute panic reshoots, Buzz believed was a new level of maturity in his directing and storytelling. Without hesitation, he told the

San Francisco International Film Festival committee that at the Masonic Auditorium he would like them to screen *For Me and My Gal.*

And so began Buzz's world tour of accolades. In November, it was announced that UCLA was going to have a Busby Berkeley Film Festival, and soon thereafter Buzz and Etta left for London. Although he was kind and gracious at every feting, his very presence in public was Buzz's subtle way of saying, "I'm still here, ready to do a bang-up job for you . . . if you'd only let me."

In January 1966, the National Film Theatre in London held a tribute to Buzz. His look and his manner were described as being "more the courtly owl than the cock robin." As the owl held court, his minions listened attentively:

> I picked the girls for their eyes. Their eyes must talk to me not flirt with me. I don't need to see girls in bathing costumes to judge them. I once had 723 girls on the set looking for work. I hired just three, but they matched like pearls. I had only sixteen girls under contract to me. The real beauties were for use in the close-ups. Of course, with those extra three, I had nineteen. My girls didn't need to be dancers. So long as they could do ballroom steps . . . that was enough. What really mattered was synchronizing the rhythm to the musical playback on the set. Movie-making was quicker then because we had no fixed working hours. The only rule was we had to allow 12 hours rest between filming. Then I edited the film in the camera as I shot it—that's why I only use one camera. . . . I never had any trouble with the censor. Of course the girls in *Roman Scandals* were nude, but it was all being done to music.

And Buzz left the Londoners laughing when asked about the "Pettin' in the Park" number. With a twinkle, he responded: "Doesn't everyone pet in a park? Why, how else would boy meet girl?"

Mr. and Mrs. Berkeley didn't stay long in England, nor did they tour the continent. They headed back to the desert in January, where, eleven months later, a dismayed Buzz had nothing professional in the offing. At home on Saturday evenings, Buzz and Etta enjoyed Jackie Gleason's variety show on CBS. The June Taylor Dancers were regularly featured, and as part of their routine, they positioned themselves in the patterns Buzz had made famous thirty years before. A high-mounted camera captured the old familiar formations. One night, totally unexpectedly, "The Great One" came onstage after the June Taylor Dancers finished: "Well, I just want you to know we didn't introduce that. It was originated in Hollywood by Busby Berkeley who, in my book, I consider the best musical-comedy director ever." Buzz wired Gleason the next day: "You're the best in my book, too, Jack."

Additional tributes forced the sedentary Buzz to venture out of Palm Desert. In February 1967, the University of Southern California, following UCLA's lead, ran two hours of Berkeley clips, and Buzz and Ruby were reunited onstage. He said little, but Ruby was as self-effacing as ever: "You're in for a treat in this second half—you'll get to hear me sing! Tell 'em Buzz. It was those microphones, wasn't it?" The next stop for the Buzz and Ruby show took place in September as they ventured to Vancouver, where the classic clips were followed by a Q and A.

The city of Chicago welcomed Buzz and Ruby to the opening-night festivities of the third Chicago International Film Festival, held on November 11 at the Carnegie Theatre. During his two-day stay, Buzz didn't see much of the city (he had seen plenty of it during his stage years), and he and Etta unsociably retired to their hotel room each evening. Ruby basked in the attention from the Chicago press, and was seen dining in some of the city's swankier eateries.

The annual effrontery, the DGA's membership dues form, arrived in February. Buzz wrote that he was retired and had no DGA-related earnings in the previous year. In December, Buzz and Etta headed to New York to the Bouwerie Lane Theatre for an off-Broadway premiere. The show, originally titled "Gold Diggers Afloat at the Caffe Cino" in its incubatory stage, had been christened *Dames at Sea* by opening night. The show was a pastiche of the Busby Berkeley Warner Brothers musicals of the 1930s. Even the lead character was named "Ruby." In the glow of nostalgia, the production was well reviewed, and leading lady Bernadette Peters went on to win a Drama Desk award. Buzz never gave his review of the show, though it's likely he and Etta were charmed.

"There's something obscene about the sight of an energetic man in full possession of his faculties forced to remain idle," wrote William Murray about Buzz for the *New York Times* in March 1969. He went on to describe Buzz as "a big man in his early seventies and the first adjective that comes to mind is gray. Gray eyes, gray hair, a gray suit, gray skin." He remarked that whether sitting or standing, Buzz sags. "His stomach bulges, his lower lip is pendulous, and his nose seems squashed against his face." Buzz mentioned that he and Etta were financially secure, which prompted Murray to assume that the opposite was true. "Hell, I've had loads of real propositions," said Buzz, "but they never get all the money up." In April, it was reported that a financed film with the curious title *The Phynx* would reunite Buzz and Ruby Keeler. It made serendipitous sense to shoot it at the Burbank Studios of Warner Brothers.

17

The Figurehead

Harry Rigby, the Broadway producer, loved the films of Busby Berkeley. In the 1930s, his well-to-do Philadelphia family routinely gave him movie money that he spent eagerly every Saturday. Harry particularly enjoyed Ruby, Joan, Ginger, and other musical stars of the day, but the films of Berkeley remained at the top of his list: "I was mad for them."

Harry was not what you would call a successful producer. In 1951, his first production, *Make a Wish,* closed in fewer than three months. It was especially painful to Harry as his family and friends had provided a good portion of the backing. Two years later, a revue Harry produced with two others called *John Murray Anderson's Almanac* fared no better. The show ended after 229 performances. In 1959, after a six-year absence, he produced two short plays to be run "in limited engagement." Nineteen performances later they confirmed their booking pronouncement. A demoted "gopher," Harry now found himself on the low rung of the production ladder, working as a production associate on Edward Albee's *Ballad of the Sad Café.* He regained producer status with the moderately successful *Half a Sixpence* in 1965. Jane Nusbaum, an associate producer of the show, worked well with Harry, and together they produced a new musical for the spring of 1967 with the catchy title *Hallelujah, Baby.* It wasn't a big financial success despite its winning the Tony Award for best musical of the season.

Harry didn't have a project in mind, but he had Buzz Berkeley on the brain. He asked a show business friend of his to contact Mr. Berkeley in California to see if he would be interested in working on a Broadway show. The word back to Harry was that the great man was "ready, willing, and able." Harry called Buzz directly upon hearing the news, and together they mapped out a promising future. Harry told Buzz that he and Jane wanted to revive a number of musicals from the 1920s and 1930s, among them *Good News* and *No, No, Nanette.* The first production, however, would be a restaging of the short-lived musical *Divorce Me, Darling,* written by Sandy Wilson, who had a big hit with *The Boy Friend* in 1954. *Divorce* didn't do as well and closed after a brief initial run in London.

Buzz was no stranger to the Broadway and Hollywood pitchmen who called him with empty offers to direct. Now in his seventies and enjoying his new notoriety, he greeted them affably and pronounced his enthusiasm for their proposals. Everything looked promising until *Dames at Sea* opened, making Harry rethink his whole concept. He felt a production directed by the "real deal" would only draw a comparison. The fact that *New York Times* theater critic Clive Barnes spoke glowingly about *Dames at Sea* while making disparaging remarks about *The Boy Friend* in its treatment of nostalgia only made matters worse.

Jane Nusbaum, who handled the financial end of her and Harry's production team, made a decision to leave Broadway to produce in Hollywood. With an intuition for a likely failure, Harry dropped *Divorce Me, Darling* as a project. Unfortunately, he had to keep Buzz waiting in the wings. A new money man was needed, preferably one willing to invest in a speculative Broadway enterprise. Harry found such a money man in the guise of Mrs. Cyma Rubin.

Cyma Rubin (née Saltzman) was married to Sam Rubin, a multimillionaire and the founder and president of Fabergé, who had sold the perfume company in 1964 for $26 million. Cyma was a patron of the arts, and together with legendary orchestra conductor Leopold Stokowski, her Rubin Foundation raised funds for the ultimately successful American Symphony. She was an avid theater attendee as well, and with the accolades she received on behalf of her work with the symphony, Cyma decided she wanted to invest in a show and wanted to meet someone who could help. Through producer Joseph Papp (whose New York Shakespeare Theater was the recipient of grants from the Rubin Foundation), Cyma met Jane Nusbaum and Harry Rigby. All three seemed to get along well, but Jane's plans were already leaning toward California. Harry and Cyma continued without Jane's services and worked on ideas for a new show.

In the summer of 1969, Harry called Buzz and told him *Divorce Me, Darling* was not going to be produced. Might Mr. Berkeley be interested in one of the shows mentioned earlier, specifically Vincent Youmans,

Irving Caesar, and Otto Harbach's *No, No, Nanette?* Buzz replied that
he had directed a local production some forty years before, and the old
show still had some "legs." He told Harry he would love to do it. Harry
was thrilled, but he knew legal obstacles regarding rights to the show had
to be overcome first. Cyma, who knew little of the Berkeley legend save
for the national nostalgia craze that surrounded him, was nonplussed at
the news of his willingness to be part of the show. In a polite letter to
Buzz dated October 6, 1969, she made known her initial plans:

> Dear Mr. Berkeley,
>   Just a word to let you know that Harry and I are working
> at the plan to present *No, No, Nanette* this season if possible.
> We have met with all the parties involved and are attempting
> to acquire the rights. If and when this takes place, we will im-
> mediately send you a contract as the director and choreographer
> of the production. I deeply appreciate the interest and assistance
> you have given us thus far and I am looking forward to meeting
> you and I hope to have the pleasure of working with you. I will
> keep you informed as the project progresses.

In spite of Cyma's not-so-subtle escape clause of "if and when this takes
place," Buzz accepted her invitation graciously:

> Dear Cyma Rubin:
>   It was so nice to receive your letter. . . . I had imagined that
> you were in the midst of getting the rights cleared—that's why
> Harry didn't call me as he said he would or get off "that" letter
> he has promised me. But with it all I think he's a great guy and
> I am very fond of him—incidentally I think he's a damn good
> showman. So give the old b——d my best. I too am waiting to
> meet you Cyma and I feel working with you will be, shall we
> say, a most "happy marriage."
>   Warm regards,
>   Busby Berkeley

A number of Vincent Youmans tunes had becomes standards over the
years (most notably *No, No, Nanette*'s "Tea for Two" and "I Want to

be Happy"), but others remained in the trunk, and Cyma wanted to revive them for *Nanette*. Buster Davis, who had worked with Harry on a number of productions, was brought in as *Nanette*'s musical director. With the whirl and excitement of a new production breathing life, Cyma sent Buzz a short status letter the following month:

> Dear Mr. Berkeley,
>
> Just to let you know that we are into the final stages of closing contracts on *Nanette* and have sent along a proposal to [your agent] for you. Harry is beside himself with anxiety and thus far all reports are very enthusiastic on the revival. We will be getting together in the next few weeks just as soon as the last ends are tied. In the meantime, please begin to clear your calendar because we're all going to be very busy—soon. Harry says that he is flattered by your compliments and he sends his love.
>
> Me too,
> Cyma

More than two months passed before Buzz replied to Cyma, though in his defense he thought he had answered her but apparently hadn't:

> Harry called me on the phone Sunday night, had a lovely talk and we are taking care of the contract ourselves. [My agent] no longer represents me. Harry and I talk the same language and we get along great, so we do not need a third or outside party. Expect to receive the new contract from Harry within the next few days as soon as his lawyer has drawn it up. Can't wait to meet you and jump back into the harness once again. It will be a lot of hard work, but I'm sure it will all be very much worthwhile.
>
> Most sincerely,
> Buzz

Madison Avenue, by way of comic Stan Freberg and a can of soup, took notice of Buzz's public reemergence. In a minute's time, a national television commercial written and directed by Freberg for Heinz's Great American Soup introduced Busby Berkeley to a new generation. A husband (Dave Willock) walks into his kitchen and comments to his wife: "Boy am I hungry. (*He notices the soup can.*) "What kind of soup is that?" Emily, his wife, played by Ann Miller, replies: "Make way for The Great American Soup." "Can you give me that again?" asks the husband. And just like the desks in the opening of the "Dames" number, the stage props split horizontally revealing a Berkeley-type set as Miller taps and spins her way around a giant soup can that rises from the floor. She sings: "Up at the Ritz they passed the word to 42nd Street. Make way for the Great American Soup." Throw in a patented top shot with platinum blond dancers in formation and some fast taps on the lid of the soup can and the set reassembles as the husband gets the last laugh: "Emily, why do you have to make such a big production out of everything?" The commercial, the most expensive ever made at that time, was a big hit and ran for the better part of a year. Ironically, the soup didn't sell well, and Heinz eventually discontinued the product.

Buzz signed an agreement with Rubin and Rigby productions on February 25, 1970, as director and choreographer for the revival of *No, No, Nanette*. In his earliest discussions with Harry, Buzz had mused that it would be fun to work with Ruby Keeler again. Despite the fact that he had been with Ruby at the three film festivals that paid him tribute, he knew in his heart that she wouldn't go for it. Ruby Keeler Lowe was now the wife of industrial builder John H. Lowe, as well as a retired grandmother, a mother of two sons (one adopted) and three daughters. She didn't want to leave her beloved family or California's sunbathed golf courses (where her score was routinely in the eighties) for the Broadway footlights that held no interest for her.

Things changed for Ruby in 1969. He beloved husband passed away on February 11. With the realization that her children, now grown, had their own lives and were either living elsewhere or were married, Ruby decided to downsize. The three homes she shared with John were sold, and Ruby took residence in a Corona Del Mar apartment. But a revitalization of her fabled career was still not even a possibility. She hadn't done anything related to show business in almost twenty years. Famed movie fan Ken Murray had a weekly television series, and he contacted Ruby in 1950 to see if she would be interested in a two-week stint at New York's Roxy Theater. *Variety* praised her performance, making mention of Ruby's "still-slim gams and chassis." A supporting role as a "tipsy witch" in the 1968 Chicago production of *Bell, Book and Candle* was met with less-than-stellar reviews. Ruby wasn't all that enthused about taking the role in the first place, telling a member of the Chicago press that she "thought it might be a mother part, with kids, something very simple." That's what Ruby wanted—nothing big and nothing splashy. She left for the West Coast immediately when her three-week engagement ended.

Buzz called Ruby and discussed *No, No, Nanette*. Ruby was nice, polite, and firm in her resolve. She eventually acquiesced to a reading of the script. She wasn't convinced the role of Mrs. Jimmy Smith was right for her. It was written as a straight drama and didn't play to Ruby's dancing and singing strengths. Her kids, however, were thrilled at the idea, especially Kathy, the youngest. They didn't want their mother to be a lonely widow when bigger things were beckoning. Yet here was her old friend (and lately film festival companion) Buzz Berkeley at the other end of the phone line, boasting of his new director's credit at almost seventy-five. Ruby knew of Buzz's dream of one more show, one more opening. His dream was now being realized. Ruby Keeler would join him.

With the legendary director in their midst, the New York press was eager for quotes, and Buzz was most obliging. "Age doesn't mean anything to me," he pontificated; "I claim that a person doesn't grow old by living a certain number of years; a person grows old by deserting his ideals. In my book, you're as young as your faith, and as old as your doubt. You're as young as your self-confidence and as old as your despair." In commenting about the new decade, Buzz reflected on what he had done, and more importantly, what he could do with a 1970s budget:

> You know, if someone came along today and made a "Gold Diggers of 1970" he'd make himself a bloody fortune. And I'd like to do it. Wow! What I could do with widescreen and color! I didn't have those things back in the Thirties; I had to stage the numbers in black and white on a normal screen. . . . Yes I know the studios are down on musicals because they cost too much money. But they don't have to. I hear *Hello, Dolly!* cost $20 million. I could have made it for $10 million, if they had just given me the chance. . . . One of the problems with movie musicals

today is that the studios won't take a chance on original stories. They wait until a hit shows up on Broadway and they buy it. In my day the story was the least important thing. What we wanted to know was, who's going to write the score? It was the songs that sold the pictures.

Buzz's assessment was generally accurate (and the dig at *Hello, Dolly!* might have been unintentionally aimed at its director, Gene Kelly). But his last sentence was pure modesty, for one could argue that it was his treatment of those songs that sold the pictures.

Soon after signing his contract, Buzz made the papers again when it was announced that *Gold Diggers of 1935* and *Footlight Parade* were to be given a short theatrical run. A daughter of one of the old Berkeley gals, Mrs. Melba Marshall Quenzer, presented Buzz a certificate of appreciation at the reopening. Twenty of Buzz's beauties, some of whom he hadn't seen in thirty-five years, attended the little ceremony at the Lido Theatre.

Columnist Joyce Haber leaked a story about an upcoming television special called *Tippy-Tap-Toe* based on dances from the 1930s. Evidently Buzz had been signed to an exclusive contract and would be designing "one of his legendary musical numbers" and would be acting as the special's technical adviser. It mattered little to him that the project never took off.

The Phynx limped its way in and out of theaters in May 1970. It was an unfunny spy spoof, where Buzz, Ruby, and assorted old-time stars are kidnapped by the crazed dictator of Albania. The United States comes up with the idea to send a famous rock band to the country in an effort to free the hostages. The fabricated group known as The Phynx weaves its way throughout Europe and eventually plays a command performance for the king of Albania (George Tobias) and his wife (Joan Blondell). Offering his chicken at tableside is Colonel Sanders, one of the unfortunate kidnappees along with George Jessel, Butterfly McQueen, Edgar Bergen, Charlie McCarthy, Xavier Cugat, Johnny Weissmuller, and others. Later, the "guests" are introduced and take their seat, waiting for the band to begin. Ruby walks out with Dorothy Lamour and Rudy Vallee, and a snazzy Busby Berkeley is followed by a group of his original dance girls. With the help of Bowery Boys Leo Gorcey and

Huntz Hall, the hostages hide in a half-dozen radish carts. By the time the carts reach the city walls, The Phynx comes to the rescue and plays so loud that the walls, like in Jericho, tumble down, allowing the Hollywood aged to escape their captors. The studio had, for good reason, so little faith in the film that it was released and withdrawn within a fortnight. Buzz and Ruby's silent contribution amounted to little other than their name recognition in the credit list.

Ruby protested the dramatic role in *No, No, Nanette* to Harry Rigby, saying that she was a dancer and there were no dances with the part. Harry told her that dances would be added to the show just for her. "And songs, too," said Harry. With a response that could almost be imagined in the shy, lilting, inquisitive voice that made her and *42nd Street* a hit, Ruby, noncommittal and emotionless, told her producer, "I guess . . . I could . . . try it." Other cast members were soon signed to the production. Bobby Van, who hadn't seen Buzz since the *Small Town Girl* days, was to play the role of Billy, and Helen Gallagher was cast as Lucille. The inimitable Patsy Kelly, who had just garnered some nice reviews for her work in *Rosemary's Baby,* and who knew Ruby from way back, was also given a contract.

When it came to Busby Berkeley, Cyma Rubin knew she had a bargain. She brought herself up to speed and learned of Buzz's past dalliances and ignominies. It wasn't out of the realm of possibility that she used this knowledge as leverage. He didn't command the top dollar of his early days, so Cyma could use his services as director and choreographer while paying him only one salary. Buzz's contract stipulated a fee of five thousand dollars to be paid in five, nine-hundred-dollar installments with five hundred dollars payable at signing, along with a per diem of forty dollars when the show was in out-of-town tryouts. Additionally, he was to be given a percentage of the play's gross receipts: 2 percent until the show's investment was repaid, and 3 percent thereafter.

Upon Buzz's agreement, the wheels of publicity began to turn. Merle Debuskey, a publicist who had worked with Harry and who knew Cyma, was hired. Debuskey went to work arranging interviews with the local press.

Buzz and Etta flew to New York to meet Harry and Cyma a few weeks after he signed his contract. Harry was at the airport to greet the couple. As the passengers began to disembark, Harry, with a shock, saw the director with his wife behind him. He had that gray appearance exactly as described by *New York Times* writer William Murray. In the corridor near the airline gate, Buzz walked toward Harry holding his briefcase in his right hand. A big smile emanated from Harry as the men approached each other. Then, in a startling accident, Buzz removed his briefcase from his hand, placed it on the ground, and fell to the floor in a giant heap where the briefcase stood. The sound of the fall reverberated in the airport corridor. "He's all right, he's all right," assured Etta as she bent down to assist her husband. "He has a spastic colon, and he took a painkiller on the plane. It just made him dizzy." Etta took one arm and Harry the other, and they lifted Buzz off the floor. A cut across Buzz's nose bled, and a blue bruise was noticeable on his forehead. "I'm all right, I'm all right," Buzz protested as he waved his arms free of his helpers. After a short moment, Buzz fully regained his equilibrium, and all three exited the terminal and went into Harry's waiting car. Harry drove the couple to the Algonquin Hotel, where later Buzz and Etta met with Cyma and Sam Rubin. Cyma was quoted as saying her reaction to meeting and speaking with Buzz was "worse than terror" and that she was relieved only by the fact that up to that point she hadn't spent much money on him.

Cyma told Harry that it had been a mistake to hire Berkeley. She thought that maybe using his name was all the contribution Buzz could make. Harry reassured Cyma that he would get a real performance out of him. Harry said that Etta had made a promise to him. Cyma was incredulous at hearing this. In his contract, Buzz was allowed two assistants, so Harry promised Cyma to hire a codirector or a cochoreographer. Cyma, on her own, went looking and chose Donald Saddler, a choreographer with roots in ballet. He would assist in staging the dances and musical numbers. Saddler, for his part, wouldn't be a "co" anything and insisted that he alone would receive the choreographer credit, Busby Berkeley notwithstanding. Harry certainly knew Saddler, having worked with him on *John Murray Anderson's Almanac,* but the prospect of another professional association was not something Harry embraced. He expressed his opinion of Saddler to Cyma, and she responded with forceful vulgarity: "I don't give a shit what you want at this point. It's my money and I'm going to close the fucking checkbook, Harry! Because going the way you're going, we are going no place." Cyma made Harry call Saddler and offer him the job. Now the play had two dance directors, each chosen by a different producer. The fact that Donald Saddler was not going to work for the low rate that Buzz was receiving made Cyma bristle all the more. She didn't begrudge Saddler the money, but regretted that anything was being spent on the Hollywood relic who seemed to add nothing but name recognition to the production.

In July, Buzz was ready, with Harry's assistance, to select some of the girls who would make up the group of chorines who would be credited as the "Busby Berkeley girls." The first auditions took place on Buzz's turf in California. The Berkeley edict was still in force; girls had to be "gorgeous, not just beautiful." Out of the dozens who auditioned and sang "That's Entertainment" to the accompaniment of an old upright piano, five met Buzz's standards. They signed contracts and were given airplane tickets to New York. In an interview with a *Newsweek* reporter held during the West Coast auditions, Buzz revealed his criteria for selecting the right girl: "Beautiful eyes. I can picture a girl through her eyes. They mirror the soul."

The following month, Buzz made the trip back east, but Cyma, Donald Saddler, Harry, and others had begun auditions of their own, selecting a few performers for the show without his knowledge. Buzz was unfazed by the usurping of authority and said nothing on the record to the contrary. On September 1, an open call for dancers created a miniature riot scene. The news media showed up, egged on by Buzz's celebrity and his eagerness to return to Broadway.

More interviews came Buzz's way, and he refused none. Seated in the center of the front row, he spoke with a reporter from the Associated Press who, apparently, was interested in learning which movie stars got their break in his films. Buzz thought for a moment and yelled back to Harry: "Who were some of the other stars I discovered? Lucille Ball . . . Betty Grable." Harry added Paulette Goddard, while Buzz appended the list with Ginger Rogers and Ann Dvorak. Etta sat toward the back of the theater during his interviews. She explained, "He has been asked the same questions so many times," and went on to say that Buzz attended a film festival in Michigan against doctor's orders and that he recently threw out his back at home.

It was a charade that Buzz had any real influence in the casting. Donald, Cyma, and Harry chose 18, with Harry occasionally running toward Buzz to confirm a selection of a semifinalist the three had just made. Television crews were there to film Buzz as he walked past each hopeful asking brief background questions. He moved from his front-row seat, where he was miked, toward the few steps leading to the stage. He looked as if he were caught on something and wildly waved his arms. A member of the chorus helped unhook Buzz's lavalier microphone, and he completed his ascent without incident. Buzz asked the girls the standard questions: "What's your name?" "Where are you from?" "How long have you been in the business?" Over and over, he went down the line with each of the 18. When he was finished he turned to the cameraman and asked, "Was it all right?" "It was beautiful," said the cameraman. Barking, Buzz replied: "I don't care if it was beautiful. Was it all right?" He took residence in the third row, where, after a spell, he was seen dozing. That night the local newscasts featured Buzz watching the tapping of auditioning dancers. An interview Buzz gave to the Associated Press was fed nationally with accompanying photographs. A typical whitewash, it nonetheless presented him in a favorable light: "Preparing for a comeback on Broadway, Berkeley auditioned 350 starry-eyed dancers. . . . 'I look at the personality, the looks, the face, and the figure. . . . I talk to them. I can feel pretty quickly if they've got that verve,' said the white-haired director who launched the careers of stars such as Betty Grable, Lucille Ball and Ginger Rogers."

On September 28, Ruby Keeler arrived at 10 a.m. and gathered with cast members in the two rehearsal halls on the fourth floor of the Broadway Arts Studio. Ruby told Harry she had been driven to the studio by a "nice cab driver." "It's a good omen," replied Harry. Ruby was a bit nervous: "This is kind of fun, but I would probably feel more at home if I ran with the chorus; anyway, it's going to be interesting." The first day not much was accomplished except the signing of forms. Ruby filled out her Social Security number and received the "Actors Equity Rules for shows." Ruby remembered when chorus girls were not paid for rehearsals. She remarked that "the benefits today are great." Buzz didn't arrive for rehearsals until three that afternoon. He had attended the emplacement of a bronze plaque in memory of Vincent Youmans on the corner of Sixty-first Street and Central Park West, the site of Youmans's birthplace.

A few days later, the publicity people arranged for Ruby and Buzz to appear on David Frost's talk show. Cyma Rubin was anxious that the world would see the frail man and urged the television director not to show Berkeley walking onstage. Instead, after interviewing Ruby, the show took a commercial break and Buzz magically appeared at the host's side. Only the studio audience (and Cyma) saw the doddering director slowly make his way to the interview chair during the commercials. David Frost, who, in his enthusiasm, sometimes appeared as if he were elevated an inch above his chair, asked Berkeley how he got the idea for the girls on the piano number. "Well, David," Buzz replied, "ideas don't come easy, you know. But one day I was out driving and I got this idea to have a hundred girls dancing on pianos." "Fantastic . . . just fantastic," said Frost in his affable British inflection. A follow-up question about Buzz's filming a dancer's feet from below met with this response: "Well, that was interesting. I had the studio get me a piece of glass, oh, about this thick. And I put the camera underneath and had the man dance on it."

Cyma was incensed. After the Frost interview, she viewed Buzz as a museum piece. She told Harry she wanted Buzz out. Harry pleaded Buzz's case, and begged Cyma to keep the legendary man with the production. The following day, Cyma called Broadway director Burt Shevelove and explained the situation to him before offering him the director's job. She stated that Berkeley was too old to direct the play. Shevelove wanted to know what Buzz's role was. "We're working on that," replied Cyma. "Just one thing," added Shevelove; "keep him out of my way. There is not going to be time for politics or for worrying about hurt feelings."

Burt Shevelove was a moderately successful director whose biggest hit to date was *A Funny Thing Happened on the Way to the Forum*, in which he adapted the book and directed the production. Coincidentally, he had worked with Harry in *Hallelujah, Baby!* All in all, he seemed a perfect fit. However, he was not going to play the figurehead as Berkeley had been doing. He was to be totally hands-on with the production. Shevelove insisted on having the final word in all decisions concerning the play's direction. His agent struck a hard bargain with Cyma Rubin, asking for wages five times the union minimum, along with the highest per diem of any member of the show. When Cyma went through the show's percentage tally she realized that something needed excising. The show's weekly gross would pan out as follows:

Busby Berkeley: 2%

Burt Shevelove: 1.5%

Donald Saddler: 1%

Ruby Keeler: 2.5%

Other production personnel would get various amounts. All together, the percentages were staggering. Consequently, Cyma insisted that Buzz's financial deal be rewritten. She controlled the purse strings, and Harry had no choice but to follow orders. A short time later, a new contract was sent to Buzz that stated "the previous agreement is hereby cancelled, terminated, and of no further force and effect." Buzz's role in the production would be changed. He was no longer the show's director and choreographer. A nondescript title of "consultant and advisor" was bestowed. His 2 percent gross deal was cut in half. A five-thousand-dollar fee was changed to five hundred dollars per week for five weeks as an advance against any future royalties. He couldn't even choose his own associates as the new contract plainly stated that the producers had sole and absolute control of all personnel to be engaged (cast, director, choreographer). He was also to agree "to cooperate in attending press conferences, publicity interviews, and so forth." The final insult came in the show's credits. "Entire production staged by Busby Berkeley" was to be changed to "Production supervised by Busby Berkeley." Buzz asked Harry to include the word "Entire" to the credit, but it was not to be. If it had been up to Cyma Rubin, she would have sent Buzz packing, but she was persuaded to keep him on for the name recognition alone, to say nothing of the press scandal that would have resulted from his dismissal.

The new contract was signed, and Buzz, uncomfortably, had to be introduced to the man who would be replacing him. Ruby Keeler needed assurances from Harry that Buzz was still a part of the production. After all, Buzz was the hook that had brought her back to the stage, however reluctantly. At a dinner party in which Cyma had assembled the principals of the play, Buzz had another unforeseen brush with his balance. As everyone was getting up from the dinner table, Buzz stood and promptly slid down on Cyma's floor. Harry and Etta immediately rushed to Buzz's aid and lifted him. As at the airport, Buzz gave a gruff, "I'm all right, I'm all right" while he was being assisted out the door to a waiting cab.

Burt Shevelove noted that there was a whole different feeling about the production from that point forward.

During the subsequent tryouts, Buzz could be seen sitting on a folding chair, onstage, behind the girls. Donald Saddler was in front of the dancers, giving constant eye contact to Buzz as if to seek approval. One of the girls in the group of those rejected stood out of line and handed a piece of paper to Buzz. He didn't read it and gave it to Etta, who whispered the words into his ear. Buzz nodded, but said nothing. On the paper was written, "My mother was in the chorus of No, No, Nanette in 1924."

With Buzz on his folding chair, the rehearsals proceeded in earnest. The dancers danced in front of Donald Saddler, and he often asked them to turn around and do it one more time for Mr. Berkeley. Cyma, in the wings, was fuming. She whispered loudly to Harry that Berkeley wasn't being paid to be an audience.

Whenever Ruby Keeler was interviewed about No, No, Nanette, she came across as aloof or worse, uninterested. On NBC radio's Monitor program, she responded to a question regarding her enthusiasm about a return to Broadway: "I'm not terribly excited about being back to do the show. As a matter of fact, sometimes I feel like I just want to go home to California." When Ruby went backstage to visit Ethel Merman (who was starring in Hello, Dolly!), Ethel asked her if she was excited about doing Nanette. "No, not yet," she wearily responded. Ruby would be at the theater each day at three as the daily call sheet demanded and do a few dance steps. Afterward she would walk aimlessly around the theater and take part in whatever conversation was brewing.

During a chorus break, Etta told those around her (more than once) that Buzz was working on his autobiography, but that he was too busy now to continue. Last year, she went on, her husband was asked to go on a lecture tour to fifty "or maybe a hundred" schools. By this time, Etta had been asked politely not to attend rehearsals as her nonstop chatter made it difficult for some cast members to concentrate.

Burt Shevelove was actively rewriting Nanette's script. When he finished act 1, the news was applauded by cast members and Buzz alike. He misspoke when he promptly asked for a copy of "Strangelove's" script! Buzz took the daily script pages and with a three-hole punch at a table beneath a gooseneck lamp, he dutifully bored his own little holes in the paper. According to chorus boy Kevin Daley, everyone was "sick" at the way Berkeley was treated: "To have a man of his stature, his reputation, sit there day after day and give him script pages and a punch so that he could make holes for the three-ring binders. Really, it was sickening."

Buzz would occasionally stop what he was doing to yell advice to some of the dancers, imploring them to "smile and work harder." Tolerating Busby Berkeley and giving credence to his directions were different things. He added his comments during the rehearsal of the show's most famous number, "Tea for Two." It appeared somewhat static, but Shevelove wanted to stage it as a lovely ballad as performed in the original show. "Don't you think there should be some movement?" asked Buzz. "The boy should go this way, and the girl should follow him, and then she should go that way, and he should follow her." Buzz's suggestion fell on deaf ears. A few weeks later, a rumor had spread throughout the cast that Buzz was holed up in his hotel room for a couple of days due either to illness or to Shevelove's edict that he leave the theater.

The director's script had not met with universal approval. At a script run-through, Ruby quietly objected in her usual nonconfrontational manner. She didn't like a Shevelove line and responded, "It's one thing to look bad onstage because I'm an old woman, but it's another thing to look bad because I've been given bad material."

No, No, Nanette was going to Boston and other cities first before it played on Broadway. Buzz had regained his health (if, indeed, that's what had kept him away from the theater) and was ready to accompany the cast. The five-hour train ride was exhausting, and Buzz dozed during most of the trip as Etta watched the scenery from her window. While still in New York, Buzz taped an interview with a Boston station that was to broadcast when the cast settled there. It was Buzz, perfunctory as ever:

"Mr. Berkeley, in the film where pianos danced across the stage, there were men in black beneath each piano, pushing them around. Did you have to rehearse much with them to get the pianos into the right position?"

"Oh, no."

"How did they know where to go?"

"Well, we just told each one where to go and then we practiced a lot before we filmed it."

The first night in Boston a run-through was scheduled, but Buzz was not asked to be present because Burt Shevelove would "blow up" if he saw him. Buzz kept his distance and did not interfere or otherwise upset the contracted director.

The first Boston matinee in the fall of 1970 took place at the ornate Shubert Theatre at 2:30 p.m. Buzz sent a huge rose bouquet to Ruby's dressing room. Their scent filled the air, which was already thick with anticipation and excitement. The audience was enthralled with the show. Ruby Keeler had received the lion's share of adulation, and her performance was met with vociferous approval from the matinee crowd. She tapped as if a day hadn't passed since she was seen in a bib-top and wooden buck shoes brushing her hair from her face. Harry Rigby, beside himself with joy, embraced everyone and gave Buzz a bear hug of gratitude. In its second week, *No, No, Nanette* was sold out. The three cities scheduled after the Boston run—Toronto, Philadelphia, and Baltimore—saw advance ticket sales rising as a result of the Boston reviews.

In November, as the cast came to Philadelphia, Harry planned a party for Buzz's seventy-sixth birthday. He wanted to take Etta, Ruby, and Patsy Kelly along for the celebration. When the show opened to the same raves as in Boston and Toronto, lyricist Irving Caesar ran up to Buzz with ebullient praise. A realist, Buzz said: "I don't know why everyone keeps congratulating me. I didn't do it all by myself." According to reports, there was a standard response that cast members were obliged to give when the media asked about working with the legendary Busby Berkeley. "He was marvelous, so kind and knowledgeable" or "His presence—all those years of creativity and imagination—it was just an inspiration to us all" were the tendered noncommittal replies per the edict of Cyma Rubin.

Burt Shevelove didn't take Berkeley's accolades in stride. In those days of nostalgic revival, the name Busby Berkeley meant more than a simple credit. In some reviews, Shevelove wasn't even mentioned as they deferred instead to the show's figurehead. Burt was particularly enraged when the *Philadelphia Bulletin*'s critic wrote that "the 1925 musical had been recreated by Shevelove, with the help of Busby Berkeley, the old movie choreographer."

Just as the show was preparing to go to Broadway, Harry was having major problems with Cyma. On Rubin & Rigby Productions, Ltd.

stationery she wrote him an angry letter, reprimanding him for his wasteful spending and unauthorized days away from the office. Harry took it in stride, knowing full well his contract stipulated his agreement with Cyma could not be terminated until after April 1, 1971, with 180 days written notice. In Baltimore, on Christmas Day of 1970, Harry received a special-delivery letter signed by Cyma:

> Dear Mr. Rigby,
>   You are hereby notified that you are removed as a director of Rubin & Rigby Productions, Ltd., effective as of this date.

Sam Rubin immediately moved to take Harry's name off the credits. Now the show would be presented by "Pyxidium, Ltd." instead of "Cyma Rubin and Harry Rigby." David Merrick, the Broadway impresario whose legend rivaled that of Florenz Ziegfeld, spoke plainly and accurately when he remarked, "Everybody in the business knows that Harry Rigby put the show together and that Mrs. Rubin bankrolled it."

During their stay in New York, the Berkeleys attended one of the hottest shows on Broadway, the self-described "tribal rock musical" *Hair*. Buzz fell asleep during the show: "It looked like hodgepodge to me. All those kids coming out in the aisle, lying down on their bellies, then running back onstage. What a bore!" Buzz believed he could take a property as controversial as *Hair* and give it the old "show doctor" treatment. "And we wouldn't need all that nudity." Buzz told writer Hal Wingo of the ethos that had made him the toast of Broadway and a big man in the Hollywood heyday: "You put 12 girls in a line doing kicks and so forth and it's all very nice, of course, but I figured you put 48 girls on a stage doing the same thing and it becomes spectacular. . . . We would have these meetings with producers, directors and all the rest and I would start walking around the room waving my hands to explain how I wanted a number to go. Well, they didn't know what the hell I was talking about and at the end they would say, 'Hey Buzz, that's great!' But how could they know what was in my mind? They had to wait and see my ideas on the screen."

No, No, Nanette had its first Broadway preview on January 6, 1971, and its official opening thirteen days later at the Forty-sixth Street Theatre. It quickly garnered a reputation as the hottest ticket in town.

Scalpers were getting fifty dollars for ten-dollar upper-balcony seats. The first-nighters included Zero Mostel, Gwen Verdon, and Marlene Dietrich. Despite his dismissal, Harry Rigby came as Buzz's guest.

The crowd was ecstatic. When Ruby broke into her tap dance to "I Want to Be Happy" and the tempo of the song and dance increased, so did the applause and cheers. Someone in the back of the theater yelled, "That a girl, Ruby!" During the curtain calls, Patsy Kelly (who didn't dance in the show) did a crazy gyration on center stage that ended with an exuberant high kick. She turned her head toward the grinning Ruby and yelled, "Eat your heart out!" The audience went wild. After the show, family, friends, and well-wishers crowded into Ruby's dressing room. Buzz came in and kissed the reluctant star still in makeup. "Oh, thank you Buzz," she said. He nodded and replied tiredly, "I'm worn out with this one . . . worn out."

The reviews were rapturous. According to one report, "audiences cheer the first notes of *Tea for Two* and *I Want to be Happy*. Most nights, there is a moment of near hysteria when Ruby Keeler appears . . . when she starts to tap dance, shouts of affection bounce through the theater." Clive Barnes of the *New York Times* wrote: "For everyone who wishes the world were fifty years younger—and particularly, I suspect, for those who remember it when it was fifty years younger —the revival of the 1925 musical *No, No, Nanette* should provide a delightful, carefree evening. It also has a certain amount of taste and imagination. One of the show's many charms is the amount of dancing—not unexpected, when it is remembered that the production has been supervised by the great Busby Berkeley, who once made Hollywood a world fit for tap dancers, and stars Ruby Keeler, who, way back when, was sent on that stage by Warner Baxter, an unknown, and came back a star. Ruby still is a star." *New York* magazine critic John Simon was one of the play's dissenters. His readers (and even those who simply heard of the bad review) responded with nasty, negative letters to the critic, "impugning everything from my virility to my religion," according to Simon.

Buzz and Etta attended two parties to celebrate the Broadway opening, Harry Rigby's and Cyma Rubin's. The next morning they packed for a return trip to California. A quick detour brought Buzz to the *What's My Line?* television show, where he was the mystery guest. On

March 21, Buzz appeared on a West German variety show called *New York, New York* with Ruby Keeler, designer Bill Blass, and actress Carol Channing.

Back in the desert, Buzz went through his mail and corresponded with old friends. Actress Joan Crawford was one of Buzz's well-wishers on *Nanette*'s opening night, and he was touched:

> My dear Joan,
> Have just arrived home here in the Desert and am starting to catch up on my overdue mail. To begin with, thanks a million for your lovely wire on the opening night of "No No Nanette." You don't know how much I loved it . . . especially from you. Yes, I guess we did give Broadway a big smash hit for which I am very grateful after the long hard work. Etta joins me in much love to you Joan.
>
> Fondly,
> Busby Berkeley

Happy to have Buzz out of the way, Burt Shevelove took one final offensive jab. He demanded that the large photograph of Buzz, which hung outside the theater along with photos of the rest of the cast, be removed. With a bitter disregard for the truth, he said, "No one knows who that old man is."

Harry Rigby immediately brought suit against Cyma Rubin to reclaim his *Nanette* credit. On Christmas, one year after the delivery of his termination letter, Cyma instructed her lawyers to offer Harry a settlement. Harry took the cash, but walked away without the producer's credit.

Helen Gallagher, Patsy Kelly, and Donald Saddler won Tony Awards in 1971. Burt Shevelove was nominated for best direction of a musical, but lost to Harold Prince for *Company*.

On February 3, 1973, *No, No Nanette* closed on Broadway after 861 performances. Busby Berkeley's contribution to the play remained largely misunderstood, but it made good "nostalgia triumphs" copy for the public and the press.

The Berkeleys remained in Palm Desert, where, according to Etta, Buzz was working on the finishing touches to his autobiography. Both were enjoying the escalating weekly stipends that *No, No, Nanette* produced. Despite Cyma Rubin's intention to wipe Buzz's name from the show, she could not escape the fact that it was the famous director's reputation that had brought the rebirth of *No, No, Nanette* to prominence and profitability. In a *Life* magazine tribute to nostalgia, published around the same time as *No, No, Nanette*'s opening, Buzz revealed a thinly disguised rebellion to retirement: "They used to complain it was too expensive to do my kind of show. But all my pictures made barrels of money. I never had a failure in my life. And if some producer today had the foresight and confidence to say, 'Let's do it again,' I'd show them. I guarantee you that."

The lion in winter: still roaring and raring.

18

The Palmy Days

Buzz and Etta flew to West Berlin for the city's film festival in 1971. Still riding the wave of his newfound notoriety, Buzz accepted the Unicrit Prix Award, which was inscribed: "To Honour Busby Berkeley Master Musical Maker/A Tribute from Unicrit Berlin Film Festival 1971." Buzz pontificated in his authoritative voice about beauty and his girls while the festival's international press took notes: "I always named 'em the Berkeley Girls, and no one picked any girls but me. I picked 'em all. Always. Once a producer came up to me and said, 'Buzz, that one on the end looks cute,' and I said, 'Oh, sit down.' People have the damnedest ideas about beauty." One generalized question brought forth a moment of honest self-reflection. What did he think of his career? "Well, I just say to myself, 'Buzz, you must have done a hell of a good job; they all like it.'"

In July, film critic Richard Schickel interviewed Buzz for the television special "The Movie Crazy Years." Schickel felt that the usual give-and-take between interviewer and subject was lacking. Buzz's responses were often terse with little explanation. In the editing room, Schickel worried that he'd have no useful footage of Buzz. Working with his team of editors, Schickel was surprised to find that not only was every single word Buzz said usable, but that Buzz scarcely uttered a wasted word. According to Schickel, Buzz's responses suggested "an orderly, logical way to present examples of his work." In assessing Buzz's viability, he said, "I haven't the slightest doubt that if you gave Berkeley a camera (and a traveling crane, of course) and a hundred girls he could still, at 76, stage one of his patented production numbers."

The Thalians, a charitable organization, began in 1955 as a means for Hollywood celebrities to reverse some of the town's negative press by devoting their time and money to children with mental health problems. Buzz, a Thalians supporter, was the honoree at their all-star gala in

1971. The entertainment program that evening was a tribute to Buzz titled "The Busby Berkeley Years." Debbie Reynolds (president of the Thalians since 1957) and Carleton Carpenter were there re-creating their "Aba Daba Honeymoon" number. Buzz's bronze-colored plastic trophy had a small statuette of Goofy the dog affixed to its base and read, "The Thalians, Mr. Wonderful, Busby Berkeley, 1971."

Some exciting news made the trades in August. It was announced that Buzz's life would be brought to the screen by producers Jack Haley Jr. and Jim Terry. The screenplay, based on Buzz's memoirs, was to be written by Jerry Mayer, a television writer with many credits. Haley would direct the film, budgeted at an estimated $5 million. Sounding a bit like the prepress for *No, No, Nanette,* it was reported that Buzz himself would "be in charge" of all the musical numbers and would choose all the girls in the picture personally. To that end, a nationwide contest was planned to find new and fresh Berkeley girls. The stars who worked with Buzz in his glory days would soon to be contacted for cameo appearances. And according to *Boxoffice* magazine, Buzz's memoirs would be published soon.

In one of life's sweet non sequiturs, Buzz and Etta flew to New York in March of the following year. He had been contacted by Bloomingdale's upscale chocolate shop, "Au Chocolat," to autograph candy boxes for a new item dedicated to him. Chocolatier, entrepreneur, and purported producer of Buzz's life story Jim Terry named the chocolate "Phudge" and said it was named after "musical producer Busby Berkeley." A wire photo shows Buzz (candy in mouth) alongside Terry. It's no doubt that the Berkeleys' luggage was heavier on the return flight, weighed down with the six different varieties of Phudge available exclusively at Au Chocolat.

Buzz's palmy days were spent in idle pursuits. There was the occasional round of golf, but he was no scratch player. The sweltering summers kept him housebound, and the phone rang infrequently. Though it appeared that Hollywood's biography of Buzz was stagnating, Jim Terry had an offer up his sleeve more ambitious than Phudge. He and writer Tony Thomas would collaborate with Buzz on a large photo-filled book covering his years in Hollywood. Buzz consented, and with a dedication to Etta, *The Busby Berkeley Book* was published in September 1973 by the New York Graphic Society. Coinciding with the publication was an exhibit staged by Don Smith at the Pub Theatrical Restaurant in New York titled "Hooray for Hollywood." It was announced that Buzz would attend the invitational preview on September 25, but he never made it. In late summer, he suffered a debilitating stroke.

During his convalescence, Buzz was given still another award, this time for the reissue of his popular eye-popping *The Gang's All Here*. Dated one day after the invitational preview, the certificate came from the Southern California Motion Picture Council and states, in part, that the film is of "outstanding merit."

Buzz was confined to his home, and Etta spent her days doting on her husband. The interviews stopped, his phone went silent, and the motion picture of his life story went no further than the announcement stage. In May 1975, writer Joyce Haber reported that the new project of movie producers Robert Chartoff and Irwin Winkler was to be *Busby* for 20th Century Fox. Buzz, according to Haber, would be acting as the technical adviser. No actors were identified for the lead, but it would be "a top name," according to Chartoff. "We're just about to sign our writers," he said. "Once we do, we'll know more about the casting." Haber also mentioned that Buzz had *eight* wives and that a couple of his unions were remarriages! In July, the producers said they expected a year's-end start date, but Buzz was still recovering from the stroke and everything depended on his lucidity.

It might have been Gertrude who persuaded her son to keep and treasure his career collectibles. Buzz maintained scrapbooks with hundreds of articles, newspaper clippings, and photographs. His fan mail, resurgent in the early 1970s, was carefully answered in handwritten responses and later typed by his secretary. Various versions of his replies were stapled to the original documents for recordkeeping. Buzz kept his membership cards (if not the memberships themselves) to the Director's Guild and the American Federation of Television and Radio Artists, among others. In his black leather wallet were his business cards and miscellaneous handwritten notes. A mustard yellow address book etched with Buzz's signature had among its listings the numbers and addresses of Jack Warner, Joan Blondell, Rudy Vallee, the Brown Derby Restaurant, the Hollywood Pet Cemetery, and Bullock's department store in Westwood. In his living room, Buzz tamped his cigarettes in a square glass ashtray with "Buzz" engraved on the bottom. Etta saved his anniversary cards to her. One had this handwritten sentiment: "*I love you, love you, love you / Your own devoted boy, forever and ever, Buzz.*"

On his wall hung a magnificent 32 × 38" oil-on-canvas painting of himself in shades of blue and aqua. The artist, Beatrice McCulley, was the daughter of the famed novelist Johnston McCulley (*The Mark of Zorro*). And what might have been Buzz's magnum opus rested undisturbed in a monogrammed briefcase. On loose-leaf notebook paper were written, in his own hand, his memoirs, titled "Girls, Glamour, and Glory." Its three-hundred-plus pages contained humorous and scandalous anecdotes.

Early Sunday morning, March 14, 1976, Etta made a frantic emergency phone call. Her husband could not be awakened. Paramedics from nearby Eisenhower Hospital made the six-mile trip in haste, but they needn't have rushed or run their sirens. Eighty-year-old Buzz had succumbed not by his own hand as he had tried thirty years earlier, nor from cirrhosis, which cuts short many an alcoholic's existence. At 6:35 a.m., a combination of acute fatal dysrhythmia and generalized arteriosclerosis saw to it that, despite the paramedics' valiant efforts, an all-enveloping eclipse cast a permanent shadow over the palmy days of Busby Berkeley.

Epilogue

Riverside County's certificate of death, like so much of Busby Berkeley's public record, was rife with errors. Etta provided what little factual information it contained. His name was not "Busby NMN Berkeley" as reported; his father was not William Enos; and his parents' birthplaces were not unknown.

Buzz was interred at Wiefels and Son Funeral Directors in Palm Springs. "Professional and Personal Services" including the casket, memorial card printing, certified copies of the death record, filing fees, and taxes came to a total of $1,283.69.

On March 29, the will of Busby Berkeley (signed on March 8, 1971) was filed for probate. After revoking all wills and codicils of previous wills, Buzz stated the following (capitalized as written): "My true full name is BUSBY BERKELEY WILLIAM ENOS."

Etta was named as executor and sole beneficiary of her husband's estate, which was valued at $100,000 even. Five local bank accounts with a cumulative total of $141,229.99 were declared in the will's attachment to be the community property of Buzz and Etta.

Eight years after Buzz's death, he was paid tribute during the opening ceremonies of the 1984 Olympic Games at the Coliseum in Los Angeles. Under the colonnade at the peristyle end of the Coliseum were eighty-four men seated at white baby grand pianos playing Gershwin's "Rhapsody in Blue." Also, every spectator held a card and when the cards were turned over en masse, the images of flags of the participating nations were revealed, the same effect Buzz had employed as far back as *42nd Street*.

Etta Dunn Berkeley lived on for more than two decades after her "devoted boy's" passing, well into her nineties. Sadly, financial hardship may have been the instigating factor in her decision to auction off most of Buzz's personal property. On October 27, 1998, at 7:30 p.m., the

Los Angeles auction house Butterfields held an auction titled "Property
from the Estate of Mrs. Busby Berkeley." Buzz's many awards, his press
clippings, biographical cassette tape recordings, typed anecdotes and
memoirs, the McCulley oil painting, letters to Gertrude, photographs of
his childhood and the mansion at 3500 W. Adams, his driver's license,
monogrammed ashtray, and even his heartfelt handwritten anniversary
cards were fodder for the gavel. The sentimentalist in Etta had deferred
to reality.

Although Gertrude had died some thirty years before her son, her
strong-armed influence was felt long after her passing. Had it not been
for Etta's abiding love, companionship, and overshadowing of the iconic
Gertrude, it's almost certain that Buzz would have chosen to spend
eternity in Ohio adjacent to his parents. In the purchasing of two side-
by-side plots in Cathedral City's Desert Memorial Park (minutes from
his Peppergrass house), Buzz had at last declared his independence from
Gertrude's lifelong hold. A walk down the aisle of section A-14 first
reveals Etta's headstone. There's a single engraved rose on the left and
an interesting, accurate, self-identifying epitaph on the right. It reads:

Etta Dunn Berkeley
Beloved Wife of Busby
1902 ✝ 1997

To the left is Buzz's headstone, tarnished and eaten a bit by surface rust.
The epitaph is also quite interesting for what it conceals:

Busby Berkeley
2D LT US ARMY
World War 1
1895 1976

His occupation is unmentioned. However, if one scrutinizes the words
on a deeper level, a nod to his professional life is revealed. Never in his
military career did he abandon his legal surname. It wasn't until Buzz's
early days on the stage that he removed the "William" and the "Enos"
to create the alliterative moniker of international renown. His headstone
expresses a duality, revealing a man deeply proud of his service to his

country and, obliquely, his connection to the most popular art form of the twentieth century.

Years after his passing, Hollywood and cable channels such as Turner Classic Movies remembered Buzz whenever a tribute to the heyday of 1930s musicals was held. A three-hour television special titled "Happy Birthday Hollywood" ran on the ABC network in May 1987. Introducing what turned out to be a ten-minute tribute to Buzz's work, Debbie Reynolds abbreviated a quote Gene Kelly had once made. In full, he said: "Berkeley showed what could be done with a movie camera. A lot of that is made fun of nowadays; sometimes laughed at. But he was the guy who tore away the proscenium arch. He tore it down for movie musicals. Many get credit for that, but it was Berkeley who did it. And if anyone wants to learn what can be done with a movie camera, they should study every shot Busby Berkeley ever made. He did it all."

In 1999, on volume 3 of a three-disk "concept" recording by the Magnetic Fields, a group fronted by Stephin Merritt, is the song "Busby Berkeley Dreams." It was a hit for the band and is readily available on Web sites catering to video downloads. Interesting that in 1999 Berkeley had all but disappeared from public consciousness (the DVDs of his films wouldn't arrive for seven more years), and the target audience must have been a bit baffled as to the meaning of the song's reference.

Variety columnist Army Archerd reported in his column of May 5, 2000, that a new musical was being readied called "BUZZ!!" (with two exclamation points), written by Larry Gelbart, David Zippel, and Alan Menken. Two years later, a follow-up story by Robert Hofler added the names of Marty Ehrlichman (producer) and Robert Jess Roth (director) to the production. The ninety-minute show was to chronicle Berkeley's life through ten "gold diggers style production numbers" and was shopped at various Las Vegas hotels as well as Broadway. The project never materialized.

Buzz's contributions to *42nd Street, Gold Diggers of 1933,* and *Footlight Parade* were honored when the Library of Congress added the films to the National Film Registry. In Hollywood, nothing could be more appropriate than the inclusion of "Busby Berkeley" to the Hollywood Chamber of Commerce's Walk of Fame. A bronze star on terrazzo near 6730 Hollywood Boulevard (where Ruby Keeler is remembered eternally) awaits his name.

For three consecutive years, Buzz was nominated for an Academy Award in the now-defunct "Dance Direction" category. For a man who single-handedly revived a cinema genre; saved a studio from collapse; provided Depression-era work for his friends; was esteemed reciprocally by his colleagues; for a man whose work is neither dated nor dismissible; for such an unparalleled craftsman, an honorary Oscar is long past due. Should one overlook the flawed, disquieting nature of his personality? What conclusions can be drawn about the military school scamp, the AWOL soldier, the choleric tyrant, the cavalier spender, the serial nuptualist, the suicidist, the drunkard, and the accidental killer? Award him for his irreproachable artistry, and accept him fully and nonjudgmentally for all he was.

The man who was . . . Buzz.

On Busby Berkeley's Memoirs

A fortunate convergence of timing and happenstance brought Busby Berkeley's memoirs to my attention in the fall of 2009. While this book was being written, author and musical historian Miles Kreuger phoned me with the exciting news that famed cinema historian Marc Wanamaker of Los Angeles's Bison Productions had presented him with the memoirs.

As noted within, Berkeley's memoirs went up for auction in 1998, and I had assumed that they were in the possession of the anonymous highest bidder. The auction house (Butterfields) would not reveal the disposition of the memoirs much less the identity of the auction winner, so the search for the unique document ended before it started.

I later learned that there was no highest bidder. After the auction, the memoirs were returned to Etta Berkeley. She placed them in Buzz's monogrammed briefcase and banished both to her small garage. After Etta's passing, her house was being readied for sale, and—reminiscent of the final sequence of *Citizen Kane*—the garage was emptied without regard for the treasures it held. A nearby neighbor grabbed the briefcase and gave it to his friend Mr. Wanamaker, and it remained in his possession until Mr. Kreuger informed him of the work I was doing.

As stated, the memoirs amounted to some three hundred typed, double-spaced pages and were meant for publication as Busby Berkeley's autobiography to be titled "Girls, Glamour, and Glory." The pages contained proofreader's notations, marginal additions, and crossed-out redundancies. Berkeley's proficiency as an author was not evident, and one can assume that a skillful editor would have proffered numerous improvements.

The memories recounted in the memoirs were seen through Buzz's rose-colored glasses. Although elucidating tidbits regarding his family, military history, Broadway days, films, marriages, and suicide attempt were gleaned for this book, there were lapses in details and a complete disregard of important events that research illuminated. He shared little of his 1935 car accident and avoided comment on his dipsomania, multiple arrests, and other nefarious aspects of his interesting life. His memoirs were less a mea culpa than a rollicking visit to yesteryear Hollywood, where humorous anecdotes were prodigiously recounted. In short, the final word on his life was not his own. The running thread throughout the memoirs was Etta. It was her amity and unwavering loyalty that resulted in the happiest, most stable time of Buzz's life, and it can be stated unequivocally that Busby Berkeley's memoirs were a direct result of their abiding love.

Appendix: The Works of Busby Berkeley

Stage Works

The information about Busby Berkeley's stage work was gathered from Berkeley's memoirs; Tony Thomas and Jim Terry, with Busby Berkeley, *The Busby Berkeley Book* (Greenwich, Conn.: New York Graphic Society, 1973); Martin Rubin, *Showstoppers: Busby Berkeley and the Tradition of Spectacle* (New York: Columbia University Press, 1993); and assorted *Playbills* and similar theater handouts.

Circa 1919
THE MAN WHO CAME BACK

A drama by Jules Eckert Goodman. Buzz played an unidentified dramatic role in the out-of-town production that ran for a year.

Circa 1921
IRENE

A musical comedy in two acts. MUSIC: Harry Tierney. BOOK: James Montgomery. LYRICS: Joseph McCarthy. Buzz played the role of Madame Lucy.

Circa 1922
PINWHEEL REVEL

An exploration of the dance. DESIGNER AND DIRECTOR: Michio Itow. STAGE MANAGER: Busby Berkeley. Buzz also appeared as an actor.

1923
THE GREENWICH VILLAGE FOLLIES

A revue in two acts. STAGE DIRECTOR: Busby Berkeley.

HITCHY KOO 1923

A musical revue. Buzz starred in the touring version and was director and performer.

Circa 1924

MARY

A musical in two acts. ARLINGTON SQUARE THEATER, Boston. MUSIC: Louis A. Hirsch. BOOK: Otto Harbach and Frank Mandel. LYRICS: Otto Harbach. DIRECTOR: Busby Berkeley.

1925

HOLKA POLKA

A musical in three acts. LYRIC THEATRE, New York, N.Y., October 14– October 31 (21 performances). PRODUCER: Carl Reed. MUSIC: Will Ortman. BOOK: W. Walzer. ADAPTATION: Bert Kalmar and Harry Ruby. TRANS-LATOR: Derick Wulff. LYRICS: Gus Kahn and Raymond B. Egan. MUSI-CAL DIRECTOR: Max Steiner. STAGING: Oscar Eagle. DANCES AND ENSEMBLES: Busby Berkeley. ENTIRE PRODUCTION AND COSTUME DESIGNER: Livingston Platt.

GOING UP

A musical comedy in three acts. Circa October. MUSIC: Louis A. Hirsch. BOOK AND LYRICS: Otto Harbach and James Montgomery. Buzz directed for the Somerville Theater Stock Company when it played in Fitchburg, Mass.

CASTLES IN THE AIR

A musical play. SHUBERT OLYMPIC THEATRE, Chicago, opened November 22. After nearly a year, one unit from Chicago went to Broadway at the SELWYN THEATRE on September 6, 1926 (160 performances in New York). PRODUCERS: John Meehan and James W. Elliott. MUSIC: Percy Wenrich. LYRICS AND BOOK: Raymond W. Peck. STAGING: John Meehan. ENSEM-BLES: Busby Berkeley (listed only for the Chicago run). DANCES: John Boyle. SCENERY: Rothe Studios.

1926

THE WILD ROSE

A musical in two acts. MARTIN BECK THEATRE, New York, N.Y., October 20–December 11 (61 performances). PRODUCER: Arthur Hammerstein. BOOK: Otto Harbach and Oscar Hammerstein II. LYRICS: Otto Harbach and Oscar Hammerstein II. MUSIC: Rudolf Friml. MUSICAL DIRECTOR: Herbert Stothart. ASSISTANT MUSICAL DIRECTOR: Mario Agnolucci. STAGING: William J. Wilson. CHOREOGRAPHY: Busby Berkeley. SCENIC DESIGN: Josef Urban. COSTUME DESIGN: Mark Mooring.

SWEET LADY

A musical comedy in three acts. December 1926–March 1927 (closed after a series of out-of-town tryouts). PRODUCER: Thomas Ball. MUSIC: Delos Owen and Thomas Ball. LYRICS: Bud Green. BOOK: Mann Page and Jack McGowan. DIRECTOR AND STAGING: William Caryl. MUSICAL NUMBER AND DANCE STAGING: Busby Berkeley.

1927

LADY DO

A musical in a prologue and two acts. Liberty Theatre, New York, N.Y., April 18–June 4 (56 performances). PRODUCER: Frank L. Teller. MUSIC: Abel Baer. BOOK: Jack McClellan and Albert Cowles. LYRICS: Sam M. Lewis and Joseph Young. MUSIC ORCHESTRATION: Frank E. Barry. MUSICAL DIRECTOR: Louis Gress. DIRECTOR OF ORCHESTRA: Frank E. Barry. PRODUCTION REVISION AND STAGING: Edgar J. MacGregor. DANCE AND ENSEMBLE STAGING: Busby Berkeley. COSTUME DESIGN: Karyl Norman and Ellis Porter. SCENIC DESIGN: Louis Kennel and Gus Wimazal.

A CONNECTICUT YANKEE

A musical in two acts adapted from the work of Mark Twain. Vanderbilt Theatre, New York, N.Y., November 3, 1927–October 27, 1928 (421 performances). PRODUCERS: Lew Fields and Lyle Andrews. MUSIC: Richard Rodgers. BOOK: Herbert Fields. LYRICS: Lorenz Hart: MUSICAL DIRECTOR: Paul Parnell. MUSIC ORCHESTRATION: Roy Webb. DANCES: Busby Berkeley. STAGING: Alexander Leftwich. SCENIC DESIGN: John Hawkins and John F. Hawkins Jr. COSTUME DESIGN: John F. Hawkins Jr. COMPANY MANAGER: Harry B. Nelmes. STAGE MANAGER: Murray Jay Queen. ASSISTANT STAGE MANAGER: John Creighton. ART DIRECTOR: Herbert Ward.

THE WHITE EAGLE

A musical play in a prologue and three acts. Casino Theatre, New York, N.Y., December 26, 1927–February 4, 1928 (48 performances). PRODUCER: Russell Janney. MUSIC: Rudolf Friml. BOOK: Brian Hooker and William H. Post. LYRICS: Brian Hooker and William H. Post. Adapted from the play *The Squaw Man* by Edwin Milton Royle. MUSICAL DIRECTOR: Anton Heindl. MUSIC ORCHESTRATION: Joseph Majer. STAGING: Richard Boleslavsky. CHOREOGRAPHER: Busby Berkeley. DIRECTORS: Russell Janney and Olga Treskoff. SCENIC DESIGN: James Reynolds. COSTUME DESIGN: James Reynolds. LIGHTING DESIGN: Ray Barnet.

1928

THE LITTLE SPITFIRE

A play in three acts by Myron C. Fagan. A production of THE BUSBY BERKE-LEY PLAYERS in Plainfield, N.J. Buzz acted in and directed the production.

PRESENT ARMS

A musical in two acts. LEW FIELDS' MANSFIELD THEATRE, New York, N.Y., April 26–September 1 (155 performances). PRODUCER: Lew M. Fields. MUSIC: Richard Rodgers. LYRICS: Lorenz Hart. BOOK: Herbert Fields. MUSICAL DIRECTOR: Roy Webb. STAGING: Alexander Leftwich. CHO-REOGRAPHY: Busby Berkeley. SCENIC DESIGN: Herbert Ward. COSTUME DESIGN: Milgrims.

EARL CARROLL VANITIES [Seventh Edition]

A revue in two acts. EARL CARROLL THEATRE, New York, N.Y., August 6, 1928–February 2, 1929 (200 performances). PRODUCER: Earl Carroll. LYR-ICS: Grace Henry. MUSIC: Morris Hamilton. BOOK: W. C. Fields, Paul Ge-rard Smith, Joe Frisco, Robert T. Tarrant, and Herman Meyer. ADDITIONAL MUSIC: George Bagby, G. Romilli, Michael H. Cleary, George Whiting, Louis Alter, Mario Savino, Jesse Greer, Ernie Golden, and Abner Silver. MUSICAL DIRECTOR: Ray Kavanaugh. ADDITIONAL LYRICS: Paul Jones, Ned Washington, Joe Burke, Raymond Klages, Ernie Golden, Jack LeSoir, and Roy Doll. DIRECTOR: Earl Carroll. CHOREOGRAPHY: Busby Berkeley. STAG-ING: Edgar J. MacGregor. MACHINERY BALLET created and staged by the Marmein Sisters. SCENIC DESIGN: Hugh Willoughby. COSTUME DESIGN: Mabel E. Johnston and William H. Matthews. ART AND TECHNICAL DI-RECTION: Bernard Lohmuller.

GOOD BOY

A musical in two acts. Hammerstein's Theatre, New York, N.Y., September 5, 1928–April 13, 1929 (253 performances). PRODUCER: Arthur Hammerstein. MUSIC: Herbert P. Stothart. BOOK: Otto Harbach, Oscar Hammerstein II, and Henry Myers. LYRICS: Bert Kalmar and Harry Ruby. MUSICAL DIRECTOR: Herbert P. Stothart. DIRECTOR: Reginald Hammerstein. CHOREOGRA-PHY: Busby Berkeley. SCENIC DESIGN: John Wenger. COSTUME DESIGN: Mark Mooring. MECHANICAL AND TREADMILL EFFECTS: Peter Clark, Inc. and Edward Dolan.

RAINBOW

A musical in two acts. GALLO OPERA HOUSE, New York, N.Y., November 21–December 15 (29 performances). PRODUCER: Philip Goodman. BOOK: Laurence Stallings and Oscar Hammerstein II. LYRICS: Oscar Hammerstein

II. MUSIC: Vincent Youmans. MUSICAL DIRECTOR: Max Steiner. MUSIC ORCHESTRATION: Max Steiner. CHOREOGRAPHY: Busby Berkeley. STAGING: Oscar Hammerstein II. PRODUCTION SUPERVISION: Philip Goodman. SCENIC DESIGN: Frank E. Gates and Edward A. Morange. COSTUME DESIGN: Charles LeMaire. RESEARCH AND TECHNICAL DIRECTOR: Leighton K. Brill.

HELLO, DADDY!

A musical in two acts based on a farce adapted from the German by Frank Mandel. LEW FIELDS' MANSFIELD THEATRE, New York, N.Y., December 26, 1928–January 1929. GEORGE M. COHAN'S THEATRE, New York, N.Y., January 21, 1929–May 1929. ERLANGER'S THEATRE, New York, N.Y., May 6, 1929–June 15, 1929 (198 performances). PRODUCER: Lew M. Fields. BOOK: Herbert Fields. LYRICS: Dorothy Fields. MUSIC: Jimmy McHugh. PRINCIPAL DANCE ROUTINES: Buddy Bradley. HARMONY ARRANGEMENTS OF THE GIERSDORF SISTERS' SONGS: Arthur Johnston. MUSIC ORCHESTRATION: Maurice De Packh, Stephen Jones, Fod Livingston, and Hans Spialek. STAGING OF MUSICAL NUMBERS: Busby Berkeley. STAGING OF BOOK: Alexander Leftwich. SUPERVISION OF ENTIRE PROJECT: John Murray Anderson. SCENIC DESIGN: Hermann Rosse. COSTUME DESIGN: Charles Le Maire.

1929

PLEASURE BOUND

A revue in two acts. MAJESTIC THEATRE, New York, N.Y., February 18–June 15 (136 performances). PRODUCERS: Lee and J. J. Shubert. MUSIC: Muriel Pollock. BOOK: Harold Atteridge. LYRICS: Max Leif, Nathaniel Lief, and Harold Atteridge. ADDITIONAL MUSIC: Phil Baker, Maurice Rubens, and Peter DeRose. ADDITIONAL LYRICS: Moe Jaffe, Sid Silvers, Charles Tobias, Irving Kahal, and Sidney Clare. MUSICAL DIRECTOR: Harold Stern. MUSIC ORCHESTRATION: Emil Gerstenberger and Archey Bleyer. STAGING: Lew Morton. CHOREOGRAPHY: Busby Berkeley and John Boyle. SCENIC DESIGN: Watson Barratt. COSTUME DESIGN: Ernest Schrapps.

A NIGHT IN VENICE

A revue in two acts. SHUBERT THEATRE, New York, N.Y., May 21–circa September. MAJESTIC THEATRE, September 16–October 19 (175 performances). PRODUCERS: Lee and J. J. Shubert. MUSIC: Lee Davis and Maury Rubens. LYRICS: J. Keirn Brennan and Moe Jaffe. FEATURING SONGS by Vincent Youmans. ADDITIONAL ORCHESTRATIONS: Vincent Youmans. FEATURING SONGS with lyrics by Oscar Hammerstein II. MUSICAL DIRECTOR: Max Meth. DIRECTORS: Lew Morton and Thomas A. Hart.

CHOREOGRAPHY: Busby Berkeley and Chester Hale. SCENIC DESIGN: Watson Barratt. COSTUME DESIGN: Erté, George Barbier, and Ernest Schrapps.

BROADWAY NIGHTS

A revue in twenty-four scenes. 44th STREET THEATRE, New York, N.Y., July 15–August 17 (40 performances). PRODUCERS: Lee and J. J. Shubert. MUSIC: Sam Timberg, Lee David, and Maurice Rubens. LYRICS: Moe Jaffe. BOOK: Edgar Smith. MUSICAL DIRECTOR: John McManus. FEATURING SONGS by J. Fred Coots, Ralph Erwin, and Phil Svigals. FEATURING SONGS with lyrics by J. Keirn Brennan, Sam M. Lewis, Joe Young, and Clifford Grey. DIRECTOR: Stanley Logan. CHOREOGRAPHY: Busby Berkeley and Chester Hale. SCENIC DESIGN: Watson Barratt. COSTUME DESIGN: George Barbier and Ernest Schrapps.

THE STREET SINGER

A musical in two acts. SHUBERT THEATRE, New York, N.Y., September 17, 1929–February 1930. ROYALE THEATRE, New York, N.Y., February 17, 1930–March 7, 1930 (191 performances). PRODUCER AND DIRECTOR: Busby Berkeley. MUSIC: John Gilbert, Nicholas Kempner, and Sam Timberg. BOOK: Cyrus Wood and Edgar Smith. LYRICS: Graham John. FEATURING SONGS by Richard Meyers with lyrics by Edward Eliscu. MUSICAL DIRECTOR: Pierre De Reeder. SCENIC DESIGN: Watson Barratt. COSTUME DESIGN: Orry-Kelly and George Barbier.

THE DUCHESS OF CHICAGO

A blend of operetta and musical comedy. November 1929–December 1929. Closed after tryouts in Springfield, Newark, Philadelphia, Baltimore, and Boston. PRODUCERS: Lee and J. J. Shubert. MUSIC: Emmerich Kalman. LYRICS: Edward Eliscu. ADDITIONAL NUMBERS: Maurice Rubens and Sam Timberg. BOOK: Julius Brammer and Alfred Gruenwald. DIRECTOR OF DIALOGUE: Stanley Logan. STAGING: Busby Berkeley.

1930
RUTH SELWYN'S NINE FIFTEEN REVUE

GEORGE M. COHAN'S THEATRE, New York, N.Y., February 11–15 (7 performances). PRODUCER: Ruth Selwyn. CHOREOGRAPHY: Busby Berkeley and Leon Leonidoff. STAGING: Alexander Leftwich.

LEW LESLIE'S INTERNATIONAL REVUE

A revue in two parts. MAJESTIC THEATRE, New York, N.Y., February 25–May 17 (95 performances). PRODUCER: Lew Leslie. MUSIC: Dorothy

Fields and Jimmy McHugh. BOOK: Nat N. Dorfman and Lew Leslie. LYRICS: Dorothy Fields and Jimmy McHugh. DIRECTORS: Lew Leslie and E. C. Lilley. CHOREOGRAPHY: Busby Berkeley and Harry Crosley.

NINA ROSA

A musical play. MAJESTIC THEATRE, New York, N.Y., September 20, 1930–January 17, 1931 (137 performances). BOOK: Otto Harbach. MUSIC: Sigmund Romberg. LYRICS: Irving Caesar. PRODUCERS: Lee and J. J. Shubert. STAGING OF ENTIRE PRODUCTION: J. C. Huffman.

**

NOTE: Buzz commented to authors Tony Thomas and Jim Terry (*The Busby Berkeley Book*) that he worked on this show. Author Martin Rubin (*Showstoppers*) writes that Berkeley's name was not seen in the program when *Nina Rosa* opened on Broadway, nor was Buzz named in any New York review. Rubin surmised that a possible falling out had occurred between Buzz and the Messrs. Shubert prior to the Broadway opening. The sheet music for one of the songs ("Your Smiles, Your Tears") does list "Dances by Busby Berkeley."

SWEET AND LOW

A revue in two acts. CHANIN's 46TH STREET THEATRE, New York, N.Y., November 17, 1930–April 1931 (184 performances). PRODUCER: Billy Rose. SKETCHES: David Freedman. MUSICAL DIRECTOR: William Daly. FEATURING SONGS by Harry Archer, Oscar Levant, Charlotte Kent, Harry Warren, Vivian Ellis, William C. K. Irwin, Louis Alter, George M. Cohan, Dana Suesse, Phil Charig, and Joseph Meyer. FEATURING SONGS with lyrics by Edward Eliscu, Ira Gershwin, Billy Rose, Malcolm McComb, and Ballard McDonald. CHOREOGRAPHY: Danny Dare. ADDITIONAL DANCES: Busby Berkeley. STAGING: Alexander Leftwich. SCENIC DESIGN: Jo Mielziner. COSTUME DESIGN: James Reynolds.

1944

GLAD TO SEE YOU

A musical comedy in two acts. SHUBERT THEATRE, Philadelphia, November. PRODUCER: David Wolper. MUSIC: Jule Styne. LYRICS: Sammy Cahn. BOOK: Fred Thompson and Eddie Davis. STAGING AND DIRECTION OF ENTIRE PRODUCTION: Busby Berkeley. DANCES AND ENSEMBLES: Valerie Bettis. SETTINGS AND LIGHTING DESIGN: Howard Bay. COSTUME DESIGN: Travis Banton.

**

NOTE: The show attempted an eventual Broadway run but folded after out-of-town tryouts in Philadelphia and Boston. Buzz left the show after the Philadelphia run.

1971

NO, NO, NANETTE

A musical in three acts. Revival originally conceived for production by Harry Rigby. 46TH STREET THEATRE, New York, N.Y., preview January 6, 1971; January 19, 1971–February 3, 1973 (13 previews; 861 performances). PRODUCER: Pyxidium, Ltd. MUSIC: Vincent Youmans. LYRICS: Irving Caesar and Otto Harbach. BOOK: Otto Harbach and Frank Mandel. BOOK ADAPTATION: Burt Shevelove. MUSICAL DIRECTOR: Buster Davis. VO-CAL ARRANGEMENTS: Buster Davis. MUSIC ORCHESTRATION: Ralph Burns. DANCE ARRANGEMENTS: Luther Henderson. INCIDENTAL MUSIC: Luther Henderson. PRODUCTION SUPERVISOR: Busby Berkeley. DIRECTOR: Burt Shevelove. MUSICAL STAGING: Donald Saddler. CHORE-OGRAPHY: Donald Saddler. PRODUCTION DESIGN: Raoul Pène Du Bois. LIGHTING DESIGN: Jules Fisher. SOUND DESIGN: Jack Shearing. PRIN-CIPALS' COIFFURES: Vidal Sassoon. BERKELEY GIRLS' COIFFURES: Bruce Steier. SCENIC ASSISTANT: Mason Arvold. COSTUME ASSISTANT: David Toser. GENERAL MANAGER: Gatchell & Neufeld, Ltd. ASSISTANT COMPANY MANAGER: James Mennen. PRODUCTION MANAGER: May Muth. STAGE MANAGER: Robert Schear. ASSISTANT STAGE MANAGER: John H. Lowe III. AT THE TWIN PIANOS: Colston and Clements. COPY-IST: Lilette Hindin. MUSIC CONTRACTOR: Morris Stonzek: ASSISTANT CONDUCTOR: Charles Coleman: MUSIC CONSULTANT: Robert Lissauer.

Film Works

The credit Berkeley received is displayed in italics. Sources for the short synopses are the author and the American Film Institute Database. The musical numbers listed are those Berkeley worked on. Some films had songs that were filmed by others; for example, "I've Got To Sing a Torch Song" (music by Harry Warren; lyrics by Al Dubin), featured in *Gold Diggers of 1933*, was not filmed by Berkeley.

1930

WHOOPEE!

STUDIO: Goldwyn/United Artists. CREDIT: *Dances and ensembles staged by.*
SYNOPSIS: Western sheriff Bob Wells is preparing to marry Sally Morgan; she loves part-Indian Wanenis, whose race is an obstacle.
MUSICAL NUMBERS:
"Makin' Whoopee": Music by Walter Donaldson; lyrics by Gus Kahn
"My Baby Just Cares for Me": Music by Walter Donaldson; lyrics by Gus Kahn
"The Song of the Setting Sun": Music by Walter Donaldson; lyrics Gus Kahn
"Cowboys": Music by Walter Donaldson; lyrics by Gus Kahn

"A Girl Friend of a Boy Friend of Mine": Music by Walter Donaldson; lyrics by
Gus Kahn

"Stetson": Music by Walter Donaldson; lyrics by Gus Kahn

1931

KIKI

STUDIO: United Artists. CREDIT: *Dances staged by.*

SYNOPSIS: A scheming, high-spirited chorus girl gets between her boss and
his wife.

PALMY DAYS

STUDIO: Goldwyn/United Artists. CREDIT: *Dances and ensembles by.*

SYNOPSIS: Musical comedy antics in an art deco bakery with Eddie Cantor as
an assistant to a phony psychic.

MUSICAL NUMBERS:

"Bend Down, Sister": Music by Con Conrad; lyrics by Ballard MacDonald and
David Silverstein

"Yes, Yes (My Baby Said Yes, Yes)": Music and lyrics by Con Conrad and Cliff
Friend

"Dunk Dunk Dunk": Music by Con Conrad; lyrics by Ballard MacDonald

***

NOTE: Buzz can also be seen as a nonspeaking extra in the early fake séance scene.

FLYING HIGH

STUDIO: MGM. CREDIT: *Dances created by.*

SYNOPSIS: A harebrained inventor invents a new flying machine but can't figure out how to land it.

MUSICAL NUMBERS:

"I'll Make a Happy Landing (the Lucky Day I Land You)": Music by Jimmy
McHugh; lyrics by Dorothy Fields

"We'll Dance until the Dawn": Music by Jimmy McHugh; lyrics by Dorothy
Fields

"It'll Be the First Time for Me": Music by Jimmy McHugh; lyrics by Dorothy
Fields

1932

SKY DEVILS

STUDIO: United Artists. CREDIT: *Dance director.*

SYNOPSIS: Wilkie and Mitchell, trying to desert their draft into the army, stow
away on a ship that takes them into the war zone. While AWOL, the rivals
for Mary's affections accidently destroy an ammunition dump.

NIGHT WORLD

STUDIO: Universal. CREDIT: *Dances staged by.*

SYNOPSIS: "Happy" MacDonald and his unfaithful wife own a Prohibition-era nightclub. On this eventful night, he is threatened by bootleggers, and the club's star dancer falls in love with a young socialite who drinks to forget a personal tragedy, among other incidents.

MUSICAL NUMBER:

"Who's Your Little Who-Zis": Music and lyrics by Ben Bernie

BIRD OF PARADISE

STUDIO: RKO. CREDIT: *Uncredited native-dance director.*

SYNOPSIS: An island visitor falls for a Polynesian beauty slated for sacrifice to the gods.

THE KID FROM SPAIN

STUDIO: Goldwyn/United Artists. CREDIT: *Numbers created and directed by.*

SYNOPSIS: An innocent man accused of robbing banks masquerades as a bullfighter to escape the police.

MUSICAL NUMBERS:

"But We Must Rise (The College Song)": Music and lyrics by Harry Ruby and Bert Kalmar

"In the Moonlight": Music and lyrics by Harry Ruby and Bert Kalmar

"Look What You've Done": Music and lyrics by Harry Ruby and Bert Kalmar

"What a Perfect Combination": Music and lyrics by Harry Ruby and Bert Kalmar

1933

42ND STREET

STUDIO: Warner Brothers. Credit: *Dances and ensembles created and staged by.*

SYNOPSIS: Julian Marsh, a successful Broadway director prone to nervous breakdowns and left virtually broke in the Depression, directs a new show, in spite of his doctor's warnings. The show's backing comes from a rich lecher who is in love with Dorothy Brock, the star of the show. But she doesn't return his affection because she is still in love with her old partner. At the night before the premiere, Brock breaks her ankle, and one of the chorus girls, Peggy Sawyer, takes over her part, and goes out a "youngster" and comes back a "star."

MUSICAL NUMBERS:

"Forty-Second Street": Music by Harry Warren; lyrics by Al Dubin

"You're Getting to Be a Habit with Me": Music by Harry Warren; lyrics by Al Dubin

"Shuffle Off to Buffalo": Music by Harry Warren; lyrics by Al Dubin
"Young and Healthy": Music by Harry Warren; lyrics by Al Dubin

***

NOTE: The film mistakenly shows two copyright dates, 1933 (on the first title card) and 1932 (on "The End" title card). The film was released in 1933.

GOLD DIGGERS OF 1933

STUDIO: Warner Brothers. CREDIT: *Numbers created and directed by.*
SYNOPSIS: Barney Hopkins is producing a new show on Broadway, but the day before it opens, the set and costumes are confiscated due to unpaid bills. Three showgirls conspire to sweet-talk their way into getting backing for the show.
MUSICAL NUMBERS:
"The Gold Diggers Song (We're in the Money)": Music by Harry Warren; lyrics by Al Dubin
"Shadow Waltz": Music by Harry Warren; lyrics by Al Dubin
"Pettin' in the Park": Music by Harry Warren; lyrics by Al Dubin
"Remember My Forgotten Man": Music by Harry Warren; lyrics by Al Dubin

***

NOTE: Buzz is seen briefly as the "call boy" ordering the dancers to ready themselves for the "Forgotten Man" number.

SHE HAD TO SAY YES

STUDIO: Warner Brothers. CREDIT: *Directed by Busby Berkeley and George Amy.*
SYNOPSIS: A secretary pads her salary by dating prospective buyers for her company.

FOOTLIGHT PARADE

STUDIO: Warner Brothers. CREDIT: *Numbers created and directed by.*
SYNOPSIS: A producer of theater prologues fights labor problems, financiers, and his greedy ex-wife to put on a show.
MUSICAL NUMBERS:
"Sitting on a Backyard Fence": Music by Sammy Fain; lyrics by Irving Kahal
"Honeymoon Hotel": Music by Harry Warren; lyrics by Al Dubin
"By a Waterfall": Music by Sammy Fain; lyrics by Irving Kahal
"Shanghai Lil": Music by Harry Warren; lyrics by Al Dubin

***

NOTE: The Internet Movie Database incorrectly identifies Berkeley as playing an uncredited drug store clerk early in the film.

ROMAN SCANDALS

STUDIO: Goldwyn/United Artists. CREDIT: *Production numbers directed by.*
SYNOPSIS: Eddie (Eddie Cantor) gets hit by a wagon and while unconscious he
dreams he is in ancient Rome.
MUSICAL NUMBERS:
"Build a Little Home": Music by Harry Warren; lyrics by Al Dubin
"No More Love": Music by Harry Warren; lyrics by Al Dubin
"Keep Young and Beautiful": Music by Harry Warren; lyrics by Al Dubin
"Put a Tax on Love": Music by Harry Warren; lyrics by Al Dubin

1934

FASHIONS OF 1934

STUDIO: Warner Brothers. CREDIT: *Numbers created and directed by.*
SYNOPSIS: A con artist and his beautiful assistant take on the fashion world.
MUSICAL NUMBER:
"Spin a Little Web of Dreams": Music by Sammy Fain; lyrics by Irving Kahal

WONDER BAR

STUDIO: Warner Brothers. CREDIT: *Numbers created and directed by.*
SYNOPSIS: The denizens of a Parisian night club deal with murder and romance.
MUSICAL NUMBERS:
"Don't Say Goodnight": Music by Harry Warren; lyrics by Al Dubin
"Goin' to Heaven on a Mule": Music by Harry Warren; lyrics by Al Dubin

DAMES

STUDIO: Warner Brothers. CREDIT: *Numbers created and directed by.*
SYNOPSIS: Family members financially beholden to a stodgy rich uncle do their
best to hide the fact from him that their daughter is the lead in a so-called
scandalous Broadway show.
MUSICAL NUMBERS:
"Dames": Music by Harry Warren; lyrics by Al Dubin
"I Only Have Eyes for You": Music by Harry Warren; lyrics by Al Dubin
"The Girl at the Ironing Board": Music by Harry Warren; lyrics by Al Dubin
"When You Were a Smile on Your Mother's Lips and a Twinkle in Your Daddy's
Eye": Words and music by Irving Kahal and Sammy Fain

1935

GOLD DIGGERS OF 1935

STUDIO: Warner Brothers. CREDIT: *Directed by* and *Dances Created and
Staged by.*

SYNOPSIS: A socialite is bamboozled into producing a charity stage show at the luxury hotel where she summers, while her daughter rejects her arranged marriage partner for the arms of a hotel employee.
MUSICAL NUMBERS:
"I'm Going Shopping with You": Music by Harry Warren; lyrics by Al Dubin
"Lullaby of Broadway": Music by Harry Warren; lyrics by Al Dubin
"The Words Are in My Heart": Music by Harry Warren; lyrics by Al Dubin

IN CALIENTE

STUDIO: Warner Brothers. CREDIT: *Numbers created and directed by.*
SYNOPSIS: At a Mexican resort, a fast-talking magazine editor woos the dancer he's trashed in print.
MUSICAL NUMBER:
"The Lady in Red": Music by Allie Wrubel; lyrics by Mort Dixon
"In Caliente": Music by Allie Wrubel; lyrics by Mort Dixon
"Muchacha": Music by Harry Warren; lyrics by Al Dubin

BRIGHT LIGHTS

STUDIO: First National/Warner Brothers. CREDIT: *Directed by.*
SYNOPSIS: Husband-and-wife vaudeville stars separate when success goes to his head.
MUSICAL NUMBERS:
"She Was an Acrobat's Daughter": Lyrics by Bert Kalmar; music by Harry Ruby
"You're an Eyeful of Heaven": Music by Allie Wrubel; lyrics by Mort Dixon
"Nobody Cares If I'm Blue": Music by Harry Akst; lyrics by Grant Clarke

I LIVE FOR LOVE

STUDIO: Warner Brothers. CREDIT: *Directed by.*
SYNOPSIS: A socialite tries to break into show business.
MUSICAL NUMBERS:
"I Live for Love": Music by Allie Wrubel; lyrics by Mort Dixon
"Mine Alone": Music by Allie Wrubel; lyrics by Mort Dixon
"A Man Must Shave": Music by Allie Wrubel; lyrics by Mort Dixon

STARS OVER BROADWAY

STUDIO: Warner Brothers. CREDIT: *Numbers staged and directed by, sharing credit with Bobby Connolly.*
SYNOPSIS: An aggressive agent turns a hotel porter into an overnight sensation.
MUSICAL NUMBER:
"At Your Service, Madame": Music by Harry Warren; lyrics by Al Dubin

1936

STAGE STRUCK

STUDIO: Warner Brothers. CREDIT: *Directed by.*
SYNOPSIS: Broadway hopefuls put on a show.
MUSICAL NUMBERS:
"Fancy Meeting You": Music by Harold Arlen; lyrics by E. Y. Harburg
"In Your Own Quiet Way": Music by Harold Arlen; lyrics by E. Y. Harburg

THE SINGING KID

STUDIO: Warner Brothers. CREDIT: *Uncredited director of the numbers*
   "You're the Cure for What Ails Me" (Music by Harold Arlen; lyrics by E. Y.
   Harburg) and "My How This Town Has Changed" (Music by Harold Arlen;
   lyrics by E. Y. Harburg).

CHANGING OF THE GUARD

STUDIO: Warner Brothers. CREDIT: *Uncredited role as dance coach to actress*
   Sybil Jason.

GOLD DIGGERS OF 1937

STUDIO: Warner Brothers. CREDIT: *Musical numbers created and directed*
   by.
SYNOPSIS: A group of insurance salesmen try to get into show business.
MUSICAL NUMBERS:
"With Plenty of Money and You": Music by Harry Warren; lyrics by Al Dubin
"Life Insurance Song": Music by Harold Arlen; lyrics by E. Y. Harburg
"Speaking of the Weather": Music by Harold Arlen; lyrics by E. Y. Harburg
"Let's Put Our Heads Together": Music by Harold Arlen; lyrics by E. Y. Har-
   burg
"All's Fair in Love and War": Music by Harry Warren; lyrics by Al Dubin

1937

THE GO GETTER

STUDIO: Warner Brothers. CREDIT: *Directed by.*
SYNOPSIS: A U.S. Navy veteran with one leg fights to make himself a success.

THE SINGING MARINE

STUDIO: Warner Brothers. CREDIT: *Musical numbers created and directed*
   by.
SYNOPSIS: A young marine develops an inflated ego after winning a talent
   contest.
MUSICAL NUMBERS:
"The Song of the Marines": Music by Harry Warren; lyrics by Al Dubin

"You Can't Run Away from Love Tonight": Music by Harry Warren; lyrics by Al Dubin

"Night over Shanghai": Music by Harry Warren; lyrics by Johnny Mercer

VARSITY SHOW

STUDIO: Warner Brothers. CREDIT: *Finale created and directed by.*
SYNOPSIS: A Broadway producer puts on a show at his alma mater.
MUSICAL NUMBERS INCLUDED IN THE FINALE:

"On with the Dance": Music by Richard Whiting; lyrics by Johnny Mercer

"You've Got Something There": Music by Richard Whiting; lyrics by Johnny Mercer

"Have You Got Any Castles, Baby?": Music by Richard Whiting; lyrics by Johnny Mercer

"Love Is on the Air Tonight": Music by Richard Whiting; lyrics by Johnny Mercer

"Boola Boola": Written by Allan M. Hirsh

"On, Wisconsin!": Music by William T. Purdy and Carl D. Beck; lyrics by J. S. Hubbard and Charles D. Rosa

"Fight On": Music by Milo Sweet; lyrics by Milo Sweet and Glen Grant

"The Notre Dame Victory March": Music by Michael J. Shea; lyrics by John F. Shea

"The Maine Stein Song": Music by Albert Sprague; lyrics by Lincoln Colcord

"Come Join the Band": Composer unknown

"On, Brave Old Army Team": Written by Philip Egner

"Anchors Aweigh": Music by Charles A. Zimmerman; lyrics by Alfred Hart Miles and R. Lovell

"Old King Cole": Music by Richard Whiting; lyrics by Johnny Mercer

1938

HOLLYWOOD HOTEL

STUDIO: Warner Brothers. CREDIT: *Directed by.*
SYNOPSIS: A small-town boy wins a Hollywood talent contest.
MUSICAL NUMBERS:

"Hooray for Hollywood": Music by Richard Whiting; lyrics by Johnny Mercer

"Sing, You Son of a Gun": Music by Richard Whiting; lyrics by Johnny Mercer

"I'm Like a Fish out of Water": Music by Richard Whiting; lyrics by Johnny Mercer

"Silhouetted in the Moonlight": Music by Richard Whiting; lyrics by Johnny Mercer

"Let That Be a Lesson to You": Music by Richard Whiting; lyrics by Johnny Mercer

"I've Hitched My Wagon to a Star": Music by Richard Whiting; lyrics by Johnny Mercer

GOLD DIGGERS IN PARIS

STUDIO: Warner Brothers. CREDIT: *Musical numbers created and directed by.*
SYNOPSIS: Three showgirls travel to Paris in search of rich husbands.
MUSICAL NUMBERS:
"I Wanna Go Back to Bali": Music by Harry Warren; lyrics by Al Dubin
"A Stranger in Paree": Music by Harry Warren; lyrics by Al Dubin
"The Latin Quarter": Music by Harry Warren; lyrics by Al Dubin
"Daydreaming (All Night Long)": Music by Harry Warren; lyrics by Johnny Mercer

MEN ARE SUCH FOOLS

STUDIO: Warner Brothers. CREDIT: *Directed by.*
SYNOPSIS: An ambitious secretary uses the men in her life to turn herself into a radio star.

GARDEN OF THE MOON

STUDIO: Warner Brothers. CREDIT: *Directed by.*
SYNOPSIS: A nightclub owner and a bandleader compete for the lead singer's heart.
MUSICAL NUMBERS:
"The Lady on the Two Cent Stamp": Music by Harry Warren; lyrics by Al Dubin and Johnny Mercer
"Love Is Where You Find It": Music by Harry Warren; lyrics by Al Dubin and Johnny Mercer
"The Girl Friend of the Whirling Dervish": Music by Harry Warren; lyrics by Al Dubin and Johnny Mercer
"Confidentially": Music by Harry Warren; lyrics by Al Dubin and Johnny Mercer

COMET OVER BROADWAY

STUDIO: Warner Brothers. CREDIT: *Directed by.*
SYNOPSIS: A stage star's rampant ambition leads to murder.

1939

THEY MADE ME A CRIMINAL

STUDIO: Warner Brothers. CREDIT: *Directed by.*
SYNOPSIS: A young boxer flees to farming country when he thinks he's killed an opponent in the ring.

BROADWAY SERENADE

STUDIO: MGM. CREDIT: *Finale number created and directed by.*
SYNOPSIS: Career conflicts threaten a singer's marriage to a young composer.

MUSICAL NUMBER:
"None but the Lonely Heart": Music by Pyotr Ilyich Tchaikovsky; English lyrics by Gus Kahn

THE WIZARD OF OZ

STUDIO: MGM. CREDIT: *Uncredited for "If I Only Had a Brain" number (later deleted for the release). Music by Harold Arlen; lyrics by E. Y. Harburg.*

BABES IN ARMS

STUDIO: MGM. CREDIT: *Directed by.*
SYNOPSIS: A group of second-generation entertainers puts on a show to launch their careers.
MUSICAL NUMBERS:
"Babes in Arms": Music by Richard Rodgers; lyrics by Lorenz Hart
"Where or When": Music by Richard Rodgers; lyrics by Lorenz Hart
"Good Morning": Music by Nacio Herb Brown; lyrics by Arthur Freed
"You Are My Lucky Star": Music by Nacio Herb Brown; lyrics by Arthur Freed
"I Cried for You": Written by Gus Arnheim, Abe Lyman, and Arthur Freed
"Daddy Was a Minstrel Man": Written by Roger Edens
"God's Country": Music by Harold Arlen; lyrics by E. Y. Harburg

FAST AND FURIOUS

STUDIO: MGM. CREDIT: *Directed by.*
SYNOPSIS: Married book-dealers Joel and Garda Sloane get mixed up with murder during a beauty pageant.

1940

BITTER SWEET

STUDIO: MGM. CREDIT: *Uncredited director for the final number "Zigeuner (The Gypsy)" written by Noel Coward.*

FORTY LITTLE MOTHERS

STUDIO: MGM. CREDIT: *Directed by.*
SYNOPSIS: A teacher at an all-girls' school stumbles on an abandoned baby.

STRIKE UP THE BAND

STUDIO: MGM. CREDIT: *Directed by.*
SYNOPSIS: A high-school band sets out to win a national radio contest.
MUSICAL NUMBERS:
"Strike up the Band": Music by George Gershwin; lyrics by Ira Gershwin
"Our Love Affair": Music by Roger Edens; lyrics Arthur Freed
"Do the La Conga": Music and lyrics by Roger Edens

"Nobody": Music and lyrics by Roger Edens
"The Gay Nineties": Music and lyrics by Roger Edens
"Nell of New Rochelle": Music and lyrics by Roger Edens
"Drummer Boy": Words and music by Roger Edens

1941

BLONDE INSPIRATION

STUDIO: MGM. CREDIT: *Directed by.*
SYNOPSIS: A pulp-fiction writer tries to land a job with an unscrupulous publisher.

ZIEGFELD GIRL

STUDIO: MGM. CREDIT: *Musical numbers directed by.*
SYNOPSIS: Three showgirls in the Ziegfeld Follies face romantic trials on their way to the top.
MUSICAL NUMBERS:
"Minnie from Trinidad": Music and lyrics by Roger Edens
"You Stepped out of a Dream": Music by Nacio Herb Brown; lyrics by Gus Kahn
"Ziegfeld Girls": Music and lyrics by Roger Edens
"You Gotta Pull Strings": Music by Walter Donaldson; lyrics by Harold Adamson
"Caribbean Love Song": Music by Roger Edens; lyrics by Ralph Freed
"You Never Looked So Beautiful": Music by Walter Donaldson; lyrics by Harold Adamson

LADY, BE GOOD!

STUDIO: MGM. CREDIT: *Musical numbers directed by.*
SYNOPSIS: Married songwriters almost split up while putting on a big show.
MUSICAL NUMBERS:
"Lady Be Good": Music by George Gershwin; lyrics by Ira Gershwin
"The Last Time I Saw Paris": Music by Jerome Kern; lyrics by Oscar Hammerstein II
"Fascinating Rhythm": Music by George Gershwin; lyrics by Ira Gershwin
"Your Words and My Music": Music by Roger Edens; lyrics by Arthur Freed

1942

BABES ON BROADWAY

STUDIO: MGM. CREDIT: *Directed by.*
SYNOPSIS: Show-biz hopefuls stage a benefit for an orphanage.
MUSICAL NUMBERS:
"Babes on Broadway": Music by Burton Lane; lyrics by E. Y. Harburg

"How About You?": Music by Burton Lane; lyrics by Ralph Freed
"Anything Can Happen in New York": Music by Burton Lane; lyrics by Ralph Freed
"Hoe Down": Music by Roger Edens; lyrics by Ralph Freed
"Franklin D. Roosevelt Jones": Music and lyrics by Harold Rome
"Waiting for the Robert E. Lee": Music by Lewis F. Muir; lyrics by L. Wolfe Gilbert
"Bombshell from Brazil": Music and lyrics by Roger Edens

BORN TO SING

STUDIO: MGM. CREDIT: *Finale "Ballad for Americans" Directed by.*
SYNOPSIS: Fledgling entertainers put on a show for Uncle Sam.
MUSICAL NUMBER:
"Ballad for Americans": Music by Earl Robinson; lyrics by John Latouche

CALLING ALL GIRLS

STUDIO: Warner Brothers. CREDIT: *Musical numbers created and directed by.*
SYNOPSIS: A short compilation film featuring Buzz's classic numbers: "Don't Say Goodnight," "Lullaby of Broadway," "Shadow Waltz," "By a Waterfall," and "Shanghai Lil."

FOR ME AND MY GAL

STUDIO: MGM. CREDIT: *Directed by.*
SYNOPSIS: An unscrupulous song-and-dance man uses his partner and his best friend to get ahead.
MUSICAL NUMBERS:
"For Me and My Gal": Music by George W. Meyer; lyrics by Edgar Leslie and E. Ray Goetz
"Ballin' the Jack": Music by Chris Smith; lyrics by Jim Burris
"When You Wore a Tulip and I Wore a Big Red Rose": Music by Percy Wenrich; lyrics by Jack Mahoney

1943

CABIN IN THE SKY

STUDIO: MGM. CREDIT: *Uncredited director for the number "Shine." Music by Ford Dabney; lyrics by Cecil Mack.*

GIRL CRAZY

STUDIO: MGM. CREDIT: *"I Got Rhythm" Number Directed by.*
SYNOPSIS: A womanizing playboy finds true love when he's sent to a desert college.

MUSICAL NUMBER:
"I Got Rhythm": Music by George Gershwin; lyrics by Ira Gershwin

THE GANG'S ALL HERE

STUDIO: 20th Century Fox. CREDIT: *Directed by* and *dances created and directed by.*
SYNOPSIS: Playboy Andy Mason, on leave from the army, romances showgirl Eadie Allen overnight to such effect that she's starry-eyed when he leaves the next morning.
MUSICAL NUMBERS:
"Brazil": Music by Ary Barroso; English lyrics by S. K. Russell
"You Discover You're in New York": Music by Harry Warren; lyrics by Leo Robin
"The Lady in the Tutti Frutti Hat": Music by Harry Warren; lyrics by Leo Robin
"A Journey to a Star": Music by Harry Warren; lyrics by Leo Robin
"No Love, No Nothin'": Music by Harry Warren; lyrics by Leo Robin
"Paducah": Music by Harry Warren; lyrics by Leo Robin
"The Polka Dot Polka": Music by Harry Warren; lyrics by Leo Robin

1946

CINDERELLA JONES

STUDIO: Warner Brothers. CREDIT: *Directed by.*
SYNOPSIS: A woman can claim inheritance only if she marries a genius.

1948

ROMANCE ON THE HIGH SEAS

STUDIO: Warner Brothers. CREDIT: *Musical numbers created and directed by.*
SYNOPSIS: A singer on a Caribbean cruise gets mixed up in a series of romantic problems.
MUSICAL NUMBERS:
"It's Magic": Music by Jule Styne; lyrics by Sammy Cahn
"The Tourist Trade": Music by Jule Styne; lyrics by Sammy Cahn
"Brazilian Rhapsody" aka "Cuban Rhapsody": Music by Jule Styne, Ray Heindorf, and Oscar Levant
"Put 'em in a Box, Tie 'em with a Ribbon and Throw 'em in the Deep Blue Sea": Music by Jule Styne; lyrics by Sammy Cahn
"It's You or No One": Music by Jule Styne; lyrics by Sammy Cahn
"I'm in Love": Music by Jule Styne; lyrics by Sammy Cahn
"Run, Run, Run": Music by Jule Styne; lyrics by Sammy Cahn

1949

TAKE ME OUT TO THE BALL GAME

STUDIO: MGM. CREDIT: *Directed by.*
SYNOPSIS: A beautiful woman takes over a turn-of-the-century baseball team. Musical numbers were staged by Gene Kelly and Stanley Donen.

1950

TWO WEEKS WITH LOVE

STUDIO: MGM. CREDIT: *Musical numbers staged by.*
SYNOPSIS: Two sisters find romance during a turn-of-the-century family vacation.
MUSICAL NUMBERS:
"Aba Daba Honeymoon": Music by Walter Donovan; lyrics by Arthur Fields
"My Hero": Music by Oscar Straus; lyrics by Hugh Stanislaus Stange
"Row, Row, Row": Music by James V. Monaco; lyrics by William Jerome
"A Heart That's Free": Music by Alfred G. Robyn; lyrics by Thomas Railey

1951

CALL ME MISTER

STUDIO: 20th Century Fox. CREDIT: *Dances staged by.*
SYNOPSIS: G.I. Sergeant Shep Dooley, former stage star awaiting discharge in postwar Tokyo, meets his estranged love Kay when she arrives to entertain the troops.
MUSICAL NUMBERS:
"Japanese Girl Like 'Merican Boy": Music by Sammy Fain; lyrics by Mack Gordon
"I'm Gonna Love That Guy (Like He's Never Been Loved Before)": Written by Frances Ash
"Lament to the Pots and Pans": Written by Earl K. Brent; lyrics by Jerry Seelen
"Going Home Train": Written by Harold Rome
"I Just Can't Do Enough for You, Baby": Written by Sammy Fain; lyrics by Mack Gordon
"Military Life": Written by Harold Rome; revised lyrics by Jerry Seelen
"Love Is Back in Business": Written by Sammy Fain; lyrics by Mack Gordon

THE BLUE VEIL

STUDIO: RKO. CREDIT: *Uncredited dance director.*
MUSICAL NUMBER:
"Daddy": Written by Bobby Troup

TWO TICKETS TO BROADWAY

STUDIO: RKO. CREDIT: *Musical numbers created and directed by.*
SYNOPSIS: A small-town girl finds love on the road to Broadway stardom.
MUSICAL NUMBERS:
"The Worry Bird": Written by Jule Styne and Leo Robin
"Big Chief Hole-in-the-Ground": Written by Jule Styne and Leo Robin
"The Closer You Are": Written by Jule Styne and Leo Robin
"Baby, You'll Never Be Sorry": Written by Jule Styne and Leo Robin
"Pelican Falls": Written by Jule Styne and Leo Robin
"Are You a Beautiful Dream?": Written by Jule Styne and Leo Robin
"Let's Make Comparisons": Written by Sammy Cahn and Bob Crosby
"There's No Tomorrow": Written by Al Hoffman, Leo Corday, and Leon Carr
"Prologue from 'Pagliacci'": Written by Leoncavallo
"Manhattan": Written by Richard Rodgers and Lorenz Hart

1952

MILLION DOLLAR MERMAID

STUDIO: MGM. CREDIT: *Fountain and smoke numbers staged by.*
SYNOPSIS: The story of Annette Kellerman, the world's first great swimming
   star.
Music orchestrated by Alexander Courage.

1953

SMALL TOWN GIRL

STUDIO: MGM. CREDIT: *Musical numbers staged by.*
SYNOPSIS: A sheriff's daughter falls for a playboy arrested for speeding.
MUSICAL NUMBERS:
"I've Gotta Hear That Beat": Music by Nicholas Brodszky; lyrics by Leo Robin
"Take Me to Broadway": Music by Nicholas Brodszky; lyrics by Leo Robin
"Fine, Fine, Fine": Music by Nicholas Brodszky; lyrics by Leo Robin
"My Gaucho": Music by Nicholas Brodszky; lyrics by Leo Robin
"The Fellow I Follow": Music by Nicholas Brodszky; lyrics by Leo Robin

* * *

NOTE: André Previn composed the instrumental track that plays during Bobby
Van's "Street Dance" number.

EASY TO LOVE

STUDIO: MGM. CREDIT: *Musical numbers created and directed by.*
SYNOPSIS: Two men vie for the heart of a Cypress Gardens swimming star.

MUSICAL NUMBERS:

"Easy to Love": Music and lyrics by Cole Porter

"Spring, Beautiful Spring (O Frühling, wie bist du so schön)": Written by Paul Lincke

"Look Out! I'm Romantic": Music by Vic Mizzy; lyrics by Mann Curtis

"Didja Ever": Music by Vic Mizzy; lyrics by Mann Curtis

"Coquette": Music and lyrics by Gus Kahn, Carmen Lombardo, and Johnny Green

"That's What a Rainy Day Is For": Music by Vic Mizzy; lyrics by Mann Curtis

1954

ROSE MARIE

STUDIO: MGM. CREDIT: *Musical numbers staged by.*

SYNOPSIS: A trapper's daughter is torn between the Mountie who wants to civilize her and a dashing prospector.

MUSICAL NUMBERS:

"The Right Place for a Girl": Music by Rudolf Friml; lyrics by Paul Francis Webster

"Mounties": Music by Rudolf Friml; lyrics by Otto A. Harbach and Oscar Hammerstein II

"Free to Be Free": Music by Rudolf Friml; lyrics by Paul Francis Webster

"Rose Marie": Music by Rudolf Friml; lyrics by Otto A. Harbach and Oscar Hammerstein II

"I'm A Mountie Who Never Got His Man": Music by George Stoll; lyrics by George Stoll and Herbert Baker

"Indian Love Call": Music by Rudolf Friml; lyrics by Otto A. Harbach and Oscar Hammerstein II

"I Have the Love": Music by Rudolf Friml; lyrics by Paul Francis Webster

"Totem Tom-Tom": Music by Rudolf Friml and Herbert Stothart; lyrics by Otto A. Harbach and Oscar Hammerstein II

1954–1955

BIG TOWN

Television series. CREDIT: *Directed by.*

***

NOTE: The Internet Movie Database credits Berkeley with directing four episodes of the police drama. One, "The Lovers," was discovered and screened for this book. The copyright was 1954, and the database shows it aired on February 14, 1955. Note also that the episodes did not reveal their titles. Other unconfirmed episodes include "Boys Week" (air date December 27, 1954); "The Airplane Story" (air date January 10, 1955); and "The School Teacher" (air date January 17, 1955).

1962

JUMBO (aka BILLY ROSE'S JUMBO)

STUDIO: MGM: CREDIT: *Second unit director.*

SYNOPSIS: Pop and Kitty Wonder are the owners of the Wonder Circus. Because of Pop's addiction to gambling, they are constantly in debt and the creditors are ready to foreclose. Meanwhile the circus's star attraction, an elephant named Jumbo, is desired by a rival circus owner.

MUSICAL NUMBERS:

"Over and Over Again": Music by Richard Rodgers; lyrics by Lorenz Hart

"Little Girl Blue": Music by Richard Rodgers; lyrics by Lorenz Hart

"The Most Beautiful Girl in the World": Music by Richard Rodgers; lyrics by Lorenz Hart

"Circus on Parade": Music by Richard Rodgers; lyrics by Lorenz Hart

"Why Can't I?": Music by Richard Rodgers; lyrics by Lorenz Hart

"This Can't Be Love": Music by Richard Rodgers; lyrics by Lorenz Hart

1970

THE PHYNX

STUDIO: Warner Brothers. Busby Berkeley's name is in the cast list.

SYNOPSIS: Show business people are kidnapped by the Communist country of Albania. To infiltrate the country and release the famed hostages, a faux rock group is formed called "The Phynx." The group plays in the castle for the head of the country, and the loud music causes the walls to collapse, providing freedom for the captives.

Notes

1. Actress and Son

6   *William Gillette history:* Peter T. Loffredo, producer and director, *William Gillette, A Connecticut Yankee and the American Stage,* documentary (Middleton, Conn.: Connecticut Heritage Productions, 1985).

7   *Wilson Enos reviews for* Shenandoah: *Hawaiian Gazette,* November 26, 1897.

7   *Notes on the Kansas City years:* Felicia Hardison Londré and David Austin, *The Enchanted Years of the Stage: Kansas City at the Crossroads of American Theater, 1870–1930* (Columbia: University of Missouri Press, 2007).

10   *Gertrude Berkeley's breakdown:* Noted in *Kansas City Star,* and reprinted in Frank Enos's hometown newspaper, the *Mansfield (Ohio) News,* March 22, 1901. Note the mention of "her little son, Busby." It's the first time Buzz is mentioned in the press, and it underscores the fact that his first name was not William, as so many sources claim, but Busby, as first mentioned in Tony Thomas and Jim Terry, with Busby Berkeley, *The Busby Berkeley Book* (Greenwich, Conn.: New York Graphic Society, 1973).

10   *Columbia Theatre Stock Company in Brooklyn:* Weldon B. Durham, ed., *American Theatre Companies, 1888–1930* (Westport, Conn.: Greenwood Press, 1987).

11   *Gertrude's standing ovations in* Hearts Are Trumps: *Kansas City Journal,* August 24, 1902.

12   *Letter from Busby to his hospitalized father:* This letter was part of a general auction of Berkeley memorabilia in 1998 (see the epilogue of this volume for details on the auction).

12   *My darling Busby, pray . . . pray as you have never prayed before:* Gertrude's response to the telegram, from Berkeley's memoirs. The original story was that Gertrude received and read the telegram while waiting in the wings and stoically went onstage immediately thereafter. Berkeley's memoirs specifically state that his mother read the telegram in her dressing room after playing her scene.

13   *Frank Enos's funeral arrangements: Mansfield (Ohio) News,* February 29, 1904.

13   *Gertrude's reaction to her husband's death:* Thomas and Terry, *The Busby Berkeley Book.* For the contrarian view of events, see *Mansfield (Ohio) News,* February 29, 1904.

13   *Gertrude fainting backstage during* The Master Builder: *New York Times,* November 2, 1907.

13   *Negative reviews for* Myself Bettina: *New York Tribune,* November 6, 1908.

14   *Buzz's prank with the alarm clocks:* Thomas and Terry, *The Busby Berkeley Book.*

14   *By hook and crook:* Bob Pike and Dave Martin, *The Genius of Busby Berkeley* (Reseda, Calif.: CFS Books, 1973).

15   *Nazimova pulling Buzz onstage:* Thomas and Terry, *The Busby Berkeley Book.*

15   *George Enos's death:* George's death was reported in a few publications, but the coincidence of his having died in Plattsburgh, New York, is noted in Thomas and Terry, *The Busby Berkeley Book,* and in Berkeley's memoirs.

15   *She sobbed, she cried, she screamed in utter agony and grief:* Berkeley's memoirs.

16   *Buzz's Athol jobs:* Richard J. Chaisson, "1930s Hollywood Trial Had Athol Angle," *Worcester (Mass.) Telegram and Gazette,* July 24, 1994.

16   *Excerpts from* The Soul of the Violin *by Margaret Manton Merrill: New England Magazine* 13, issue 6 (February 1893).

17   *I learned a lot about show business that night:* Thomas and Terry, *The Busby Berkeley Book.*

19   *Signed Busby Berkeley Enos:* Another piece of evidence of his moniker. His signature (with the "Berkeley" squeezed in) is clear and unambiguous on the military registration card.

2. In Formation

The Busby Berkeley Book and Berkeley's memoirs were of profound help in this chapter.

20   *Naked Buzz and his bugle:* Thomas and Terry, *The Busby Berkeley Book.*

21   *Pierre Dreyfus at the Saumur School:* Berkeley's memoirs.

22   *It was quite something to see:* Thomas and Terry, *The Busby Berkeley Book.*

25   *In his zeal to flee the ship he had run past his own mother:* Berkeley's memoirs.

3. The Show Fixer

27   *Accidental meeting of John Cromwell:* Thomas and Terry, *The Busby Berkeley Book.*

28   *You're the worst dramatic actor:* Berkeley's memoirs.

28   Irene: *The Busby Berkeley Book,* by Thomas and Terry, errs in its reported time frame for *Irene.* Buzz's own recollections (in Pike and Martin, *The Genius of Busby Berkeley*), along with newspaper accounts of the day, pinpoint his involvement from late 1920 through 1922. Thomas and Terry's *The Busby Berkeley Book* incorrectly places him in 1923 for both *Irene* and *Michio Itow's Pin Wheel Revel.*

28   *Review of Buzz's Madame Lucy performance: Daily Kennebec (Maine) Journal,* May 20, 1921.

29   *Buzz in Mansfield, Ohio: Mansfield (Ohio) News,* October 24, 1921. Buzz must have been idly musing on his future to the anonymous writer, hence the mention of the newspaper business. There is no record of Busby Enos purchasing any newspaper company in his lifetime.

29   *Irene Dunne and the raw oyster:* Thomas and Terry, *The Busby Berkeley Book.*

30   *Review of* Going Up: *Fitchburg (Mass.) Daily Sentinel,* October 15, 1923.

30   *The producers of the company:* Buzz uses the term "they" in his interview with Dave Martin in Pike and Martin, *The Genius of Busby Berkeley,* and it's assumed he meant the producers.

31   *Buzz staged . . . his first musical:* Alas, the name of the musical remains unknown.

31   *Buzz directs the musical* Mary: *Fitchburg (Mass.) Sentinel,* February 14, 1924.

31   *Mention of the Berkeley Comedians:* ibid., March 1, 1924. The named troupe was a first for Buzz (his mother's "The Gertrude Berkeley Players" undoubtedly provided the inspiration), though this is the only time the troupe was mentioned in print.

32   *Buzz in Baltimore directing* Seduction: Thomas and Terry, *The Busby Berkeley Book.*

32   *His unusual creative style:* ibid.

32   *Review of* Holka Polka: *New York Times,* October 15, 1925. The *Holka Polka* finale was described as a "Charleston variation with a Czech ac-

cent" by Martin Rubin in *Showstoppers: Busby Berkeley and the Tradition of Spectacle* (New York: Columbia University Press, 1993).

33   *Additional information about* Lady Do: Brooks Peters, "King of Queens: Karyl Norman," July 21, 2009, www.brookspeters.com.

33   Sweet Lady: This show is also notable for featuring an English dancer named Archie Leach, who went on to fame and fortune as Cary Grant.

34   A Connecticut Yankee: The colloquial quote from the script comes from Frederick Nolan, *Lorenz Hart: A Poet on Broadway* (New York: Oxford University Press, 1994).

34   *Buzz assisted by Seymour Felix during tryouts: Variety,* October 12, 1927.

34   *Buzz bluffing his way in the five positions of the dance:* Anecdote from Buzz in the Dave Martin interview from Pike and Martin, *The Genius of Busby Berkeley,* and repeated almost verbatim in Thomas and Terry, *The Busby Berkeley Book.*

35   *Dancers prancing over tables:* Quote by critic Gerald Bordman in Geoffrey Holden Block, *Richard Rodgers* (New Haven: Yale University Press, 2003).

35   *Robert Coleman's column: New York Mirror,* November 8, 1927.

35   *"Rialto Fame Comes Suddenly to Young Director of Dances":* Rob White and Edward Buscombe, *British Film Institute Film Classics* (New York: Routledge, Taylor and Francis Group, 2002), 203–17.

35   *[Buzz] purchasing the twenty-four-room mansion:* Web site for Dover Public Library, Dover, N.H., http://images.dover.lib.nh.us/DoverHistory/sawyer_mansion.htm.

36   *Spectacular stage numbers:* Rubin, *Showstoppers.*

36   *Plot for* Present Arms: White and Buscombe, *British Film Institute Film Classics.*

37   *Buzz's comment on his unusual dance step: New York Times,* March 17, 1970.

37   *The Shakespeare Foundation of Stratford-on-Avon would be offering a series of the folk dances of various nations:* "Tamiris and Busby Berkeley's Troupe Are to Give Europe American 'Folk Art,'" *New York Times,* May 20, 1928. "Tamiris" refers to Helen Tamiris, the esteemed American choreographer, teacher, and dancer.

38   *Someday I'll do that with fifty . . . :* Thomas and Terry, *The Busby Berkeley Book.*

38   *Short background on revues:* Martha Schmoyer LoMonaco, *Every Week a Broadway Revue: The Tamiment Playhouse, 1921–1960* (Westport, Conn.: Greenwood Press, 1992).

38   *Rehearsal anecdote for* Earl Carroll Vanities of 1928: Sidney Skolsky, "*Earl Carroll Redivivus*," *New York Times*, August 5, 1928.

38   *Review of* Earl Carroll Vanities of 1928: Pierre de Rohan, "Creditable Revue Offers Beautiful Girls as Features," *New York American*, August 7, 1928.

38   *Some descriptions of the numbers in* Earl Carroll Vanities of 1928: Rubin, *Showstoppers*.

38   *Pat Lee, a dancer in the show:* Sheila Weller, *Dancing at Ciro's: A Family's Love, Loss, and Scandal on the Sunset Strip* (New York: St. Martin's Griffin, 2003), mentions Pat Lee as the reigning Miss America, but that fact is not corroborated by the pageant's list of past winners.

39   *Comparison to Fritz Lang's* Metropolis: Rubin, *Showstoppers*.

39   "*If you can pick up anything, fine*" and "*I thought that was wonderful*": Dave Martin interview, in Pike and Martin, *The Genius of Busby Berkeley*.

39   *Synopsis of* Good Boy: Rubin, *Showstoppers*.

39   "*I Wanna Be Loved by You," by Helen Kane:* Kane did the voice of Betty Boop in the animated series.

40   Rainbow *opening-night mishaps:* Mark N. Grant, *The Rise and Fall of the Broadway Musical* (Boston: Northeastern University Press, 2004).

40   *Arthur Hammerstein calling Buzz to Springfield, Mass., to fix* The Wild Rose: Thomas and Terry, *The Busby Berkeley Book*. The dates, however, are dubious. Buzz claimed that *The Wild Rose* and *Pleasure Bound* opened on Broadway within a week of each other, when in fact *The Wild Rose* opened years earlier in 1926. It's possible that *The Wild Rose* in a new form did play Broadway at the same time as *Pleasure Bound*, but there is no corroborating evidence.

41   *Ted Healy and His Stooges:* The act later dropped Ted Healy and became known as The Three Stooges.

41   *Jungle scenes, a wrestling bear:* Rubin, *Showstoppers*.

41   *Show opened in Newark:* Morris Fineburg, with G. P. Skratz, *Larry the Stooge in the Middle* (San Francisco: Last Gasp of San Francisco, 1984).

41   A Night in Venice: Thomas and Terry, in *The Busby Berkeley Book*, incorrectly claim that *A Night in Venice* was Berkeley's first Broadway show as a director. Lew Morton and Thomas A. Hart shared that credit.

41   *Smitten [with Esther Muir] from the moment she walked onstage:* Thomas and Terry, *The Busby Berkeley Book*.

41   *Esther Muir was previously married and divorced: New York Times*, November 27, 1929. Sources have long asserted incorrectly that Buzz was her first husband. The name Richard Brown is mentioned in the *Los*

Angeles Times obituary of August 14, 1995, but no date was given for their wedding. Quote from Esther (who obviously includes Buzz here): "My work helped compensate for my poor choice of husbands." Esther Muir lived to be ninety-two.

41   *"The Big Railroad Year" in musicals:* Gerald Bordman, *American Musical Theater: A Chronicle* (New York: Oxford University Press, 1978).

42   *Shortest chorus girl at the end of the line:* Larry Billman, *Film Choreographers and Dance Directors: An Illustrated Biographical Encyclopedia with a History and Filmographies, 1893 through 1995* (Jefferson, N.C.: McFarland, 1997).

42   *He would design the dance numbers, direct the show, and command the credit "Presented by Busby Berkeley":* Thomas and Terry, in *The Busby Berkeley Book,* note that Buzz paved the way for choreographers Jerome Robbins, Michael Kidd, and Gower Champion, who eventually staged their own shows.

42   *The fastest-stepping throng:* Thomas and Terry, *The Busby Berkeley Book.*

42   *Quote from Gilbert Seldes:* ibid.

44   *What a damn fool you are:* J. J. Shubert quoted in Thomas and Terry, *The Busby Berkeley Book.*

44   *Wedding:* The *New York Times,* November 27, 1929, reported the wedding, giving Buzz's name as "William Berkeley Enos," a name Buzz did use in addition to the two others mentioned previously.

44   *Background of* Ruth Selwyn's Nine Fifteen Revue*:* Rubin, *Showstoppers.*

45   *George Gershwin quote:* by Joel Harris, a fan of Ruth Etting: www .ruthetting.com (a site maintained by Cheryl Spelts, a granddaughter of one of Ruth Etting's cousins).

45   *Disastrously disorganized:* Rubin, *Showstoppers.*

45   Description of the musical numbers in *Lew Leslie's International Revue:* Pre-opening reviews in *New York Times,* February 10, 1930; *Newark Ledger,* February 11, 1930; and *Newark News,* February 11, 1930. Also reviewed in Rubin, *Showstoppers.*

45   *Buzz and Esther at the Cotton Club:* John Edward Hasse, *Beyond Category: The Life and Genius of Duke Ellington* (New York: Simon and Schuster, 1993).

45   Nina Rosa: Although Buzz is described in Thomas and Terry, *The Busby Berkeley Book,* as having been associated with *Nina Rosa,* it appears that his involvement ended at Sigmund Romberg's midnight audition.

Though it is possible Buzz worked uncredited, he is not mentioned in the show's program or in any New York review.

46   *Buzz and William Grady:* Pike and Martin, *The Genius of Busby Berkeley.*

46   *Conversation about coming to Hollywood for* Whoopee!: Pike and Martin, *The Genius of Busby Berkeley.* The story is told somewhat differently in Thomas and Terry, *The Busby Berkeley Book*, but the principles are the same.

4. A Cyclopean Vision

48   *Background notes on* Whoopee!: A. Scott Berg, *Goldwyn: A Biography* (New York: Riverhead Books, 1989); Herbert G. Goldman, *Banjo Eyes: Eddie Cantor and the Birth of Modern Stardom* (New York: Oxford University Press, 1997).

48   *Ziegfeld knew Berkeley:* According to Buzz, Ziegfeld wanted him for an unnamed show. Around the time of *Earl Carroll Vanities*, Ziegfeld was producing *The Ziegfeld Follies of 1927, Show Boat, Rosalie,* and *The Three Musketeers.* Buzz could have been referring to any of those shows (Pike and Martin, *The Genius of Busby Berkeley*).

48   *Buzz to Goldwyn, "I know I can":* Berkeley's memoirs.

49   *Buzz on the "single eye" of the camera:* Thomas and Terry, *The Busby Berkeley Book;* and Pike and Martin, *The Genius of Busby Berkeley.*

52   *Buzz asking for leotards for the horses:* Pike and Martin, *The Genius of Busby Berkeley.*

52   *Technicolor in* Whoopee!: The Technicolor in this film has often been labeled as "two-strip." *Whoopee!* was shot using black-and-white negative film that alternately recorded red and green colors. A more accurate term is "two-component Technicolor." Three-strip Technicolor (introduced in 1932) used multiple film stocks, whereas two-strip did not.

52   *The top shot:* Busby Berkeley did not invent the top shot, but he remains its most successful artistic proponent. The high location, the camera pointed downward, and the resultant effects born in Berkeley's prolific imagination were used in a number of pictures prior to *Whoopee!* MGM's *The Hollywood Revue of 1929* features a high shot of dancers standing in a circle during the song "Lon Chaney Is Going to Get You." A top shot is featured one hour and twelve minutes into the Marx Brothers' *The Cocoanuts* in the "Dream Ballet" number. The *Wall Street Journal* of May 27, 1929, makes mention of its interesting perspective: "One scene, however, in which a dance number is photographed from a point directly above the ensemble, giving the movements of the dancing group a kaleidoscopic appearance, though without color, is novel."

52   Sweet and Low: The title was originally *Corned Beef and Roses*, but was
      changed by Billy Rose after critics panned the show. From Frank Cul-
      len, with Florence Hackman and Donald McNeilly, *Vaudeville Old and
      New: An Encyclopedia of Variety Performers in America*, vol. 1 (New
      York: Routledge, Taylor and Francis Group, 2007).

53   *Review in* New York Times: November 18, 1930.

54   *Information on* Palmy Days: Herbert G. Goldman, *Banjo Eyes: Eddie
      Cantor and the Birth of Modern Stardom* (New York: Oxford University
      Press, 1997).

55   *Buzz mentioning his role as an actor in the film:* Pike and Martin, *The
      Genius of Busby Berkeley.*

55   *Buzz on the number of natural blondes:* Lowell *(Mass.) Sun,* October 9,
      1931.

56   *Fanchon and Marco quote from* Variety: Reva Howitt Clar, *Lollipop:
      Vaudeville Turns with a Fanchon and Marco Dancer* (Lanham, Md.:
      Scarecrow Press, 2002).

56   *Dress-ripping incident:* syndicated AP story, July 8, 1931.

59   *Headline "Rex Lease and Esther Muir to Wed":* New York Times, Janu-
      ary 4, 1932.

59   *Esther litigated for alimony:* Syracuse (N.Y.) Herald, August 19, 1932.
      The headline read "Berkeley Must Help Ex-Wife, Court Decrees."

59   *Chains idea:* Berkeley's memoirs. The show was advertised in the *Los
      Angeles Times* movie section, January 4, 1932.

59   *Norman Taurog to direct retakes of* Girl Crazy: *Variety,* February 2,
      1932.

59   *Buzz contributed to* Girl Crazy: *Variety,* February 16, 1932.

62   *Petty cash vouchers:* The quoted voucher of twenty-five dollars is from
      September 9, 1932 (signed "Busby Berkeley"). It is now owned by a pri-
      vate collector.

62   *Eddie Cantor learning about Ziegfeld's illness:* Goldman, *Banjo Eyes.*

64   *In January, Warner Brothers posted losses of $7,918,604:* Mark A. Vieira,
      Sin in Soft Focus: Pre-Code Hollywood (New York: Abrams, 1999).

5. The Cinematerpsichorean

66   *Buzz on casting his* 42nd Street *chorines by looking at their knees:* Dan
      Thomas, syndicated column, December 2, 1932.

66   *Warren and Dubin:* Many sources incorrectly state that Warren and Du-
      bin's first collaboration was *42nd Street.* In 1926, along with Billy Rose,
      they wrote the song "Too Many Kisses."

67   *The Warner house style:* Each studio's films had a "look," or what is known as a house style. MGM's was generally ornate with lavish sets, while Paramount's was more sophisticated. Warner Brothers, in its constant effort to cut costs, featured contemporary, socially conscious stories (*I Am a Fugitive from a Chain Gang, Public Enemy, Little Caesar*). This house style carried over into the timely musicals with their snappy repartee and Busby Berkeley's stark black-and-white numbers.

71   *Buzz invents "the monorail":* Description and quotes from Pike and Martin, *The Genius of Busby Berkeley.*

72   *42nd Street Special train.* A film was made at the time of departure and is featured on the *Gold Diggers of 1933* DVD.

72   *What few knew:* Zanuck's plans for making *42nd Street* a musical was unknown even to the Warner brothers. A dubious story has Jack Warner at a screening of the film totally surprised when he found out *42nd Street* was a musical. "What will I tell Harry?" asked Jack. Although Jack might have been caught unawares, *Variety* of November 8, 1932, reported, "Harry Warner picked *42nd Street* as special after seeing but six reels." Also, the film's budget (more than $300,000) surely would have raised questions (White and Buscombe, *British Film Institute Film Classics*).

72   *Buzz attached to the film* Blondie Johnson: Warner Brothers Archives, School of Cinematic Arts, University of Southern California.

79   *Long Beach earthquake . . . Buzz dangling by one hand:* ibid.

80   *Joan Blondell's voice dubbed by Jean Cowan:* Historians Rudy Behlmer and Miles Kreuger, along with Leonard Maltin, brought this tidbit to light.

80   *Etta Moten:* Etta made history when she became the first African American singer/actress to perform at the White House. The occasion was President Roosevelt's birthday. At his request, she sang "Remember My Forgotten Man."

80   *Notes on costuming for* We're in the Money: Arthur Hove, ed., *Gold Diggers of 1933* (Madison: University of Wisconsin Press, 1980).

80   *Coins duplicated in chocolate:* moviediva.com.

80   *Hoop skirt . . . two thousand yards of white China silk:* Arthur Hove, ed., *Gold Diggers of 1933* (Madison: University of Wisconsin Press, 1980).

82   *She Had to Say Yes:* Buzz's quotes: Thomas and Terry, *The Busby Berkeley Book.*

83   *Merna Kennedy wearing a ring "the size of a chunk of coal":* Wire reports, June 28, 1933.

83   *Buzz's letter and check to Samuel Goldwyn, Inc.:* Warner Brothers Archives, School of Cinematic Arts, University of Southern California.

84   *Gentlemen, include me out!:* Berg, *Goldwyn.*

90   *Buzz mentioning Eleanor Holm and "By a Waterfall":* Sheboygan *(Wisc.) Press,* October 10, 1933. Sadly, Miss Holm fought the same demons as Buzz. She was suspended from the 1936 Olympics for acute alcoholism.

90   *Buzz telling Ruby Keeler how to do a porpoise dive:* from Cass Warner Sperling and Cork Millner with Jack Warner Jr., *The Brothers Warner: The Intimate Story of a Hollywood Studio Family Dynasty"* (Warner Sisters, 2008).

90   *Buzz's quote about the pool and the* Bremen: *Dance Magazine* 42 (February 1968).

90   *Milo Anderson's swimming "costume":* Described in Deborah Nadoolman Landis, *Dressed: A Century of Hollywood Costume Design* (New York: HarperCollins, 2007).

90   *George Groves anecdote:* www.georgegroves.org.uk.

91   *A thirty-two-hour day was nothing:* Madison Lacy quoted in John Kobal, *People Will Talk* (New York: Knopf, 1986).

92   *Lorena Layson:* Lorena Layson was later known as Mrs. Louis B. Mayer.

92   *Buzz moved on to the next setup:* William Witney (prodigious director of films for Republic Pictures) learned how to stage his fight scenes by watching Buzz filming a dance sequence: "He was lining up all the girls for just one little movement. He got it perfect. Then he would rehearse another little movement, shoot it, and then maybe a few close-ups later to put in between those shots" (William Witney, *In a Door, into a Fight, out a Door, into a Chase: Moviemaking Remembered by a Guy at the Door* (Jefferson, N.C.: McFarland, 2005).

93   New York Times *review of "Footlight Parade":* October 6, 1933.

93   *Standing ovation for "By a Waterfall" at the New York premiere:* Daniel Bubbeo, *The Women of Warner Bros.* (Jefferson, N.C.: McFarland, 2001).

93   Roman Scandals: Ruth Etting had previously worked with Buzz, singing "Get Happy" in the short-lived *Ruth Selwyn's Nine Fifteen Revue.*

95   *Lucille Ball anecdote:* Lucille Ball, *Love Lucy* (New York: G. P. Putnam's Sons, 1996).

96   *Buzz leaving for New York looking for new chorus girls:* Louella Parsons, syndicated column, September 21, 1933.

96   *Buzz and Merna at Sardi's: New York Times,* December 27, 1933.

97   *Buzz to direct musical numbers for "Hot Air": New York Times,* January 7, 1934. The project was abandoned.

97 *Buzz's letter to Warner Brothers requesting that 50 percent of his salary go to Gertrude:* Warner Brothers Archives, School of Cinematic Arts, University of Southern California.

98 *Description of Gertrude's home in Redlands, Calif.:* Thomas and Terry, *The Busby Berkeley Book.*

98 *Buzz wanting "something new, something different" for "Wonder Bar":* Sheboygan *(Wisc.) Press,* March 29, 1934.

99 *Background of the Production Code:* David Boxwell's online journal, "Sense of Cinema," September 2002.

101 *Buzz's description of the "Don't Say Goodnight" number:* Pike and Martin, *The Genius of Busby Berkeley.*

102 *Recording-technique information for "Goin' to Heaven on a Mule":* George Groves, sound department employee and Vitaphone master at Warner Brothers.

102 *"Goin' to Heaven on a Mule" excised in theaters patronized by minority audiences:* I had heard a rumor that when *Wonder Bar* played in the southern United States, the "Goin' to Heaven on a Mule" number was excised from southern theaters with black audiences. In correspondence with film critic and scholar Jonathan Rosenbaum (whose grandfather owned a number of southern theaters in the 1930s), I asked him if such a thing had occurred, but he could not confirm the rumor. A more recent, albeit subtle, case of censorship is found in the DVD box set *The Busby Berkeley Collection* (Warner Home Video, 2006). Included in the set is *The Busby Berkeley Disc,* a compilation of Buzz's most famous numbers from his early Warner Brothers period. Originally released as a laserdisc, the DVD version is identical except for one thing—"Goin' to Heaven on a Mule" was purposely not included. On July 20, 2009, *Wonder Bar* was released in its unexpurgated form as both a DVD and digital download from Warner Brothers.

104 *Sam Goldwyn's lawsuit against Warner Brothers:* UP wire stories, April 20; May 5, 8, 12, and 18, 1934.

105 *Lou Brock's claiming Buzz stole his Hawaiian bolero:* Louella Parsons, syndicated column, April 23, 1934. The film was eventually released as *Down to Their Last Yacht.*

110 *Joan Blondell commenting on Buzz working her "to the bone":* John Kobal, *Gotta Sing, Gotta Dance: A Pictorial History of Film Musicals* (London: Hamlyn, 1970).

111 *Yeah . . . a pool of Goldwyn's blood:* Harrison Carroll, syndicated column, King Features Syndicate, July 2, 1934.

111 *Joseph Breen's letter of acceptance to Jack Warner:* Thomas Schatz, *The*

Genius of the System: Hollywood Filmmaking in the Studio Era (New York: Pantheon Books, 1989).

111   And She Learned about Dames: Warner Bros. Production Corp. and The Vitaphone Corp., 1934.

112   *Elinor Troy:* UP wires, October 16, 1934.

113   *Whitey Wilson obtaining pianos: New York Times,* November 25, 1934.

116   *George Groves's sound-recording anecdote:* georgegroves.org.uk.

116   *Alice Brady's unscheduled leave of absence:* Wood Soanes, syndicated column, December 7, 1934.

116   *The surviving Warner brothers:* Sam Warner had passed away the day before *The Jazz Singer* was to premiere in New York. He was forty.

117   *Buzz on wedding proposals:* syndicated newspaper item, April 21, 1935.

119   *I'd like some pigs, two or three:* John Kobal, *People Will Talk* (New York: Knopf, 1986).

119   *Buzz took his ire out on Sol Polito, the director of photography:* Footage of Buzz yelling at Sol Polito was included in a short film that Warner Brothers made for its employees titled *Breakdowns of 1935.* The film was a collection of outtakes in which foul outbursts from the likes of James Cagney and Bette Davis were treated, internally, as comedy. It was never intended for public consumption, and it was obvious that Buzz was unaware that the camera kept rolling after he yelled, "Cut."

120   *Buzz hanging the dollies:* syndicated newspaper item, April 21, 1935.

120· *She smothered a sob in her handkerchief:* Berkeley's memoirs.

120   *Merna Kennedy suing Buzz for separate maintenance: Los Angeles Times,* June 27, 1935.

6. The Cancerous Tire

Thomas and Terry, in *The Busby Berkeley Book*, mention that Berkeley was dragged unconscious from his burning car. The detailed description of Buzz at William Hudson's car and later at the café disproves this.

126   *The green convertible roadster was indistinguishable from charred metal:* Kenneth Anger, *Hollywood Babylon II* (New York: Dutton, 1984), identifies the car's color as white, but newspaper accounts of the accident agree that it was green.

126   *Background information on Jerry Giesler:* Jerry Giesler, as told to Pete Martin, *The Jerry Giesler Story* (New York: Simon and Schuster, 1960).

129   The Singing Kid: Edward Jablonski, *Harold Arlen: Rhythm, Rainbows, and Blues* (Boston: Northeastern University Press, 1996), claims that

Buzz directed Al Jolson's self-parody "I Love to Singa," but the daily production reports confirm that it was directed by William Keighley.

131 *Bryan Foy's comments about Buzz, "He's very high strung"*: syndicated UP story, December 18, 1935.

131 *Buzz's sobriety:* The stars and coworkers who took the stand on Buzz's behalf uniformly testified to his sobriety. It is worth considering that they were paid employees of the same studio as the defendant. It was in all their best bottom-line interests to tow the line, even if Buzz had been inebriated at the time he left the party.

134 *Jack Warner wired Buzz after the trial:* Bernard F. Dick, *Hal Wallis: Producer to the Stars* (Lexington: University Press of Kentucky, 2004).

134 *"Save Me Sister":* This interesting blackface number (featuring Wini Shaw under brown makeup) has an affinity with Buzz's previous work (large crowds, big set, shadow play on the walls), but there's nothing in Warner's daily production reports that links the number to him.

134 *Studio memos:* Unless otherwise noted, all studio memos are from the Warner Brothers Archives, School of Cinematic Arts, University of Southern California.

135 *Judge Burnell's threatening phone call and its aftermath:* Oakland Tribune, March 12, 1936, and a similar story from the same date in the Fresno Bee.

136 *Nobody but you will ever know that I worked on this picture:* Sybil Jason recounted the anecdote to me. The quote was given years after Al Jolson had passed, making Buzz's statement quite correct.

137 *Background on the short* Changing of the Guard: Sybil Jason, *Five Minutes More* (Duncan, Okla.: BearManor Media, 2007).

141 *Joan Blondell's assessment of Buzz and the anecdote of filming "All's Fair in Love and War" when a chorus girl became ill:* Kobal, *People Will Talk.*

142 *Joan Blondell and Dick Powell's wedding aboard the yacht* Santa Paula: Matthew Kennedy, *Joan Blondell: A Life between Takes* (Jackson: University Press of Mississippi, 2007).

7. Post-Traumatic Inspiration

143 *Buzz's comments after the trial:* Thomas and Terry, *The Busby Berkeley Book.*

144 *I was the best of the bestest:* Pike and Martin, *The Genius of Busby Berkeley.*

147   *Josef Goebbels's diary entry:* Peter Jelavich, *Berlin Cabaret* (Cambridge: Harvard University Press, 1993).

147   *Leni Riefenstahl anecdote:* Told to me by the author and film scholar John Russell Taylor. Riefenstahl's comments about Berkeley come from a 1960s interview that Mr. Taylor conducted for *Sight and Sound* magazine.

148   *Description of the Beaux-Arts mansion: Architectural Digest,* April 2000 (complete with beautiful black-and-white photos of some of the interiors). The mansion is still standing and is just as elegant as it appeared when Buzz purchased it. It is now owned by the Movement of Spiritual Inner Awareness, Peace Theological Seminary and College of Philosophy.

148   *Buzz taking girls into his office:* Anecdote related by former Berkeley girl Lois Lindsay in Kobal, *People Will Talk.*

148   *Carole Landis background:* Eric Gans, *Carole Landis: A Most Beautiful Girl* (Jackson: University Press of Mississippi, 2008).

149   Varsity Show: The film was reissued to theaters in 1942, and for that release, the film was cut to eighty minutes in length. These cuts were made to the original camera negative, and the discarded footage was not saved.

152   *Louella Parsons blaming Buzz Berkeley's drinking:* David Wallace, *Lost Hollywood* (New York: St. Martin's Griffin, 2001).

152   *Louella and the chamber pot:* Kobal, *People Will Talk.*

153   *Ted Healy's funeral:* The controversy stems from Healy's manner of death. The story goes that he was beaten to death in a bar by Academy Award–winning actor Wallace Beery, gangster Pat DiCicco, and DiCicco's cousin Cubby Broccoli (who eventually became the producer of the James Bond film series). After Healy's death, Louis B. Mayer and other powerful Hollywoodians conspired to cover up the real story with a story about some college kids who beat the man to death. The studio sent Beery to Europe for four months in an effort to protect their investment.

154   Gold Diggers in Paris: Two songs by Harry Warren and Johnny Mercer, "Daydreaming" and "My Adventure," were credited but never used.

157   *Letter from Mervyn LeRoy to Arthur Freed regarding Buzz and* The Wizard of Oz: Hugh Fordin, *M-G-M's Greatest Musicals: The Arthur Freed Unit* (Cambridge, Mass.: Da Capo Press, 1996).

158   *Louella Parsons mentions Buzz and* The Wizard of Oz: syndicated column, June 20, 1938.

159   *Buzz and Kay Francis playing a stunt before some visitors from Kansas:* Sheilah Graham's column of May 24, 1943, in which Alice Faye recounted the story that Buzz told her.

159   *Buzz, Irving Wheeler, and Carole Landis in court:* E. J. Fleming, *Carole Landis: A Tragic Life in Hollywood* (Jefferson, N.C.: McFarland, 2005).

160   *Ann Sheridan and Buzz playing a trick on John Garfield:* Robert Nott, *He Ran All the Way: The Life of John Garfield* (New York: Proscenium, 2003).

162   *Buzz taking the whole cast to the St. Mary's–Loyola football game:* Harrison Carroll, syndicated column, October 19, 1938, King Features Syndicate.

8. Buzz's Babes

164   *Buzz and the Scarecrow dance from* The Wizard of Oz: Buzz's complete version is available on the DVD *That's Dancing* and in the sixtieth anniversary release of the film on DVD and Blu-Ray.

164   *Victor Fleming's complimentary note to Buzz about the scarecrow number:* Berkeley's memoirs.

166   *Buzz and Oomph Girl campaign story:* Daniel Bubbeo, *The Women of Warner Brothers* (Jefferson, N.C.: McFarland, 2001).

167   *Reteaming of Mickey Rooney and Judy Garland:* They had been in *Thoroughbreds Don't Cry* and *Love Finds Andy Hardy.*

167   *The show was available for pennies:* Fordin, *M-G-M's Greatest Musicals.*

168   *Note regarding "God's Country."* A segment of the number featured Mickey Rooney impersonating FDR while Judy Garland imitated First Lady Eleanor. In the 1948 reissue of *Babes in Arms,* this segment was removed from all 35mm prints in deference to the president, who had died in 1945. That portion of the number remained lost until the 1990s, when an old 16mm print was discovered that contained it. The DVD of *Babes in Arms* (Warner Home Video, 2007) has the restored number, but the quality is reflective of the 16mm source.

169   *Judy lost a day to shoot retakes for* The Wizard of Oz: Thomas Schatz, *The Genius of the System: Hollywood Filmmaking in the Studio Era* (New York: Pantheon Books, 1988).

169   *Buzz requiring crew to have musical background:* "Theaters" column, *Circleville (Ohio) Daily Herald,* November 6, 1939.

170   *Mickey Rooney called Buzz "impossibly demanding":* Mickey Rooney, *Life is Too Short* (New York: Villard Books, 1991).

170   *Studio grip Harry Walden:* Anecdote from *Private Screenings: Mickey Rooney* (Turner Broadcasting System, 1997).

170   *Buzz, you have done a magnificent job with these two kids:* Berkeley's memoirs.

171   *It sounds so patriotic:* Fordin, *M-G-M's Greatest Musicals.*

173   *Party given for Buzz by the "Fast and Furious" crew:* syndicated column, October 29, 1939.

173   *Buzz uses and credits an understudy:* syndicated column, October 30, 1939.

174   Forty Little Mothers *and Wallace Beery:* One wonders if Buzz rejected Beery's adopted daughter's pictures outright due to Beery's alleged link to the death of Buzz's friend Ted Healy.

175   *Buzz encouraged Veronica Lake:* Veronica Lake, interview by Wood Soanes, *Oakland Tribune,* January 27, 1942.

179   *Roger Edens on filming "Do the La Conga":* Albert Johnson, "Conversation with Roger Edens," *Sight and Sound* 27, no. 4 (Spring 1958).

179   *Buzz's contribution to the finale of* Bitter Sweet: Edward Baron Turk, *Hollywood Diva: A Biography of Jeanette MacDonald* (Berkeley and Los Angeles: University of California Press, 2000).

180   *Will the girl with the balls please step down two steps?:* Roy P. Drachman Sr., memoir, "Just Memories," www.parentseyes.arizona.edu/drachman, created November 2004.

180   *"You Stepped Out of a Dream" number was retooled per his specifications:* Laura Wagner, "A Conversation with Tony Martin," *Classic Images* magazine, vol. 272, February 1998.

181   *Buzz [was] treated for a painful case of piles:* Berkeley's memoirs.

181   *Shirley Temple going to MGM:* Arthur Freed's mentioning of the Topsy and Eva number for Shirley and Judy Garland must've amused Buzz. A good guess is that Buzz told Arthur of his brief association with the Duncan sisters back in the 1930s.

181   *"Fascinating Rhythm":* The film *That's Entertainment III* features a behind-the-scenes look at Buzz directing the opening portion of the number.

184   *Buzz received an ultimatum from Freed:* Fordin, *M-G-M's Greatest Musicals.*

185   *Mickey Rooney on Buzz:* While commenting on the "Hoe Down" number in the compilation film *That's Entertainment,* Mickey Rooney respectfully mentions his mentor: "When our movies took off at the box office we found our budgets taking off too. So they moved Judy and I out of the backyard and into the barn then to the high school gym and later to a Broadway stage that would never have fit in a real theater. Where we got all that energy I'll never know. But a lot of it was inspired by our director, a genius, Busby Berkeley."

187   *To Roger Edens's chagrin, the minstrel number fell flat:* Fordin, *M-G-M's Greatest Musicals.*

187   *Complimentary letter from Oscar Hammerstein to Arthur Freed:* ibid.

187   *Buzz was high up on the set:* "Flashes from Hollywood," syndicated item, November 2, 1941.

189   Babes in Hollywood *was on the drawing board as the sequel to* Babes on Broadway: Louella Parsons, syndicated column, December 4, 1941.

189   *Buzz marries Claire James:* As recounted in Thomas and Terry, *The Busby Berkeley Book,* Buzz's memory of the events following his marriage to Claire James doesn't match the on-the-record reports and timeline of what occurred. According to Buzz, after the ceremony Claire (who had never had a drink in her life) was so inebriated that she spent their wedding night unconscious. He woke her up the next day in time to catch the next plane to Los Angeles. "I took her home to her mother. A few days later she called to say that she didn't want to be married, so it was annulled." The fact that she had dated a known alcoholic for years and was a complete teetotaler seems unlikely, as does the quick exit out of town provided her by her new husband on the day after the ceremony. The madness of it all certainly follows Buzz's life trajectory, but all was not as cut-and-dried as he claimed.

190   *Arthur Freed quote:* Thomas and Terry, *The Busby Berkeley Book.*

191   *Judy talking about Buzz in* For Me and My Gal: syndicated UP column, December 23, 1942.

192   *Information about the reshooting:* Alvin Yudkoff, *Gene Kelly: A Life of Dance and Dreams* (New York: Back Stage Books, 1999); and Fordin, *M-G-M's Greatest Musicals.*

193   *Buzz's comment about the picture being his favorite:* Pike and Martin, *The Genius of Busby Berkeley.*

193   Buzz said, *"Nice work Jack. Now where is Bennie?":* Gabriella Oldham, *First Cut: Conversations with Film Editors* (Berkeley and Los Angeles: University of California Press, 1992).

193   *William Saroyan's memories of Buzz:* William Saroyan, *Obituaries* (Berkeley, Calif.: Creative Arts Book Company, 1979).

193   *Orson Welles played cards for two or three days:* Simon Callow, *Orson Welles,* vol. 2, *Hello Americans* (New York: Viking Penguin, 2006).

195   *Roger Edens fighting with Buzz over "I Got Rhythm":* Albert Johnson, "Conversation with Roger Edens," *Sight and Sound* 27, no. 4 (Spring 1958). It should be noted that, in retrospect, Roger Edens confessed admiration for Berkeley's direction of "I Got Rhythm": "And I must say that this scene, with all those things I disliked looks wonderful now on TV."

195   *"I Got Rhythm" . . . $60,000 over budget:* Schechter, *Judy Garland: The Day-by-Day Chronicle of a Legend.*

195   *Hedda Hopper on Buzz's treatment of Judy:* John Fricke, *Judy Garland: World's Greatest Entertainer* (New York: Holt, 1992).

196   *Quote from Dona Massin:* John Fricke, *Judy Garland: A Portrait in Art and Anecdote* (New York: Bulfinch Press, 2003).

196   *Judy was exhausted, and her weight had dropped to ninety-four pounds:* Schechter, *Judy Garland: The Day-by-Day Chronicle of a Legend.*

197   *Judy called me "Uncle Buzz":* Fricke, *Judy Garland: World's Greatest Entertainer.*

197   *Claire James-Berkeley instructed her lawyer:* syndicated AP story, February 13, 1943.

197   *Claire refused to listen to any talk of reconciliation:* Louella Parsons, syndicated column, March 11, 1943.

9. Art and Audacity

198   *Buzz and Mother rode in a limousine chaperoned by a man identified as "Gene":* Berkeley's memoirs.

198   *Buzz's road trip with Gertrude:* Thomas and Terry, *The Busby Berkeley Book.*

198   *Buzz purchasing an Oklahoma cattle ranch:* ibid.; and *Architectural Digest,* April 2000.

199   *He and Sally were also seen at Slapsy Maxie's:* Louella Parsons, syndicated column, April 26, 1943.

201   *He had her thrown off [the set] by her own father, who worked as a studio watchman:* Hedda Hopper, syndicated column, June 12, 1943.

204   *Hookay. Thees time make with the careful! Knock one banana off my head and I will make of you de flat pancake:* The quotes attributed to Carmen Miranda are found in several sources, including Harry Haun, *The Cinematic Century: An Intimate Diary of America's Affair with the Movies* (New York: Applause Books, 2000); the Web pages "Carmen.mi randa.nom.br" and "bombshell.com" (the latter is on the page dedicated to Carmen Miranda); and Thomas and Terry, *The Busby Berkeley Book,* which credits the story to *Detroit News* reporter Harold Heffernan, who was on the set and reported the story.

207   *Description of shooting "The Polka Dot Polka" scene:* Robbin Coons, syndicated column, August 25, 1943.

208   *MGM packaged Buzz with studio stalwart Joan Crawford, and made a double deal with Warner Brothers:* J. Hoberman, "42nd Street," in

White and Buscombe, *British Film Institute Film Classics*, vol. 1, *The Best of International Cinema, 1916–1981*.

208   *He's back on the Warner lot to stay:* Louella Parsons, syndicated column, July 15, 1943.

208   *Buzz placed a "sparkler" on Lorraine's proper finger:* Louella Parsons, syndicated column, August 6, 1943.

10. The Stage Debacle

211   *Buzz was still sporting a sling:* Louella Parsons, syndicated column, January 19, 1944.

212   *Gertrude in car accident:* "Busby Berkeley's Mother Injured in Auto Accident," *Los Angeles Times,* June 3, 1944.

213   *Buzz in Atlantic City:* Dorothy Kilgallen, "The Voice of Broadway" syndicated column, September 21, 1944.

214   *Myra Steffens, "the girl with the velvet skin":* Thomas and Terry, *The Busby Berkeley Book.*

214   Program for *"Glad to See You":* Under "Members of the Ensemble," the program lists three groups: *Those with the Gift of Dancing, Those with the Gift of Singing,* and *Those with the Gift of Beauty.* In the latter, alphabetically adjacent are the two future Mrs. Berkeleys, identified as "Marge Pemberton" and "Myra Stephens." The spelling of Myra's surname changes from source to source. In Thomas and Terry, *The Busby Berkeley Book,* it's spelled "Steffin," and in a 1944 AP Wirephoto (and Berkeley's memoirs), it's "Steffens."

214   *Review from "Billboard":* Maurie Orodenker, November 25, 1944.

214   *Details on the short-lived show:* Wood Soanes, syndicated column, *Oakland Tribune,* January 9, 1945.

215   *Myra admitted honestly "the marriage was a big mistake. We will be better off apart":* Walter Winchell, syndicated column, May 24, 1945; and "The American Scene," syndicated column, June 5, 1945.

215   *One of the bad things about Los Angeles is that there are two sets of prices:* Thomas and Terry, *The Busby Berkeley Book.*

216   *Buzz removed from directing* Till the Clouds Roll By *because of the drunk-driving charge:* Sheilah Graham, "Hollywood Today," syndicated column, November 6, 1945.

11. Inconsolable

218   The date of Gertrude's death is listed in some sources as June 15, 1946,

but was confirmed as June 14 in Thomas and Terry, *The Busby Berkeley Book*, and in *The New York Times* and other newspapers that reported the story the day following her death.

218   *Almost deranged me:* Pike and Martin, *The Genius of Busby Berkeley.*

219   *I'll be right back, Mother . . . just as soon as I finish shooting:* Berkeley's memoirs.

219   *Buzz lost the New Hampshire mansion in a tax foreclosure:* "We Remember Dover," http://doverpl.wetpaint.com/page/Busby+Berkely.

220   *The judge fined him only ten dollars because he was told that was all the money Buzz had:* Fleming, *Carole Landis.*

220   *I'm a has-been and know it:* Anger, *Hollywood Babylon II.*

221   *After all I had been through:* Buzz's quote and the amount of $750 that Buzz was left with in Thomas and Terry, *The Busby Berkeley Book.*

221   *Claire James married William Girard: New York Times*, February 19, 1947.

222   *The Curtiz Company has engaged Busby Berkeley to do the song routines for* Romance in High C: Thomas Brady, syndicated column, *New York Times*, June 13, 1947; and Louella Parsons, syndicated column, June 13, 1947.

222   *The [girls on the set are] "better than ever":* Patricia Clary, syndicated column, United Press, December 7, 1947.

223   *Buzz directed the trailer: Boxoffice* magazine, October 4, 1947.

224   *Jack gave him a job when he was down and out and needed a hand:* Louella Parsons, syndicated column, November 14, 1947.

12. One Last at Bat

225   "Boys and Girls Like You and Me" is a song that was supposed to be in *Take Me Out to the Ball Game.* Originally composed for the 1943 production of *Oklahoma!* by Richard Rodgers and Oscar Hammerstein II, it was dropped from the show before its premiere, and MGM wound up buying it for Judy Garland to be used in *Meet Me in St. Louis.* It didn't last there, either, having been cut before the first preview. The next stop for the homeless tune was *Take Me Out to the Ball Game*, where Sinatra was supposed to sing it to both Esther Williams and Betty Garrett. Deemed too slow, it fell to the editor's scissors. A happy ending of sorts saw its rebirth in the 1996 Broadway revival of *State Fair.* The "of sorts" refers to the closing of the show after only three months.

226   *His was a very special talent and at this time in his life he couldn't afford to fail:* Thomas and Terry, *The Busby Berkeley Book.*

227   *You know something? This sonofabitch even* sits *tall!:* Esther Williams and Digby Diehl, *The Million Dollar Mermaid* (New York: Simon and Schuster, 1999).

227   *Buzz had all kinds of marvelous ideas, not just for this film, but for others as well:* ibid.

227   *"Baby Doll":* The song was eventually used in MGM's *The Belle of New York* (1952).

228   *"Yes Indeedy":* How these lyrics made it past the censors is a mystery:

I kissed a gal down in Mississippi.
A southern belle name o' Emmy Jo.
I thought for once love had got me dippy.
She called me Lucky Seven,
Said my kisses were from heaven,
Then I learned she was eleven,
And I had to go!

229   *In a volume louder than a whisper, Gene said, "Yeah, back to 1930":* Yudkoff, *Gene Kelly.* It's worth noting that the disparaging comments about Buzz that were uttered by Gene Kelly, Judy Garland, Mickey Rooney, Arthur Freed, and others in the course of their long careers were balanced with reverential plaudits. One may chalk up the disparity to human nature, for Busby Berkeley contained within him traits that were both loathed and loved.

229   *Too epicene and flamboyant to take seriously:* Lawrence J. Quirk and William Schoell, *The Rat Pack: Neon Nights with the Kings of Cool* (Dallas, Tex.: Taylor, 1998).

229   *Like "beauty is what beauty does," Buzz just is:* Thomas and Terry, *The Busby Berkeley Book.*

229   *Drunk-driving charge:* syndicated INS story, October 11, 1948.

230   *Buzz mentioned for the director's job in* Annie Get Your Gun: Thomas F. Brady, *New York Times,* December 7, 1948.

230   *[Judy] went into a "weeping rage" and refused to work with the man again:* Hedda Hopper with James Brough, *The Whole Truth and Nothing But* (New York: Doubleday, 1962–63).

231   *Tax loan to Berkeley:* Lowe's letter, March 30, 1949.

232   *A plagiarism suit was later filed against the studio:* According to the American Film Institute database, a November 1951 news item reported that writer Erroll Joe Palmer (also known as Erroll Paul) filed a $150,000 suit against MGM, charging that *Take Me Out to the Ball Game* was in part plagiarized from his original script "Base-Hits and Bloomers." The outcome was not made public, a sign that the suit had not been won if it ever made it to court.

232   *Anyone who gave Berkeley an unlimited budget would be out of his mind: Hollywood Reporter*, March 8, 1949.

233   *"Buzz was a bad drunk"*: Scott Eyman, *Lion of Hollywood: The Life and Legend of Louis B. Mayer* (New York: Simon and Schuster, 2005).

233   *Buzz had no conception of what this was all about*: Fordin, *M-G-M's Greatest Musicals*.

233   *Walters was "appalled" with the footage already in the can*: Paul Donnelley, *Judy Garland* (London: Haus, 2007).

233   *Buzz to direct* Summer Stock: *New York Times*, May 4, 1949.

234   *Judy received a letter from studio vice president, L. K. Sidney*: Schechter, *Judy Garland: The Day-by-Day Chronicle of a Legend.*

13. Jumping, Tapping, Diving

236   *[Buzz] to assume the role as "producing director" of the musical once known as* The Bowl of Brass: *New York Times*, March 29, 1950.

242   *Tony was strapped on a camera boom thirty-five feet high, and was thoroughly relieved when shooting was finished*: Laura Wagner, *A Conversation with Tony Martin* (Muscatine, Iowa: Classic Images, 2009).

243   *RKO to produce* The U.S.O. Story: *New York Times*, January 16, 1951.

243   *Buzz worked on* The Blue Veil: Confirmed in Kennedy, *Joan Blondell.*

244   *Annette Kellerman info*: Cullen, Hackman, and McNeilly, *Vaudeville Old and New.*

244   *So it was to be Berkeley and LeRoy, their first film together since their alchemic collaboration in* Gold Diggers of 1933: Technically, they did work together briefly on *The Wizard of Oz.*

245   *Esther Williams's accident*: Landis, *Dressed.*

246   *Anecdote of Buzz filming the "smoke" number*: André Previn, *No Minor Chords: My Days in Hollywood* (New York: Doubleday, 1991). The quote is presented verbatim, though he has Buzz asking, "can't you dance any faster?" when he probably meant, "can't you swim any faster?" as there is no dancing per se in the "smoke" number.

247   *New information about "All the Beautiful Girls"*: *New York Times*, June 16, 1952.

248   *Ox incident*: Previn, *No Minor Chords.*

249   *Ann Miller's comments*: Private Screenings: Ann Miller (Turner Classic Movies, 1997); and *The Masters behind the Musicals*, directed by Peter Fitzgerald (Warner Home Video, 2004).

253 Buzz and the dangerous numbers endured by Esther Williams: Williams with Diehl, *The Million Dollar Mermaid.*

14. Out of Sight

257 *Gross-Krasne signing Buzz for* Big Town: *Boxoffice* magazine, October 2, 1954.

257 *Buzz's use of close-ups:* Even allowing for the poor resolution of mid-1950s television sets, the abundance of close-ups was an obvious directorial choice and remains quite jarring.

258 *Buzz arrested again for drunkenness:* syndicated UP report, December 13, 1954.

258 *Either Marjorie Mae Berkeley was divorced from her husband in April 1946, as numerous wire stories reported, or she wasn't:* This mystery was never solved definitively on the record, and Buzz didn't mention the discrepancy in his memoirs. There are, however, enough clues to allow one to draw a reasonable conclusion. Due to the limited range of years of California's divorce records, a certificate of the supposed 1946 divorce is unobtainable. Two existing photos solidify the story that Marge remained married to Buzz until the 1950s. One is the Sam Spiegel/New Year's photo mentioned previously, and another is a picture taken of Buzz and Gene Kelly during the filming of *Take Me Out to the Ball Game,* where Buzz is clearly wearing a wedding ring. That evidence, along with the 1950s account of the divorce, leads one to believe that Buzz and Marge remained married far longer than just one year. It's anyone's guess why the wire services announced the divorce in the 1940s as if it were a fait accompli.

259 *Buzz's marriage to Etta Judd: Oxnard (Calif.) Press-Courier,* January 24, 1958.

260 Money from Home *game show:* Thomas and Terry, *The Busby Berkeley Book.*

260 The Count of Ten *was written around this time by William L. Penzner:* The unpublished script was auctioned in 1998 as part of a general auction by Etta Berkeley of her late husband's possessions.

261 Chartroose Caboose *information:* American Film Institute database.

15. The Ringmaster

262 *The winters are delightful:* Thomas and Terry, *The Busby Berkeley Book.*

262 *Now for the first time in my life I know what a home really means:* Berkeley's memoirs.

263   *Billy Barty's reminiscences:* Joe Collura, *Billy Barty: Born a Giant* (Muscatine, Iowa: Classic Images, 2009).

265   *Buzz's quotes on* Jumbo: Pike and Martin, *The Genius of Busby Berkeley.*

16. Remember My Forgotten Director

266   *Buzz directing stunt work at MGM for* A Ticklish Affair: Bob Thomas, syndicated AP column, March 4, 1963.

266   *Paul Henreid to star as Svengali:* AP syndicated column, May 14, 1963.

267   *I've got a great idea for a number with 60 dancing copper cuspidors:* Hal Humphrey, "Television and Radio" column, December 2, 1963.

268   *Quotes from Buzz and Ruby Keeler at the San Francisco Film Festival:* From Howard Thompson, "Busby Berkeley Recalls the Glitter of the '30's; Spectacles' Director Will Attend Series at Museum Here," *New York Times,* November 20, 1965.

269   *Buzz in London for the National Film Theatre tribute:* Alexander Walker, syndicated column, January 3, 1966.

270   *Jackie Gleason's comments and Buzz's wired reply:* Mike Steen, *Hollywood Speaks: An Oral History* (New York: G. P. Putnam's Sons, 1974).

270   *There's something obscene about the sight of an energetic man in full possession of his faculties forced to remain idle:* William Murray, "The Return of Busby Berkeley" *New York Times,* March 2, 1969.

17. The Figurehead

In correcting the unintentional inaccuracies that defined (and overemphasized) Busby Berkeley's contribution to *No, No, Nanette,* I am indebted to Don Dunn's on-the-record account of the production in his *The Making of No, No, Nanette* (Secaucus, N.J.: Citadel Press, 1972). A number of quotes used in whole or in part are attributable to Dunn's text.

277   *Age doesn't mean anything to me: New York Times,* March 17, 1970.

278   Tippy-Tap-Toe *mention:* "Joyce Haber's Hollywood," syndicated gossip column, March 25, 1970.

290   *Letter to Joan Crawford:* Busby Berkeley's personal collection, February 19, 1971 (the same date as the *Life* magazine article).

291   Life *magazine nostalgia issue:* In its February 19, 1971, issue, *Life* magazine proclaimed on the cover "Everybody's Just Wild about Nostalgia" with a photo of a young Ruby Keeler, among others. The issue featured stories about *No, No, Nanette,* Busby Berkeley, and other subjects of renewed and passionate interest.

291   *They used to complain it was too expensive to do my kind of show:* Hal Wingo, "Busby Berkeley's Girls Glitter Again," *Life* magazine, February 19, 1971.

18. The Palmy Days

292   *Well, I just say to myself, "Buzz, you must have done a hell of a good job; they all like it":* Kenneth Turan, "Busby Berkeley's Dance Numbers Are Still Eye-Popping," *Los Angeles Times,* August 1, 2008.

292   *Richard Schickel's assessment of Buzz:* Richard Schickel, "When Everybody Went to the Movies," *New York Times*, February 14, 1971.

293   *Buzz's Thalians Award: Boxoffice* magazine, August 16, 1971.

293   *Buzz autographing candy boxes at Bloomingdale's: Tucson Daily Citizen*, April 1, 1972. The connection of "Phudge" to Buzz isn't quite clear, but one hopes Jim Terry's tribute wasn't a reference to the dreadful *The Phynx.*

294   *In July, the producers said they expected a year's-end start date:* Marilyn Beck, syndicated column, July 25, 1975.

294   *Description of items in Buzz's home:* Auction listings of Butterfields Auction House, October 27, 1998.

Index

353

LaVergne, TN USA
23 February 2011
217740LV00003B/2/P